AF576768

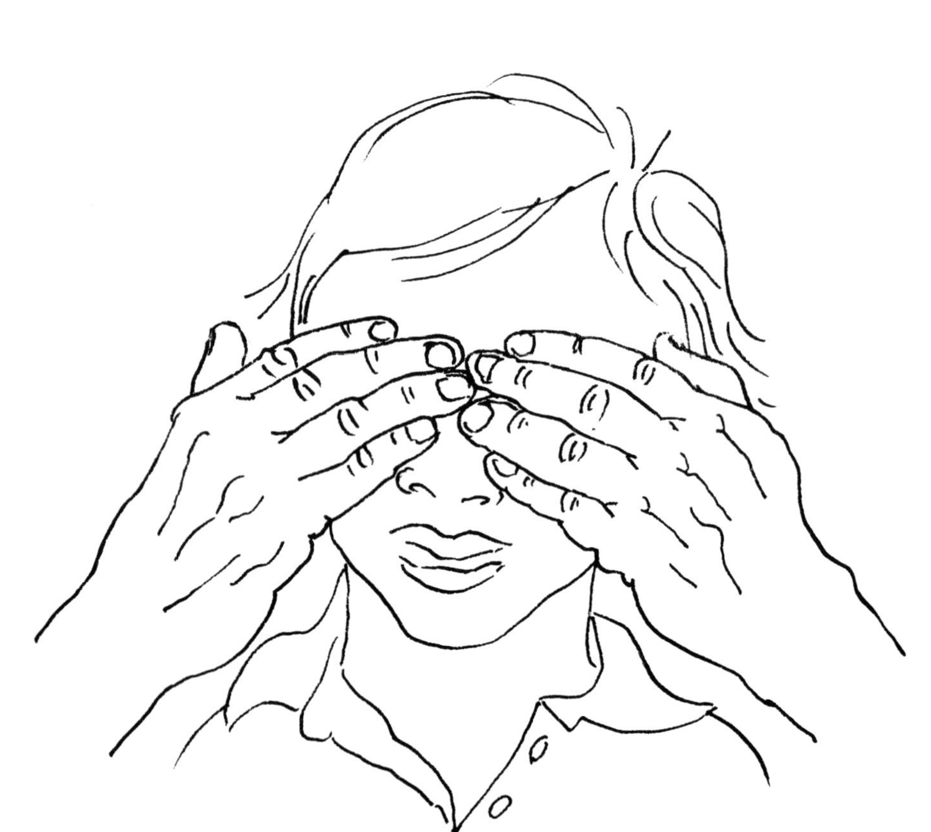

THE ART OF WONDER
A HISTORY OF SEEING

Text and watercolours by
Julian Spalding

PRESTEL
MUNICH · BERLIN · LONDON · NEW YORK

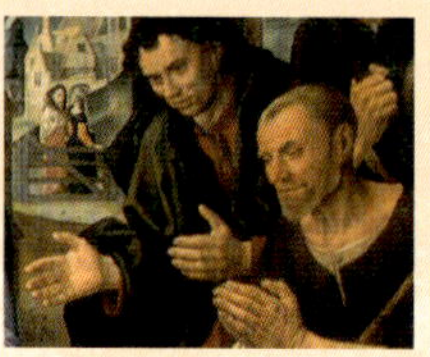

Introduction 7

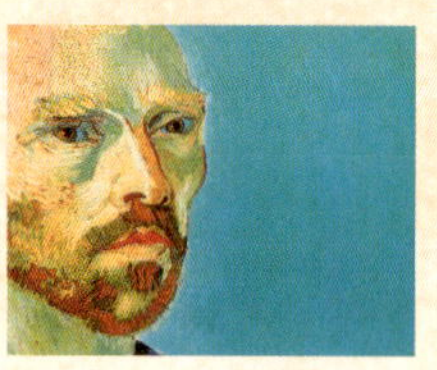

Chapter 1
The Stars in our Eyes 17

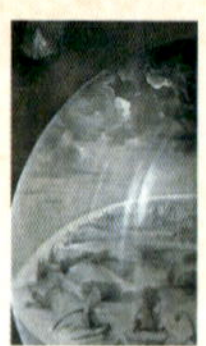
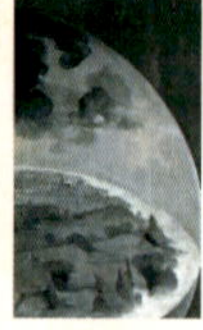

Chapter 2
When the Earth was Flat 35

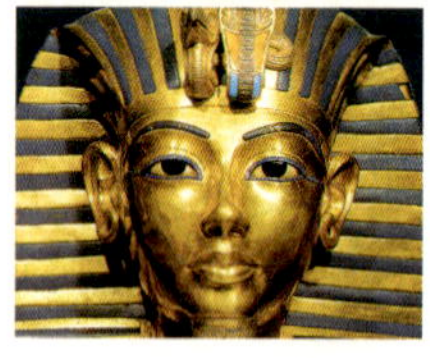

Chapter 3
Under the Sun 65

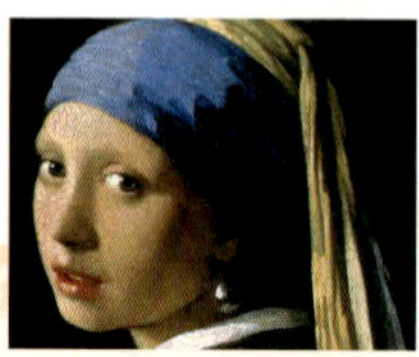

Chapter 4
Under the Moon 89

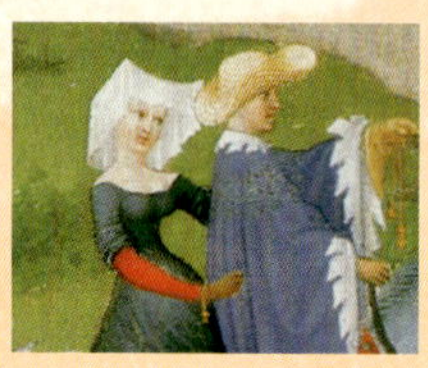

Chapter 5
Birth 115

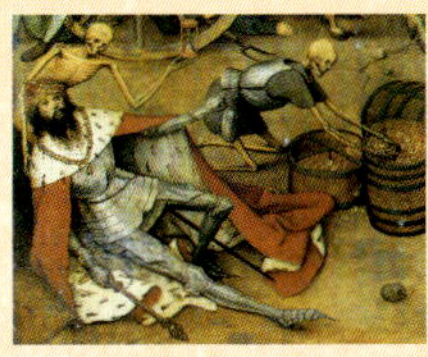
Chapter 6
Death 135

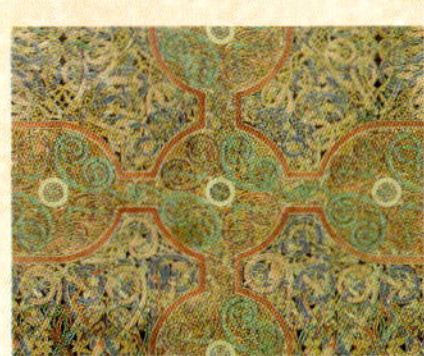
Chapter 7
Visions 157

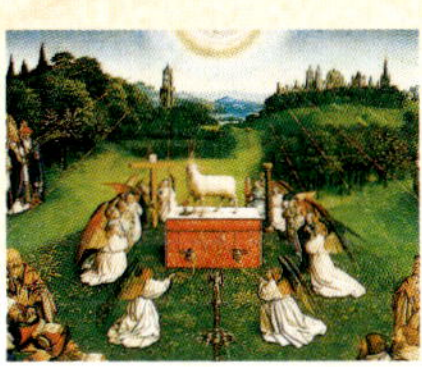
Chapter 8
The Age of Light 183

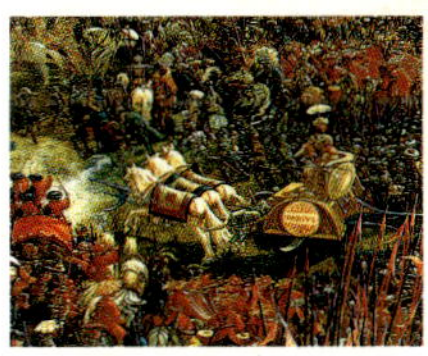
Chapter 9
The Age of Darkness 221

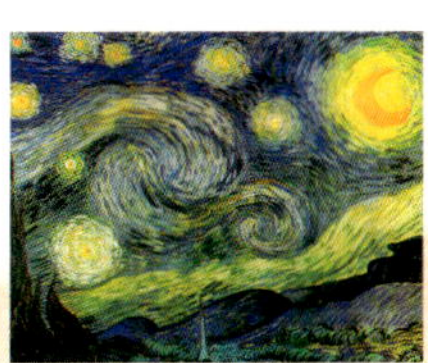
Chapter 10
Out of Sight 257

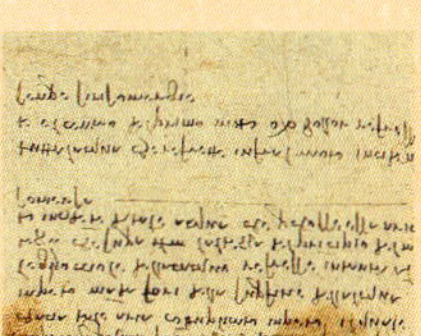
Index 284

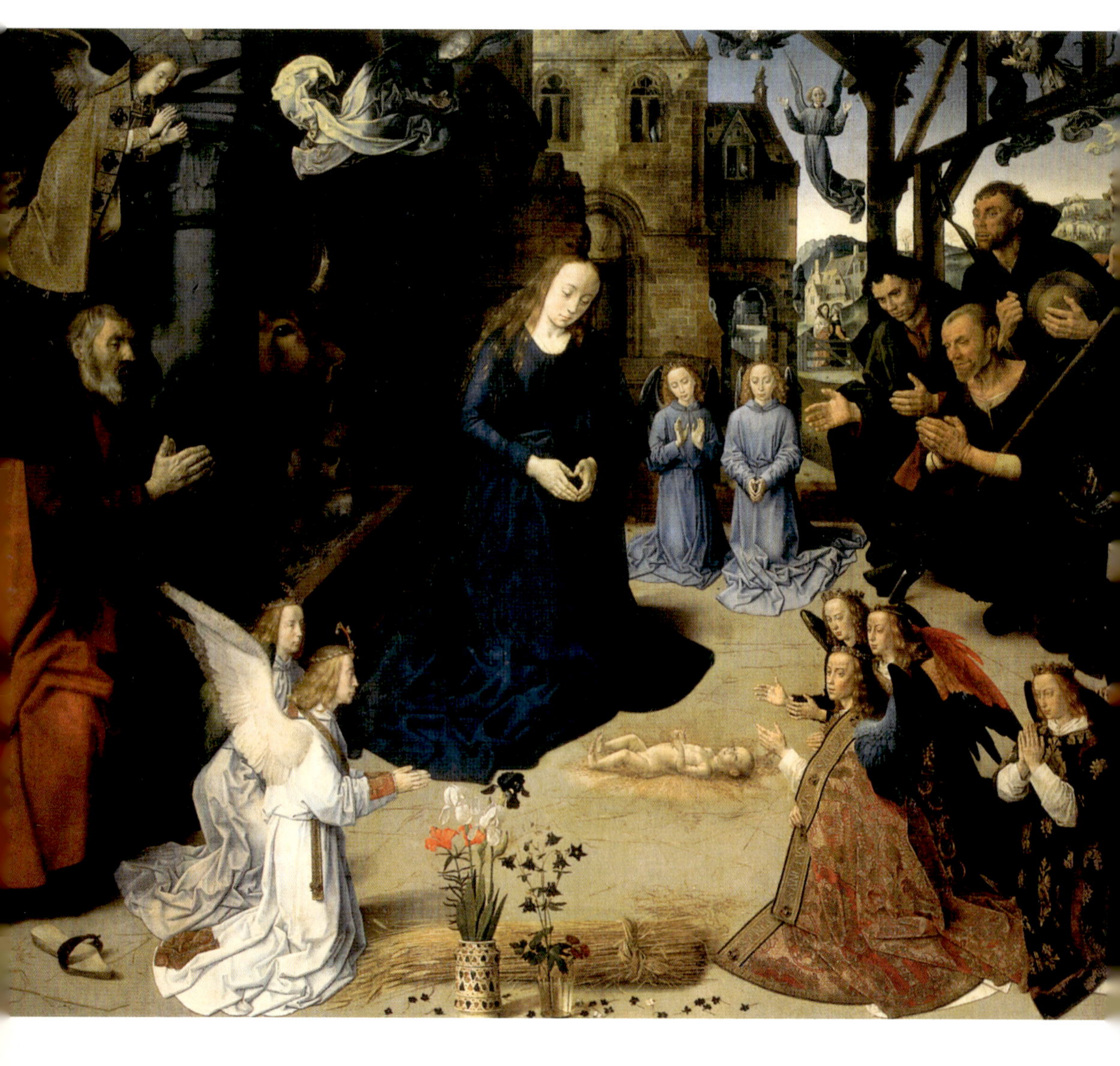

Introduction

This book looks at the art of the world in a totally fresh way. It maintains that you don't need to know about artistic styles, schools and techniques to begin to enjoy and understand art. All you have to do is to look at the world around you and respond to it emotionally. The job of artists is to give deep feelings form, whether they're carving a mask in Africa to bring to life a tree spirit, or capturing the look of joy on the face of Jesus' mother in medieval Europe, or trying to express their horror of modern warfare. People often think they can't begin to appreciate art from other cultures and ages because it's too distant, but no art is incomprehensible, because it's all made by human beings. We're exactly the same as the people who built the Pyramids and the Forbidden City and who painted pictures in Renaissance Italy. Phidias, Leonardo and Picasso had eyes, hearts and brains just like ours; they had brilliant minds, it's true, but we can go a long way to understanding their art by using our own eyes, hearts and minds. In spite of all the changes we've made to the planet, the sights of nature haven't changed, and nor have we in any fundamental way. What's changed, and changed dramatically, is what we think we're looking at when we see a sunset, a flower or a gleam in someone else's eye. To understand the art of other ages and cultures, we have to make an imaginative leap into the minds of the people who made it. And to do that we have to try to forget our modern ideas about art, history and about seeing itself. Only then will we be able to look around us again, as people did until

1 Hugo van der Goes. *Portinari Altarpiece* (centre panel), c. 1479. Oil on wood, 253 x 304 cm. Uffizi, Florence

very recently, and wonder at the miraculous appearance of the world.

Art is a recent, western invention. People in the past didn't think of art at all. Many of the most famous works of art from antiquity weren't made to be looked at by us; they were meant to be seen only by the gods. The craftsmen who fashioned Tutankhamen's golden mask would be horrified to see their handiwork exposed to public gaze. That would have seemed nothing less than sacrilegious. The idea that art can be of personal use to us is a recent western notion. Art now exists for art's sake, and it's seen as separate from religion, philosophy, politics and science. But in the past, art was in the service of all four; it illustrated our beliefs, thoughts, opinions and even our search for facts. The world's greatest works of art are, however, almost all religious. But that doesn't mean we can't appreciate them. We can sympathise with someone else's feelings even if we don't share their beliefs–so we can respond to their art. But we won't have a chance of enjoying their art fully until we understand why it was made. And we won't begin to do that if we go on thinking that all art was made for us to look at.

History is also a recent, western invention. History depends on people thinking that everything can be placed chronologically within a single time-frame. But we didn't begin seriously to pin down time until about three hundred years ago. People then started to chart the past. They collected coins and arranged them in lines according to their dates, and discovered whole dynasties and cultures that they hadn't known existed. They counted layers in sediments and discovered that the world was much older than anyone had imagined. Time opened its curtains. The dinosaurs walked on to the stage. Universal world time wasn't finally established until 1884, by the British in their naval dockyard at Greenwich, because that nation then had the power to assert its time-frame on the world. The British boasted that the sun never set on their empire, which was, for a short while, literally true.

People resisted this slavery to universal time, and some cultures still do. Many ancient religious festivals follow other, non-universal schedules. Even Christians, the most avid clock-watchers, celebrate the crucifixion and resurrection of their saviour on a date which shifts every year according to the disappearance and appearance of the moon. The calendars in Hindu homes in India are extraordinarily complex. Beneath the standard western date are a host of other data about the relative positions of the stars and planets and the most auspicious hours of the day. No Hindu would consider doing anything important, like setting a date and time for a marriage, without consulting this calendar first, and getting an astrologer's second opinion. It is only during the last hundred years that people have begun to wear an image of their new time god on their wrists, and to bow before it frequently during the day.

Before universal time there was no history, only histories. And for most people these histories were not chronological, but cyclical. Everything had its own time—there was a time for eating and for sleeping, a time for marrying and for dying, a time for working and for resting. Traditional Aborigines in Australia still conduct their lives according to these natural rhythms, when they feel them to be right. They don't have any clocks or watches. They believe all things come round again, as the sun reappears at dawn. Our ancestors were aware that there was a past, but it felt much closer to them, as if it were at their elbow. The spirits of their ancestors hung around the houses and in the forest glades. They believed that creation was, somehow, eternally ongoing. They didn't, therefore, have our sense of progress, but believed instead in recreation and reincarnation. This could be one of the reasons why the art of some cultures, like that of Stone Age Europe, ancient Egypt and imperial China, lasted for thousands of years with little apparent change. People in the past saw their world as thematic and ahistorical, and that is how time is presented in the opening chapters of this book. Chronology only clocks in when a modern concept of history begins to emerge in the West.

To date, history has tended to be literary rather than visual. Historians have valued texts above all other forms of evidence from the past, so much so that they've claimed that history proper only begins with the invention of writing; cultures that don't have writing are often dismissed as "prehistoric". But the fact that we have virtually no contemporary written accounts to corroborate our interpretations of ancient art doesn't mean that all this purely visual evidence should be dismissed. Artists anyway don't usually supply written commentaries on what they're trying to create in paint or stone. This is just as true of much art created nearer to our time, when writing was widespread. Chartres Cathedral was almost totally redesigned, within the space of a few months, after a fire in 1194, yet not one written word remains recording the fantastically elaborate thinking that went into its rebuilding. Trying to see through the eyes of artists, even modern ones (Picasso said very little about what he was actually doing) is often conjectural, but that doesn't mean it isn't worth attempting. This book is not annotated, for much of its analysis is not supported by texts—the evidence is visual and it is provided by the illustrations.

The value of art is that it preserves, in indescribable lines, shapes and colours, the feelings that went into our forefathers' thoughts. This is important because the world pictures we formed in the past were very different from the scientific, mechanistic viewpoint we assume to be universal today. We used to interpret the world poetically. We had no option but to do so, because we couldn't work out how it made sense practically. Our world pictures were at once strictly logical and at the same time totally illogical. It was logical to think that an ocean lay under the earth—as most early myths around the world maintain—because when water is poured on to the ground, it sinks through it—and it had to go somewhere. It was also logical to think that the earth was surrounded by an ocean—as most early people also believed. Every journey in every direction seemed to end at a coast—except to the north, in the northern hemisphere, which led to snowy wastes and seas of ice. But what was under and beyond these oceans no-one knew, and virtually no-one was concerned to ask. The Epic of Gilgamesh, written in ancient Mesopotamia and the oldest surviving written story in the world, states: "There has never been any way across the sea, not since the remotest times. No-one but the Sun God, Shamash, can cross the Waters of Death." What was beyond sight was not our concern, partly because what was in sight was so unfathomably interesting.

Our sense of wonder was prompted mostly by what we could see. Of course the other senses contain elements of wonder. Eve and Adam wouldn't have picked the apple if they hadn't wondered what it would be like to touch, smell and taste it and what effect its ingestion would have on their minds. But most of our senses give us experiences we can touch. It's true that we can hear at a distance—but what we could hear was usually something whose source we would have been able to get close to and understand its cause—a man knapping flints in an adjacent cave or a pack of wolves howling on the mountain-side. Only thunder and echoes remained mysterious until modern times. Sight, however, unveiled endless wonders. Our eyes carried us effortlessly far beyond our reach – to the top of the luminous clouds, up into the ineffably deep blue dome of the sky and beyond even these to the ever-changing, mysterious moon, which no-one imagined any human being would ever walk upon, at least not while they were living in the world below. Many people believed that spirits walked there, but not men with heavy feet.

That didn't mean that the visual arts were more wonderful than music and poetry. Far from it, for music and poetry can lift us on to planes of existence that do not exist in nature. The mere sound of music must have been magical in the past, especially given the eerie silence that seemed to underlie all nature. The effect of church bells calling the faithful to prayer, of bugles calling soldiers to battle, even of a shepherd playing his flute in the fields must have fallen on the ears of listeners like a drink of water after a journey across a desert. The crescendo of the chorus in the theatre of Epidaurus was probably awe-inspiring, though we can only guess at this from the tantalising scraps of ancient Greek music that survive. But it's a big step down from the sound of a massed choir and orchestra to the thrill of hearing a bird sing, and a chasm divides both of these experiences from the everyday noises of life which barely break into our consciousness.

In the visual arts this relationship between what people created and what had been created around them was reversed. Artists could never paint a sunset that was more magical than a real one, or carve in marble flesh that was as fabulous to touch as a lover's. The Bible made it absolutely clear: "Consider the lilies of the field, how they grow; they toil not, neither do they spin: And yet I say unto you, that even Solomon in all his glory was not arrayed like one of these." Nature couldn't and shouldn't be imitated, because it was god's handiwork. This is why early art often tends to be abstract, like music. This was not just because there was no point in seeking to emulate what you could see. It was more that such arrogance was bound to lead to failure, and possibly divine retribution. But despite this disregard of appearances, most early art is, in essence, a hymn of praise to the wonders of nature. This is why early art, even when it appears to be totally abstract or fanciful, provides us with so many insights into how our ancestors saw the world.

This book is not, in any conventional sense, a *history* of *art*. Instead, it tells the story of how the way we've seen the world has changed, and how those changes have affected the art we've made. It explains how modern art was born out of the wreckage of this ancient way of seeing. All civilisations before our modern age were founded on the assumption that the earth was flat and fixed in space. This affected what people thought they were looking at. No-one knew why the sun rose and fell or where it went to at night. Everything our ancestors looked at—from the dew sparkling in the morning to the snow shining on the mountains, from the dark, cold waters in the oceans to the stars twinkling in heaven—was wonderful because it could not be explained.

Seeing itself was a mystery. Most people used to believe that the eye emitted rays—and many still do. The way you looked did good or ill; hence the widespread belief in the evil eye. But most of us no longer think we see with our eyes at all. Eyes are just lenses. We see, now, with our brains. How our brain sees is still mysterious. Scientists have only recently discovered, for example, that it takes us a fraction of a second to see anything; so our brains must play tricks with time in ways we don't understand, because we think we see instantaneously and act as though we do. It is in such elusive areas of consciousness that we find mysteries. But for our ancestors the simple act of seeing was a mystery in itself. For them, looking was a religious activity fraught with dangers. Hindus today still go to the temple for *darshana*—which literally means "seeing"—and they do so particularly at those times when the gods are decked with flowers and are even more beautiful and therefore more beneficent to look at. Seeing for them is an act of giving and receiving. For Leonardo—a precursor of modern western man—seeing was primarily a means of thinking. This way of looking survives in the English language when we use "I see" to mean "I understand". Both these uses of seeing—as a way of praying and a way of understanding—are ways of looking that we've lost. This book tells the story of that loss.

Our forefathers used to look at the world around them very differently from the way we do today. Seeing itself was a wonderful gift from heaven, and wonderful were the things this gift enabled us to see. But now wonder is something that has receded almost out of sight. If today we see an adult gazing with wonder, we tend to assume that he must be a bit simple-minded. One can still see wide-eyed amazement on the faces of children, and some adults, in Disney's theme parks—and one reason for their success is that they attempt to provide wonder in a wonder-less age. But theirs are the grins of gratified enjoyment and lack the element of mystery that gives birth to real wonder. Not even the most protected child can believe that Mickey Mouse is actually shaking his hand. True wonder is inspired when the magical mixes with day-to-day reality.

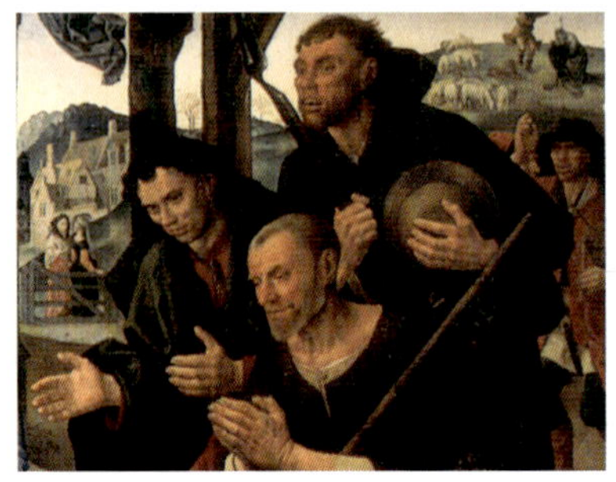
2 Hugo van der Goes. *Portinari Altarpiece*, detail, cf. p. 6, The Three Shepherds

Wonder can be seen here on the faces of the shepherds in the *Portinari Altarpiece* (ill. 1, 2), painted by the Netherlandish artist Hugo van der Goes (died 1482). Like his compatriot Vincent van Gogh four centuries later, Hugo was a devout Christian and suffered from bouts of madness, perhaps triggered by the intensity of his ardour and his art. Few artists have ever painted ordinary people so vividly. His shepherds gaze with wonder at the Madonna and the new-born Christ child (ill.3). The expressions reveal a childlike innocence and spontaneity. True wonder can't be premeditated or posed. And there is a smile of pleasure about their faces, too, for wonder, while it lasts, obliterates suffering. Nevertheless, each of their expressions is subtly different. In the face of the shepherd on the lower left, wonder is turning into admiration and love, while in the one on the right wonder is melting into praise. Their eyelids are lowered. But the young shepherd at the top gazes wide-eyed at the whole scene. He can't believe his eyes. True wonder, so beautifully encapsulated here, is always an uplifting sensation of delight held tremulous with doubt.

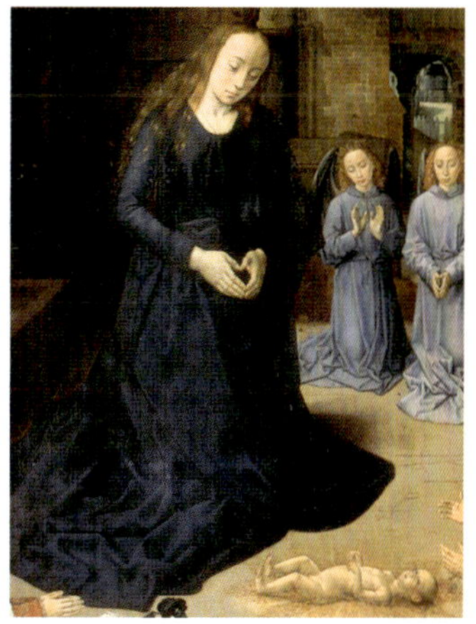

3 Hugo van der Goes. *Portinari Altarpiece*, detail, cf. p. 6, The Madonna and Child

This book tells the story of wonder–of how our wonder gave rise to our religious beliefs, to our arts and sciences and to many of our social structures. It tells the story of how, gradually, we lost our sense of wonder, and ends by wondering if we are just beginning, with great difficulty, to discover this sense again.

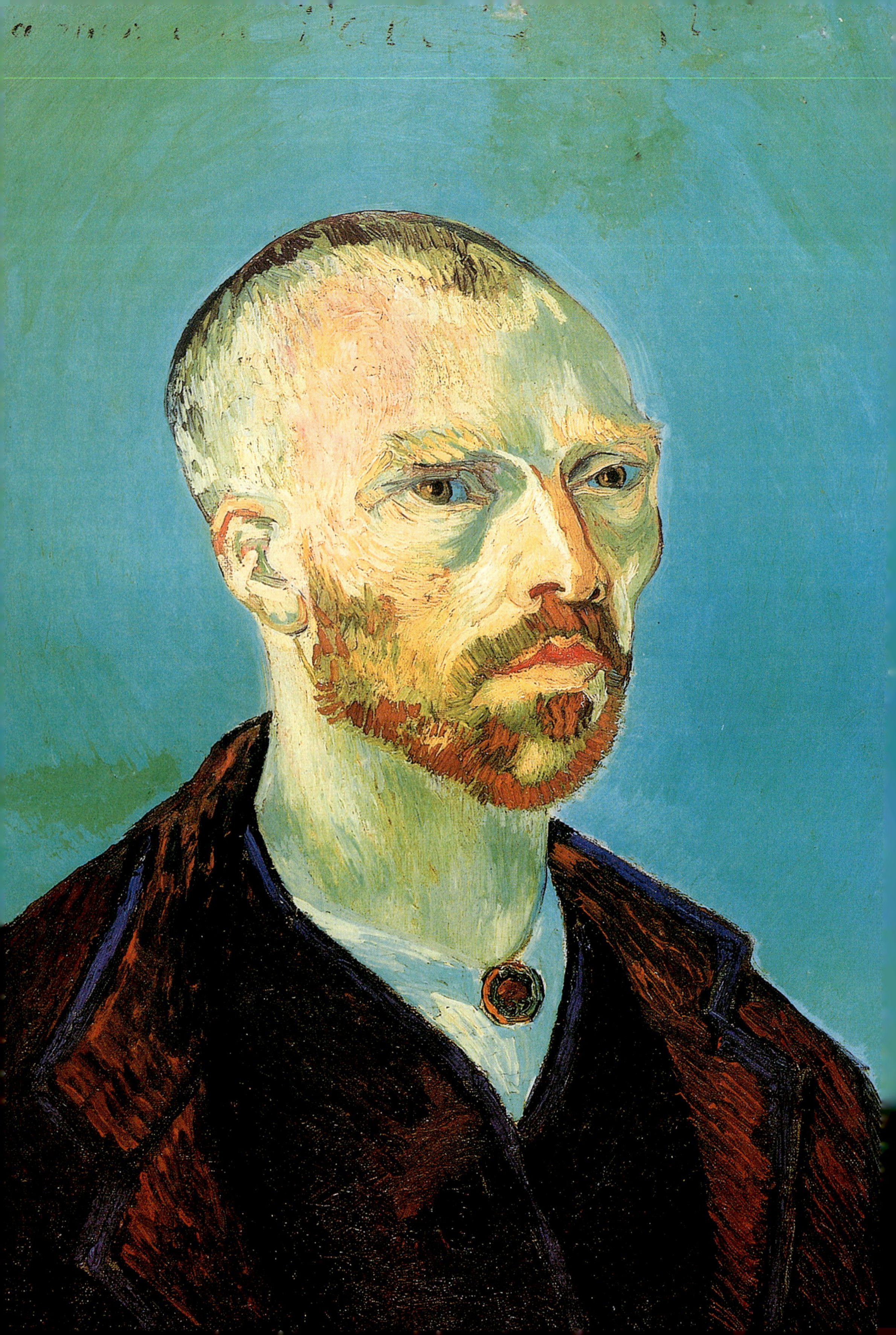

Chapter 1

The Stars in our Eyes

What do you see when you look into someone's eyes? There seems to be a light there–the spark of life that goes out when a person dies. Many people used to think that the light in their eyes–indeed the very fact that they could see at all–was a gift from heaven. Light, they thought, had its home up there. That's why fire, the source of light on earth, always rises, to return to the place where it was born. Flames can flare up but cannot rest below. It was logical, therefore, to think that the spark of life we can see in each other's eyes was a flicker of celestial fire. Some ancient Greek philosophers went further, and believed that all the stars in the night sky were souls waiting to be born. They were shaken down, from time to time, by celestial winds, and fell to earth to give each person his or her life spirit. People believed that there were, literally, stars in their eyes. Van Gogh painted everyone, including himself (ill. 1), as if they were, as he put it, "stars in the depths of an azure sky". The Buddha told his favourite disciple, with his dying breath: "Be the light of yourself"–be guided by your own divine ray.

We don't see heaven in people's glances any more. If we see someone's eyes shining, we're most likely to wonder what drug they're taking. The light in people's eyes is seen to be the product of a chemical reaction. If you're trying to read someone else's mind or find out what makes them tick–the modern equivalent of searching for someone's soul–you tend to look for clues in their body language or behaviour. You would never think that you could tell a person's true nature merely by looking into their

1 Vincent van Gogh. *Self-Portrait*, 1888. Oil on canvas. 60 x 49,9 cm. Fogg Art Museum, Harvard University, Cambridge, Mass. Bequest-collection of Maurice Wertheim, Class of 1906

eyes, though people still attempt to do so when they think someone's lying to them. They look them straight in the eye. It rarely works today, because even children learn quickly how to throw back a defiant gaze. Naughty children, surely, have always done so; but divine punishment lay in wait for anyone who played hide-and-seek with their soul. And eyes, in the past, were windows to the soul.

Seeing is now mechanical, not spiritual. We talk of lenses and light waves, retinas and optic nerves. But these are all recent scientific discoveries. A century and a half ago, the very existence of eyes was used to attempt to prove that the theory of evolution was wrong. If the first creatures had been blind, as Darwin maintained, how could the eye have evolved, when nothing knew that there was anything to see? The only way to explain sight was that it was a gift from outside—from an all-seeing god. Seeing was, therefore, a god-given ability, and people used their eyes with much greater care and respect than it would ever occur to us to do today. How people use their eyes doesn't matter much any more. So we find it very difficult to understand why merely setting eyes on the emperor of China could have been an act punishable by death. But then we don't regard seeing as an act at all.

Until only a couple of centuries ago, seeing was believed to be an active, not a passive process. Even the ancient Greeks, who questioned everything, thought that seeing was an emission from the eye, like a ray sent out to touch what it saw. The idea was still prevalent five hundred years ago. Leonardo da Vinci (1452–1519) observed in his notebooks how "the sun, as soon as it appears in the east, immediately reaches to the west with its rays", and he compared this to the eye which "as soon as it opens, sees all the stars". Eyes were miniature suns and saw, as the sun was thought to see, by emitting rays that illuminated all they touched. The fact that you couldn't see the eye's rays was not problematic. You couldn't see the wind–but you could feel it and watch it flutter leaves and lift hair. The inconvenient fact that the sun's rays could sometimes be seen streaming through a gap in the clouds or through a chink into a darkened room was explained by the sun's much greater power. Even when you couldn't see the sun's rays, you could feel their heat burning into your skin. Eye light was like sunlight filtered through clouds: it was too feeble to cast shadows; you couldn't see it or feel its warmth. The sun was so powerful that it could illuminate the whole world. Our eyes were much weaker: they could only illuminate our souls. But both the rays from the sun and those from our eyes were believed to be capable of penetrating darkness.

The rays from our eyes touched what they saw. This touch could be life-enhancing or annihilating. People used to be much more wary of where and how they looked in their daily lives. It's only during the last three hundred years that scientists have worked out that the eyes are soft receptors of light waves. Nothing shines out of them at all. We still find this difficult to accept, because we are so accustomed to using our eyes to express our feelings and to interpret other people's looks. Many people still believe that they can make someone aware of their presence just by staring at them from behind, even though there's no scientific basis for this. And many people still avoid looking directly at other people in public, and especially at anyone who is acting aggressively, for fear that any eye contact will be interpreted as a challenge. In sexually potent situations, the briefest exchange of glances can be an invitation to intimacy. We think we are making eye contact; in fact we are making extremely rapid assessments of the body language around the focus of our attention. The most intense visual experiences many people have are when they are in

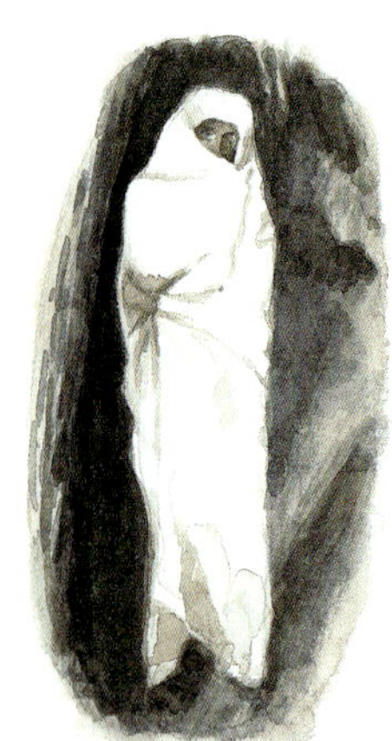

2 After Edward S. Curtis. *Waiting in the Forest*, 1911, detail. Photograph from *The North American Indian*, vol. VI, 1911

love. They can then go to untold lengths just to catch sight of their beloved, to ease the unbearable visual hunger that often accompanies sexual desire. It was traditional among the Native American Cheyenne for love-sick youths (ill.2) to disguise themselves in white blanket shrouds, leaving only a slit for their eyes. They would then linger about the edges of the encampment at night, like ghosts, hoping to catch a glimpse of their sweethearts. Seeing is heightened when we are in love or when we are frightened, and these experiences help us appreciate what the everyday business of seeing must have meant to people who believed that a mere glance could, in itself, be good or evil.

Millions of people around the world still protect themselves against the Evil Eye by wearing magic amulets, such as cowrie shells (ill.3). These small, rare shells were valued wherever they were found on beaches, and were treasured in cultures far from the sea. They were often bartered as an early form of currency. It was mysterious enough that they had been created under the waves, but it was their appearance that made them magical. A cowrie shell looks like a closed eye when viewed horizontally, and like a vagina when held vertically. It's also like a clenched fist, looked at from the palm side. So it was the perfect amulet to protect its wearer from the Evil Eye, from that invisible, harmful, dark emission that came towards you through the air from another's gaze, and was most probably sexually or covetously motivated.

A lecherous man could defile a woman just by leering at her, which is why so many women around the world wear veils. A thief could rob you by just stealing a glance, which is why the pockets of the tunics of the Berber people are designed in the shape of elegant, pointed lances (ill.4), to pierce any prying eye. People with evil intentions could, without warning, lay the Eye on you: a curse that could lead to an accident, sickness or death

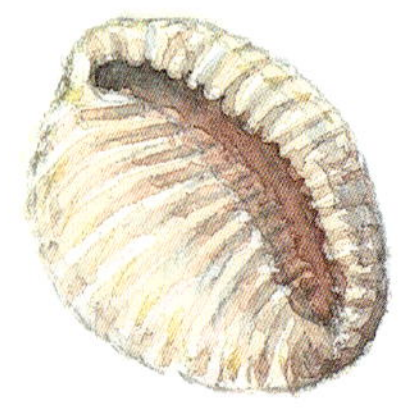

3 Cowrie shell

from which there was little chance of escape. Many people don't believe in the Evil Eye any more, and gaily flaunt their wealth and flesh, but almost all of us still take care how we look into another person's eyes. It's difficult for us to get used to the notion—despite our increasingly mechanistic view of life—that our skulls are set with a pair of surveillance cameras, not two mysterious shining orbs.

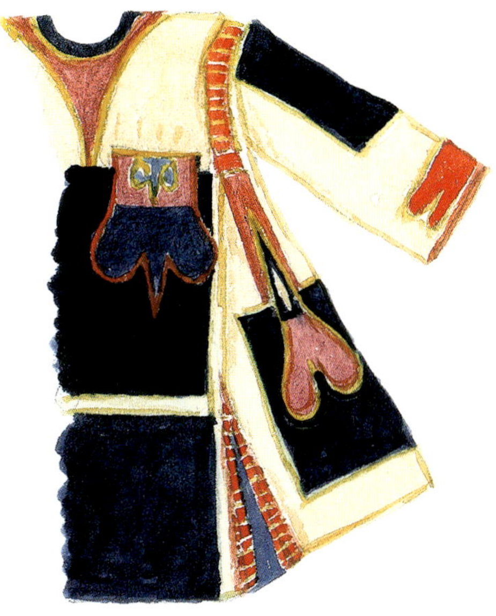

4 Detail of a pocket on a military tunic (*jibba*) worn in the Sudan in the late 19th century. British Museum, London

We're so used to thinking that the world is a globe, the moon is a lump of rock and the sun is an on-going nuclear explosion, that it's extremely difficult for us to imagine a time, not that long ago, when it was perfectly reasonable to think that the moon became pregnant every month, and the sun travelled underground at night by boat and was drawn across the sky by a team of invisible horses by day. Such ideas seem so ludicrous to us that we tend to think that nobody could seriously have countenanced them. But to our ancestors they were simply common sense. Everything, for example, *had* to give off wafer-thin images, as a flower wafts scent, because you could see these images caught in shiny surfaces like a pool of water. People soon made mirrors to catch these ghostly emanations. They had no idea they were reflections. No-one imagined that one day light—the most elusive and magical substance of all—would be discovered to bounce off surfaces like a ball.

This doesn't mean to say that everyone went round all day with their jaws hanging open, gaping with wonder. Most people in the past must surely have taken the world for granted most of the time, just as we do—especially as they grew older and wiser and realised that there was little they could do to change any-

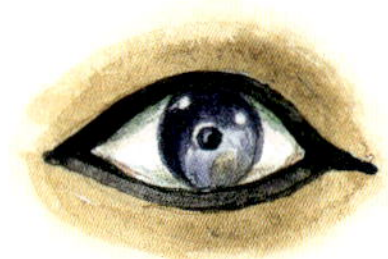

5 Detail of eye of Prince Rahotep, 2620–2560 B.C.E. Painted limestone. The Egyptian Museum, Cairo

thing. The Roman poet Lucretius (c. 100–c. 55 B.C.E.) composed the vividly realistic and beautiful epic poem *On the Nature of the Universe.* It's a passionate exhortation to encourage his readers to admire the wonders of nature. But when Lucretius looked at his fellow men he regretted their lack of interest in the world around them. He commented that "the pure and undimmed lustre of the sky and all that it enshrines" was "a sight which no-one now, you will admit, thinks worthy of an upward glance". He attributed this lack of interest to people's growing tiredness. Lucretius believed, along with many others, that the world was dying and humanity was dying with it. He'd have been very surprised that we're still here. But many of our ancestors did wonder. And they came up with theories about how the universe worked that are so wildly different from our own that it's difficult to imagine how the world appeared to them. But fortunately we have one great advantage when we attempt to do this because we are essentially, despite our myriad differences, the same people who painted in caves 35,000 years ago.

6 Statue of chief ritualist Kaaper, known as "Sheikh el-Beled", c. 2560 B.C.E. Wood, copper and stone, height 1.10 m. The Egyptian Museum, Cairo

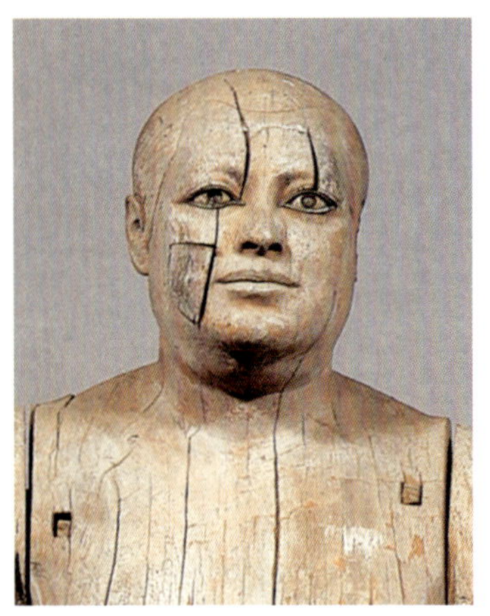

When we encounter faces from the past, we almost always recognise the look in their eyes. It's our look–the look of a human being. The ancient Egyptians were masters at making life-like eyes. The archaeologist who first shone his torch on the statue of Rahotep, in 1871, ran terrified from the tomb because he thought the statue was alive and was looking at him. The white of the eye had been made of milky quartz and the iris of rock crystal. But the masterstroke was the nail head sunk at the back of the iris to indicate the pupil. It was this that reflected the torch beam, as if a light were streaming out of the statue's eye (ill. 5). When workers dug up the statue of Kaaper (ill. 6), an ancient Egyptian head of rituals, they were so surprised by its likeness to their local mayor, Sheik el-Beled, that they named it after him, even though the statue portrayed someone who had lived 4,500 years before. This time the eyes' pupils were made of black stone. We now appreciate that it's not, in fact, the eyes that give this portrait its life-like appearance. It's the look that the sculptor has magically conjured around them that makes the statue come alive—the slight smile playing on his lips, even the swell of flabby skin under his chin all combine to give this portrayal its entirely realistic "look". We recognise this look immediately: it's one of questioning awareness. It's the look that, as far as we can tell, distinguishes us from all other animals—a self-conscious responsiveness, a very human look.

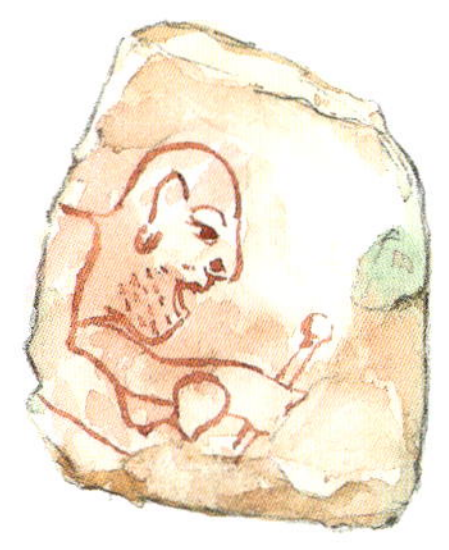

7 Unshaven stonemason. c. 1200–1153 B.C.E. Painted limestone, flake, 150 x 135 cm, from Deir-el-Medina. Fitzwilliam Museum, Cambridge

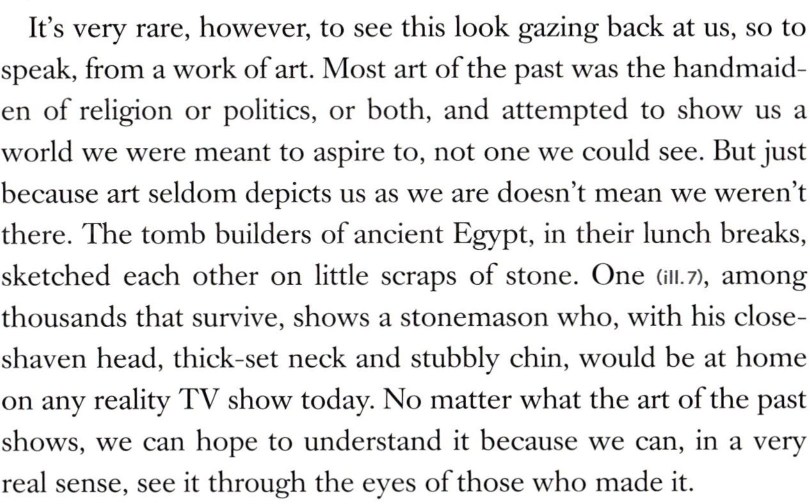

It's very rare, however, to see this look gazing back at us, so to speak, from a work of art. Most art of the past was the handmaiden of religion or politics, or both, and attempted to show us a world we were meant to aspire to, not one we could see. But just because art seldom depicts us as we are doesn't mean we weren't there. The tomb builders of ancient Egypt, in their lunch breaks, sketched each other on little scraps of stone. One (ill. 7), among thousands that survive, shows a stonemason who, with his close-shaven head, thick-set neck and stubbly chin, would be at home on any reality TV show today. No matter what the art of the past shows, we can hope to understand it because we can, in a very real sense, see it through the eyes of those who made it.

Until very recently we were all looking at the same nature. It's only during the last century that we've come to see ourselves as a blight on the planet, and to treasure the few pockets of wildness left. Now our so-called countryside—from America to China—is in fact an open factory, with field after field of sterilised crops, many of them grown under plastic. But the odd hedgerow or copse, motorway or railway verge, or strip of jungle, desert or

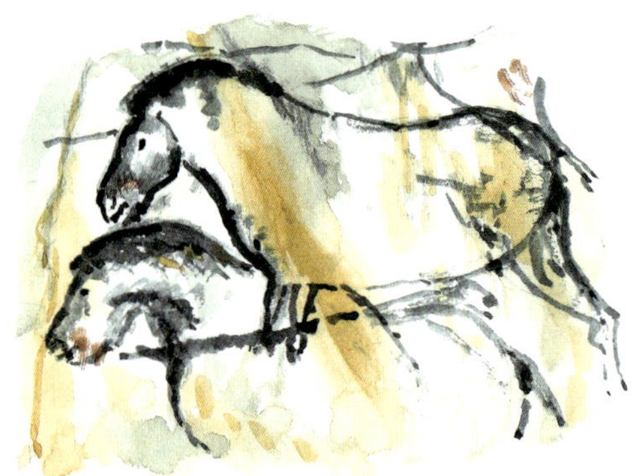

8 Horses on the left of the central niche, c. 32,000 B.C.E. Chauvet cave, France

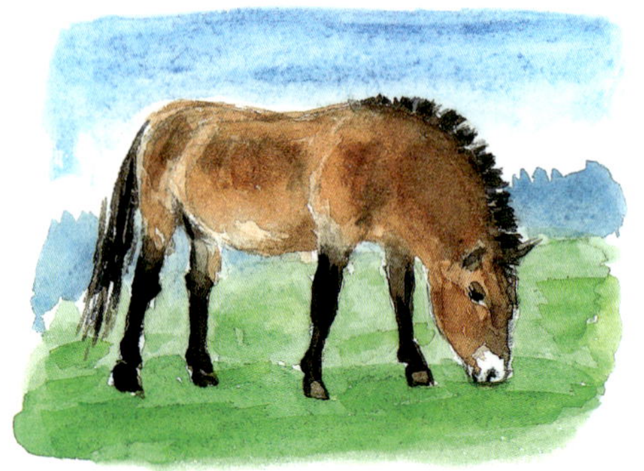

9 Przewalski's horse, living today

swamp—depending on where you live—still contains exactly the same flowers and trees, insects, small mammals and birds that our ancestors saw. One just has to multiply these a million-fold in one's mind, and populate the wilderness with the larger beasts we have almost entirely exterminated—then one can imagine exactly the same landscape our ancestors saw when they first began to gaze with wonder at the world around them. The horses depicted in the Chauvet cave (ill. 8)—the oldest painted cave in the world, which was only discovered in 1994—are identifiably the wild Przewalski's horse (ill. 9) which only survives in zoos.

There was another world hidden from us during the day—the magical world of the stars. We had invented animal-fat candles by the time we began painting in caves 35,000 years ago, but street lighting has only existed for little more than a hundred years. Now many people have never seen a night sky full of stars. But in the past people's daylight hours were lapped by darkness. Every day, when the sun set, a curtain opened on to a celestial theatre that held our ancestors in awe. If you're in an area far from light pollution, you can see that the stars are not twinkling pin-pricks of white light but glow with all the colours of a muted rainbow. The night is not black but filled with an ethereal light. As the poet Shelley put it, writing two hundred years ago, as the mystery of the cosmos was being unravelled: the stars that fill the heavens are a "million pieces of coloured glass" which "stain the white radiance of eternity".

David Malin, working at the Anglo-Australian Observatory in New South Wales, Australia, at the end of the twentieth century, took a remarkable series of photographs of the night sky using very long exposures in starlight (ill.10). His pictures show the subtle, jewel-like colours of stars that have not been dimmed by pollution and stained by sodium glare. These colours are precisely those used by Paddy Japaljarri Sims in his *Night Sky Dreaming* (ill.11). A twentieth-century scientist and a representative of the world's oldest continuous culture both see the same stars, but interpret what they see in very different ways. The Australian Aboriginal culture dates back at least 35,000 years. One reason why it has survived so long is that these people were, until recently, totally cut off from the rest of mankind. Another reason could be that traditional Aborigines have no sense of chronology – and no need to mark the passage of time by doing something new. They follow the call of the spirits that live all around them and within them. They believe the world began, and still exists, in Dreamtime. There is no other time. Dreamtime was, and is, when the spirits moved, as they still move, through the land creating the hills, plants, animals and waterholes. The spiritual task of every traditional Aborigine is to keep these dreams alive. If they stop dreaming, they believe the world will die.

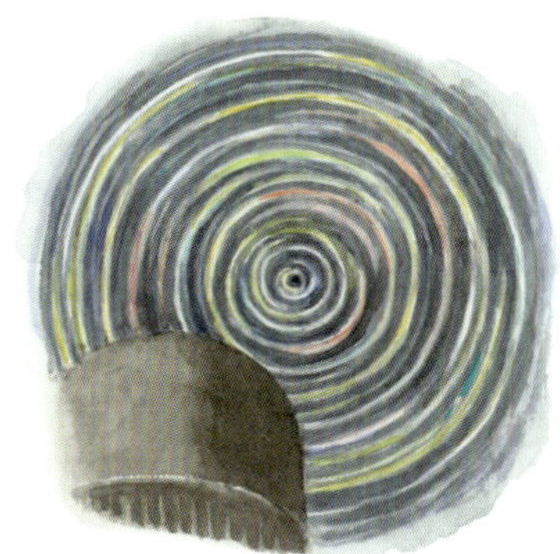

10 After David Malin. Nine-hour exposure of star trails around the south pole

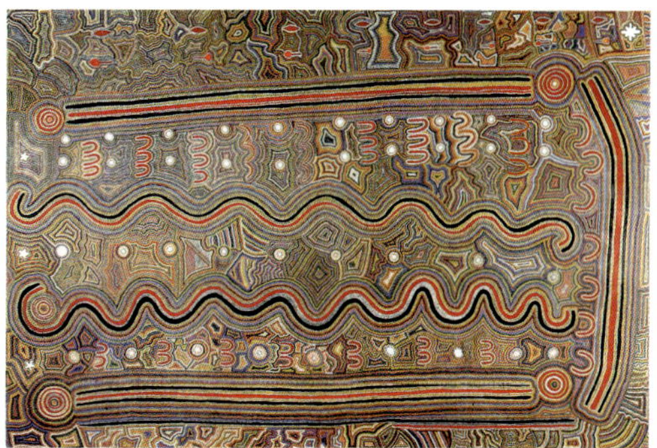

11 Paddy Japaljarri Sims. Night Sky Dreaming, 1993. Acrylic on canvas, 281 x 486 cm. Gallery of Modern Art, Glasgow

Paddy Japaljarri Sims is a senior figure in the Warlpiri community at Yuendumu, northeast of Alice Springs. He is responsible for *Night Sky Dreaming*, which tells an immensely complex tale of the spirits who formed the heavens. This picture was painted, with the help of about thirty relatives and friends, during a month-long ceremony accompanied by endless story-telling, joking and laughter, dancing and singing, much of it performed during the night, under the jewelled canopy of stars. This single painting is the product of a religious community. Huge pictures like this used to be drawn on to the ground itself—as if the sky was, for a while, reflected in a magic pool. They are now painted on to canvases laid on the ground using modern pigments. When the ceremony's over, the Aborigines have no use for the paintings that were created during it. They have no tradition of hanging pictures on walls, nor, in truth, any walls to hang them on. So the paintings are sold to earn income for the people and promote wider awareness of their traditional culture.

The rippling circles and waving bands that provide *Night Sky Dreaming* with its celestial skeleton are strikingly similar to the ancient so-called "cup and ring" marks (ill. 12) found painstakingly carved into exposed boulders on the other side of the world, in Europe. Their significance has been lost, but a plausible explanation could be that they were star-pictures particularly relevant to birth-signs of the people who lived in that region. When filled with water, some could literally have acted as star-mirrors, designed to bring the heavenly bodies down to earth, perhaps on occasions such as a birth, initiation or wedding, so that their celestial influence could be more effective. The fact that

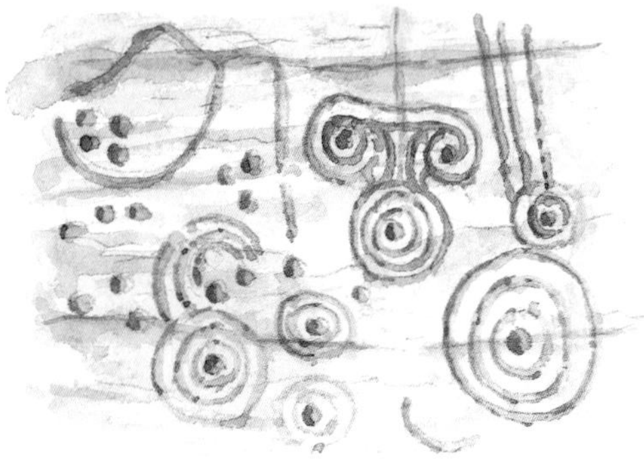

12 Cup and ring marked stone, c. 2500 B.C.E. Achnabreck, Scotland

some were carved on slopes might have enabled supplicants to re-enact the "spirit flow" from heaven to earth.

People continue to believe that their fortunes are, somehow, linked to the stars, though they follow them in newspaper columns, rather than reading their meaning in the heavens. Until Galileo turned his newly invented telescope on the night sky in 1609, people could only guess what the stars actually were. Early man must have sensed, as we do, when he looked into outer space, that he was gazing into something infinite – or at least infinitely beyond his comprehension – and he surely must have found this belittling. The Roman poet, Valerius Flaccus, expressed it well: "the very quiet of things, the silence of the world, the stars … fills us all with fear". But at the same time, the stars, particularly the brighter ones, appeared much nearer to us – eternally out of reach, but not that far above our heads. They *had* to have a meaning for us. If they didn't, why were they there?

The explanation found in many cultures around the world was that stars were the souls of those who had died and of those waiting to be born. When the Roman emperor Hadrian's favourite, Antinous, died, a new star appeared in heaven, and Hadrian was convinced it was his beloved boy's spirit. Shooting stars, which we now know to be meteorites burning on entering the earth's atmosphere, were interpreted as flying angels in medieval Europe, and, traditionally, you made a wish whenever you saw one. Australian Aborigines, on the contrary, believe shooting stars are dying spirits, and they avert their gaze with respect as soon as they see one. Changes in the heavens could augur either good or evil. But they couldn't be irrelevant, especially since such changes in the stars were extremely rare. The most famous celestial incident was the star that appeared over Bethlehem at Jesus' birth. It is rendered here in stone as a heavenly flower by the great medieval sculptor, Gislebertus (ill. 13). You can almost hear the angel whispering, as it gently touches one of the Magi's hands, "Wake up, wake up! It's time to be on your way." No eyes in art open with such fresh delight–despite the fact that this sculpture has been stripped of all its brightly coloured paint, and the eyes have lost their settings of azure glass.

The first humans must have noticed that the stars appeared to be set in fixed patterns and that they all revolved, en masse, around one of the poles (ill. 10). They were naturally tempted to see faces and creatures, humans and gods in this vast configuration of dots. In the northern hemisphere, the most familiar constellation is the Great Bear–also known as the Plough or Big Dipper (ill. 14)–not just because it's easily recognised, but because the last two stars on its "ladle" point to the North Star, which is distinguished in the night sky by its splendid isolation. To the Chinese, this pole star became very important because it provided the anchor-point for the north-south axis along which all their imperial and cere-

13 Gislebertus. *The Dream of the Magi*, c. 1125–35. Stone. Cathedral Museum, Autun, France

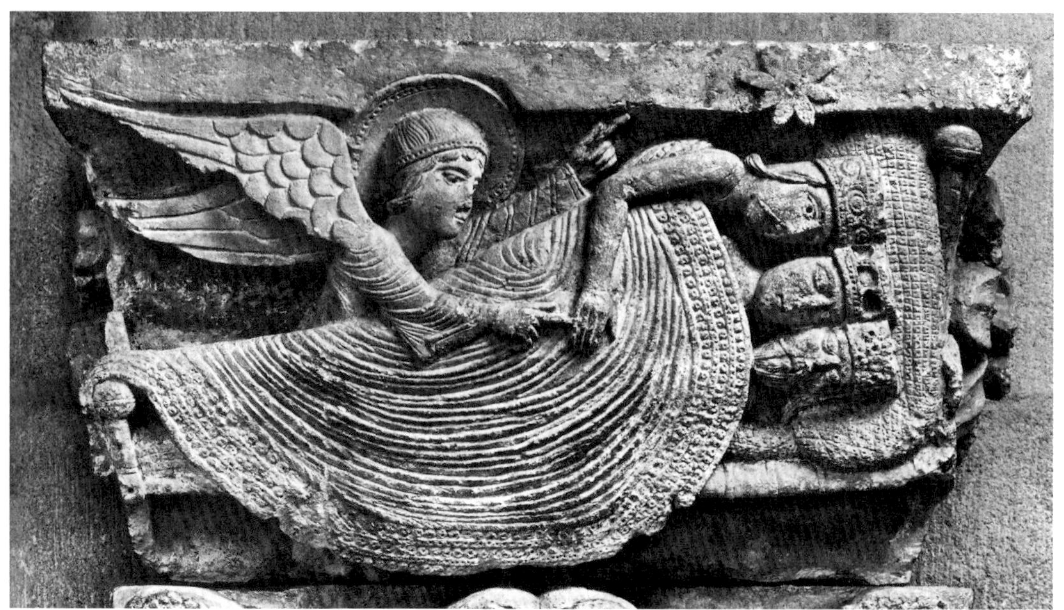

monial buildings were constructed. The garden at the extreme northern end of the Forbidden City in Beijing contains many curious stones. One has natural markings that look like a priest worshipping the Great Bear (ill.15)–the constellation that, itself, bows to the North Star.

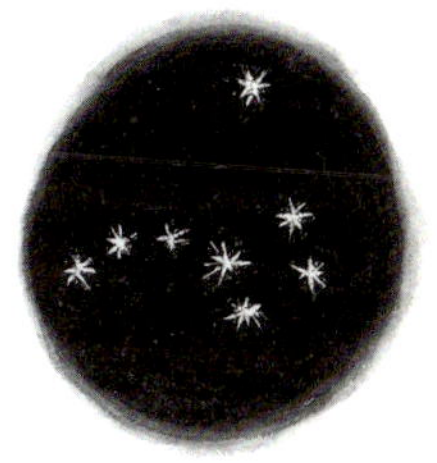

14 The constellation of the Great Bear, also called the Plough, showing the two "pointer" stars indicating the North Star

This order of stars appeared to be irrevocably fixed. Below them–and therefore closer to earth–were seven "heavenly bodies" that appeared to be free to move across the sky: the sun by day, and by night the moon and the five planets that were then visible to the naked eye. Mars, Mercury, Jupiter, Venus and Saturn together with the sun and moon still provide names in several languages for the seven days of the week. These celestial beings were thought to be above our heads, but not far off. It was observed that things became increasingly hazy the further they were away, but the sun and moon had sharp outlines, so they had to be fairly close. For the same reason, it was argued by ancient Greek philosophers that the sun and moon had to be no larger, or smaller, than they actually appear. But there was another remarkable thing about the sun and the moon. However you look at it, it's an extraordinary coincidence, in cosmic terms, that the sun and moon appear, from the earth, to be the same size. This similarity made their differences all the more remarkable. The strong light of the sun makes everything flower with colour. The weak light of the moon is veiled during the day and only emerges at night. The sun and the moon–widely believed to be the two eyes of heaven–have become so deeply ingrained in our imaginations, literature and religious symbolism that it is probably impossible to assess the extent of their influence on our history. Certainly our understanding of sexual differences–the sun is always male, the moon almost always female–would not have been the same if the earth's satellite and its sun hadn't been paired so precisely.

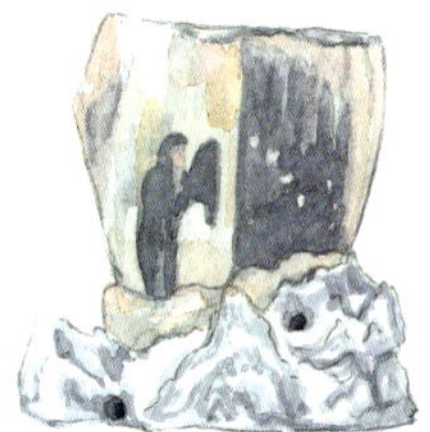

15 Natural stone mounted in the garden of the Forbidden City, Beijing

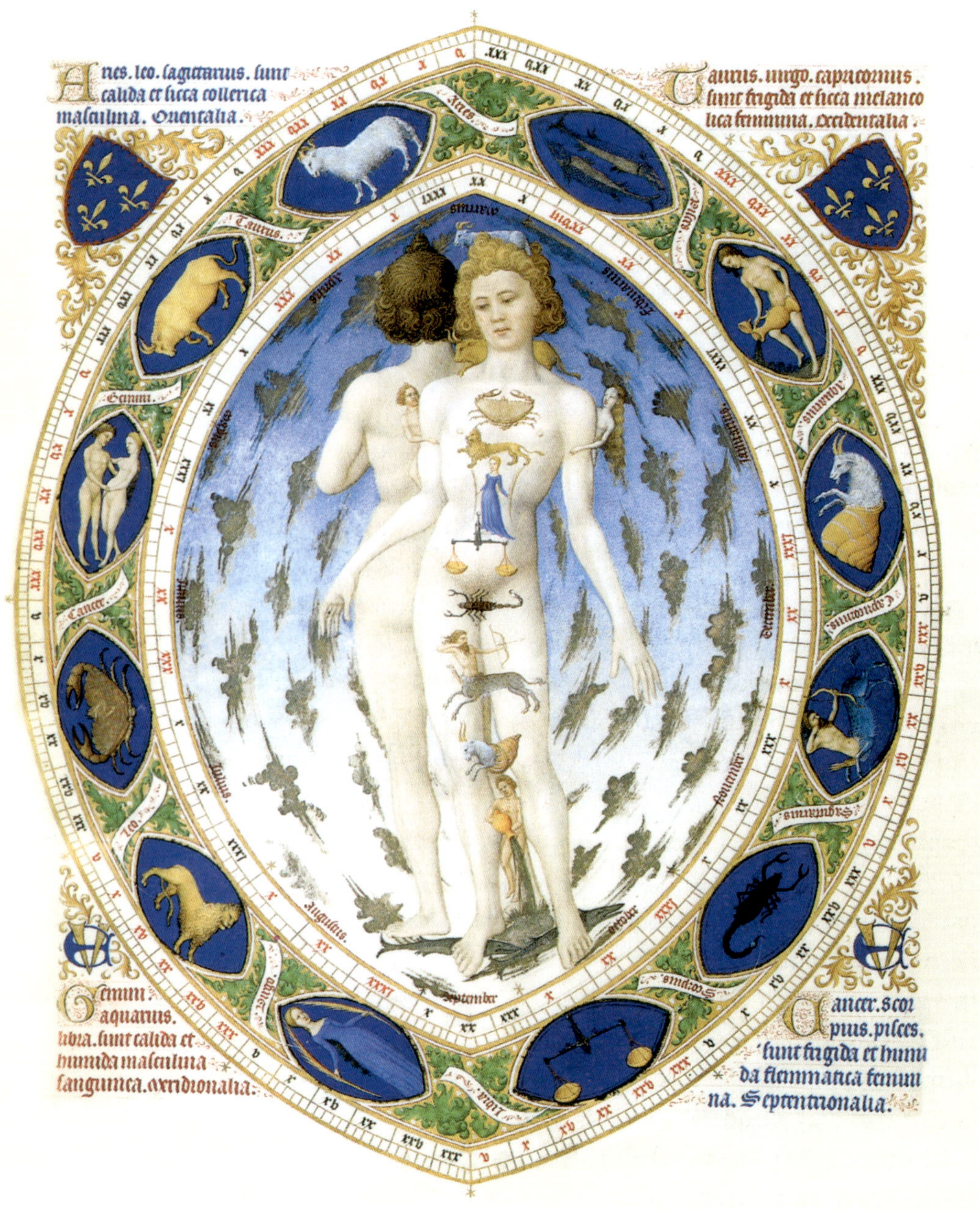

16 Limbourg Brothers. *Les Très Riches Heures du Duc de Berry*: Anatomical Man, c. 1410. Musée Condé, Chantilly, France

The five planets were observed to journey across the sky within a broad band under 12 constellations. These came to be called the zodiac–a set of stars that has had an incalculable influence on human thought. In a world governed by the zodiac, everything had to fit–there were 12 hours of the day and 12 months in the year, 12 labours of Hercules and 12 tribes of Israel, Jesus had 12 apostles, King Arthur 12 knights and the Dalai Lama 12 councillors, and there were 12 Chinese years to a cycle. In many ancient religions, these zodiacal signs were believed to have a special effect on our lives. Their conjunction with different planets at your birth shaped your character and indicated your future. This was your "star sign". Saturn imparted laziness; Mars, aggression; Jupiter, ambition; Venus, voluptuousness and Mercury, greed. Hindus added two demonic planets to the set–Ragu and Kauthu who swallowed the sun and the moon when they were eclipsed. Personifications of these nine planets–including the sun and moon–sit at the entrance to all Hindu temples.

Zodiacal divination rapidly became extremely complex, as growing armies of astrologers, from Mexico to India, France to China, earned a living wage attributing every possible feature and ailment of the body and mind to stellar influences. They are graphically depicted here in this miniature from the *Très Riches Heures* (ill. 16). Many must have doubted the efficacy of astrology, particularly if they'd paid a lot for a prediction that turned out to be wrong, but the Roman philosopher Seneca surely spoke for the majority when he asked: "Think you so many stars shine in vain? Even the smallest ones that do not appear to move have dominion over us." We looked at the stars in the sky and the stars in our eyes and wondered what it all could mean.

Many early explorers tell stories of "primitive" people looking behind mirrors in amazement, but they were almost certainly

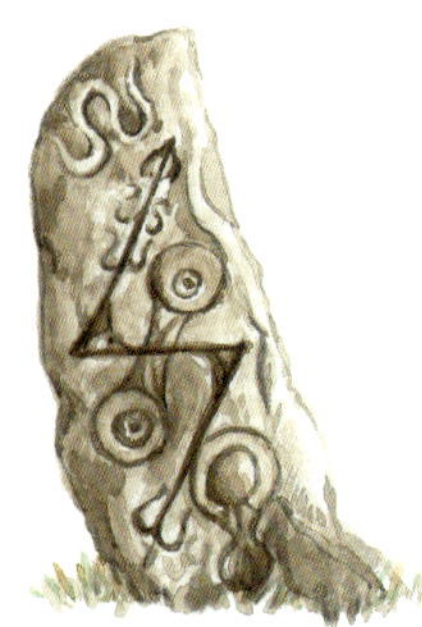

17 Pictish stone, with serpent, Z rod and mirror symbols, c. 6th–7th century C.E. Aberlemno, Scotland

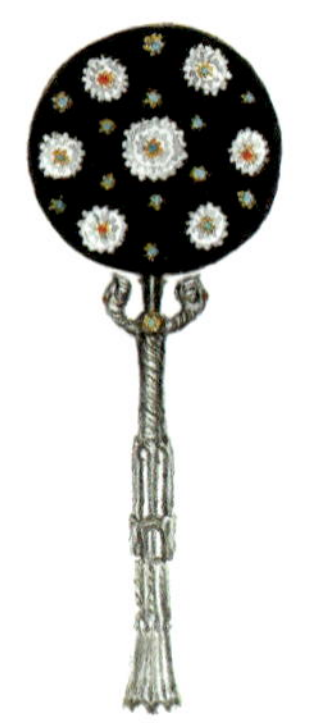

18 Mirror, 1500–50 C.E. Istanbul, Turkey. Ebony, turquoise and ruby, 26 cm long, 10.7 cm diameter. Topkapi Sarayi Museum, Istanbul

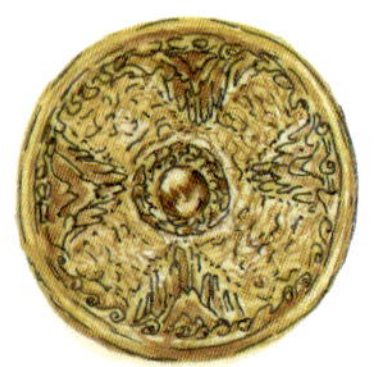

19 Bronze mirror from Horyuji, 8th century C.E., Nara period. Chinese or Japanese, 35 cm. National Museum, Tokyo

being fooled. We've been looking at our reflections from earliest times, in ponds, shiny wet surfaces, and later, when we developed the art of making them—at least 6,000 years ago—on polished stone and metal surfaces. Mirrors have been found in early burials in many parts of the world. They were possibly possessions treasured from puberty, to be taken on one's journey into the next world. We automatically associate them with vanity—but this is a modern interpretation. Appearances, in the past, were important for their own sake, and one would, after all, want to look one's best before the gods, as one did in life. Mirrors are mostly but by no means invariably associated with women. The images of mirrors found on Pictish stone slabs (ill. 17) across Scotland are thought to celebrate people of standing, and mark territorial boundaries. And we know that mirrors were carried on journeys by Chinese explorers and used to fend off evil spirits—presumably by deflecting their evil gazes back on themselves.

What did our ancestors think they were seeing when they looked at themselves in a mirror? It was a commonplace among the ancient Greeks that everything gave off images, and you could catch them yourself in a mirror. These translucent ghostly images were magical emanations of your spirit—and of its substance. For most people around the world believed, one way or another, that spirits were distillations of the stars. Nothing was solely material in our ancestors' world; it was as if god was just on the flipside of everything you looked at.

So it's on the backs of mirrors that we find clues to what people thought they were looking at on the front—a microcosm of the macrocosm, no less, because the backs of mirrors are often decorated with condensed world pictures. This Turkish mirror (ill. 18) shows the heavens in miniature, with the sun and moon and five planets and the 12 constellations as rubies and turquoise set in silver rosettes in ebony—so evocative of the real colour of stars. Many oriental mirror backs (ill. 19)—which were often hung on cords, not held in the hand—show the axial mountains of creation rising from the waters of the underworld, and reaching up to the land of the blessed. Mankind was thought to embrace, within its being, all the faculties of the universe—inanimate existence, vegetative life, sensitive life and, over and above these, the god-like faculties of reason and judgement. So looking into one's own eyes was like seeing the world in a bead of dew. The immensely refined design on the back of this Celtic mirror (ill. 20) dating from the first century C.E. can't, surely, be mere pattern-making. The designs repeat each other in ever reduced sequences—just as everything has its place in the order of creation, from the twinkling stars to your sparkling eyes.

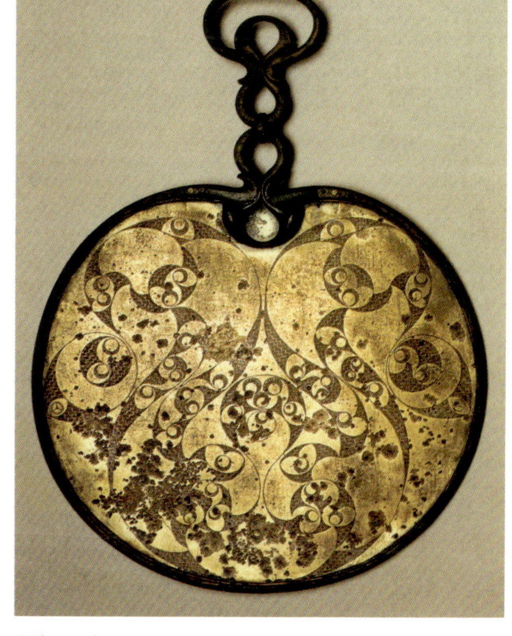

20 The Desborough Mirror. Celtic, c. 1st century C.E. Bronze, length 350 cm. British Museum, London

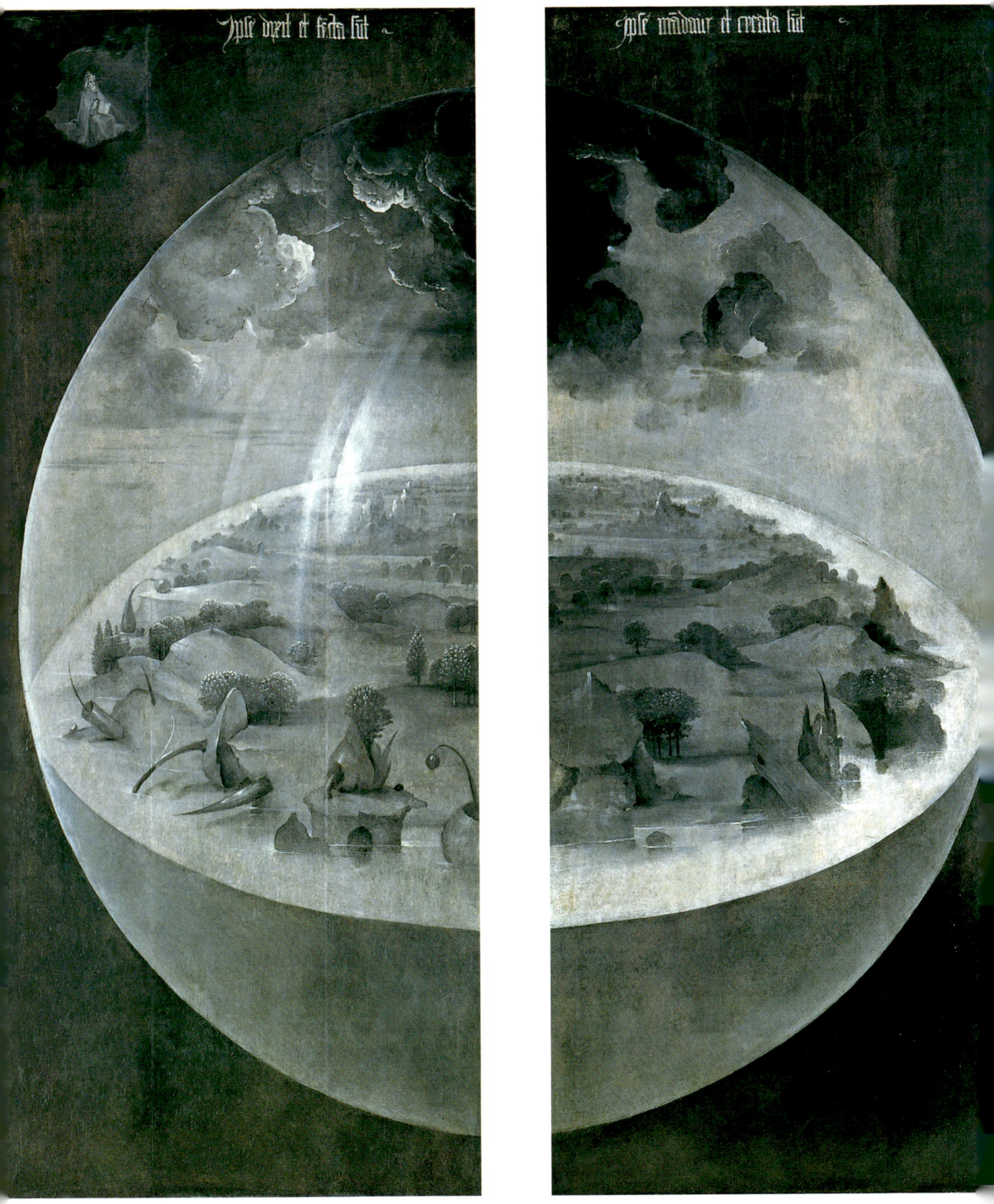

Ipse dixit et facta sunt

Ipse mandavit et creata sunt

Chapter 2

When the Earth was Flat

We first looked at the world about 150,000 years ago. Our species of humankind, *Homo sapiens sapiens*, emerged in Africa, but didn't begin to populate the rest of the globe until about 60,000 years ago. We've changed the whole planet dramatically and drastically since then – in an unbelievably short time, geologically speaking – but we haven't in any essential way evolved further ourselves. Originally we lived alongside another, older species of humankind – *Homo sapiens neanderthalensis* – who had lived in Europe for about 250,000 years. They looked different from us (ill. 2) – how subtly different is shown in a recent remarkable reconstruction at Zurich University, based on the skull of the Gibraltar 2 (Devil's Tower) Neanderthal child (ill. 3). Neanderthals were bigger-boned than ourselves; they had beetling brows and were considerably stronger and had larger brains. But there is no firm evidence that they made art. Among other traits peculiar to our species, there might have been some evolutionary advantage in the making of art. Perhaps art bound human groups closer together and made them stronger. It is possibly significant that at the same time we began to make art on any scale and in a form that lasted – approximately 40,000 years ago – Neanderthal man became extinct. Now we are the only type of humans on the planet.

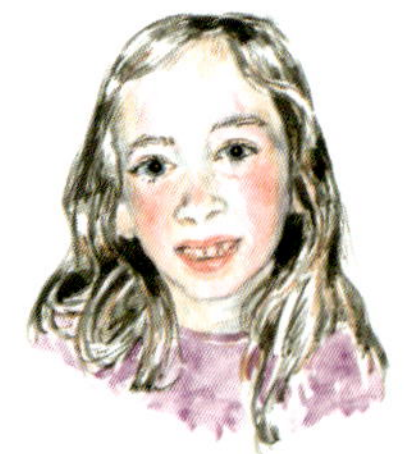

2 Isobel Johnson aged 7, 2005

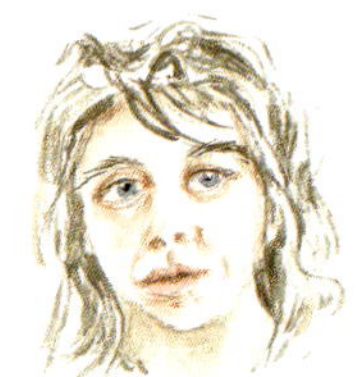

3 Reconstruction of a Neanderthal child by the Anthropological Institute of the University of Zurich, Switzerland

Our species was extremely successful, spreading along the coastlines and up the river valleys of the world with remarkable rapidity. They outwitted any opposition, and overcame all obstacles with their ingenuity. Driven largely by a need to find new

1 Hieronymus Bosch. *God Creating the World.* The external doors of *The Garden of Earthly Delights* Triptych, c. 1505, see p. 146, ill. 24, p. 214, ill. 36. Prado, Madrid. Painted just after Columbus sailed over the edge of the sea; one of the last images of a flat Earth.

hunting areas–human beings, like most other animals, are essentially territorial–they first spread across Asia to reach the islands in the Pacific and Australia. Sea levels were a hundred metres lower at that time due to the grip of the last ice age. Land masses that are now islands, like New Guinea and Malta, were linked to mainlands. Then humans moved up into Siberia and down into Europe. They ventured across the Bering Strait, which was then a glaciated land bridge, down to the tip of South America. The pattern of human occupation of the world is now becoming clearer as scientists examine DNA samples and trace people's antecedents. It's possible to do this because, though people are forced to move to survive, their inclination is to settle in one place, and, if all goes well, families will occupy one locality for hundreds of generations. People today romantically think of themselves as wanderers, but most of us have a much stronger homing instinct.

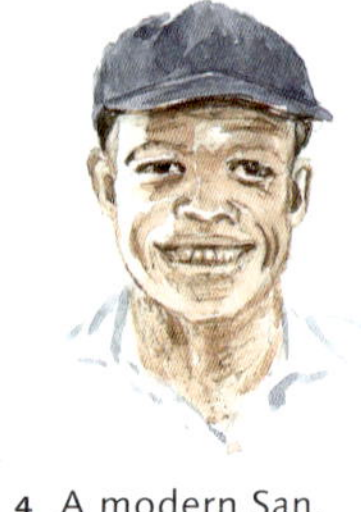

4 A modern San, Africa

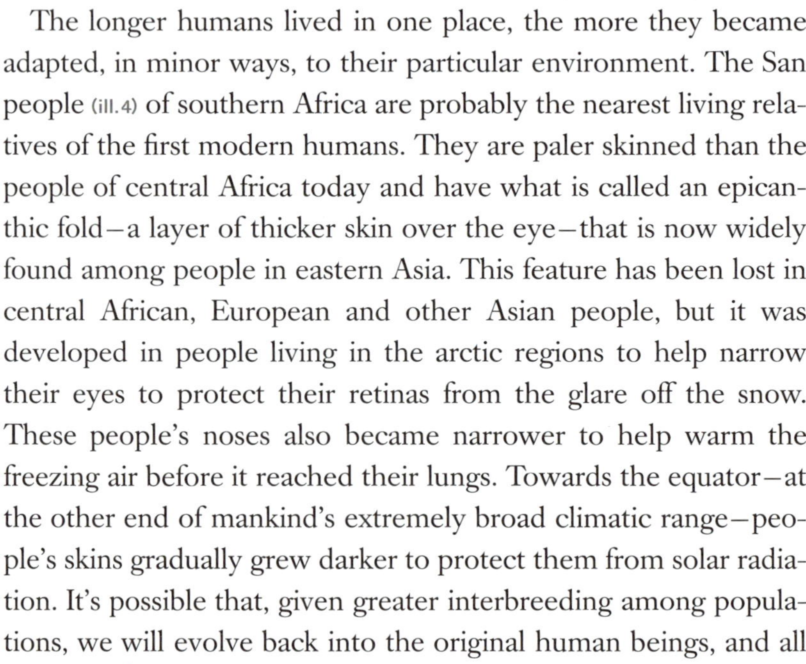

The longer humans lived in one place, the more they became adapted, in minor ways, to their particular environment. The San people (ill.4) of southern Africa are probably the nearest living relatives of the first modern humans. They are paler skinned than the people of central Africa today and have what is called an epicanthic fold–a layer of thicker skin over the eye–that is now widely found among people in eastern Asia. This feature has been lost in central African, European and other Asian people, but it was developed in people living in the arctic regions to help narrow their eyes to protect their retinas from the glare off the snow. These people's noses also became narrower to help warm the freezing air before it reached their lungs. Towards the equator–at the other end of mankind's extremely broad climatic range–people's skins gradually grew darker to protect them from solar radiation. It's possible that, given greater interbreeding among populations, we will evolve back into the original human beings, and all become San-like once again. Scientists now think the first humans were, on average, just under two meters tall, thin in build, with a fairly dark skin and slightly narrow eyes. They would not look out of place on any urban street.

As humans settled they started to domesticate animals and cultivate plants, and being naturally gregarious and feeling safer together, they began to build villages, then towns and cities. The first major civilizations grew up along the world's great fertile river valleys—the Nile in Africa, the Tigris and Euphrates in Mesopotamia, the Indus in India and the Yellow River in China. These cultures are mostly thought to have emerged about seven to eight thousand years ago, but archaeologists are beginning to discover shadowy evidence of extensive settlements in shallow waters off the coast, particularly of India, on land that was dry fifteen thousand years ago, before the sea levels rose as the polar icecaps melted at the end of the last ice age. As archaeologists begin to explore the sea bed, it seems probable that man's urban history will be found to be much older than currently estimated.

The world became more crowded and people began to fight each other for resources. Cultures clashed. Then the differences in our appearance, which had evolved over tens of thousands of years, were used to justify one group's domination over another, such is the importance we have always given to the evidence of our eyes. People who *look* different, it was totally reasonable to assume, must *be* different. A beautiful casket from 1300 B.C.E. (ill.5) was found in Tutankhamen's tomb. It was used to hold several pairs of the young Pharaoh's sandals and was decorated with scenes showing him fighting his neighbours, presumably to ensure that Tutankhamen would continue to walk over Egypt's enemies in the afterlife. One panel depicts the red-skinned Pharaoh in his chariot, his bow-string pulled back to form a perfect triangle in the centre of the composition. His pointed arrow, held horizontally, is ready to fly. The chariot's horses raise their front legs, with their magnificent feather-plumed manes held high into the air. Behind the king are ranks of red-skinned soldiers marching and riding through rows of flowers. Divine well-being is advancing. Just as the sun's spreading rays dispel the night, so the Pharaoh eradicates the forces of darkness. Before him, with his arrow poised to fly, there sprawls a panic-stricken heap of black-skinned Nubians, their legs and arms flailing in a chaotic jumble as they try to flee. The accompanying hieroglyphs tell us that Tutankhamen is "the perfect god, the image of the sun rising over foreign lands ... crushing the vile land of Kush". This was propaganda, and it worked. Archaeology is only just beginning to rescue the sophisticated Kush civilisation from the ancient Egyptian myth-making which depicted their darker-skinned southern neighbours, quite untruthfully, as disorganised barbarians. The Egyptians later suffered a similar fate: travelling people in Europe were called "gypsies" as a term of contempt.

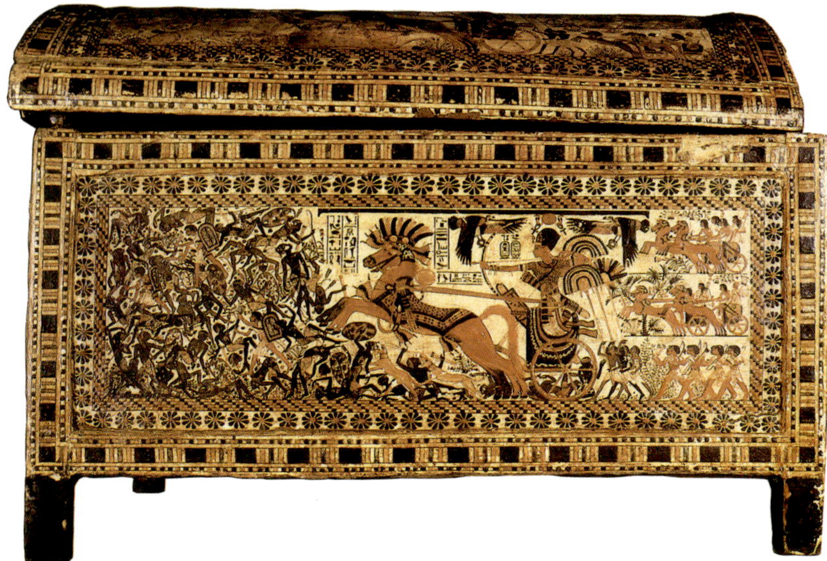

5 Tutankhamen in his chariot crushing "the Vile Land of Kush", 1300 B.C.E. Casket, stuccoed and painted wood. The Egyptian Museum, Cairo

This early example of racism wasn't just a political exploitation of difference, though we tend now to interpret it as such. The ancient Egyptians believed they were obeying a natural law. There had to be a reason why someone's skin was darker than another's. Was it perhaps that paler people were purer, and therefore closer to heaven? After all, you don't find brown in the sky. You see all the hues there, from gold to deepest purple, but never brown. It's the one colour missing from the rainbow. Brown is the colour of earth and excrement. The oldest surviving social hierarchical society in the world—the caste system in India—is fundamentally racial. The ancient Sanskrit word for caste, *varna,* means colour. At the top were the Brahmins—the priests and teachers, astrologers and healers—who were invariably pale-skinned. Next down were the Kshatriyas, kings and warriors, politicians and police. They were a little darker. Below them were the Vaishyas, the merchants and craftsmen, shopkeepers and servants. Darker still. At the bottom of the heap came the Shudras—the untouchables. They literally were so, because they performed society's unclean tasks, like shovelling excrement, clearing away corpses—and keeping pigs. They were the darkest of all. The caste system became set about 3,500 years ago, and stems from the era when fairer-skinned Aryan people began to invade India from the northwest, and conquered the indigenous, much darker-skinned Dravidian tribes who had migrated to southern India from Africa thousands of years before. But the Aryans might not have been able to assert their authority so strongly and to maintain it, had not a hierarchy of skin colour appeared so logical.

When we eventually realised, only a few hundred years ago, that we were just another species of animal, Karl Linnaeus—the man who gave his name to the system which we still use to classify all living organisms—thought he could distinguish, in 1735, four different types of *Homo sapiens*: "*American:* hair black, straight, thick; nostrils wide, face harsh; beard scanty; obstinate, content, free. Paints himself with fine red lines. Regulated by custom. *European*: Hair yellow, brown, flowing; eyes blue; gentle, acute, inventive. Covered with close garments. Governed by laws. *Asiatic:* hair black; eyes dark; severe, haughty, covetous. Covered with loose garments. Governed by opinions. *African:* hair black, frizzled; skin silky; nose flat; lips tumid; crafty, indolent, negligent. Anoints himself with grease. Governed by caprice." It's not difficult to guess to which group Linnaeus, the Swede, thought he belonged. It was the era of the slave trade that shipped millions of Africans across the Atlantic in appalling conditions, to live short lives on the cotton and sugar cane plantations of America, the Caribbean and Brazil. There had been countless slave trades around the world before then, and the practice was not formally abolished till the nineteenth century, in 1833 in Britain and 1865 in America, though brutal tribal slavery is still practised in some parts of Africa today. We now know the word "race" has no scientific basis at all. Our differences are skin deep—underneath we're all the same people. Yet the terrible myth of racism lingers because we're still, despite the advances of science, affected by differences perceived by our eyes. Seeing, from the very beginning, was the way we made sense of the world. And seeing enabled us to create art.

The earliest art produced by human beings only survives as paintings or carvings on rock—hence its name "rock art". This gives the wrong impression because it's most unlikely that this art form was the only one practised then. Art must surely have decorated perishable surfaces—the ground, mud or wooden houses, and people's bodies. Like a stick that appears bent in water, our understanding of the art of the past is skewed from the truth by our modern view of it. And that view is based on the tiny amount of art that happens to survive. The idea that it's worth keeping the art of other cultures is very recent in origin, and still not accepted in many societies. Museums as we know them today have only existed for two hundred years. Most dynasties did their best to wipe out all traces of the one that went before. The Baroque artists of seventeenth-century Europe blithely obliterated Renaissance frescoes because they thought them primitive. If our idea of the Renaissance is totally inadequate, how much more so must be our perception of the art of cultures that flourished thousands of years earlier, whose existence only survives in caves and on scraps of stone!

The meaning of rock art is now becoming much clearer since archaeologists have begun to pool their knowledge with anthropologists who have studied similar, not necessarily rock-based, art that has been produced—and in rare instances is still being produced—in communities that have remained isolated from modern man, such as the traditional Aborigines who live in the vast desert regions of Australia. Rock art is found all over the globe, from Australia (ill.6) to Sweden (ill.7) and California (ill.8). The largest painted area is to be found in China (ill.9)—the Mountain of Flow-

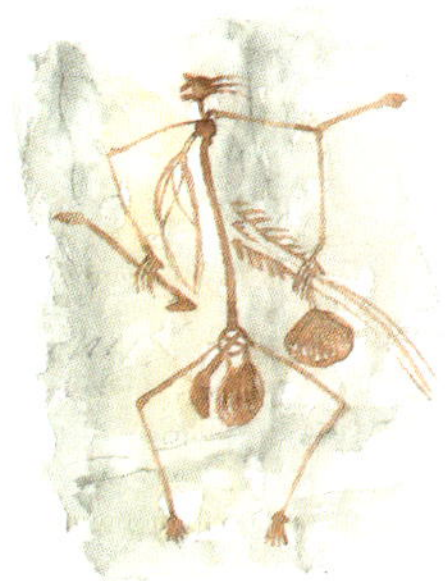

6 Rock painting at Obiri, by the East Alligator River, c. 500 C.E. Approx. 120 cm high. Northern Territory, Australia

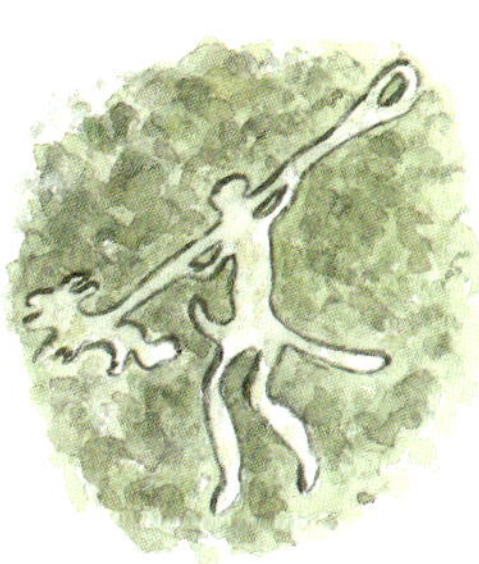

7 Petroglyphs at Fossum, c. 1000 B.C.E. Bohuslan, Sweden

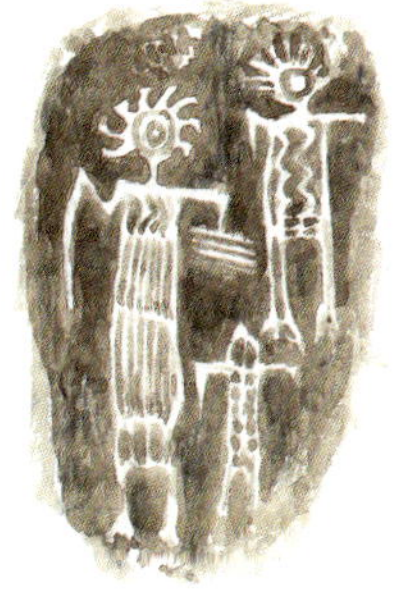

8 Incised drawings, Renegade Canyon, 1st century C.E. Coso Mountain Range, California

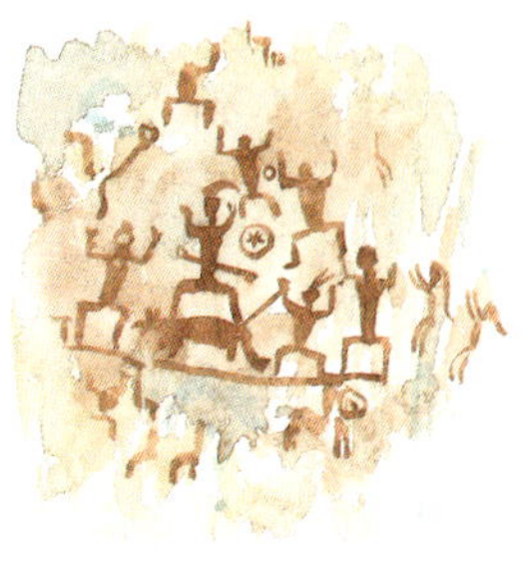

9 The Mountain of Flowers, Hua Shan, 1st century C.E. Guangxi, China

ers at Hua Shan in the southern Guangxi province. It stretches over a rock shelter 40 metres high and 200 metres long, and is decorated with images that relate to frog dances which are performed by local villagers at the base of the cliff. Frogs, which appeared at the first rains, were believed to be the offspring of the thunder god. It's probable that most rock art around the world was originally associated with dances and ceremonies, masks and costumes that have now been lost.

There is a family resemblance between these images, though they were produced by peoples who could never have known of each other's existence. These similarities spring partly from the limited means of mark-making then available to mankind: the same restricted palette of pigments—mostly vegetable dyes, earth pigments such as ochres, and charcoal—and the same basic methods of application—sticks with frayed ends used as brushes and hollow reeds used as spray guns. It's tempting to liken these early artistic efforts to young children's art which is also similar the world over. Children's art only becomes distinctive and individually expressive when the children grow up and become aware of their wider social context. But it would be totally wrong to think of rock art as being in some way the childhood art of mankind. It was the product of adults who had minds quite as mature as our own. The similarity one senses in rock art springs from the fact that it was made by people who were living in what was, give or take climatic differences, the same world, and they looked at it in the same way. People painted and carved rocks and caves because they believed that the earth gives birth.

Before our modern scientific age, anyone who started thinking about how the cosmos worked just couldn't make it out. The evidence of our senses told us that the ground we were standing on was flat, but then where did the sun go at night? What were the stars? Where did the water come from that fell from the sky? If an apple fell down, why didn't the moon? From what were creatures born? It seemed that there would never be final answers to such questions. It wasn't that our ancestors were dimmer or less inquisitive than we are. They simply didn't have the keys to unlock the secrets of nature. Until four hundred years ago there were no telescopes or microscopes to examine the macrocosm or the microcosm. Moreover, many people felt it was wrong to try to extend the range of sight their creator had given them. To the religious-minded, people were born to be bathed in mystery.

Our modern age didn't begin in earnest till Columbus tried to sail to India westwards and discovered America instead and Galileo, for the first time in history, looked at the moon through a telescope. Until then, people could do nothing but gaze at the world around them with wonder. They could have all sorts of theories about how it worked–but none could be proved. That's why scientists were called philosophers until three hundred years ago, because all they could do was add another theory to the existing mythological explanations of the universe. A handful of ancient Greek thinkers calculated that the earth could be a sphere orbiting the sun, but their ideas remained buried in obscure Byzantine and Islamic libraries known to a few priests who wouldn't have dared to whisper such opinions abroad. But for the rest of us, which was effectively all of us, wherever we were on earth, the sights of nature–the ebb and flow of the tides, the waxing and waning of the moon, the seasonal round–were all manifestations of a profound mystery. Whenever you started to think about anything you came up against a wall of wonder–just as, when you tried to look into the distance, all you could see was a mist–that encompassing screen of mystery that was, perhaps, specifically designed to cushion our existence and shield us from the unknown—the Veil of Maya that the Buddha's mother kindly threw around us to prevent us remembering our birth or foreseeing our death.

The key idea that dominated people's view of the universe was that everything we could see had a special meaning for us. Many believed that we had been given eyes for this very purpose—to interpret the sights of nature. Seeing and what we could see were both sacred. It was only a hundred and fifty years ago that Darwin discovered that natural appearances, apart from a few connected with our sex drive, were utterly irrelevant to our well-being. There wasn't even a particular type of food that had evolved its beauty especially to activate our saliva, though we've since done our best to compensate for this oversight of evolution. It was when we found out that the sights of the world weren't made for us to look at that our world picture changed utterly and forever, and our modern minds emerged. Before that, our world pictures were dominated by our attempts to understand the evidence of our senses, above all what we could see. The art and architecture of ancient cultures—these two forms of visual expression were not then divided—were, in large measure, manifestations of our ancestors' world pictures. And the more one examines these world pictures the more they have in common, though this evidence has often been overlooked because it's primarily visual and not textual.

The common assumption that underlies all early world pictures is that the earth was, despite the occasional mountain and valley, to all intents and purposes, flat. It therefore had to have an edge, or edges if it wasn't round. Many, like the Chinese, thought it was square, because the earth clearly had four directions—the east where the sun was born, the west where the sun died, the north where, if you lived in the northern hemisphere, it was cold, and the south where it was warm. Hindu ascetics, called *sadhus*—mostly aging men who have renounced all the material pleasures of life to dedicate themselves to meditation and prepare for death—still make pilgrimages in their thousands to the four cardinal extremities of India: Badrinath in the north, Puri in the east, Rameshvaram in the south and Dvaraka in the west, which were established as holy places by the great sage Adi Shankaracharya in the eighth century C.E. Many *sadhus* travel naked—clothed, as they say, in nothing but the sky—their skin often smeared with ash to remind them of their body's approaching end on the funeral pyre.

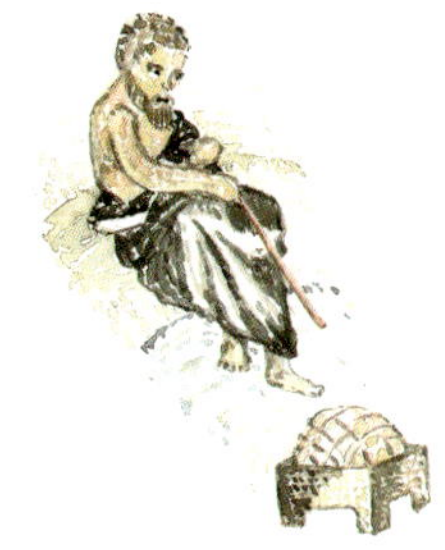

10 Detail from the *Academy of Plato* from Pompeii, 1st century C.E. Mosaic. National Archaeological Museum, Naples

The sky was a hemisphere, but how did it fit on the square earth? Our ancestors, for the most part, saw no reason to try to resolve this inconsistency. They welcomed the contradictions in nature because they thought these were poetic. They contained messages for us from the gods if we could only learn to interpret their meaning. So Plato is depicted studying a model of the world—a dome on a rectangular block—in a mosaic on a floor in Pompeii (ill. 10), while the Chinese placed mysterious Cong disc rods carved in jade (ill. 11) in the tombs of the nobility, which were almost certainly symbols of the eternal mystery of the relationship between the cylinder and the cube, the heavens and the earth, as it repeats itself through time.

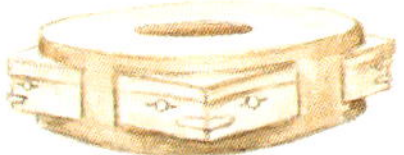

11 Cong, Liangzhu Culture, c. 2500 B.C.E. White jade, 3.4 cm high x 12.7 cm wide. British Museum, London

Clearly the world had four directions, but there were two directions that were even more important—up and down. The most potent was all around us though we could not see it: gravity, that gravest and most mysterious of forces that held everything in place. Without gravity, chaos would surely reign. All early world pictures were based on the assumption that there is an up and a down and that we are somehow caught in the middle—extraordinarily, the only creature to walk upright. The shining

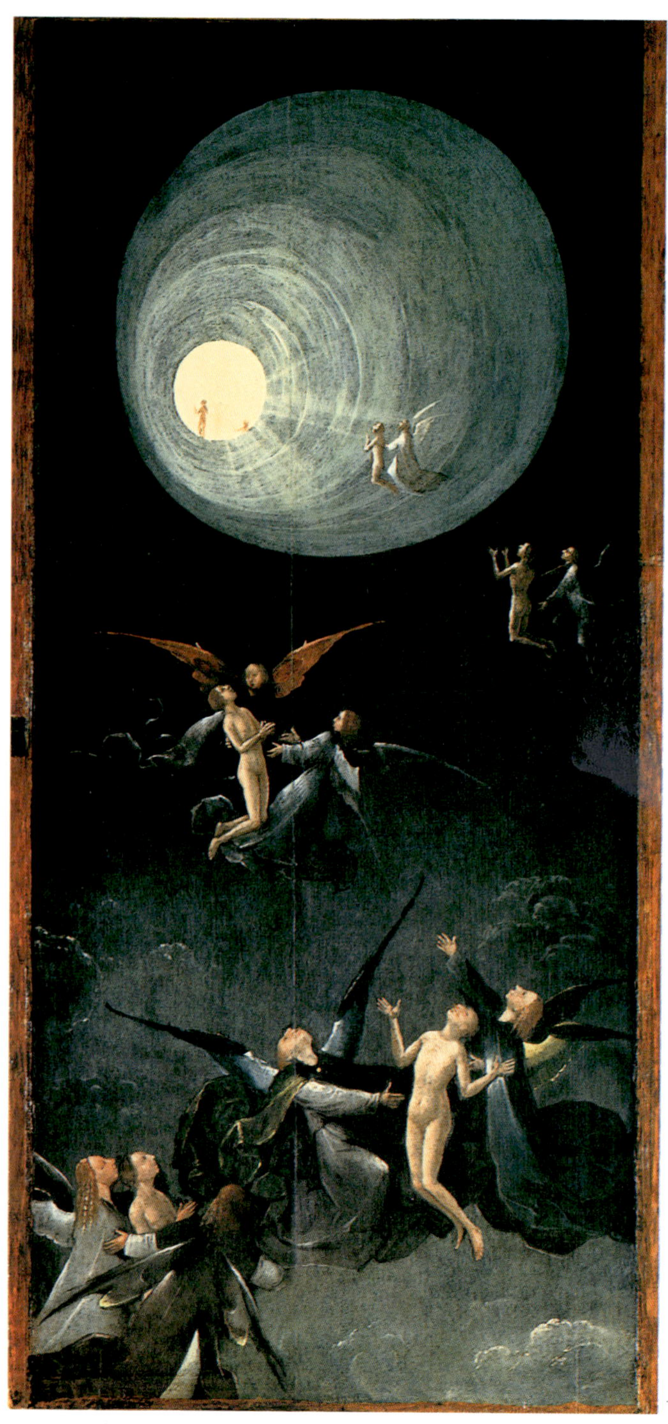

12 Hieronymus Bosch. *Souls Being Carried to Heaven by Their Guardian Angels* c. 1500–04. Right half of diptych, oil on wood. Doge's Palace, Venice

light of heaven beckoned to our soul (ill.12) while the cold grave waited for our body below. For who could deny the evidence of their senses? The body when it dies becomes cold and heavy and falls, while all that's living is warm and rises. Rising and falling were the primary motions of creation.

Some ancient Greeks, like Democritus (460–370 B.C.E.), believed that everything was made of atoms that were so tiny noone could see them, and modern science has proved them right. Lucretius described how, at the beginning of time, these atoms had fallen like rain. If they had gone on falling straight down nothing would exist. But some had fallen slightly out of true and hit each other and begun to bounce in all directions—like dust particles one sees in a shaft of sunlight across a darkened room. As they bounced about some stuck together. So, gradually, fire and water, clouds and mountains, plants and human beings were created, each with their different consistencies of mass and energy and movement. Our ancestors thought of creation in terms of contending forces, but these were primarily governed by concepts of up and down, which were strongly linked with ideas of good and evil. It wasn't until Newton worked out how an apple could fall while the moon stayed up that our thinking about the universe was totally revolutionised. That had huge implications for who we thought we were and what we thought we were doing here. Revolutions sprang from such revolutionary notions.

Before our modern age, stability, hierarchy and, above all, balance were believed to be the keys to healthy continuity. A three-dimensional cross (ill.13) underpins all the major ancient world pictures—the Christian cross is a simplification of this metaphor. There were the obvious four horizontal directions, but there were also up and down. Our ancestors had a vivid impression that heaven was hovering just above their heads. Even

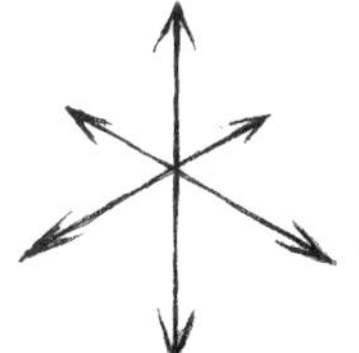

13 Three-dimensional cross

though it's now a ruin, the Parthenon on the Acropolis rock in the centre of Athens (ill.15) still shines with the light of pure grace far above the noisy, polluted city. When pristine it must have been an extraordinary beacon of clarity and harmony, high on the brow of a hill–perhaps the world's finest symbol of mankind's aspiring, god-like mind. When Sir Christopher Wren rebuilt the churches of London after the great fire of 1666, he drew a spiritual tidemark across the city. His fifty new white marble spires and towers shone brightly in the upper air, while their brick skirts were hidden in the teeming secular world below (ill.14). Until our materialist age, no worldly edifice was allowed to encroach on this celestial realm, just as no building today is allowed to rise higher than the dome of St Peter's in Rome or the god-encrusted towers of the Sri Meenakshi-Sundareshwarar Temple in the Hindu holy city of Madurai in southern India. The Islamic fundamentalists' attack on the World Trade Center in New York in 2001 was, in part, an attack on materialistic architecture.

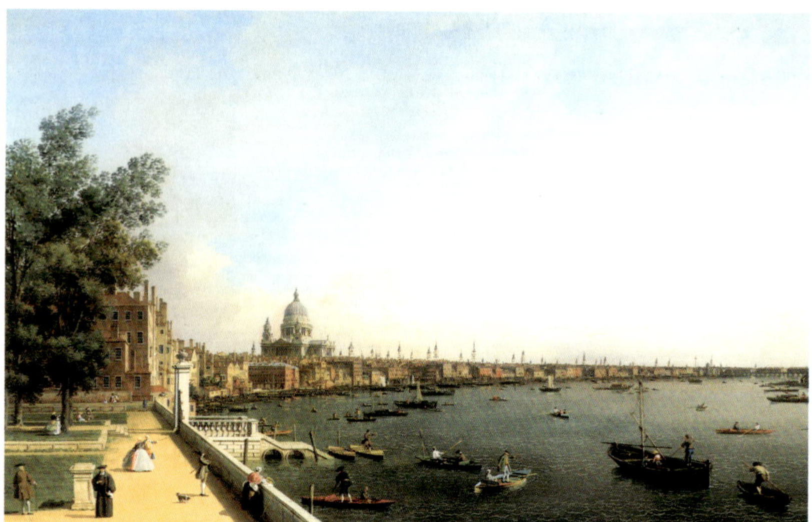

14 Antonio Canaletto. *The Thames, London, from the Terrace of Somerset House with the City of London in the Distance*, c.1750. Private collection

Countless pillars graced the ancient cities of the world, but we no longer take the few that remain, like Nelson's column in Trafalgar Square in London, as literal elevations of our heroes into the heavenly realm. But that is why the British erected this column in 1840 to the admiral who won the Battle of Trafalgar. It stands 185 feet high and four magnificent lions guard its base. Lions, facing the four directions (ill. 16) originally sat on top of dozens of Dharmastambhas–Pillars of Righteousness and Cosmic Law and Order–erected throughout India during the reign of the great king Ashoka (271–238 B.C.E.), to encourage his citizens to live an orderly life in an ordered world. In early Christianity, penitents like St Simeon Stylites (387–459 C.E.) fasted on the top of immensely tall pillars and preached to crowds of thousands. These pillars not only elevated their subjects, but represented the great tree of life that held the sky up, the pivotal axis between the world above and the world below.

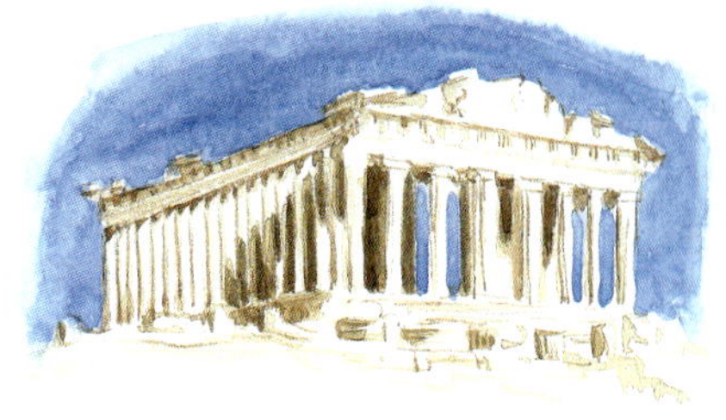

15 The Parthenon on the Acropolis from the south-west, 447–435 B.C.E. Athens

Where the three meridians crossed–east to west, north to south and up and down–was the centre of the world. Mountains were often believed to mark the exact spot. Standing at the centre of the world, on a mountain top, was obviously the quickest way up to heaven. So Abraham took his son to be sacrificed on Mount Moriah in Jerusalem, the central mound of the Jewish world. Then Solomon built a temple platform around it, so all the Jews could make their sacrifices there. Then, many centuries later, Muhammad (c. 570–c. 632 C.E.) was lifted up to heaven when he was standing on this same rocky outcrop–the faithful say you can still see the imprint of his foot in the stone. The Dome of the Rock (ill. 17), one of the earliest mosques of Islam, now covers this sacred spot. Though reconstructed over the centuries, this

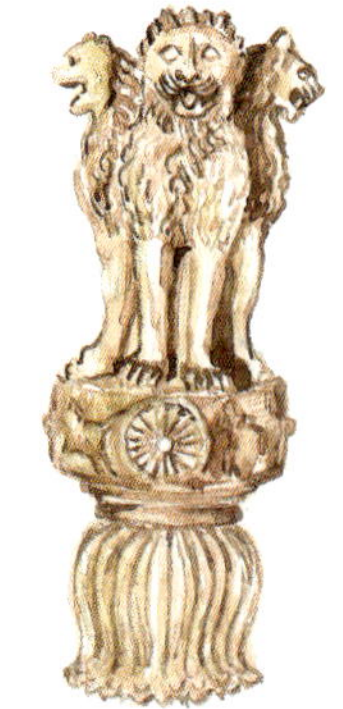

16 The Lion Capital, Ashoka Pillar, c. 250 B.C.E. Sandstone, 215 cm high. Archaeological Museum, Sarnath, India

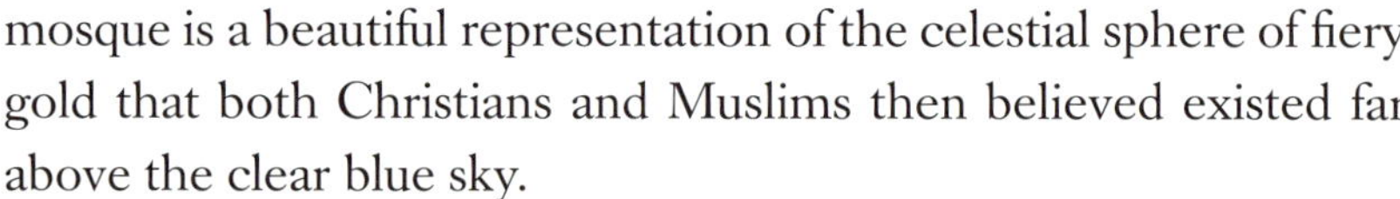

mosque is a beautiful representation of the celestial sphere of fiery gold that both Christians and Muslims then believed existed far above the clear blue sky.

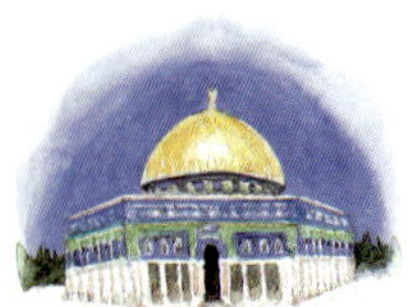

17 The Dome of the Rock, 681–691 C.E. Jerusalem

The concept of a three-dimensional axis at the centre of the world underpins the geometrical arrangement of almost all the great sacred buildings of the past, from the pyramids to Salisbury Cathedral (ill.18), from Stonehenge (p.85, ill.38) to the Taj Mahal (p.181, ill.37). They marked the spot not just where human spirits soared to heaven, but where gods came down to earth, at the crossing point of the four directions. A detail (ill.19) in Piero della Francesca's painting *The Baptism of Christ* (p.206, ill.22)–now barely visible in the original, let alone in any reproduction, because the gold leaf has worn away–shows this divine descent into the horizontal world below. At the moment when Jesus was baptised, which was the moment when Christians believe he began his mission as the Son of God, gold rays fell on him from heaven above, and began to spread out into the world in all directions, symbolised by the halo that appeared on the crown of his head.

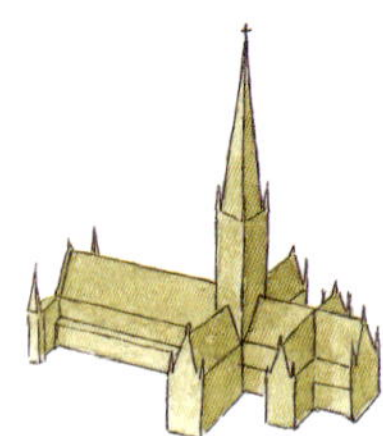

18 Diagram of Salisbury Cathedral, 1220–60 C.E. England

The Forbidden City in Beijing (ill.20) was still in ritual use until 1911. Though it is now stripped of many of its splendours, and crowded with tourists, it's still possible to glimpse the beautifully simple, profoundly humble, high solemnity of this vision of heaven on earth. The Forbidden City was at once a home for the emperor, and the religious and administrative centre of the empire. All these ancient palace temples, from the Hindu Angkor Wat and the slightly later Buddhist Angkor Thom in Cambodia (ill.21) to the Aztec Tenochtitlan in Central America (ill.22) took a similar form. They were square or rectan-

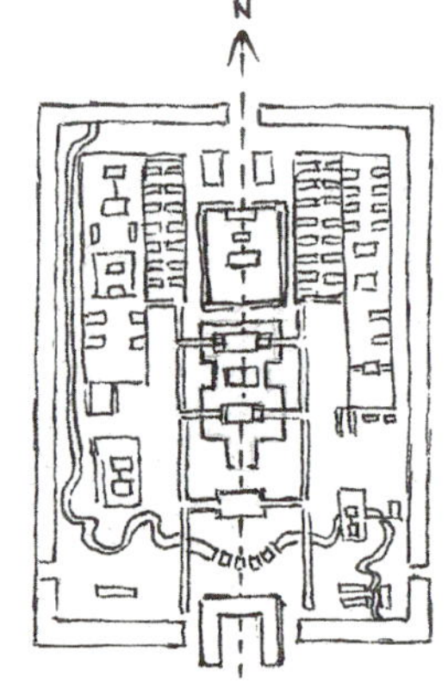

Plan of the Forbidden City

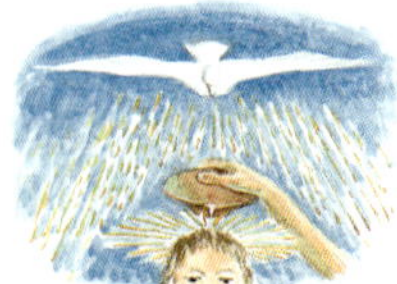

19 After Piero della Francesca. The *Baptism of Christ*, detail, c.1440. Oil on panel. National Gallery, London

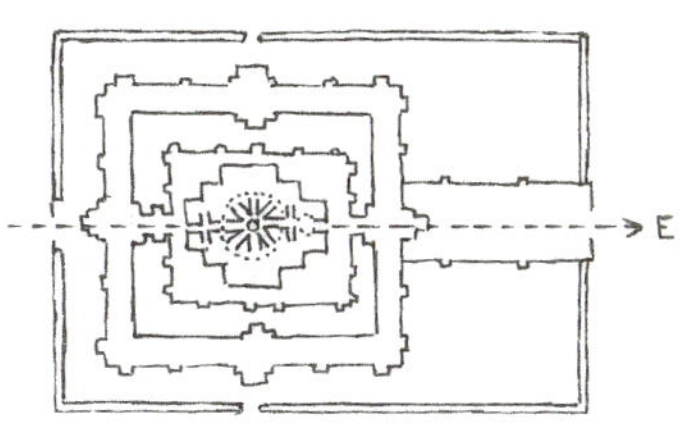

21 Outline plan of Angkor Thom, 12th century C.E. Cambodia. Each perimeter wall is over 2 kilometres long

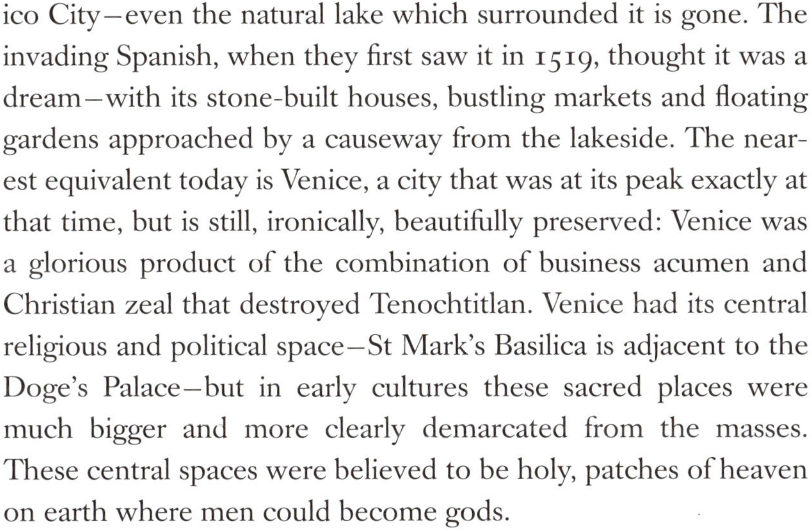

gular in shape, reflecting the earth bounded by the four cardinal points. Each palace-temple was surrounded by a wall and a moat – not just to keep unholy people out, though that was one purpose – but to symbolise the cliffs and oceans around the edge of the earth. Tenochtitlan is now totally buried under modern Mexico City – even the natural lake which surrounded it is gone. The invading Spanish, when they first saw it in 1519, thought it was a dream – with its stone-built houses, bustling markets and floating gardens approached by a causeway from the lakeside. The nearest equivalent today is Venice, a city that was at its peak exactly at that time, but is still, ironically, beautifully preserved: Venice was a glorious product of the combination of business acumen and Christian zeal that destroyed Tenochtitlan. Venice had its central religious and political space – St Mark's Basilica is adjacent to the Doge's Palace – but in early cultures these sacred places were much bigger and more clearly demarcated from the masses. These central spaces were believed to be holy, patches of heaven on earth where men could become gods.

Today we assume everyone is equal – but in the past, rulers were regarded as divine beings and, as gods, naturally lived in

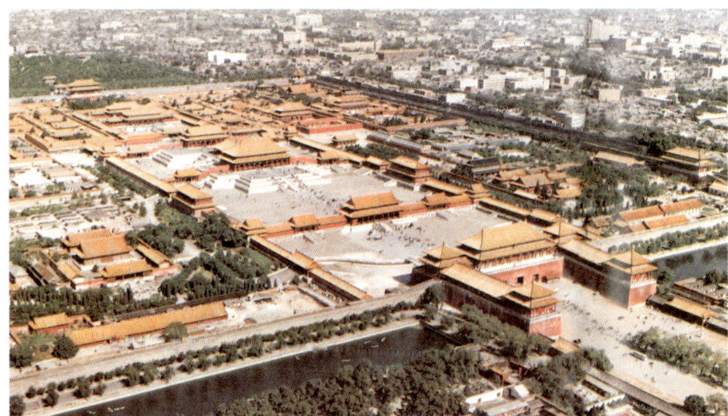

20 The Forbidden City, 1695–97 C.E. Beijing

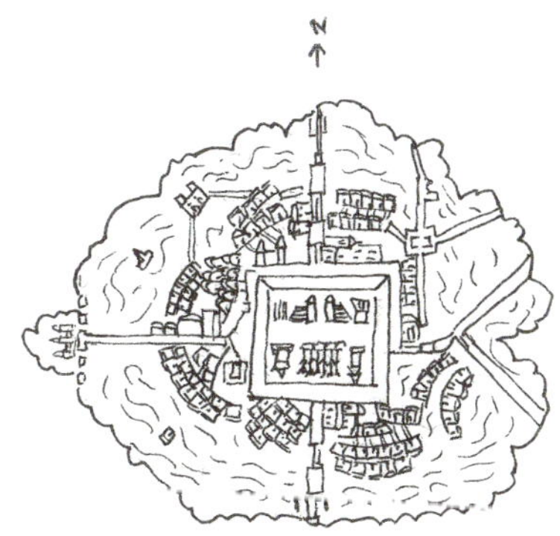

22 Tenochtitlan, from a map possibly originally drawn for Cortés, 16th century. Woodcut

compounds apart from others. Their wealth was not a flamboyant symbol of oppression but a manifestation of the well-being of the whole nation. Though some Chinese emperors, during the two thousand years the system lasted, certainly abused their absolute powers and oppressed their subjects—an aspect of their rule which has been emphasised but was nevertheless continued by certain of their communist successors—the main function of the successive Sons of Heaven was to bring peace and prosperity to the land. They did this by performing rituals and making decisions designed to maintain the harmonious balance of all creation, which they believed was manifest in heaven, and which they sought to replicate on earth. They performed these rites, except on very special occasions, within the bounds of the Forbidden City. In China, the emperor was the centre of the universe—and it moved wherever he moved. He was a god in human flesh—the conduit through which all the goodness above flowed down to the people below.

The Chinese invented the compass about 2,000 years ago. Polar magnetism revealed a profound mystery—a line of force that ran from north to south, truncating at right angles the line traced by the sun from east to west—as mysterious and invisible a power as that of gravity itself. The Forbidden City (ill.20) was believed to be located at the centre of the world where these three lines crossed. It was there that the emperor lived and breathed, made decisions and propagated his line. He had many concubines in case the empress failed to produce an heir, or a prince died. The most important single feature of the city—the axis around which everything else was arranged—was the Dragon Road. It must have been laid out with a compass because it runs absolutely straight, right through the city, from north to south. The emperor was carried along this road in a palanquin—since he was a god his feet didn't touch the ground—and performed all his sacred duties in the halls and gateways that were built along its path.

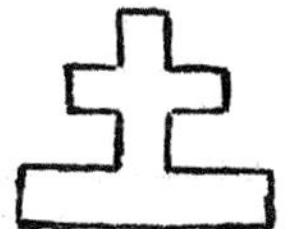

23 Chinese calligraphic sign for the earth

The emperor's daily journey began in the dark, early hours of the morning. He was carried from the north, where he lived his half-human existence, through the Gate of Heavenly Purity up the cloud-dragon ramp to the three great Halls of Preserving Harmony, Central Harmony and Supreme Harmony. Here, in a sequence of ancient rituals, he divested himself of any mortal shortcomings, became fully a god and made imperial decisions. It was in the Hall of Supreme Harmony that the emperor, on special occasions, personally presided over the final examinations to select the highest-ranking mandarins. These three halls are situated on an elevated stone pavement shaped, if looked down on from above, in the form of the Chinese character for Earth (ill.23). This is the highest place in the Forbidden City. Even today you can feel magically elated here, on a level with the surrounding treetops and gracefully curving, gold-tiled roofs. You feel, strangely, much higher than you are—as if you are walking on clouds.

When he had performed all the necessary rites in the Hall of Supreme Harmony, the emperor was then carried further south along the Dragon Road, down another cloud-dragon ramp and across a great courtyard until he arrived at the Gate of Great Harmony. There he appeared at the top of another cloud-dragon ramp to greet the officials who had arrived from all quarters of the country, just at the very moment when the sun's rays broke over the eastern horizon at dawn. It was then that he announced his edicts which were to be carried by his emissaries to the four corners of his empire. The journey the emperor had taken was profoundly symbolic—from the cold north, representing death, to

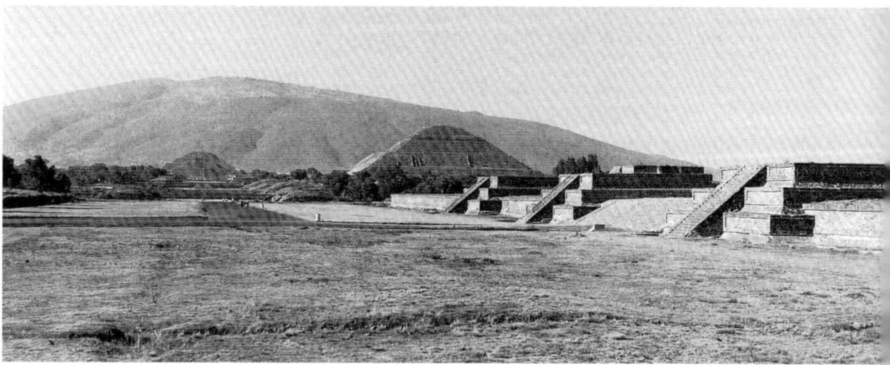

the warm south, representing life, crossing the line the sun itself would take from its daily birth in the east to its death in the west. Sacred rituals performed at the central point where the paths of heavenly and earthly life cross by someone who was half-god and half-man must, surely, help to maintain the balance and harmony of the universe from which, the Chinese believed, all goodness flowed.

We know virtually nothing about the great ghost city of Teotihuacan in Mexico. Even its name, which means "the place where men became gods", was given to it by the Aztecs five hundred years after it had fallen into ruins. But the Aztecs were the last rulers of what was essentially a continuous ancient culture, and the name they gave to this extraordinary place was probably true to its purpose, for it had many features in common with the great city, Tenochtitlan (ill.22), which the Aztecs themselves built as their capital in what is now Mexico City and which the invading Spaniards almost totally, and maliciously, destroyed. Teotihuacan was built by pre-Aztec people between about 200 B.C.E. and about 750 C.E. (ill.24). Built in about 100 B.C.E., the great Sun Pyramid is precisely aligned so that on two days of the year, in May and July, the sun is directly overhead and its eastern edge

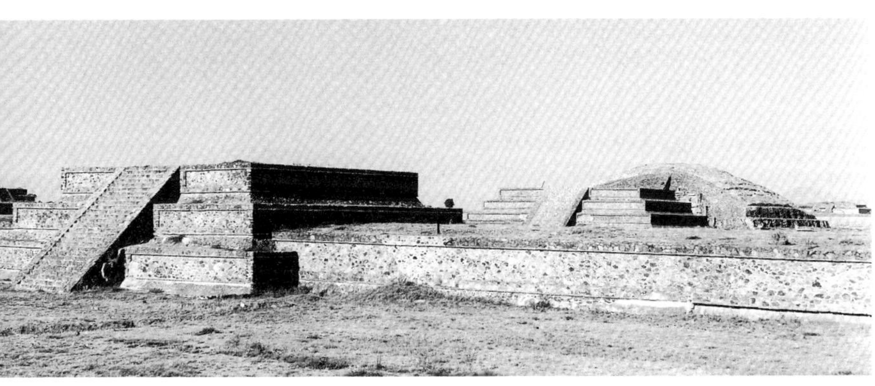

24 Teotihuacan, Mexico, c. 200 B.C.E.–c. 750 C.E.

faces directly towards the point where the sun rises on the horizon. This alignment, which is slightly off true with regard to the four cardinal points, governs the layout of the whole site, the orientation of the second, slightly smaller pyramid—believed to be dedicated to the moon—and the placing of several smaller pyramids that could be altars to planets and stars. The whole complex is possibly a celestial reflection on earth. Its meaning is lost, but the operations of the Forbidden City might give us a clue as to how this vast sacred site was used.

The current grim, almost fascist appearance of Teotihuacan owes much to its restoration in the twentieth century from heaps of rubble. Every straight edge one can see today is a fanciful reconstruction. The buildings were originally not grey, but gaily painted. The few scraps of plaster that have survived suggest that every surface was decorated with flowers, birds and butterflies—and jaguars stalking through waves of rain-lashed foliage. Walking down the main avenue—Teotihuacan's equivalent of the Forbidden City's Dragon Road—must originally have been like strolling through paradise. We know from comparative sources that sacrifices—of humans as well as animals—almost certainly took place on these high-stepped altars, but the general impression must have been of a great celebration of life, not, as it appears today, of an obsession with death. The festivals of the Aztecs and their precursors were probably more like contemporary Hindu religious rites – a better word would be riots – when everyone and everything is decked with heavy, scented garlands, though the Hindus themselves have long since abandoned blood sacrifices. Believing in egalitarianism, we like to emphasise the oppressiveness of these ancient societies, and have therefore named the main avenue in Teotihuacan "The Street of the Dead", imagining screaming slaves being dragged along it and hacked to pieces on the blood-strewn altars. Death was never denied in early cultures; it was the inevitable shadow of life. Beauty was probably celebrated much more than terror in Teotihuacan – just to what degree can be imagined if, as some scholars believe, the Pyramid of the Sun was originally covered with gold leaf and the Pyramid of the Moon with silver.

Varanasi in northern India is one of the oldest living cities in the world. Many of the religious rites still performed there probably date from at least 2,500 years ago. The city is regarded as one of the holiest in the Hindu world. It's an extraordinary ancient encrustation – riddled with narrow passages and pitted with countless shrines – high on the west bank of the River Ganges, with hundreds of steps, the famous *ghats*, leading down to the sacred waters swirling below. Every year, thousands of pilgrims bathe in these purifying eddies and fill urns to take a little home. Hindus believe the Ganges cascaded down from heaven at the beginning of time to give life to the world. The river flows from the north – from Lord Shiva's home in the Himalayas – in a southerly direction towards the sea. Varanasi is sited on an ancient crossing place that goes directly from west to east. Priests perform a fire-beacon ceremony (ill.25) on the riverbank every day

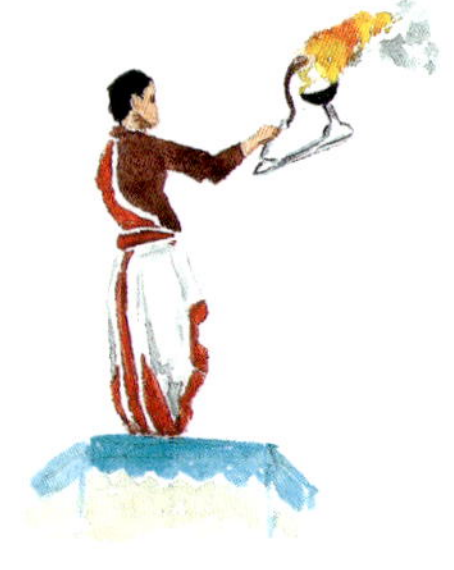

25 Ceremony greeting the rising sun, contemporary. Varanasi, India

at dawn praising the rising sun and in the evening thanking the setting rays. But surprisingly, at this crossing place, the river does not run south, as one would expect, but north, as if it were returning to Lord Shiva's home.

That is the reason why Hindus in their thousands go to Varanasi to die. Smoke from the cremation pyres rises continually along its banks. The spirits of the dead are then carried by the Ganges to Lord Shiva, whose eternal dance destroys all evil in their souls. Anyone who dies in Varanasi is guaranteed a future life as an enlightened one. But perhaps there is an even older reason for this most ancient practice, one that stems from a time before Shiva took his current form. It's fitting to cast the pale ashes of the dead into a river that runs towards the cold, white land of the north, but surely wrong to send them on a journey towards the warm, vibrant south. Varanasi is located on an exact crossing point between west and east and north and south. It is perhaps for this reason that the local priests have for centuries kept alight the Fire of Shiva, guarded by his tridents (ill.26), from which they light each funeral pyre, at the axis of the world. For Hindus believe that "the flame that leaps towards the sky leads one from the unreal to the real, from darkness to light, from death to immortality".

How fire got down to earth, presumably from the sun, was one of the greatest of all mysteries, since fire can never travel downwards. The Roman writer Lucretius describes seeing the upper branches of trees, having rubbed against one another for hours in the sunshine, suddenly bursting into flame. This must have been a much commoner sight when untended

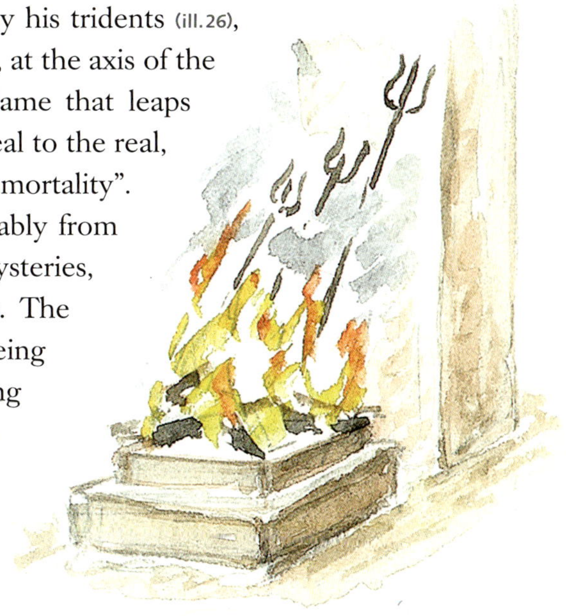

26 Shiva's tridents by the eternal flame, contemporary. Varanasi, India

woods were everywhere. Fire seemed to be contained in things and could be released as sparks, but it apparently had no natural home on earth. The most common way of making fire was by twirling the end of a dry stick in a hole made in another. There was a sexual analogy here. Early mankind must have noticed that our body temperature seems to rise when we make love–more proof, if proof were needed, that blood is a mixture of water and fire. Blood was thought to combine the two essentials of life–warmth and fluidity. Blood was liquid and fell like water, but it was also hot and red like fire. The heart–the source of blood–was the only part of the viscera left in a mummy by the ancient Egyptians because it was thought to be the vital centre–the sun in the body.

Volcanoes, where people knew of them, were generally thought to be the sites where the four "elements" of life–earth, fire, water and air–had first fallen. Earth tremors in India were believed to be caused by the elephants who held the world up shifting their feet. Earthquakes, volcanic eruptions and lightning, where they occurred together, must have struck our ancestors as having a common cause. This might explain the power of the god Pachacamac in Inca mythology. The Incas, Aztecs and Mayans–the most famous of several central and southern American early societies–are generally thought to have been sun worshippers. But this is, like so many of our interpretations of ancient religious beliefs, an oversimplification. The Incas worshipped Wizacocha, who was an immaterial presence behind the physical sun. The Huichol people, who live in the high mountain sierra in northeast Mexico, are one of the oldest native societies to have been little affected by the Spanish invasion. They praise the fire god Tatewara–the son of the sun and not the sun itself–who is not of this world but without whose warmth and protection mankind could not live. Their shaman priests carry prayer arrows for healing and seeing. Like many shamans, they close their worldly eyes when they pray so that their spiritual sight will be released, just as lightning is an arrow of fire born out of ethereal clouds.

Our ancestors saw themselves suspended on a three-dimensional cross—between dawn and sunset, north and south, and the spiritual life above and the mortal life below. But there was also the fourth dimension of time. That appeared to be a straight line, too—an inevitable procession from birth to death. But, and this was a great comfort to our ancestors, life also appeared to be cyclical. The sun appeared again, as did the moon, just as the stars revolved around the pole. But how did cycles relate to straight lines? This was the same dilemma again: how does the domed sky fit on the square earth? Was time an arrow or a wheel, or perhaps a progressive spiral? No-one had any idea how the world had begun. Buddhists and the ancient Greeks believed existence was timeless, with no beginning or end. Jews, Christians and Muslims believed that the universe had been created by god on a specific occasion only a few thousand years ago (they differ in their chosen start dates), and that time was essentially linear. Hindus believe that everything is reborn, and that time is essentially cyclical. Their different concepts of time are reflected in their religious practices. Buddhist sit still and meditate. Christians and Muslims go on pilgrimages—though often they end their journeys with perambulations around the altars of cathedrals or around the Kabah at Mecca, the rectangular block building covering Islam's sacred meteorite. Devout Hindus perfect their religious life by walking round the four sacred cardinal points of India and the sacred Kailash Mountain—the birthplace of Shiva in the Himalayas.

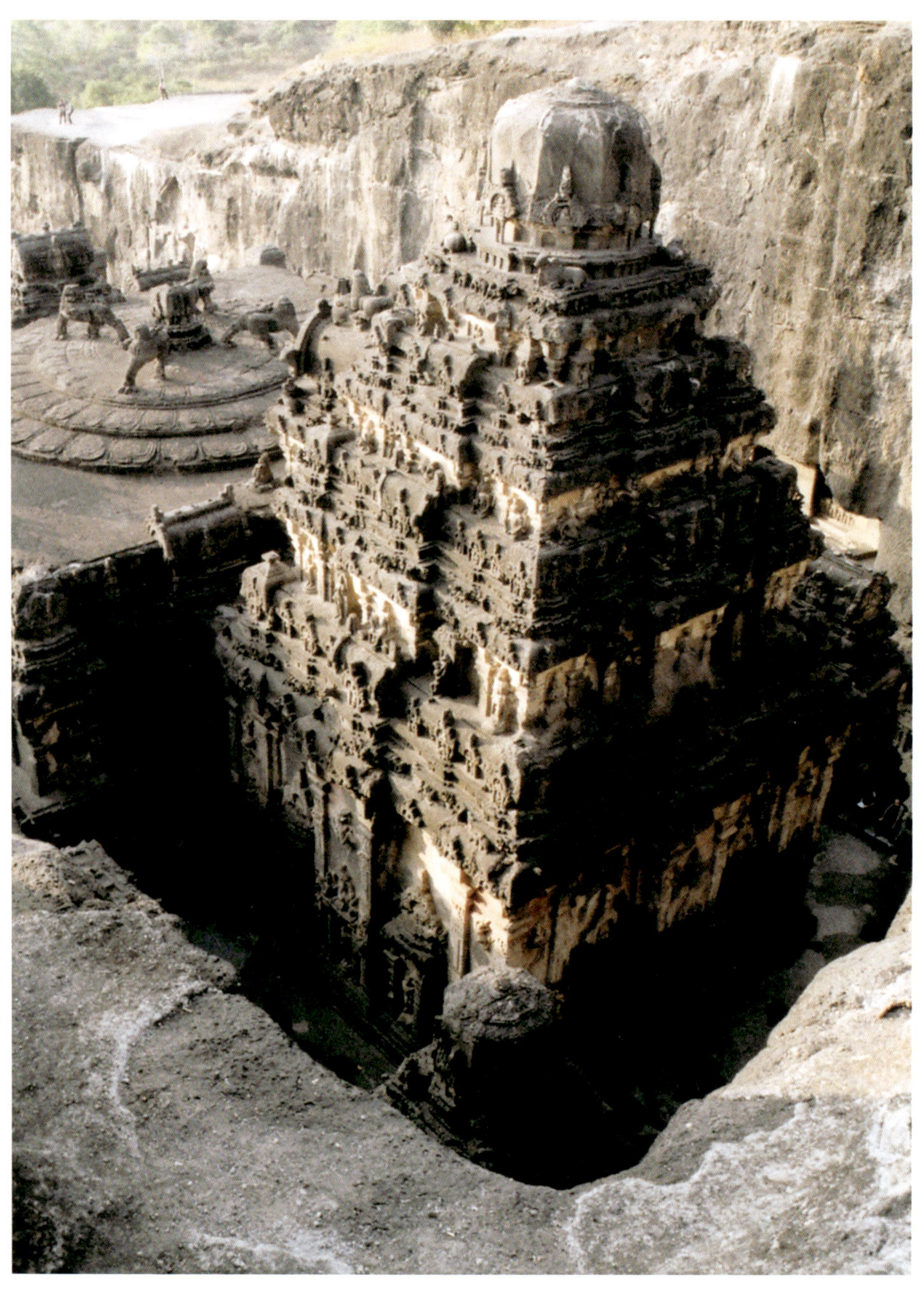

27 Kailash Temple,
8th–9th century C.E. Ellora, India

Our ancestors' world pictures were at once logical and illogical, simple and paradoxical. Above all, they were always poetic and symbolic, because people didn't believe that there would ever be a consistent, materialist explanation of all they could see. It's not surprising that virtually no complete renderings of early world pictures survive or perhaps were even attempted. They were the assumed backdrop of everyone's thoughts–and few mention what everyone takes for granted. Moreover, it just didn't occur to people then that they could look at their world from the outside. That was the prerogative of a god. We are so used to seeing the earth from outer space that we find it difficult to imagine a time, not so long ago, when the very idea of doing so would have been mind-blowing.

The Kailash Temple (ill.27) at Ellora in India was an attempt to express how Hindus conceived of their cosmos from the inside. This extraordinary rock carving would surely rank among the wonders of the world had it not been so sadly vandalised, mainly by later generations of Muslims. There's nothing like it in the world. It's difficult to photograph because the whole temple is hidden in a vast cliff. You enter at the bottom through a gateway that has been carved out of what remains of the cliff wall. Inside you find yourself in a vast chamber open to the sky, flanked on three sides by thirty-metre-high sheer rock faces that have been chiselled away. In the centre is a huge temple which looks as though it has been built out of stone blocks. The whole structure has in fact been carved out of what's left of the cliff. This colossal building, with its entrances and inner sanctuaries, tiered terraces and colonnades, is in fact one lump of sculpted rock. It took over a hundred years, from about 750 C.E., and four generations of masons to carve it, from the roof down! It must have been visualised in its entirety before the first hammer blow, by people who knew they

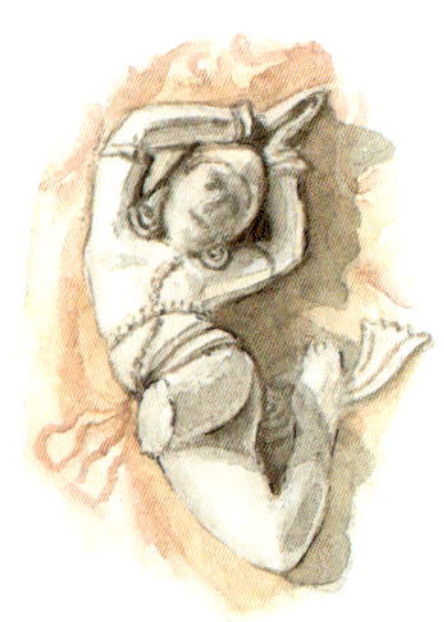

28 Devata, c. 8th century C.E. Kailash Temple, Ellora, India

would never live to see it completed. The complexity and sheer effort of realising this monumental structure is bewildering to the modern mind. Everything had to be carved in reverse and downwards, with no room for a slip of the chisel. The great Kailash Temple stands as a testament to the conviction of its makers that the world picture they were discovering within the living rock was one that, once revealed, would last forever.

The whole temple is an image of Mount Kailash, a real mountain in the Himalayas which is still worshipped by Hindus as the home of Lord Shiva, the god of creation and destruction. Mount Kailash was thought to be the divine axis between heaven and earth, and it is this aspect that is depicted in the temple at Ellora. It's topped by a vast opening lotus flower on which four huge lions prowl, guarding the four celestial gates to the east, west, south and north. The upper storeys depict heaven, the abode of the gods. Beneath this is the sky through which *devatas* (ill. 28)–the angels of Hinduism–dance and fly. Below them is the earth where humans live and gods appear from time to time to perform their miracles and get up to mischief. The whole towering edifice of earth, sky and heaven is carried on the backs of elephants–though of course it's not, which is the wonderful conceit. No elephants anywhere have been so beautifully carved–their great ears ripple delicately in the breeze while their huge feet paw through the waters of the underworld as their trunks pull up water creepers and lotus flowers–though sadly they have been so vandalised that only tantalising glimpses of their glory remain. The whole mountain must once have flowed with movement, from the paddling elephants underneath to the lions prowling on the lotus flower on top. Almost all the original painted plaster has fallen away, but what a sight this temple must have been when it was freshly decorated!

Though the Kailash Temple was carved out of solid rock, it shares something of the sensibility of the diaphanous silk banner (ill. 29) that was carried in the funeral procession of the Chinese noblewoman, Lady Dai, and afterwards laid on her coffin to waft her spirit up to heaven. Unfortunately the silk has so darkened with age that the original is virtually impossible to reproduce. At the bottom of the banner is the watery underworld, where monstrous fish circle each other slowly. Above them, a giant holds up the flat of the earth on which servants are preparing the funeral feast of Lady Dai. Higher still is the zone of the air where winds, clouds and fabulous birds are linked together in an eternal whirl. Lady Dai is already on her journey–she walks, with a stick, on top of the clouds and asks her way to heaven. Far above her head is the celestial dome of the sky, where more divine birds fly. Two gods sit guarding the gateway to heaven where the spirits of the cosmos dance between the rising sun and the crescent moon, awaiting the new arrival. No-one now knows for sure why a blackbird was associated with the sun and a toad and hare with the moon in China–perhaps they sang and danced when these heavenly bodies appeared. What we do know is that our ancestors believed that the whole of creation, from the stars in heaven to the humblest amphibian, was linked together in one flowing, flowering mystery.

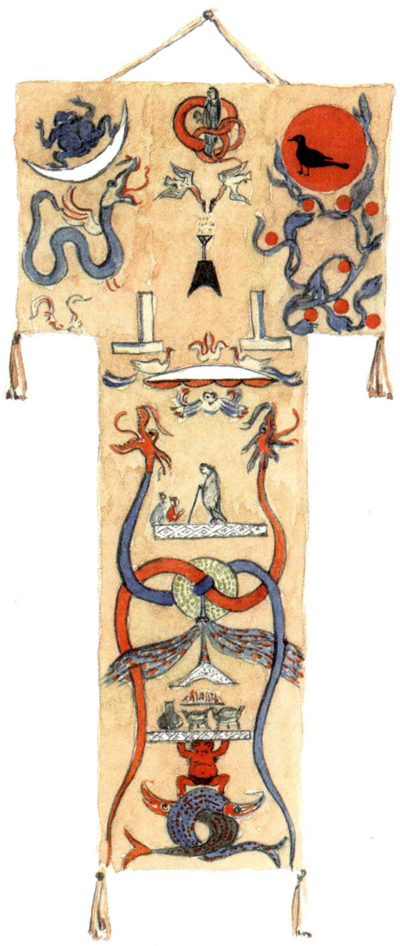

29 Funerary silk banner from the tomb of Lady Dai (Xin Chui) Mawangdui, western Hanc, 168 B.C.E. Hunan Provincial Museum, China

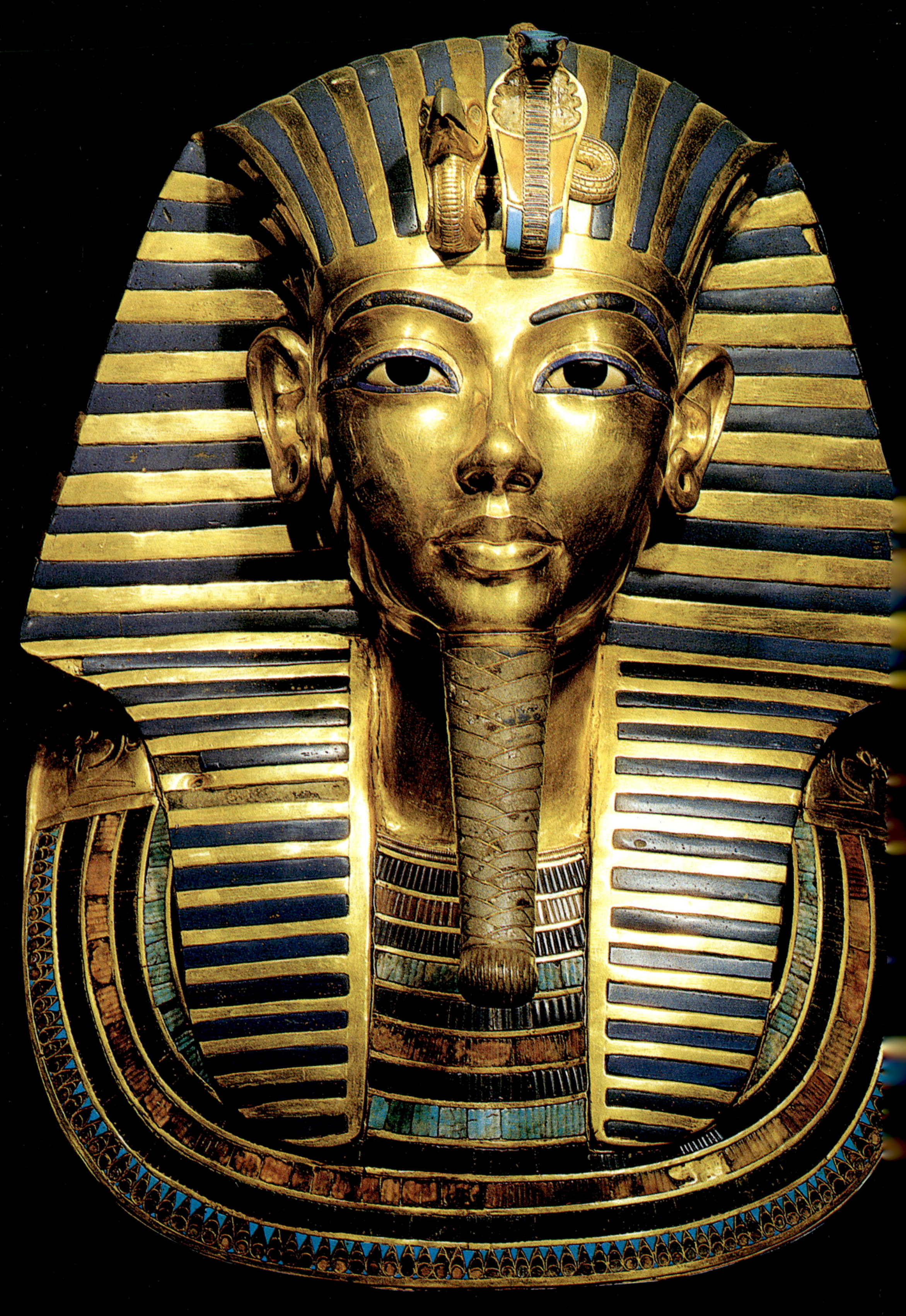

Chapter 3

Under the Sun

When the sun rises the stars are wiped out. Only the moon tries to resist—on clear days you can see its ghost lingering for a while in the morning sky. A haunting Aztec myth attempted to explain this mystery. One day Coatlicue, the fearsome earth goddess and mother of all things (p. 160, ill. 5), became enchanted by a beautiful rainbow feather that danced in the air beside her. She reached out, caught it and tucked it into her bosom. The cheeky feather took advantage of this intimacy, and Coatlicue became pregnant—with the sun. Her daughter, Coyolxauhqui, the moon, and her four hundred sons, the stars, were furious and threatened to kill their mother, complaining that the heavens were crowded enough already. The sun, hearing these threats, leapt from Coatlicue's womb, and hacked the moon to pieces. So her dismembered image (ill. 2) lay at the foot of the main sacrificial steps in all major Aztec temples.

It might seem perverse to begin an account of the influence of the sun with a story about the moon, but our ancestors believed everything was interconnected, and these connections were everything. It was out of their attempts to explain how things fitted together that the early religions and myths, arts and philosophies grew. It was self-evident to everyone that creatures had to die for others to live. Most ancient religions, therefore, involve sacrifices, of the self and of others. The sun might have dominated everything we can see, but it did not exist in isolation.

All life, obviously, depended on the sun. Nothing grew or flourished without its touch. There was light from the moon, but that

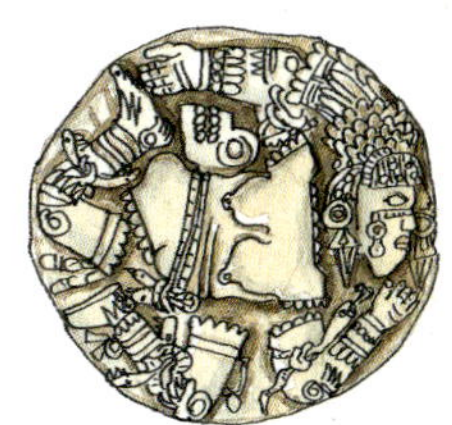

2 *The Dismemberment of Coyolxauhqui, Goddess of the Moon.* Stone, diameter 300 cm. Museo del Templo Mayor, Mexico City

1 Gold mask of Tutankhamen, c. 1350 B.C.E. Gold, faience, lapis lazuli, 540 x 39 x 49 cm. The Egyptian Museum, Cairo

was cold and pale. Only sunbeams brought warmth and colour. That was why the birds sang so gloriously when the sun appeared at dawn. All nature joined in this celebration. But what was this sun, and how did it move across the heavens, and where did it go at night before it rose again at dawn? It's doubtful if anyone in the past thought that there would ever be final answers to such questions—not even the ancient Greeks. They had more theories than most, but each tended to cancel the other out and there was no way of proving if any was right.

Lucretius, the Roman poet who dismissed all religions with contempt, favoured the idea—probably of Greek origin—that the sun didn't travel underground at night, but died every day, exhausted by its labours. In the early morning, he claimed "scattered fiery atoms" could be seen from the top of Mount Ida, gathering in the sky to create the new sun. This is possibly the idea that's depicted on the east pediment of the Parthenon (p. 49, ill. 15) in Athens. This temple was built between 447 and 433 B.C.E. to celebrate Athena, the patron goddess of the city. Few of its sculptures survive—they were destroyed when the temple was converted first into a church and later into a mosque. The fragments that remain are now mostly in the British Museum. In one corner of the pediment, horses pull the sun's chariot out of the sea in the morning. Marble waves lap around their necks as they toss their heads in rapture. In the other corner, a horse hangs its head wearily over the stone parapet (ill. 3). Its muscles and eyes bulge and its lower jaw hangs open as it gasps for breath. Some scholars think this horse pulled the chariot of the moon, but a more convincing interpretation could be that it's one of the sun's horses, exhausted after a day's work, sinking into the sea at sunset.

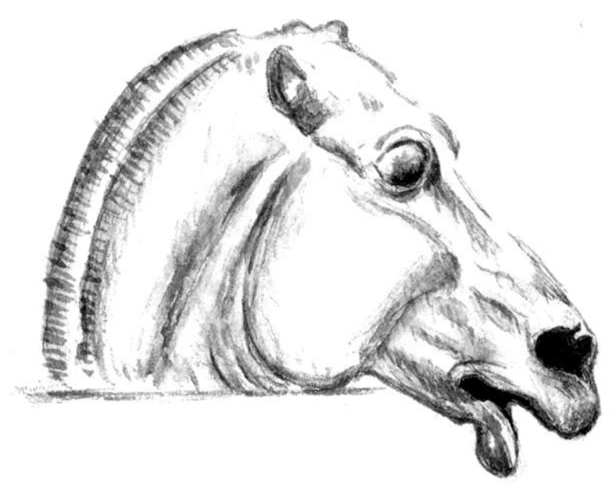

3 Right-hand horse of the east pediment of the Parthenon, 447–433 B.C.E. Marble. British Museum, London

Many early myths maintain that the sun was pulled by invisible horses across the sky. The famous four horses on St Mark's Basilica in Venice–the originals are now inside and replicas have taken their place above the portico–actually came from Constantinople and date from Roman times. They might have been used to pull a chariot of the sun–or an emperor's chariot associated with the sun, because they were gilded. Gold was always associated with sun worship, and was often stolen, which is why so little evidence of this widespread cult survives.

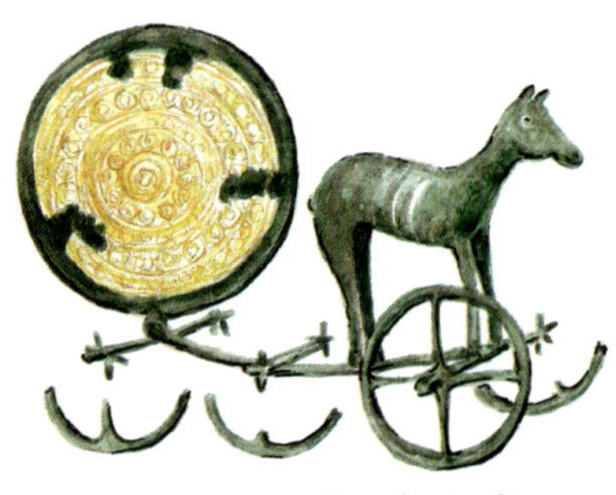

4 Sun chariot from the Trundholm bog, c.1400 B.C.E. National Museum of Denmark, Copenhagen

A rare exception is this tiny sun chariot (ill.4), which was placed in fragments, probably as some sort of sacrifice, in a bog in Denmark three and a half thousand years ago. The early people of Denmark used their dank bogs to preserve things, just as the ancient Egyptians, at the opposite end of Europe, used their dry desert sands.

This little chariot was probably a demonstration model for showing young religious initiates how the sun worked. The sun was thought to be a flat disc which shone on one side only. It was pulled across the sky by a horse. The horse and the sun are *both* on the demonstration cart. The instructor would have rolled the model from left to right showing the sun's shining side–just as the sun appears to move from left to right across the southern sky when viewed from northern Europe. Then the demonstrator turned the model round to roll the sun back to its starting point in the east, so that the initiates would see the dark side of the sun disc which was not gilded. Thus they learned why everything goes dark at night–because the sun is a flat disc that's only lit on one side.

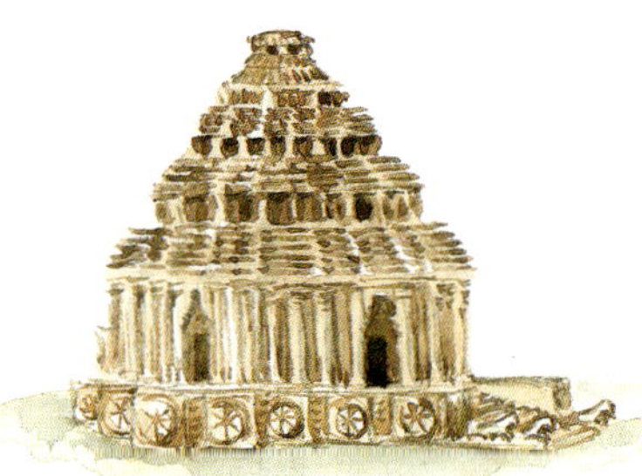

5 The remaining central tower of the Sun Temple at Konarak, 1240–56 C.E. India

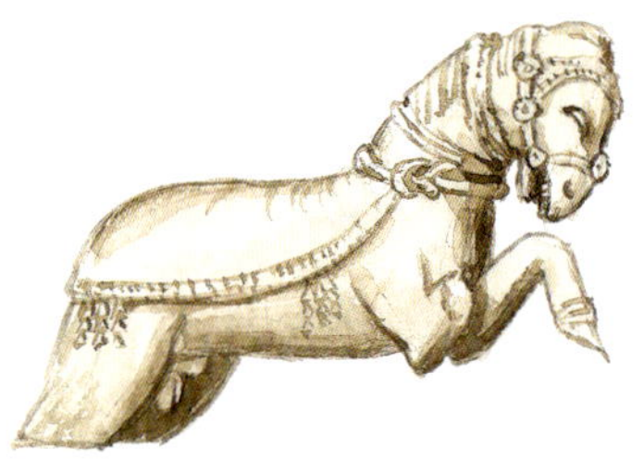

6 Detail of a horse from the Sun Temple at Konarak, 1240–56 C.E.

The great sun temple at Konarak, in India (ill.5) is a chariot, too, but on a colossal scale. The central tower is half the size of its neighbour, which was 70 metres tall until it collapsed about a century after it was completed in 1256. The temple was on the coast – the sea has now receded – on the extreme eastern edge of India. It faces due east so that the sun's first rays can strike right into the inner sanctum, where Surya the sun god stood. The whole temple is conceived as a chariot. It's being pulled by seven horses (ill.6) – one for each day of the week, and rolls on twenty-four wheels – a pair for each month of the year. It's an image of the sun returning to be reborn on the eastern horizon – and a prayer in stone to help it on its way. The sides are covered with some of the liveliest sculpture in Indian art, much of it on a minute scale, as if to praise the sun's power to inspire the most intimate stirrings of life. Herds of elephants wave their trunks and help their young, while monkeys steal fruit from trees and a buxom girl arouses an aging priest. In one tiny panel, sadly severely eroded, two lesbians make love under a mosquito net on which mice play (ill.7). Everyone is invigorated by the sun.

Many people believed that the sun, after it set, sailed back to the east across the ocean that lay under the earth. This tiny boat

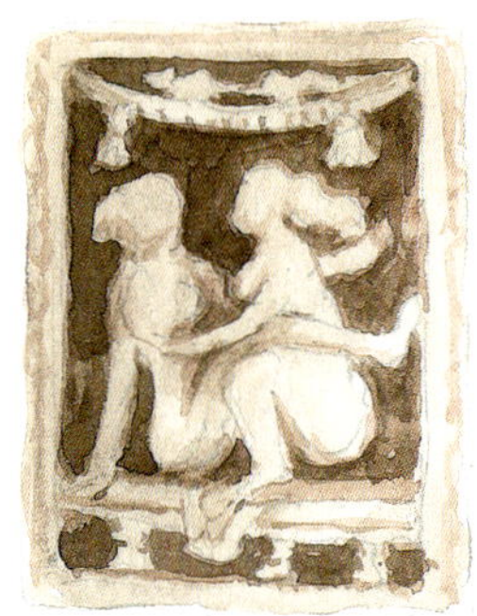

7 Sun Temple at Konarak, 1240–56 C.E., detail of a lesbian love scene. Stone relief, India

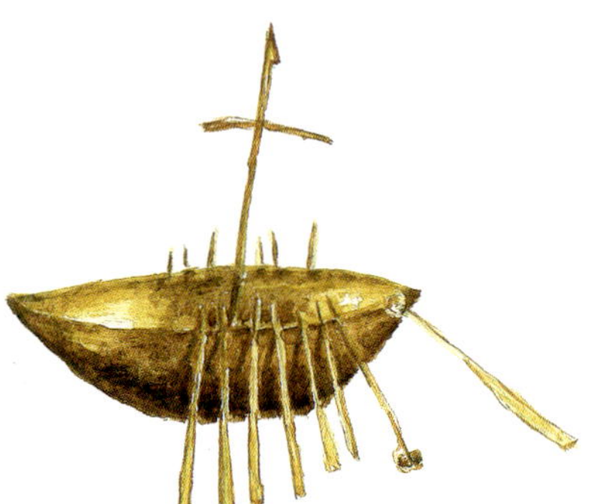

8 *Golden Boat* from the Broighter Hoard, c.1st century C.E. National Museum of Ireland, Dublin

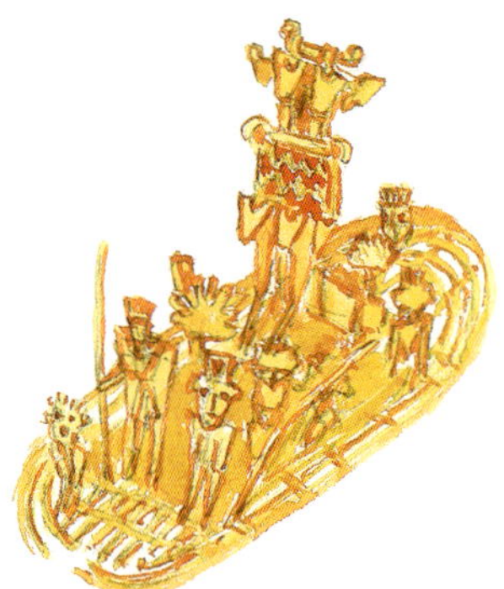

9 Gold Raft – Muisca, 1200–1500 C.E. 19.5 x 10.1 x 10.2 cm. Museo del Oro, Colombia

(ill.8) made by pre-Christian people in Ireland was possibly also a model used during initiation ceremonies to explain the mysterious journey of the sun beneath one's feet at night. The same use could have been made of this gold raft (ill.9), found in Colombia. It's also toy-size. Some scholars think it represents a ceremony of succession: when a chieftain of the Muisca people died, the next-in-line sailed into the village on a raft and made offerings of gold to the lake. This in itself could be a sun-worshipping ceremony–the new leader rose out of the east as the sun does. In the imagery of ancient people the references are usually many-layered.

If the sun travelled underground at night, how did it get down there? Some ancient Egyptians believed it was pushed into a hole by a scarab beetle, which then accompanied it on its journey so that it could push it up again at dawn. The scarab beetle in real life is a drab little insect with a remarkable instinct. It breaks off some dried cow dung which it rolls into a ball by dancing rather impressively backwards and forwards on its hind legs. It then lays its eggs in the dung ball and pushes it down a hole. This provides food for the grubs when they hatch and eventually the new scarabs crawl out–just as the sun comes up at dawn. So the ancient Egyptians sought to find a poetic metaphor that would embrace the whole of creation–from the humblest creature grubbing about in another animal's droppings to the highest being of all, sailing across the heavens. The whole story is depicted in this royal pendant (ill.10) found in Tutankhamen's tomb–the stars above, the waters of the underworld below, and the scarab standing in the solar boat ready to push the sun up at dawn. The baboons are in attendance because, in the Egyptian hills, they shriek as the sun rises. The whole of nature joins in the chorus of praise.

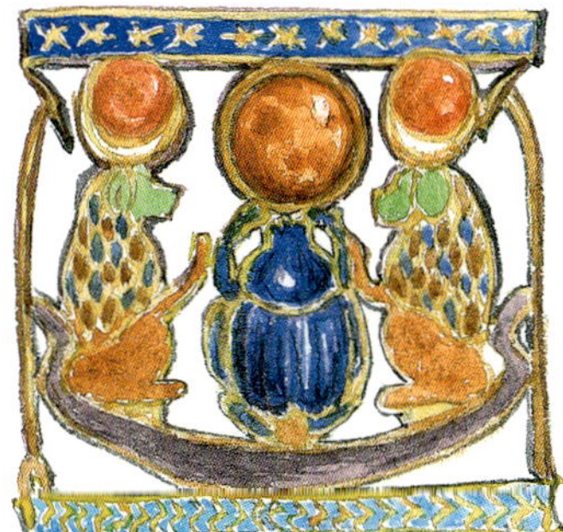

10 Pectoral pendant of the Necklace of the Rising Sun, from the tomb of Tutankhamen, c.1361–52. B.C.E. The Egyptian Museum, Cairo

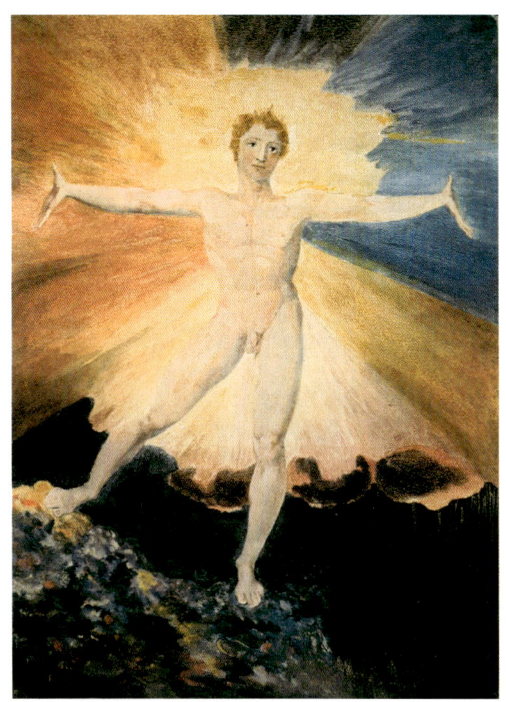

11 William Blake. *Glad Day*, c.1795. Colour print with watercolour, 36.8 x 26.3 cm. Huntington Library, San Marino, California

We see exactly the same dawn as our ancestors did, and we still associate it with revival. Its gentle, pearly colours, which can make even the most squalid urban sprawl look fresh, make such a striking contrast to the heavy-curtained reds that drape the setting sun. We now know that sunrise and sunset are just the effect of the earth turning. But we still speak of–and think of–the sun as rising. The English mystic William Blake (1757–1827) continued to insist that the sun *did* rise, even though he lived long after our modern view of the solar system had become widely accepted. An acquaintance once asked him: when you see the sun don't you see a gold disc shaped somewhat like a guinea? "No, no," replied Blake, "I see a host of angels singing alleluia!" Blake eked out a poor man's life in London composing and singing songs, writing poems, painting pictures and hand-colouring books that manifest his spiritual visions. *Glad Day* (ill.11) beautifully illustrates a line in Shakespeare's play, *Romeo and Juliet*: "Night's candles are burnt out, and jocund day / Stands tiptoe on the misty mountaintops." But the picture is also an image of the joy we can all feel, Blake believed, if we shake off our "mind-forged manacles" and allow our inner natures to blaze forth. Blake tried to revive the way the "Ancients" saw the world.

Dawn-greeting ceremonies were practised in many cultures around the globe (p.56, ill.25) though, since they were ephemeral, very little evidence of them survives. One was caught by the American photographer Edward Curtis (1868–1952). Curtis spent his life, often in great personal hardship, recording the cultures of the native peoples of America as they were being driven off their homelands into reservations, where the vast majority of them died from malnutrition, disease, alcoholism and despair. This image (ill. 12) shows a Tewa Pueblo Native American making a personal offering to the rising sun. A Lakota Native American hymn to the sun ran: "Here am I. Behold me. I am the sun. Behold me." This was not arrogance, but acceptance; just as the stars could be seen in people's eyes, so the power of the sun was in everyone, and it was replenished every day.

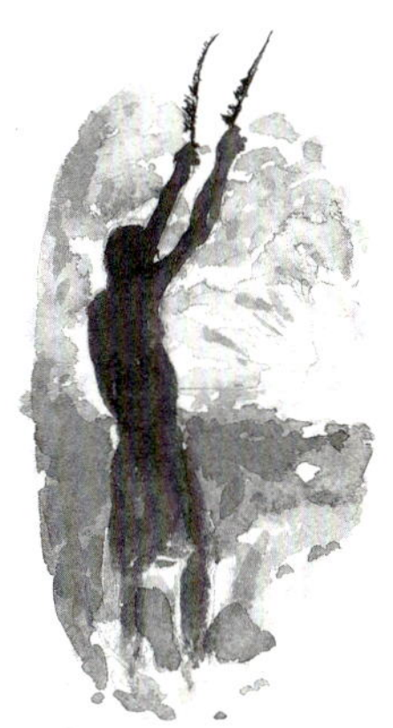

12 After Edward. S. Curtis. *Offering to the Sun, San Ildefonso*, 1926, detail. Photograph from *The North American Indian*, vol. XVII, 1926

Dawn has seeped into our subconscious as the pre-eminent symbol of rebirth. In one of the oldest of all surviving Christian churches, dedicated to Saints Cosmas and Damian, a golden mosaic above the altar shows Christ, resurrected after his execution and burial, appearing to mankind as the sun bursting through the rosy clouds of the morning (ill. 13). Christian altars are generally placed at the east end of churches not just so that the congregation can face Jerusalem. The Aztec people of Central America believed that the sun had risen in the north, south and west in previous ages, and that all of these had ended in calamity. It was during the era of the sun in the east that a few Christian adventurers arrived from Europe, soon after Columbus had proved that there was land over the edge of their ocean. Some of the Aztec priests argued that because these strange pale people came from the east, where the sun rose, they must be messengers from the sun god. This partly explains why Hernando Cortés, in 1521, was able to conquer the majestic capital of the Aztecs—then a beautiful, lake-bound, garden-strewn stone-built city with over 300,000 inhabitants—with only a few hundred men, and then systematically and ruthlessly eradicate one of the world's greatest civilisations. The east didn't only bring forth goodness.

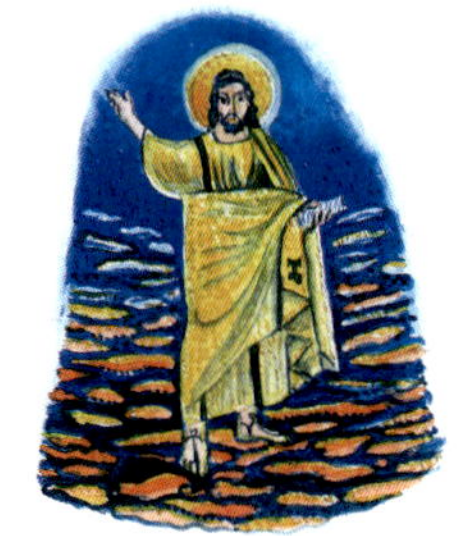

13 Christ as Dawn, 523–30 C.E., detail. Mosaic, heavily restored in the 19th century. Apse of Church of Saints Cosmas and Damian, Rome

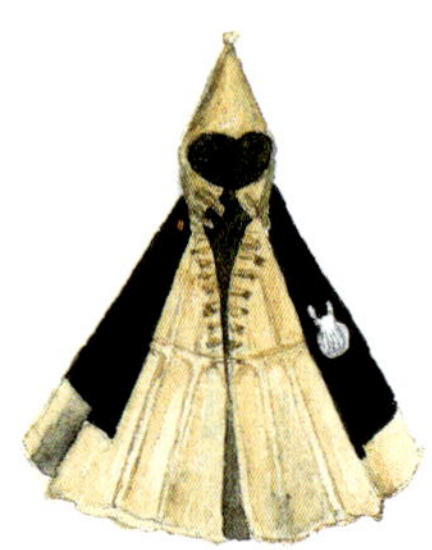

14 Stephan Prawn's pilgrim's cloak with scallop badge, c.1570 C.E. Germanisches Nationalmuseum, Nuremberg

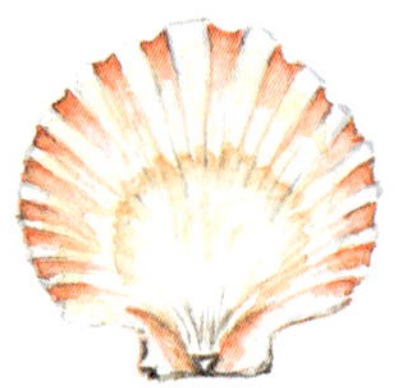

15 Scallop shell

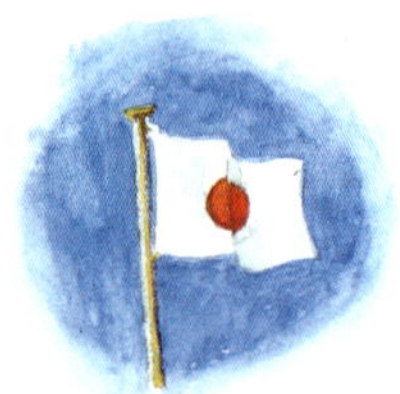

16 Japanese flag

Before Columbus made his heroic journey, Spain was thought to stand on the western edge of the known world. The second most popular pilgrimage destination in Christendom, after Rome–Jerusalem had long been Islamic–was to the Spanish city of Santiago de Compostela, where the body of St James was reputedly buried. When the Christian pilgrims arrived there–they had walked from all over Europe–the majority continued on to a tiny place on the coast called Finisterre, whose name means the end of the earth–even though it had no Christian significance. The badge the pilgrims wore on their journey was the scallop (ill.14), though this shell had no Christian significance either. It's highly probable that the crowds who made this pilgrimage every year were sustaining a much more ancient tradition of worshipping the setting sun, and praying for the coming dawn that would heal them of their afflictions. Scallop shells (ill.15) are the most perfect images in nature of the sun's rays spreading across the sky at dawn, and they rose from the then unknown depths of the sea, from where the sun also rose and to which it returned.

At the other end of the known world was Japan–the closest one could get on land to where the sun rises. The country's Japanese name, Nihon, means "the source of the sun". Though the single red sun on a white ground was not officially adopted as the Japanese flag (ill.16) until 1870, this symbol had for centuries been associated with their emperors. Japanese traditional culture, like that of ancient Egypt, believed that natural and social order radiated from the sun. A popular woodcut print captured these beneficent rays (ill.17). It was made during the period when Japan deliberately cut itself off from foreign influences for fear that western scientific ideas would undermine its traditional culture. The West forced it to reopen its doors to trade in 1854, after two hundred years of isolation. The print shows ships under full sail, laden with goods–

in the original meaning of the word–majestically entering Tempozan Harbour under a sky emblazoned with the rose-tinted rays of the rising sun. Tempozan means "mountain of heavenly peace" which, though it was the name of an actual hill created from the silt dredged to make this artificial harbour, also refers here to the celestial mountain formed by the sun's rays bursting through a cloud–a luminous phenomenon that had been given its greatest manifestation in the pyramids of ancient Egypt.

It was entirely logical for our ancestors to associate the sun with a king–because the sun rules the heavens as kings rule the earth. Emperors and pharaohs could, like the sun, punish their subjects, naturally enough, but their main role was to emanate goodness, as the sun does. The great hand-made books that recorded the events in the reigns of the Mughal emperors of India tend to have their first page decorated with a *shamsa*–an image of a flaming sun made of gold leaf. They show the sun's rays

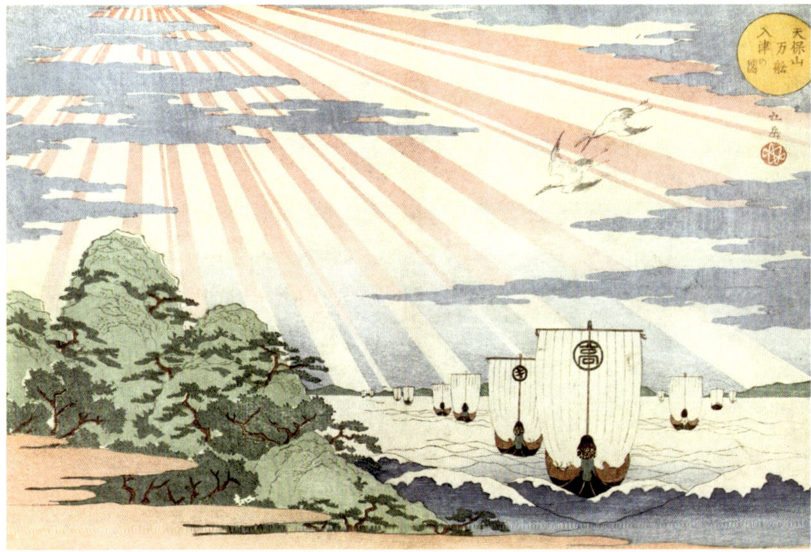

17 Gakutei. *Ships Entering Tempozan Harbour*, c.1832. 35.5 x 28 cm. Victoria and Albert Museum, London

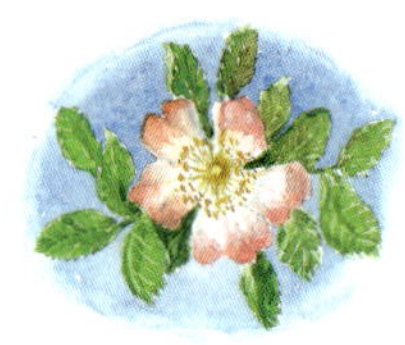

18 Wild rose

breaking up into a coronet of tiny flowers, just as the sun's rays flood through everything in nature and find their echoes in the sun-burst centres of wild flowers (ill.18) from which the bee draws nectar, the food of the gods. So the sun's beneficence was seen to seep through all creation. The honey-coloured robes worn by Hindu priests were believed to attract good spirits, as flowers attract insects. Among the greatest annual events at the Indian emperor's court were the celebrations of his solar and his lunar birthdays. On the first his weight in gold, and on the second his weight in silver, were distributed as alms to the poor. A more literal interpretation of the king as a channel for heaven's beneficence can hardly be imagined. In his imperial record book, the *Padshahnama,* for the year 1632, the emperor Shah Jahan, who became famous for building the Taj Mahal, is shown being weighed against bags of gold (ill.19). He is stripped bare to the waist except for a string of pearls, and wears the flimsiest pair of silk trousers. A halo of solar goodness radiates from his head. Each ceremony was the occasion of a great feast. One hopes the emperor ate heartily before climbing on to the scales.

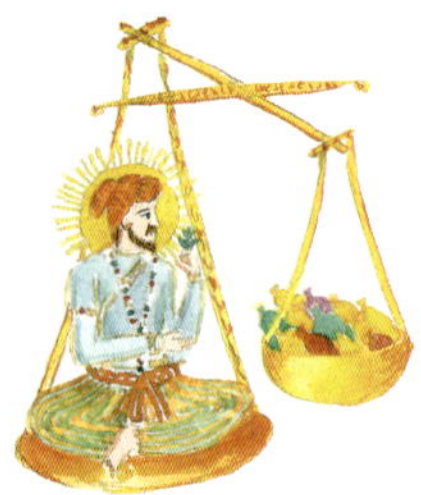

19 *The Weighing of Shah Jahan on his Birthday*, 1632 C.E., detail. Padshahnama, Royal Collection, Windsor Castle

The ancient Egyptians were an intensely religious people–the ancient Greeks thought them absurdly so–and saw divinity in all living creatures. They built temples to bulls, crocodiles and cats, though the sun-god Ra reigned supreme over all. In 1359 B.C.E., one Egyptian pharaoh, Akhenaten, tried to tidy up all these religious beliefs by declaring that there was only one true god–his own father, the sun–and all the others weren't really gods at all. Akhenaten wrote a beautiful hymn–or perhaps it's truer to say that whoever wrote it said it was by the king–praising the sun's beneficent influence on all things. He emphasised the goodness of the sun, not its destructive power. On this relief (ill.20), which probably decorated a fairly lowly official's home, Akhenaten and

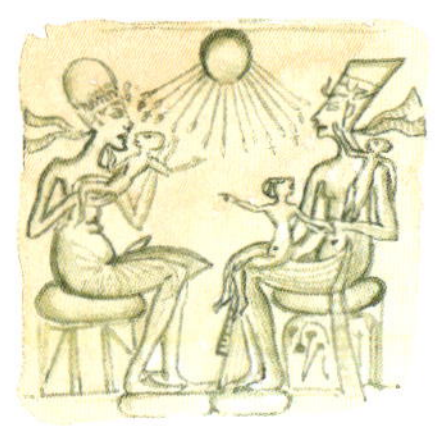

20 *The Pharaoh Akhenaten and his Queen Nefertiti Fondling their Daughters*, 1353–36 B.C.E. Limestone, 33 x 39 x 3.8. cm. Ägyptisches Museum, Berlin

his queen Nefertiti are shown fondling their naked daughters. Their son, Tutankhamen, had not yet been born. Children are portrayed as gifts—there are few happier images in the history of art. The sun's rays—each ending in a drip of golden honey—kiss each member of the royal family with the *ankh* sign—the key to eternal life.

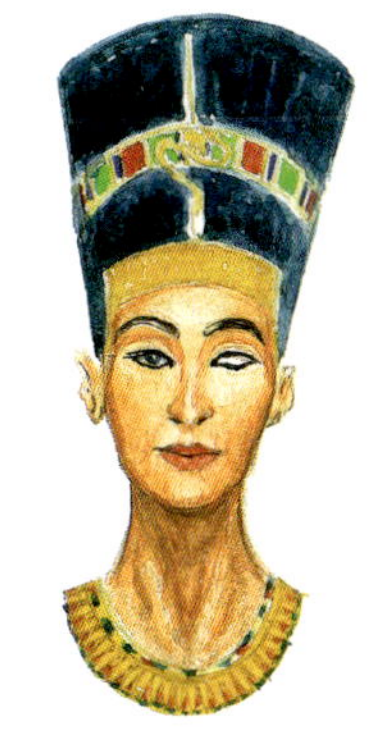

21 Bust of Queen Nefertiti, c. 1350 B.C.E. Ägyptisches Museum, Berlin

Akhenaten liked everything to be depicted as it was—as the sun had made it. His portraits show his unusually long face, sloping shoulders and exceptionally wide hips—though there is a new theory that this last feature might have been exaggerated to symbolise his role as father and mother of his people. His leading wife—he had several—was a natural beauty, as we can tell from this unfinished bust (ill. 21) found in the ruins of a workshop. Her beauty was a gift of the sun. Akhenaten's short reign ushered in what was probably one of the most wonderful flowerings of naturalistic art the world has ever seen, but unfortunately hardly any of it remains. Immediately his young son, Tutankhamen (ill. 1), took over, the old religious ways, with their hundreds of gods—and the retinues of priests who earned their living by serving them—were reinstated. Akhenaten's religion was declared a heresy and almost everything it produced destroyed.

Our ancestors were as aware as we are that the sun could not only give life but could also destroy. Nowhere is this clearer than in Egypt, where a luscious green strip of vegetation, rarely more than a couple of miles wide and fertilised every year by the regularly flooding waters of the Nile, is for over a thousand miles flanked on either side by inhospitable desert. Today you can stand with one foot on soft mud sprouting with grass, while with the other feeling through the sole of your sandal the heat of the burning sand. Evidence suggests that the climate was milder during the two thousand years of ancient Egyptian civilisation. The

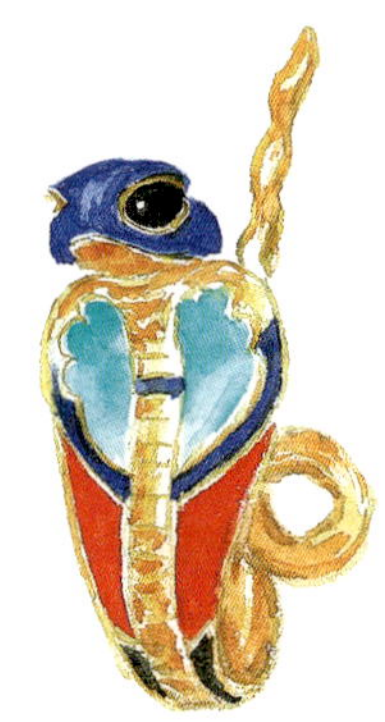

22 The ureus of Sesostris II, c. 1780 B.C.E. The Egyptian Museum, Cairo

division between desert and fertile valley was less abrupt. Grasses grew on the dunes and shepherds grazed their flocks there. But the contrast between life and death remained severe. The Egyptian pharaoh wore in his crown the *ureus*, a divine cobra (ill. 22) made of gold and lapis lazuli, which could annihilate the pharaoh's enemies with a glance from its obsidian eye–just as the sun can wither a plant in the desert or a real cobra can blind an attacker by spitting venom with lightning accuracy into its eyes. It was in the desert that the ancient Egyptians built cities for the dead–so that their ancestors could live there forever, as close neighbours of the living. Today, these ruined monuments built in stone are like the homes of ghosts–shimmering in the sand dunes–while nothing remains of the brightly painted mud and reed palaces and villas that the Egyptians actually lived in, along the palm-shaded banks of the Nile.

We see exactly the same sunsets (ill. 23) that our ancestors saw, but we no longer regard them as daily reminders of mortality. The fact that the sky turned blood red in the evening led the vast majority of people in the past to believe that the sun was in the throes of death. Australian Aborigines believe that the red stain in the evening is made by the souls of the dead escaping from and returning to the underworld, when its gates are opened to let the sun descend. In the very earliest human burials found in many parts of the world (ill. 24), the corpses were often sprinkled with red ochre, either round their heads or over their whole bodies. This is generally thought

23 J.M.W. Turner. Sunset: Rouen, c. 1829. Body colour on blue paper, 13.5 x 18.9 cm. Tate Britain, London

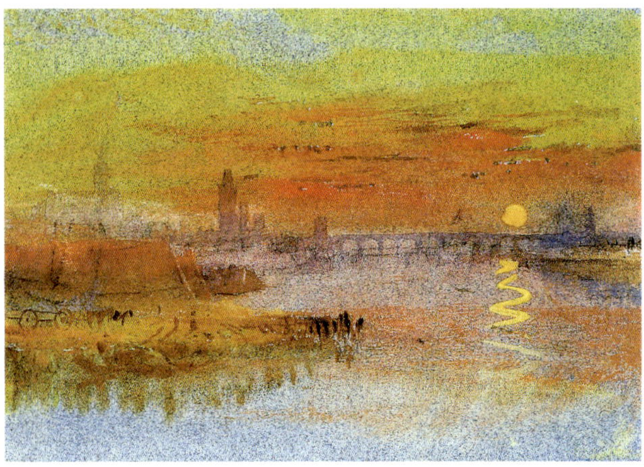

to symbolise spilt blood, but it could equally indicate sunset—and the hope of a subsequent sunrise.

It's probable that the gold masks found in the burial chambers of kings, in places as far apart as Greece and South America, were laid gently across the faces of the dead rulers to give them the power to rise again, as the sun does at dawn, not into this world but into the heavenly world above, where they could intercede for those below. The mask of this Mycenaean king from pre-classical Greece (ill.25)—wrongly thought when it was discovered to have belonged to Agamemnon—has closed eyes. Presumably they would open when the king woke in the next world. This Chimu gold mask (ill.26) was originally painted red, as the red sky stains the sun as it descends. The red was mostly scrubbed off by its finders because they thought the mask would be more valuable if it could be seen to be gold. Gold was the flesh of the sun—into which eternal, incorruptible substance the flesh of the king would be transformed. It didn't matter to its makers what the mask looked like to human eyes. This face was to be seen by the gods alone—and they would know what it was made of underneath. The mask is crying—seven emerald beads hang from each eye. Perhaps these represent the tears of the world, for all nature suffered with the passing of the earthly life of the king. And perhaps, too, they represent the power of the king's eyes, when reborn in the sun, to shed tears that will revitalise the earth below.

The ancient Egyptians believed that their king was literally the son of the sun. The future well-being of their society depended on the pharaoh's safe return to his father in heaven. Not only the pharaoh's face, but his whole body had to be transformed into sun-matter, and so did many of the accessories he would need in the afterlife—his throne and bed, his dagger and his sceptre. So much gold was used that these graves, over the centuries, were

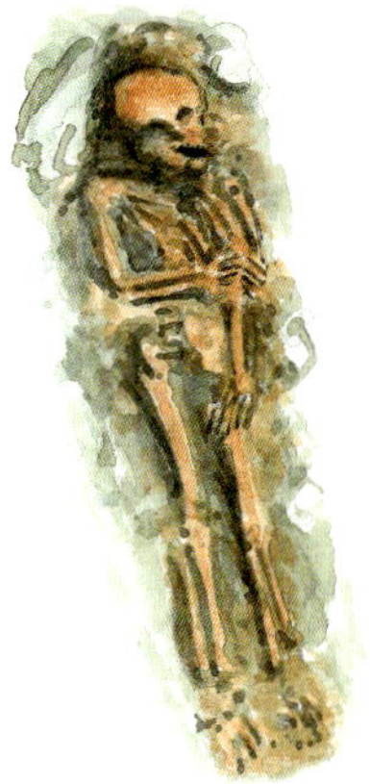

24 Burial of a boy aged between 12 and 14 found in the cave of Arene Candide, c. 20,000 B.C.E. Italy

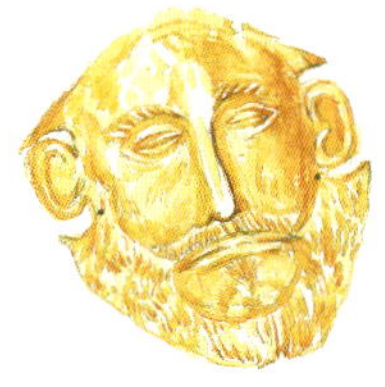

25 Mycenaean gold mask, 1580–50 B.C.E. 26 cm high. National Archaeological Museum, Athens

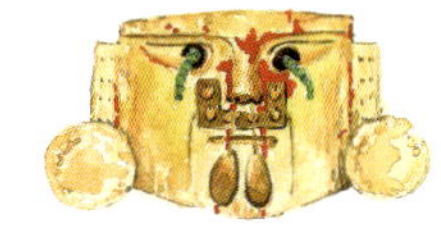

26 Gold funerary mask, Chimu culture. 31 x 60 cm. Miguel Mujica Gallo Collection, Gold Museum, Lima

robbed by unbelievers, except for the smallest one which belonged to a short-lived, soon-forgotten king. Tutankhamen's mummy (ill. 1) was encased in gold when he died so that his whole body could be reincarnated in the afterlife. X-rays of his skull reveal that this mask is only slightly idealised. We are looking here at the face of an eighteen-year-old boy transformed into the spirit-matter of the sun, to be reborn, at dawn, into eternal life. His new eyes, inlaid with translucent quartz backed with red pigment, would enable him to look into the eyes of gods. They were never meant to be seen by us.

The sun's position changed throughout the year. Nobody could explain the seasons. In temperate lands, in the northern hemisphere, where the majority of early civilisations were formed, it was observed that the sun rose higher and grew hotter in summer

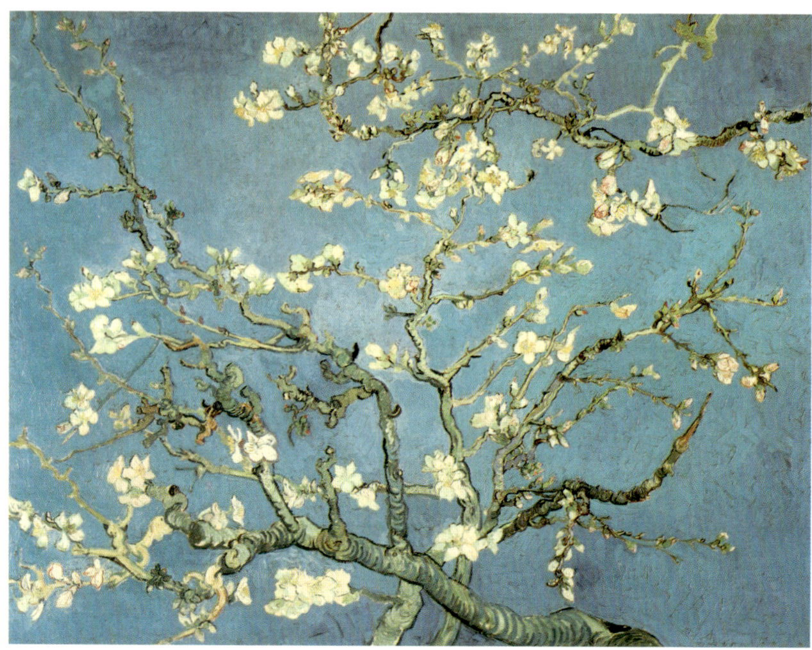

27 Vincent van Gogh. *Blossoming Almond Tree*, 1890. Oil on canvas, 73.5 x 92 cm. Van Gogh Museum, Amsterdam

and then dropped back again and grew colder in winter. What was remarkable was that this seasonal round magically reflected the ages of mankind–spring was delicate youth, summer fulsome parenthood, autumn rich maturity and winter withered old age, when one's hair turned to snow. And since winter always gave way to spring again, the implication was that mankind–and the whole of creation–would be reborn. The beginning of a new season of life was celebrated around the world. It was one of the most solemn duties of the high priest or ruler to "break the soil" after winter. Astrologers had to work out the most auspicious moment for the first seed to be sown. Kings from the Inca in Peru to the emperor in China wielded ceremonial spades, and the order was sent out that everyone could then begin planting.

Spring was a period, everywhere, of great rejoicing. In Japan, thousands of people leave the cities in April to see the wild cherry trees blossoming on the hills. Their ancient Shinto religion has long praised natural beauty. Vincent van Gogh admired Japanese artists because they looked closely at plants and the seasons, and didn't waste their time, as he put it, "measuring the distance of the moon from the earth". Inspired by Japanese prints, which became available when Japan was forced to open its doors to Western materialism, he painted this picture (ill.27) looking up through the middle of a blossoming almond tree at the blue dome of the sky above. He sent it to hang in the room of his new-born nephew, named Vincent by his loving brother, Theo. It captures the magical emergence of delicate petals from rugged, bare branches. Spring has long been associated with birth. Three and a half thousand years earlier, this fresco (ill.28), show-

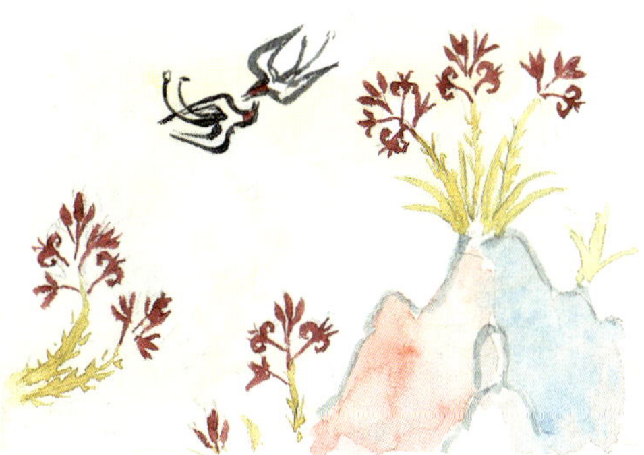

28 Spring fresco from Thera, c.1550–1500 B.C.E., detail. National Archaeological Museum, Athens

ing ragged rocks burgeoning with deep red lilies, while pairs of swallows flit and tumble in the sky, decorated what is believed to have been a child's bedroom in a palace on the Mediterranean island of Thera. It was preserved under the ash from a volcanic eruption in about 1500 B.C.E. Swallows arrive in spring. It was not known until the nineteenth century that they migrated vast distances. Before that, the most widely accepted theory was that during the winter they hibernated under the sea! Swallows, after all, swoop and dart in the air like fish under water.

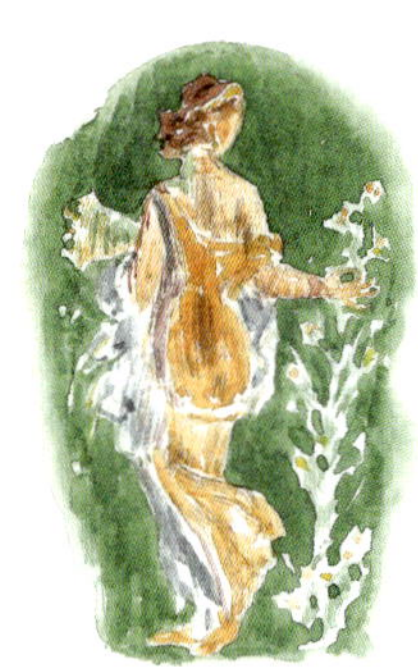

29 After *Maiden Gathering Flowers*, 1st century C.E. Fresco, 39 x 31 cm, Stabiae, Villa of Ariadne. National Museum, Naples

The eruption of Vesuvius, in 79 C.E., preserved this wall painting (ill.29) in Stabiae. It's thought to illustrate the Greek myth which explained the arrival of spring. There was a golden age, long before our own, when it was always summer. Then one day, the beautiful young goddess Persephone was innocently picking flowers, barefoot, in a meadow, when she was carried off by the god Hades to live with him in the Underworld. Her mother Demeter, the earth goddess, pleaded for her return, and Hades eventually let her come back for two-thirds of the year–our spring, summer and autumn–as long as she spent what became our winter with him. In the Christian Middle Ages, it became popular to show the baby Jesus with his mother surrounded by spring flowers–the Madonna of the Meadow.

Spring was a symbol of rebirth even nearer the equator where the seasons are not so clearly marked. The main differences there were between hot, dry seasons–the "yellow grass time" of the Australian Aborigines–and rainy seasons. When the first rains begin to fall the mudfish–shown here interlinked on the seat of a royal stool (ill.30)–suddenly emerge, magically flapping with life, from the sun-cracked river beds already rapidly turning to brown slush. They were revered by the people of the kingdom of Benin in what is today western Nigeria as messengers of the regenerating power of the Oba. This power gave the Oba dominion over the land and the waters, for mudfish could live in both.

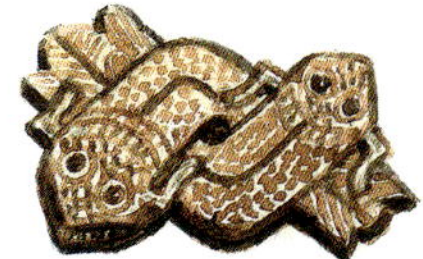

30 Intertwined mudfish design – seat of stool, Benin, Nigeria, 16th century. Bronze, 34 cm high. National Museum of Nigeria, Lagos

The pale yellow and pink-flushed flowers of spring–the primrose and wood anemone–are soon swamped by a sea of bluebells, roses and honeysuckle, and the woods become heavy with the scents and sounds of summer. Sandro Botticelli's *Primavera* (ill.31) captures this moment of spring turning into summer. The nymph Chloris is seduced by Zephyrus, the green spirit of the west wind. She immediately starts to spew flowers out of her mouth, but when Zephyrus marries her she is transformed into Flora, the goddess standing beside her, who, with one of the most seductive and knowing smiles in art, scoops flowers from a fold in her robe slung before her swelling womb and strews them across the glade. The immensely rich Florentine banking family, the Medici, probably commissioned this picture for a family wedding–it might have hung in a bridal chamber. The Medici owned an orange grove which, according to family tradition, foreshadowed their firm's fortune. If the grove cropped well, so would their profits; if not, they would suffer losses. The orange trees are bare above Zephyrus, but laden with fruit above Flora. The message of the picture was that this marriage–which was almost certainly a commercial arrangement–would bode well for the Medici's fortune.

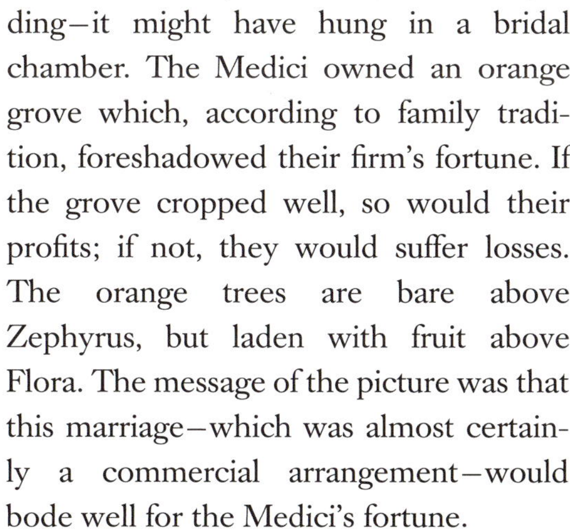

Summer turns into autumn, and that too was cause for wonder. It couldn't have been a coincidence that leaves and fruit turned gold and red–the colours of sun-

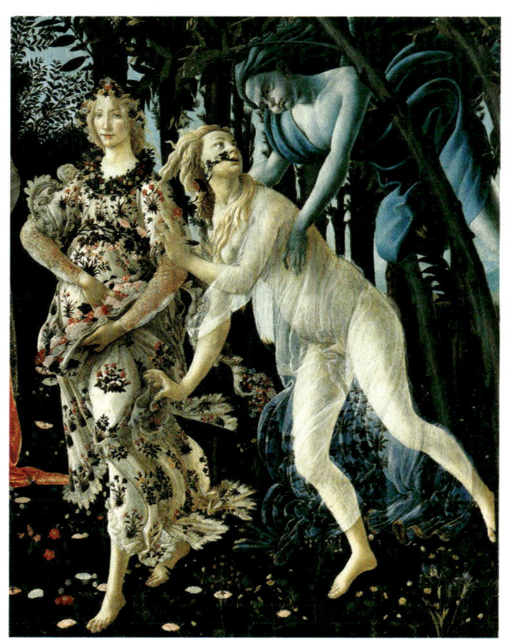

31 Sandro Botticelli. *Primavera*, c.1478, detail showing right half: Flora, Chloris and Zephyrus. Uffizi, Florence

set. This was proof, if proof were needed, that the seasons were the gift of the sun. John Keats (1795–1821) expressed this beautifully in his *Ode to Autumn*: "Season of mists and mellow fruitfulness / Close-bosom friend of the maturing sun." Keats' near contemporary Samuel Palmer expressed similar feelings in paint (ill. 32). Inspired by William Blake when he was a young man to lead the life of the "Ancients", Palmer spent nine years in an English village with friends, communing with nature, painting pictures of fecundity and playing the flute. In many cultures, autumn has long been the season for thanksgiving. It was a good time to give the gods something in return for their generosity, because there was food to spare. The end of the rice harvest is still celebrated with exuberance in India, beginning with prayers to the sun. Women get up well before dawn to paint decorations in rice flour paste on the sides of their houses (ill. 33) and on the ground before their doors. These are in part food for insects, for it's believed that every living thing should benefit from the harvest.

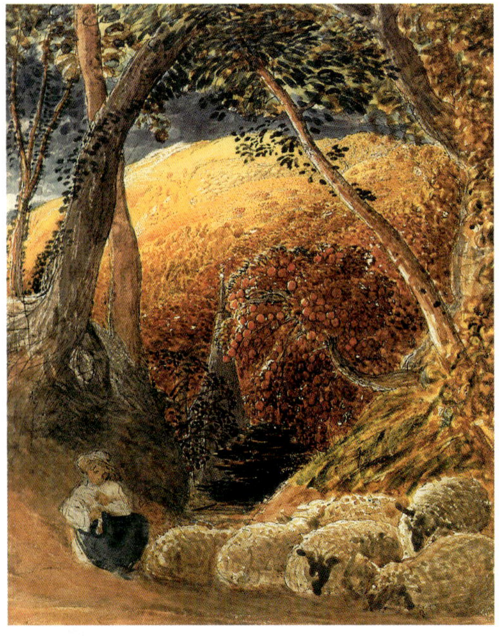

32 Samuel Palmer. *The Magic Apple Tree*. Fitzwilliam Museum, Cambridge

Harvest festivals in the U.K. are now reduced to a few offerings of food in packages and tins in local churches – our hope is only for the replenishment of supermarket shelves. Many of the plants we eat have never seen the sun – they're grown under artificial light. We used to make more significant offerings, such as one of the season's new calves (ill. 34). We no longer kill animals on altars, but that's not a sign that we've become more caring of animals. We've probably lost, perhaps forever, the extraordinary intimacy expressed here between the calf and his bearer. They seem to share the same look, as if they are both aware of the significance of the event they are taking part in. We don't know this sculpture's original context – it might show a sacrificial animal being carried to the altar of Demeter, the ancient Greek goddess of the harvest, or it might be an offering, or a prize, for a victory at the games.

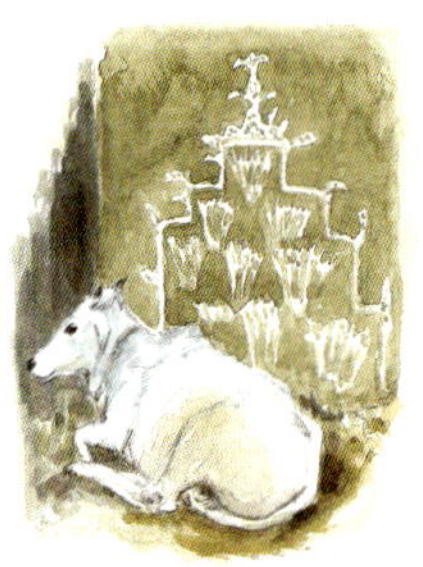

33 Rice paste design on a village house in Orissa, India

The sacrifices our ancestors made were all the greater because they knew the suffering they caused, as this quote from Lucretius shows: "Often before the fair shrines of the gods a calf has fallen … but the grieving mother many a time returns to the stall, pierced to the heart with a yearning for her calf, so long does she seek for something which she knows and which is her own." Today's factory farming methods are more brutal than anything inflicted on animals in the past, made worse by the fact that the animals' suffering is kept out of sight.

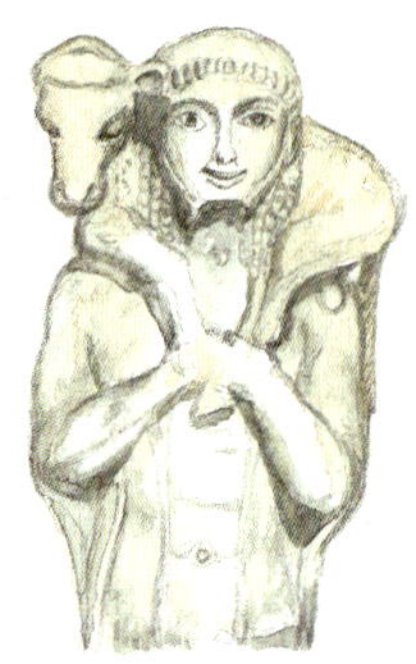

34 The Moscophoros "Calf Bearer", c. 570–60 B.C.E. Marble. Acropolis Museum, Athens

For our ancestors, the coming of winter reflected their own fate. The weak, old sun cast winter's shroud. Snow covered the ground just as hair turned white, before the deathly pallor spread throughout. White, more logically than black, is the colour of mourning in eastern cultures. The bowed head of van Gogh's *Old Man on the Threshold of Eternity* (ill. 35) says it all. His isolation is something we can understand, now that more and more old people are shovelled away into homes. Traditional cultures in the past, from China to America, treated age with respect. Living long was in itself an achievement. Lives that were completed were valued more than those that were truncated before all the stages of life could be experienced. Old people were nearer to one's ancestors and to the gods. Being good to them could be beneficial, for they might well repay your kindness by soliciting the Supreme Being for your health, longevity and success.

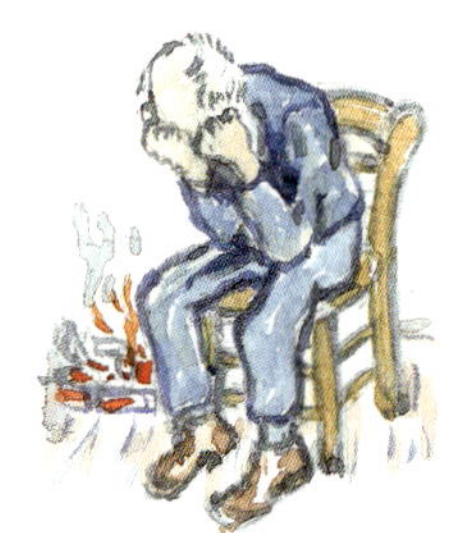

35 After Vincent van Gogh. *Old Man in Sorrow (On the Threshold of Eternity)*, 1890. Oil on canvas, 81 x 65 cm. Rijksmuseum Kroller-Muller, Otterloo, The Netherlands

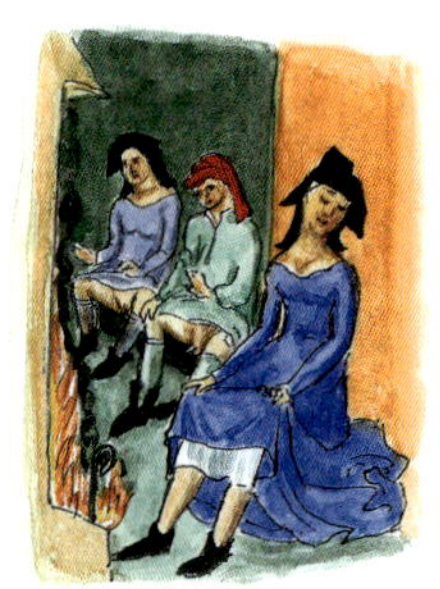

36 After the Limbourg Brothers. *Les Très Riches Heures du Duc de Berry*: February, detail, c.1410. Musée Condé, Chantilly, France

The fire can no longer warm the bones of van Gogh's old man. But the fire still invigorates the people sitting round it, in this detail (ill.36) from a medieval book of seasonal prayers. Winter, if you're young, will lead to spring. They lift their clothes to warm their naked private parts. Brueghel's *Hunters in the Snow* (ill.37) is one of the most popular paintings in the world, not just because of the glorious patterns made by the bare branches, the hunters with their dogs, and the magpie swooping down over the people playing on the ice, but also because the picture celebrates survival through winter. There are few things more comforting than being snugly dressed against the cold, knowing that a fire and feast are waiting.

The passing of deep midwinter–when the sun is at its lowest and its rays are barely warm–is celebrated, the world over, with a banquet. The much older Yule Log festival was adopted by Christians to mark the birth of their Saviour. They turned it into Christmas, but the tree has now risen again and comes, magically, into the house, laden with material blessings. If it weren't for modern consumerism, one might think the ancient gods were returning. Stonehenge (ill.38) represents the high point of native British culture before the invasion of the Romans and the introduction of Christianity. Though no records remain which indicate its use, it was almost certainly erected for rituals connected with the yearly cycle of the sun and the other heavenly bodies. Stonehenge is usually thought to celebrate sunrise on midsummer's day, but

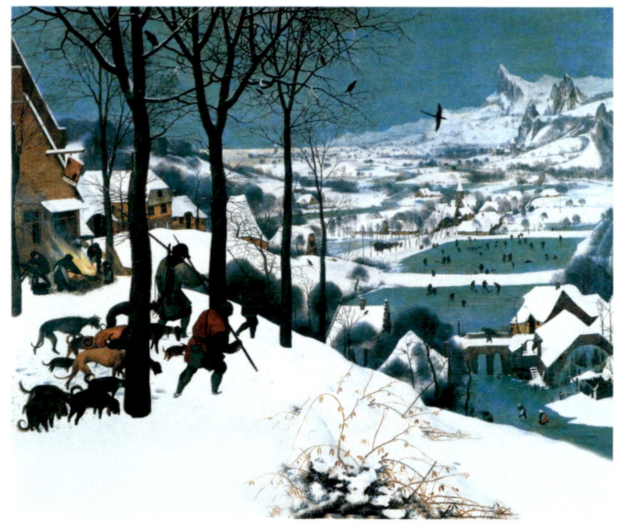

37 Peter Brueghel. *The Hunters in the Snow*, 1565. Oil on canvas, 117 x 162 cm. Kunsthistorisches Museum, Vienna

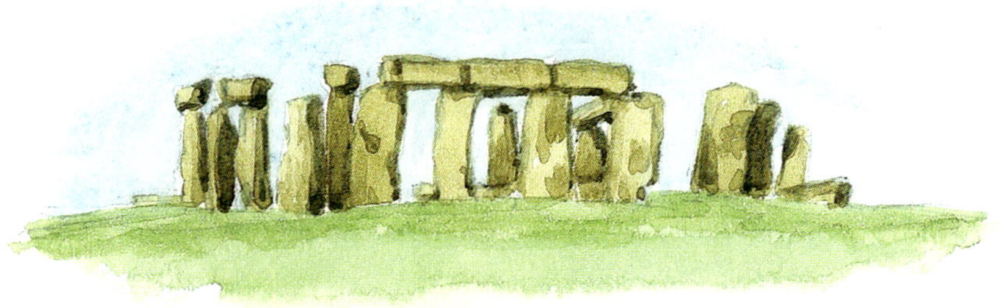

38 Stonehenge, c. 2550–1600 B.C.E. England

expert opinion now thinks it was used for rites connected with sunset in midwinter, to ensure that the sun started to rise again for the coming year.

We can perhaps catch a glimpse of how Stonehenge might have been used by looking at the sacrificial practices that survived into modern times in China. For over two thousand years – until 1911 – China was ruled by an emperor who was believed to be half divine. He was like an Egyptian pharaoh, except that he was the son of all the heavens, not just the son of the sun. When the emperor performed his religious duties, he was carried everywhere, as Egyptian pharaohs had been, because heavenly bodies – like the sun – exist above the ground. The emperor came to earth only in extreme circumstances, such as during a severe drought, to conduct ceremonies to bring rain. But in the most important ceremony of the year, at the time of the winter solstice, the emperor, accompanied by 660 attendants and guards, was carried out of the Forbidden City to the Temple of Heaven. There his palanquin was set down. The Son of Heaven then walked – on his own feet – to the centre of the Terrace for Offering Sacrifices to Heaven. This was an act of great humility, demonstrating his sympathy with the sun which, at that time of year, barely had the strength to lift itself above the southern horizon.

The Terrace for Offering Sacrifices to Heaven which exists today dates from 1530 C.E., though it was later modified in 1749 C.E. It

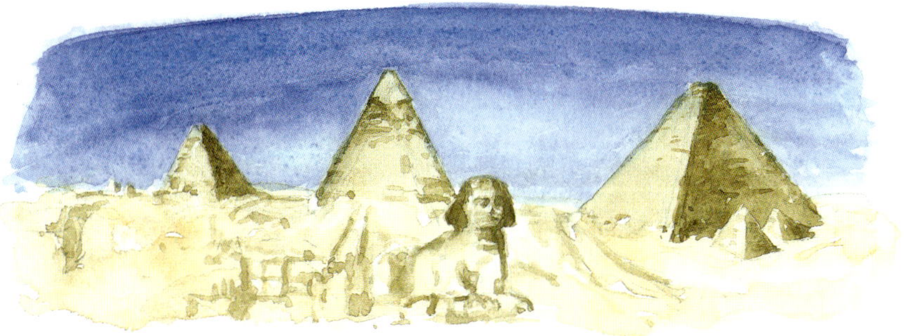

39 View of the Pyramids and Great Sphinx at Gizeh, c. 2500 B.C.E. Cairo

almost certainly reflects the shape of an older original. This sacred place is a huge square space open to the sky, bounded by four low red walls. In the middle of each wall is a cloud gateway exactly aligned to the east, west, north and south. In the centre of this enclosed area rises the sacrificial altar, a stack of three wide and low circular terraces which are also open to the sky. The floor of the topmost terrace is blue, originally made of ceramic tiles, now of stone slabs. They radiate from a central circular blue stone directly under the vault of the sky. There are no superfluous decorations, no distractions from the serious business of making the correct observances to the sun, to ensure that it would keep to its path and rise again. Our ancestors saw a simple geometry underlying the order of the world.

This divine order is most beautifully expressed in the pyramids at Gizeh in Egypt. These weren't just tombs; they were profoundly poetic symbols. Though the Egyptians undoubtedly used hired and slave labour, it now appears that people throughout society as a whole voluntarily contributed to the building of the pyramids, and the other great temples and tombs, much in the same way that wealthy merchants and landowners willingly, as a public demonstration of their faith and humility, pulled carts of stones, and of food and wine, to help the masons build the cathedrals in western Europe during the Middle Ages. Coming across the Great Pyramids (ill.39) even today–hedged in as they are by the creeping, ugly, half-finished concrete suburbs of Cairo–is an extraordinary experience. Even compared to modern skyscrapers, their scale is immense. They appear to reach up and touch the dome of heaven. But there is something else, too, which must have struck contemporaries even more forcibly than it does us–they appear not to have been made by human hands. There are no windows in their vast, uncompromising sides–nothing at all to suggest any human presence. Their very shape is inhuman. A traveller coming across the pyramids in the past might have wondered if a god had made them. When originally covered with gleaming white marble–almost all this was stripped off centuries later to build the first mosques in Cairo–and capped, as has been suggested, with gold, the brilliant, shimmering light reflected from their surfaces would have made these massive monuments seem weightless and insubstantial. They must have shone in the rolling desert sands like rays from the sun itself beaming down on the world–the perfect image on earth of the beneficent power of the sun.

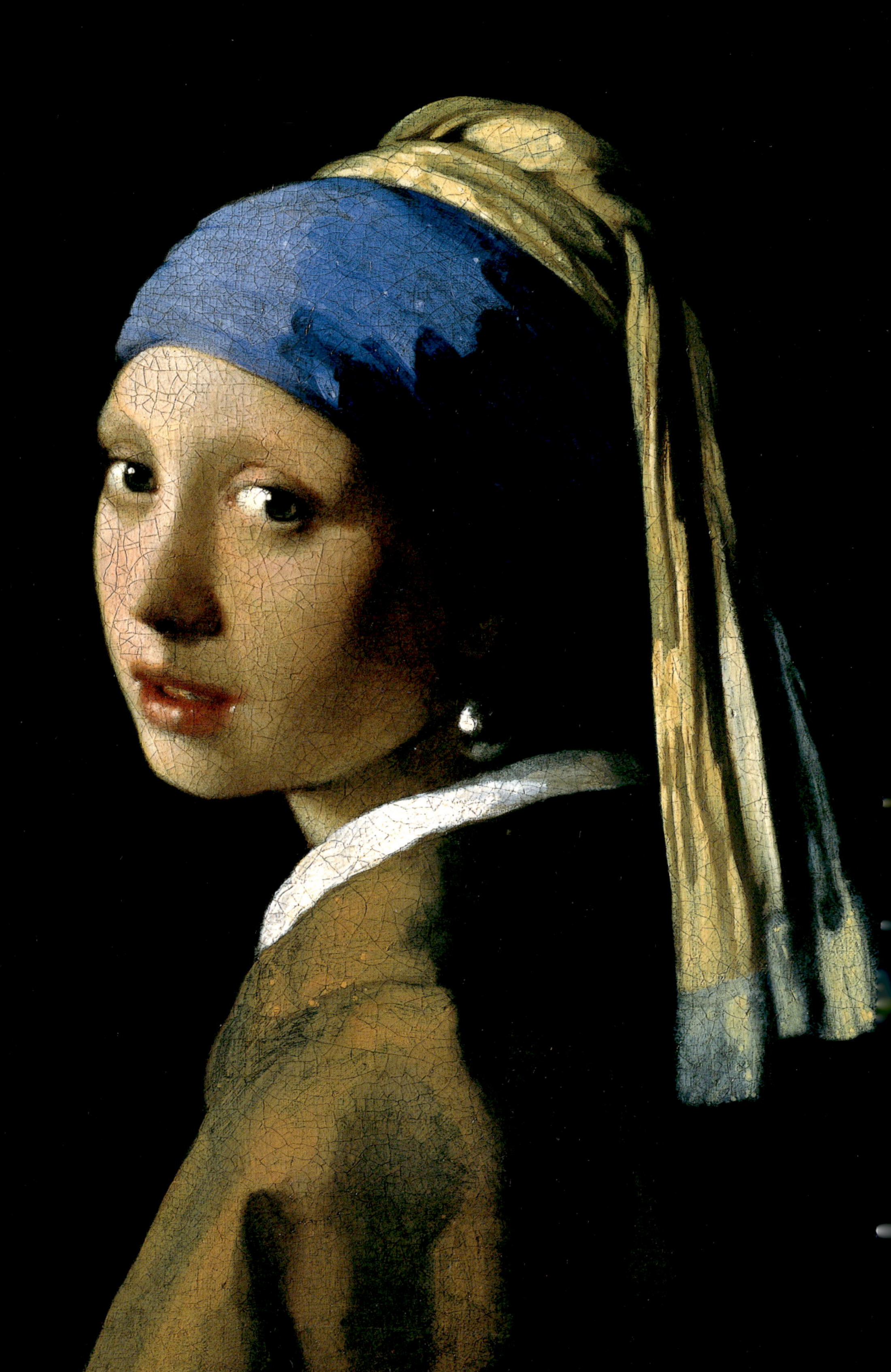

Chapter 4

Under the Moon

In 1999 a remarkable "sky disc" (ill. 2), unique in the world, was discovered in Germany. Virtually nothing is known about the people who made it apart from the fact that they lived and buried their dead about 3,600 years ago around what is now Mittelberg in northern Germany. The disc may be the earliest representation now known of an actual constellation if, as has been proposed, the group of seven stars depicts the Pleiades, a stellar cluster that was important to farmers in Europe because it appeared in the heavens at harvest time. The gold arcs at the side are believed by some to represent the seasonal shift in the appearance of the sun on the horizon. The bow was first interpreted as a sun boat, until the disc was looked at the other way up. Since then it has been thought to represent a rainbow, and the striations along its length support this theory. If this interpretation is correct, the disc could be an image not just of the sun, moon and stars but of the relationship between them.

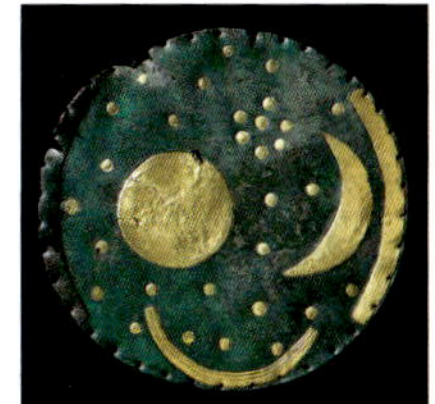

2 Nebra sky disc, c. 1600 B.C.E. Gold and bronze, 32 cm diameter. Landesmuseum für Vorgeschichte, Halle, Germany

The sun's rays bake the earth dry; the moon's cold beams draw out its moisture. It would be surprising if our earliest ancestors, given their dependence on the rhythms of nature, had *not* observed the relationship between the moon, the rise and fall of the tides and the menstrual cycle of women, which is now believed to be a biological memory of life's origin in the sea. The moon has long been associated with water. When sunlight strikes rain or water vapour, a rainbow appears. It's one of the few perfectly rounded forms in nature, like the sun and the moon, the dome of the sky (represented by this disc), the eyes of humans

1 Jan Vermeer. *Girl with a Pearl Earring*, c. 1665. Mauritshuis, The Hague

and higher animals, and the centres of many flowers. Magically, in the rainbow, all the colours of the world appear, when sunlight and the vapours of the moon combine. And at harvest time the colours of the world are at their most intense, and a red glow even tints the harvest moon.

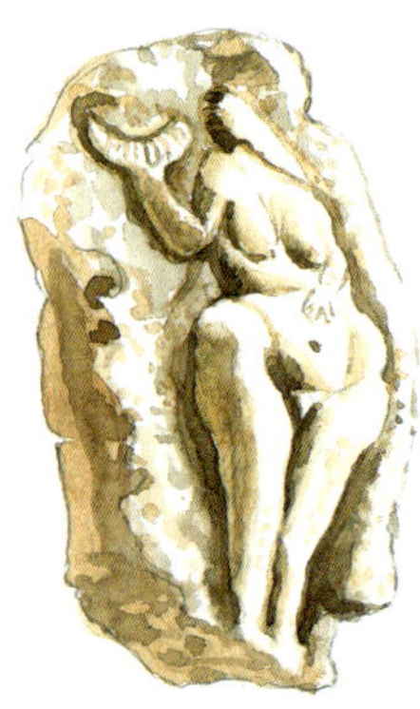

3 *Venus of Laussel*, Dordogne, France, c. 25,000–20,000 B.C.E. Limestone, 44 cm high. Musée de l'Homme, Paris

The moon is invariably female in mythology, except occasionally in India, where gods have a habit of switching sexes. Though a few ancient Greek philosophers thought moonlight was a reflection of sunlight, everyone else around the world, including most Greeks, thought the moon emitted its own pale rays which were soft, gentle and feminine in contrast to the sun's, which were fierce, strong and masculine. The sun is master of the day, so men ran public affairs. The moon is mistress of the night, so women managed private life inside the home. The moon illumined our most intimate thoughts and acts; she was associated with all things motherly–sex, tenderness and fecundity. Moreover, the moon is veiled during the day, which could be one of the original reasons why women in some cultures wear veils when they leave their houses. The wife or mother of the Chinese emperor, when contributing to affairs of state, spoke from behind a curtain. Purdah, the tradition of keeping women out of sight, which is still prevalent in many societies influenced by Islam, probably had very ancient roots.

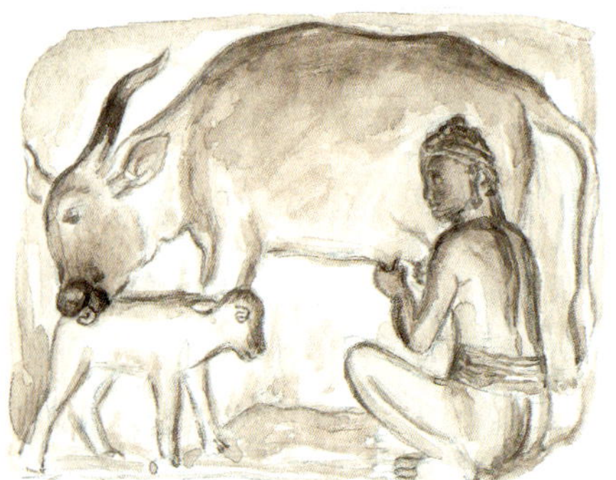

4 *Krishna Milking a Cow*, temple relief, stone, 7th–8th centuries C.E. Mamallapuram, southern India

The *Venus of Laussel* (ill. 3) was carved in a rock shelter lived in by early humans. It's one of the oldest sculptures to have come down to us, and it seems to represent an earth mother holding up a symbol of the moon goddess. Horned animals, like cattle, were associated with the moon, just as animals with manes, like lions, were associated with the sun. Cows are still sacred to Hindus in India, and they wander freely wherever their divine spirit takes them, into houses and through crowded city streets. The horn was often depicted as a cornucopia from which all goodness flowed, just as milk—as white as the moon—flowed from the udders of cows. Women's breasts swell with milk when they've given birth, just as the moon fills with light every month. A beautiful temple relief (ill.4) at Mamallapuram on the coast of southern India shows Krishna, the blue, storm-cloud god, milking a cow while the cow licks the back of her calf—a cycle of life-giving love. The temples at Mamallapuram are cut into a strange boulder-strewn landscape, the chief attraction of which is a huge ball of stone that rests precariously on folds of rock which look like the fingers of an open hand (ill.5). Local tradition holds that this is the butter-ball that Krishna stole when he was a boy, so fond was he of churned milk.

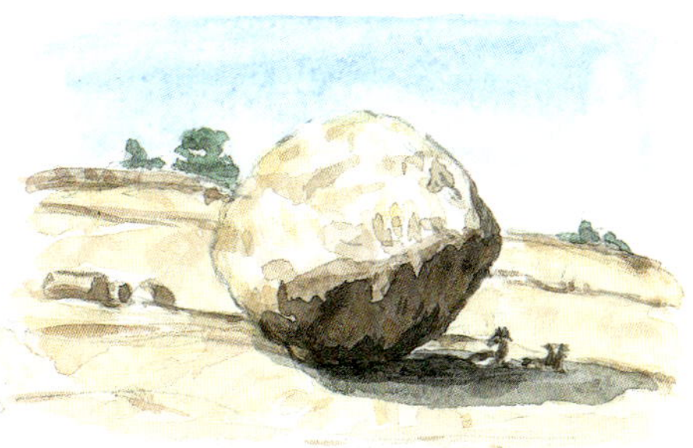

5 A natural outcrop of rock, Mamallapuram, southern India

It was widely believed that women were most fertile when the moon was full. It was then that Krishna made secret, sensual love to everyone—men were sometimes included as well as women—making sure, as he did so, that nothing would disturb the enchantment of the world. Here (ill.6), in a river under the full moon, he sports with the cow girls who tend the sacred cows, each of whom think he's making love to her alone. The moon's repeated preg-

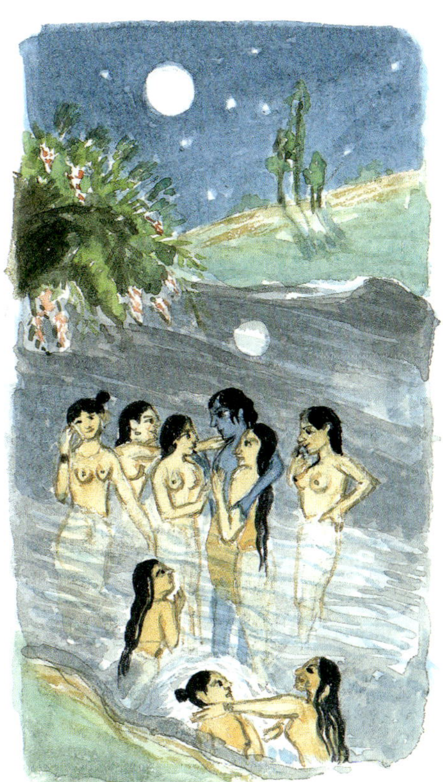

6 After Krishna Bathing with Gopis, 18th century C.E., detail, Kangra miniature. Bharat Kala Bhavan Museum, Varanasi

nancy held sway over the fertility of the earth. It was only at full moon that the Chinese emperor lay with his empress. At less auspicious times he made love to his many other wives and concubines, because a child born from a union at these times would have less chance of becoming an all-powerful Son of Heaven. Scribes took careful note of the date and hour of each imperial ejaculation. Chinese astrologers calculate horoscopes from the time of conception, more logically than those in Europe who read them at the time of birth. Their aim was to determine the secular and religious leadership potential of any resulting royal progeny. The moon became pregnant in the celestial regions, and has therefore long been associated with spiritual as well as material regeneration. The Buddha was supposed to have been born in 586 B.C.E. at the time of the full moon, and some Buddhists still make public confessions of faults to cleanse their spirits at the appearance of the new moon.

The waxing and waning of the moon was explained in different ways. In ancient Greece, India and Iran, the moon was regarded as a staging post to heaven. Souls landed on it after they'd left their mortal remains below and, when the moon was full, these were ejected from it up towards the stars. The moon is absent from the night sky for approximately three days or two nights. Significantly, Jesus Christ (c. 6 B.C.E.–c. 30 C.E.) spent three days in hell after his crucifixion, and Nanak (1469–c. 1539 C.E.) disappeared for three days before founding Sikhism out of Hinduism and Islam—a religion which worships under the sign of the crescent moon. Hindus still offer special prayers in *Amavasyas*—the days of no moon, when they believe their Lord Shiva is busy on Mount Kailash with the affairs of the universe and thus unable to attend to their demands. The major religions of the Bible—the Jewish, Christian and Muslim faiths—all adopted the lunar calendar, to varying degrees, to determine their chief ceremonies. Muhammad (c. 570–632 C.E.) told his followers not to begin fasting until they actually *saw* the new moon, an edict which still causes problems for some on cloudy nights. Christianity follows the lunar calendar too, for its Easter festival which celebrates the resurrection of Christ.

The moon was believed to be closer to us than the sun, and therefore, *under* the sun–just as women were thought to be beneath men in the hierarchy of mankind. The moon, therefore, separated heaven above from our world below. Everything under the moon was seen to be in a state of flux, as the moon itself is the only heavenly body that changes shape, swells, and then fades to nothing. The sun and moon both died, but death seemed to be integral to the moon's nature. This tiny, crescent-shaped nose ring (ill. 7) depicts a gold sun on a silver background and a silver moon on a golden background. Gold was believed among Peruvian and Central American cultures to be the tears of the sun, shed as it passed under the earth at night. Like the radiance of the sun, gold never changes–it's incorruptible. Silver was thought to be the sweat of the moon and, like the moon, it turned black until it was polished again. It was important to decorate the nostrils–for breath, in many cultures, was believed to be the very essence of life. You took your first breath when you were born and breathed out your last when you died. A whole cosmology is depicted here in this deceptively simple ornament–in the breath of life that came down to earth and gave life to everything beneath the sun and moon.

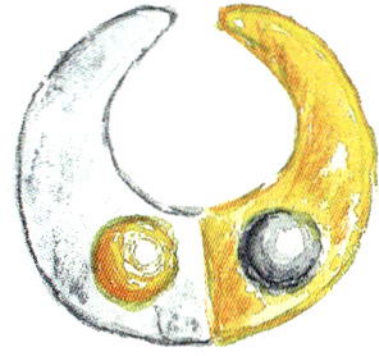

7 Sun and moon bimetallic nose ornament, Mochican, classic period, c. 500 C.E. Silver and gold. Rafael Larco Herrera Museum, Lima

The German alchemist Paracelsus (1493–1541 C.E.) believed that opals, with their elusive rainbows caught in a pearly soup, were nothing less than distilled moonbeams. It is probable that our ancestors saw a relationship between the moon and the pearl,

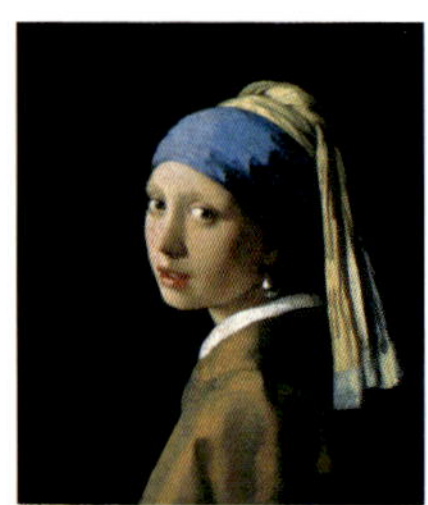

1 Jan Vermeer. *Girl with a Pearl Earring*, c.1665. Mauritshuis, The Hague

which was so close in many ways to the opal. Pearls are found under the sea in the vaginal-like, close-lipped, soft secrecy of the oyster. They can take the form, so rare in nature, of a perfect sphere, and shine with a pale, lunar brightness. The moon and pearls are almost invariably associated with women. Vermeer's *Girl with a Pearl Earring* (ill. 1) appeals to something deep in our nature. Any man who has watched someone he loves from behind, and seen her turn round, as if she felt his gaze, and glance at him at once with an immediate, reciprocal love, can understand the moment Vermeer has tried to distil for ever. The girl's loving look is pure but not virginal, for her slightly parted lips, glistening at the corner, suggest a sexual consummation. The glance in her eyes, the turn of her neck, the whole composition, pivots around the bead of light that glows in the pearl droplet. The moon, giving birth in heaven, reigned over those giving birth below. In this painting spiritual and earthly love are combined, a sublime goal for any mortal being.

In Islamic belief, probably based on theories from ancient Greece, pearls were thought to be conjunctions of water and fire. Fire and water both flowed but in all other respects they were direct opposites. Water always seeks to fall, and is cold and blue. Fire is hot and red and always seeks to rise. When they came together they vanished as steam except, so it was believed, when they turned into pearls. Then the spiritual yearning of fire combined with the earthly yearning of water—the marriage of grace with desire that we find so haunting in the picture by Vermeer.

8 Dragons dancing with pearls, 18th century C.E. Glazed tiles. The Forbidden City, Beijing

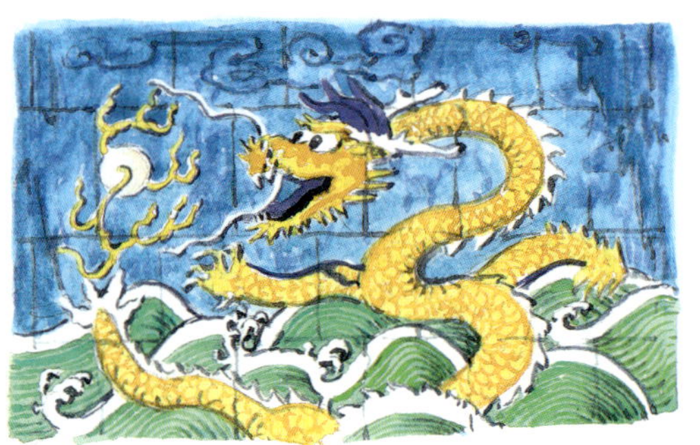

Pearls were regarded as both eternal and transient, like the moon. Spheres representing them hung above the thrones of the Chinese emperors. They symbolised the union between the celestial and mortal worlds which imperial rule encapsulated. In screens around the Forbidden City, dragons played with them (ill.8) among the waves and clouds. Here were the invisible forces of nature – the winds in the air and the currents in the sea that could be calm and gentle but, when angry, could lash the coasts with storms and crash the clouds together with thunder and lightning.

To our ancestors everything under the moon, like the moon itself, seemed to be in a state of permanent flux, so unlike the fixed, star-studded constellations in the heavens above the sun. It's true that there were snow-capped mountains on land that seemed to be permanent enough. Few can have tried to climb them, and if they had done they would have found themselves becoming inexplicably light-headed. Most believed such places reached up to heaven and were lived in by the gods. Mount Olympus, where Zeus had his throne, is a real mountain in Greece. So is Mount Kailash in the Himalayas, where Lord Shiva lives. But mountains weren't only to be found on land. The sea could also be mountainous and white-capped, without being fixed in one place for an instant. Hokusai's print of Mount Fuji, Japan's holiest mountain and home to some of its oldest gods (ill.9), has become so famous

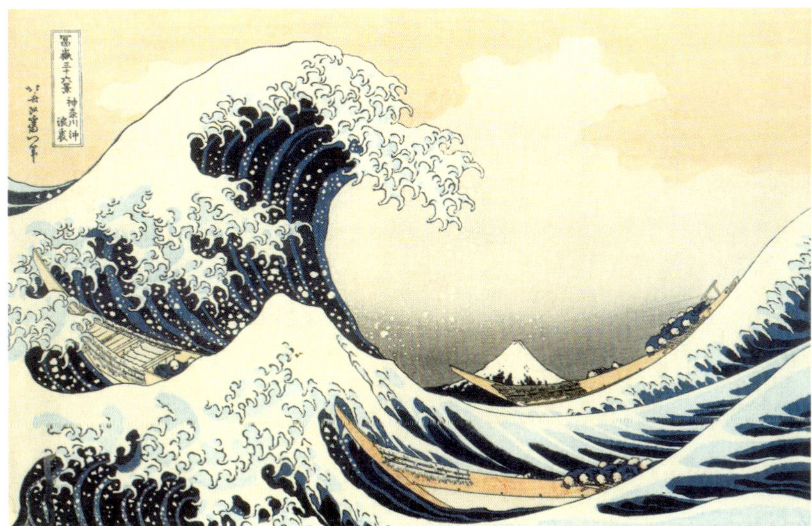

9 Hokusai. *The Great Wave off Kanegawa*, c.1828. Woodcut from *The Thirty-six Views of Mount Fuji*

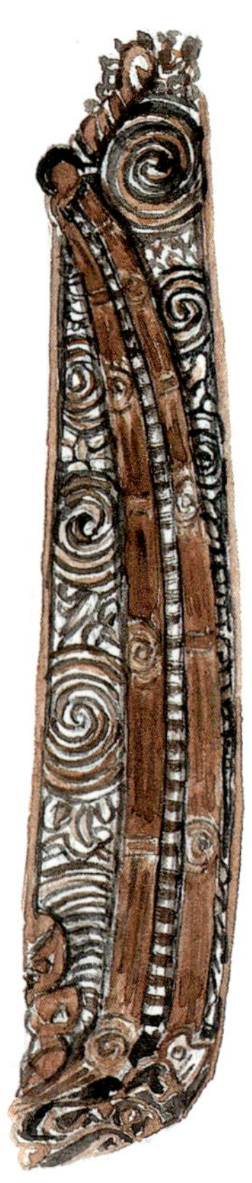

10 War canoe stem post, Koputaroa, collected 1831. Height 165.2 cm. Canterbury Museum, New Zealand

perhaps because it expresses a profound truth about the nature of our existence. It is mankind's fate to live between the mountains on land and the mountains at sea in a state of never-ending, cliff-hanging insecurity.

Human beings have long felt that they are "at sea". The Maori people settled in Aotearoa–later called New Zealand by European settlers–about 1,200 years ago. They carved elaborate prows for their war canoes which represented what they thought were the two great waves of existence: the eternal world of the gods above and the mortal world below, with the tiny figure of man, at the bottom left, caught between them (ill. 10). Beside the Great Pyramid of Cheops were buried two colossal wooden boats, only one of which (ill. 11) has yet been excavated. They were possibly intended to sail and row the dead pharaoh up and down the Nile, which the ancient Egyptians believed rose out of the waters of the underworld in the south and sank back into them in the north. A boat tossed on the open sea and a pyramid of light standing in the desert dunes–could there be two more poetic images of all mankind's profoundest fears and hopes?

Our ancestors knew that they lived precariously in an unstable world. Before scientists worked out the laws of erosion and evaporation a couple of hundred years ago, the relationship between mountains and rivers was a mystery. We guessed that the secrets of the universe might be hidden in the pebbles at our feet. In the tranquillity of their temple gardens Zen Buddhist monks would contemplate an assembly of rocks and raked gravel (ill. 12) and imagine mountains and seas melting into each other, while they recited the fifteen prayers to the Buddha that would eventually lift them out of this hopelessly unsettled and unsettling world, and on to the eternal celestial plane of spiritual enlightenment.

Clouds looked like mountains in the sky, yet they were as light as feathers, like exploded pearls. They were made of that most mysterious substance–mist, which forms when fire and water meet. Mist was thought by many to be the essential substance of all life–the melting point where matter turned into spirit. Mist is formed by our breath when the air is cold. How mist and clouds were actually created was a mystery until the late eighteenth century. It was only then that words like cirrus and cumulus entered our vocabulary. The devoutly Christian artist John Constable (1776–1837) was fascinated by the cloud theories of early meteorologists like Luke Howard, because these enabled him to paint this most elusive and wonderful aspect of God's handiwork with even more transcendent truthfulness (ill. 13).

Imperial imagery in China always involved clouds. Clouds symbolised the emperor's location in the world. Stone pillars carved with cloud shapes hedge the sacred platforms in the Forbidden City in Beijing. Records state that when these were in ceremonial use, clouds of incense billowed across their surface, making the emperor and his retinue look as though they were floating on air. At the same time water, probably scented and

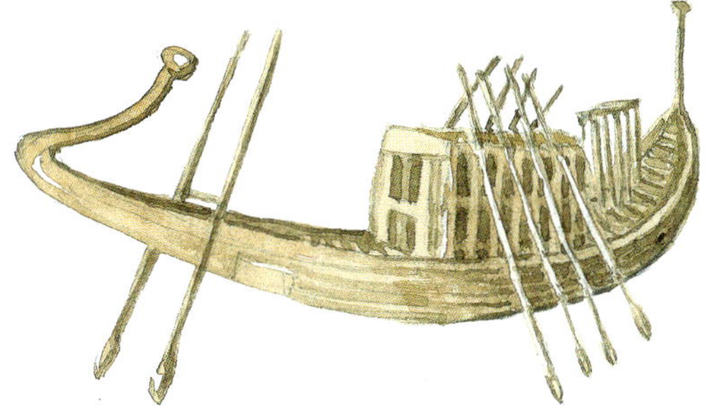

11 The Sun Boat, c. 2500 B.C.E. Cedar wood, sycamore and halfa grass, 43 metres long. Solar Boat Museum, Gizeh, Egypt

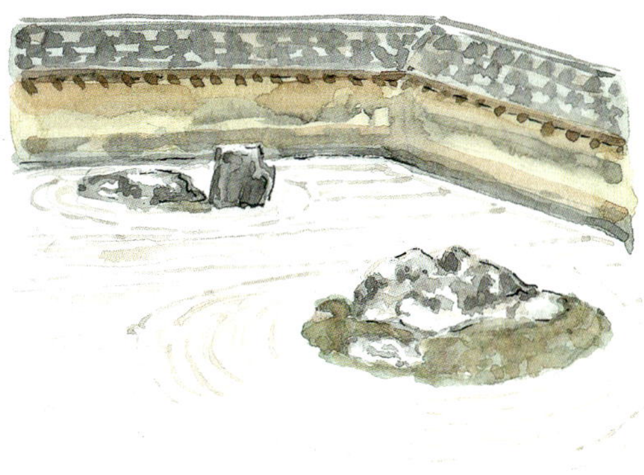

12 *Waterless stream*, Zen Garden at Ryoan-ji Temple, founded 1473 C.E. Kyoto

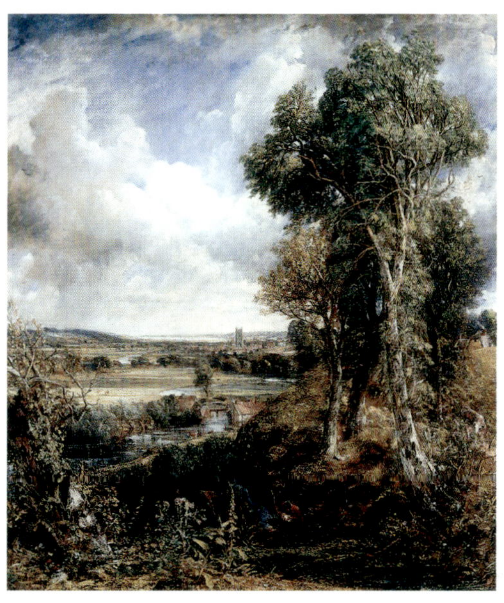

13 John Constable. *Landscape (Dedham Vale)*, 1828. Oil on canvas, 145 x 122 cm. National Galleries of Scotland, Edinburgh

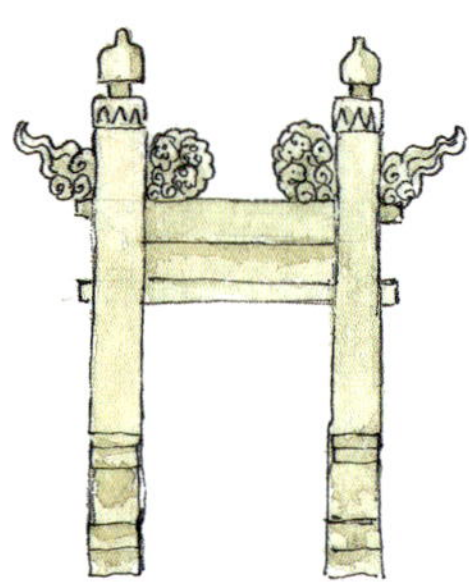

14 Cloud gateway, 1530 C.E. Stone. Temple of Heaven, Beijing

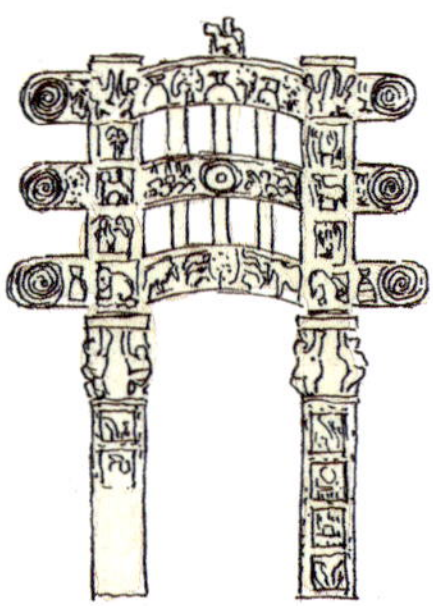

15 Gateway, 1st century B.C.E. Sandstone. The Great Stupa, Sanchi, India

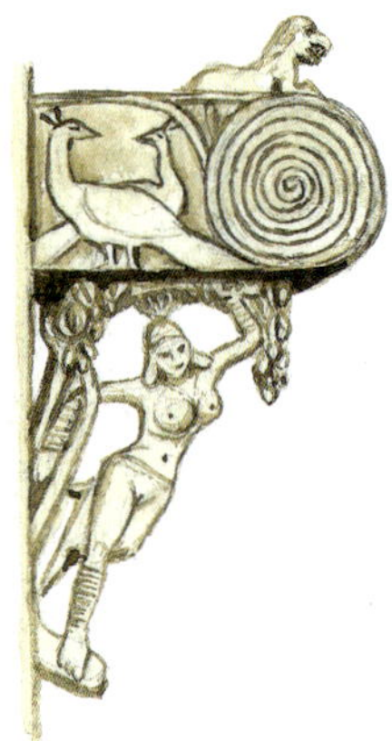

16 Gateway, 1st century B.C.E. Sandstone, detail. The Great Stupa, Sanchi, India

coloured, spurted out of the dragon spouts that surrounded these imperial platforms, as if the clouds were pouring down life-giving rain. The strange cloud gates (ill. 14) at the Temple of Heaven in Beijing were perhaps inspired by the celestial gateways (ill. 15) built around the Great Stupa at Sanchi, one of the earliest Buddhist monuments in India, dating from the third century B.C.E. Buddhism became hugely influential in China, though it largely died out in India. The gateways at Sanchi (ill. 16) are decorated with spirals, a symbol of the one leading to the many and many leading to the one—the embracing beneficence and singularity of god. Some of these spirals give birth to peacocks, as clouds give birth to rainbows and the morning mist condenses into prismatic dew.

The colouring of clouds, from pearly white to dark grey, their shifting forms, and their ability to disappear and reappear all suggested that they were emanations from the moon. Most importantly, they brought rain which, in turn, brought life. And when the rain fell on the mountains, it created rivers which magically symbolised, as the seasons did, the whole trajectory of human existence from bouncing, bubbling youth to slow, meandering old age. Everything in nature seemed to be trying to teach us something. Leonardo da Vinci looked at everything as intensely as he did because he was sure he could learn something by doing so. Mountains and the rivers that cascaded down from them were, for him, an eternal mystery, and he painted them bathed in mist (ill. 17). The Chinese had long been fascinated by the relationship between mountains, water and clouds. From very early in their history—at least by 500 B.C.E., the era of Confucius and Lao Zi, the founder of Taoism—they looked at nature poetically, not scientifically. They believed that everything was in a state of eternal flux between action and passivity, spirit and matter, life and death, encapsulated by the two complementary principles of existence, the Yang and the Yin (ill. 18), the former positive, masculine and light; the latter negative, feminine and dark. Everything is on the point of turning into its opposite – mountains with their thrusting masses were male, though dark, until snow fell on them, while the streams cascading down their sides were feminine, though light, until they formed dark pools at their base. Opposites played together in the formation of the world. Silver turned black, and the moon waxed and waned.

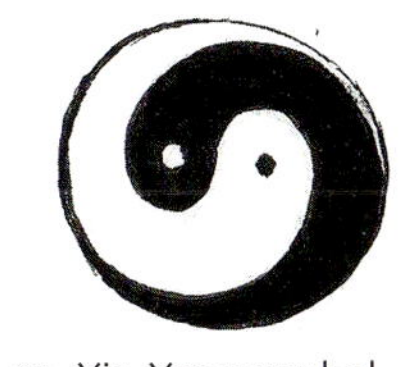

18 Yin-Yang symbol

During the highly sophisticated Song Dynasty, in the eleventh and twelfth centuries C.E. – perhaps one of the most cultured eras the world has ever witnessed – Chinese artists developed a uniquely condensed, minimalist style of watercolour painting (ill. 19). Black ink and water, brushes and white paper were all they needed to recreate the universe. Depending on how much it was diluted with water, ink could evoke everything from a mist rising in the valley to a towering mountainside, from a shimmering leaf to an old, gnarled trunk. The ink was the breath and

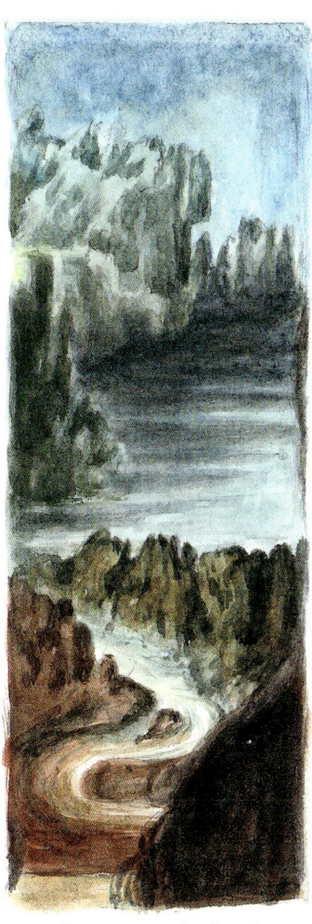

17 After Leonardo da Vinci. *Mona Lisa*, 1503, detail of the background. Louvre, Paris

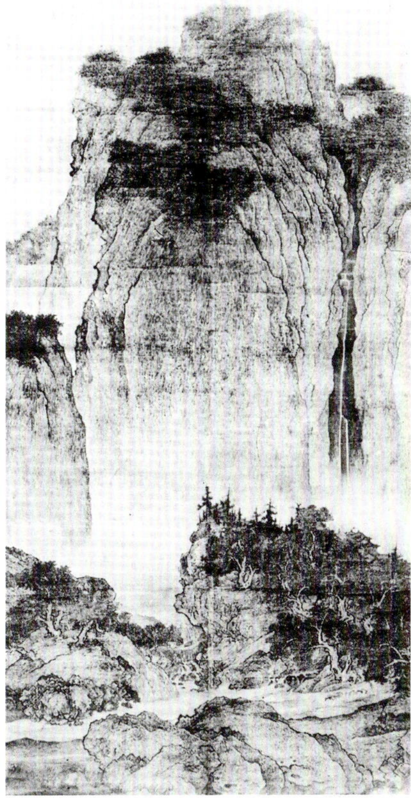

19 Fan K'uan. *Travellers among Mountains and Streams*, early 11th century C.E. National Palace Museum, Taiwan

flesh of life. Brushmarks indicated the force and direction within all creation; mountains and rivers, plants and animals, stones and clouds were all believed to contain their own life-force. The brush was the bones and strength of life. And the white paper, on which and within which this whole ballet was performed, represented the light and space of life—expanding infinitely in all directions, or concentrated into a vital spark flickering along a growing branch or dancing down a waterfall.

Machu Picchu (ill. 20) was the last city built by the Incas in the fifteenth century C.E. as they retreated further and further into the Andes to escape the invading Spaniards. It's an extraordinary, stone-terraced construction, perched on a ridge a vertical mile above the broiling, roaring brown waters of the Urubamba and Aobamaba rivers. Frequent landslides prevented human habitation lower down. The town was abandoned soon after it was built and was lost in the jungle until it was rediscovered in 1911—the survivor of an ancient culture whose buildings, art and beliefs had been almost entirely eradicated by the Spaniards. We know virtually nothing about how Machu Picchu operated, but we can make some informed guesses. We know that mountains in the past were holy places not just

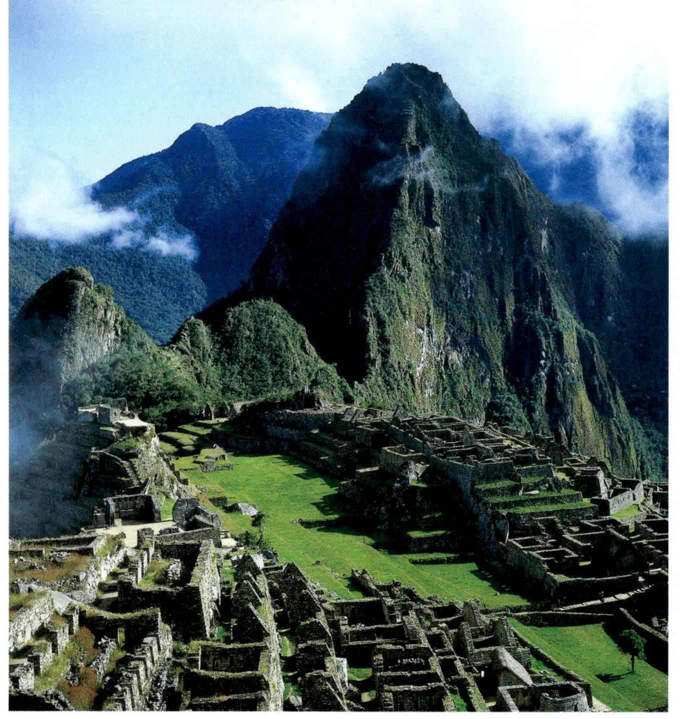

20 Machu Picchu: general view. Contemporary photograph

because they were nearest to the gods: they were thought to have a life of their own. Machu Picchu—the name means ancient mountain peak—was built on the top of a spirit-mountain. The peak of the mountain—its growing tip, where its spirit lived—rose in the heart of the city. The Incas carved this living rock to create a strange asymmetrical altar (ill.21), unique in the world.

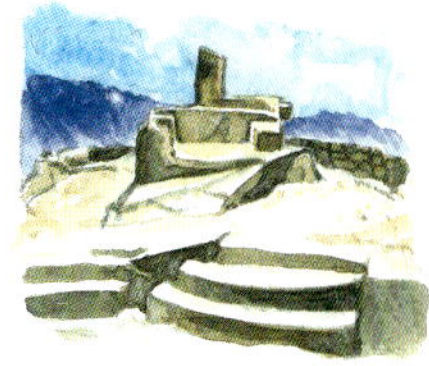

21 So-called Inti-watana (the hitching post of the sun) altar and steps cut out of the living rock, Inca, c.1450 C.E. Machu Picchu, Peru

The Incas are known to have been sun worshippers, and the Inca himself was believed to be the son of the sun. However, the theory that this mountain-top altar was some sort of a sundial or solar "hitching post" does not explain its complex form. There is in any case another building lower down in the city, with immaculately curved walls made of beautifully hewn stones, which is believed to have been a temple to the sun, for its two windows are aligned with the solar solstices. The high altar at Machu Picchu is more likely to have been the mountain spirit's home where, at religious festivals, it was fed and watered, and linked to the heavenly bodies in the sky, to ensure that the life-enhancing waters within it would flow.

Beautiful rock-cut channels conduct mountain springs throughout Machu Picchu, not just for human use and consumption—there are terraced fields and bath-houses—but also to feed the spirits, because these channels often conduct water across strange, asymmetrically-cut stone altars. Perhaps these springs represent the life-force that flows through all creation and that must be kept moving for life to flourish. The damming of a life-force, after all, leads to stagnation, illness and death. These streams perhaps had a spiritual and earthly existence, a duality that can be heard in the traditional music of the Andes, in which two players on two different sets of panpipes perform one melody. The flow between all living things and their spirits had to be maintained for the balance of creation to be sustained.

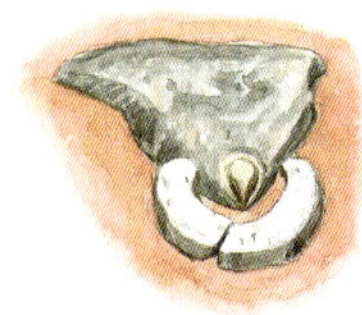

22 The Altar of the Condor, c.1450 C.E. Machu Picchu, Peru

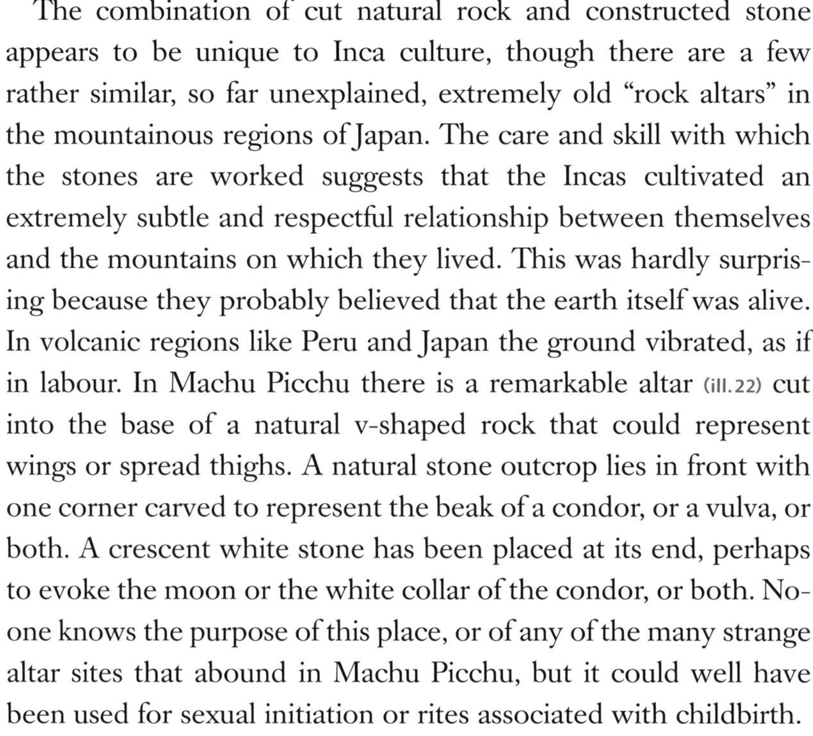

The combination of cut natural rock and constructed stone appears to be unique to Inca culture, though there are a few rather similar, so far unexplained, extremely old "rock altars" in the mountainous regions of Japan. The care and skill with which the stones are worked suggests that the Incas cultivated an extremely subtle and respectful relationship between themselves and the mountains on which they lived. This was hardly surprising because they probably believed that the earth itself was alive. In volcanic regions like Peru and Japan the ground vibrated, as if in labour. In Machu Picchu there is a remarkable altar (ill.22) cut into the base of a natural v-shaped rock that could represent wings or spread thighs. A natural stone outcrop lies in front with one corner carved to represent the beak of a condor, or a vulva, or both. A crescent white stone has been placed at its end, perhaps to evoke the moon or the white collar of the condor, or both. No-one knows the purpose of this place, or of any of the many strange altar sites that abound in Machu Picchu, but it could well have been used for sexual initiation or rites associated with childbirth.

No culture has ever dressed stone more precisely and finely or on a larger scale than the Incas, not even the ancient Egyptians. Their extraordinary asymmetrical interlocking masonry, which used no mortar, was partly developed to resist earthquakes. The walls, as they were shaken, became more tightly bound together. But this wasn't just resistance; it was also a celebration, for the earthquake was a living god–Pachacamac, the lord of underground fire. Vast and wonderful asymmetrically cut boulders were used to build a strange construction, situated just above the Incas' capital, Cuzco, in a place called Sacsayhuaman (ill.23). It took about a century to build, possibly from about 1440 C.E. It cannot have been a fortress for the citizens of Cuzco, for it is exposed to attack at the rear, nor would this use explain its

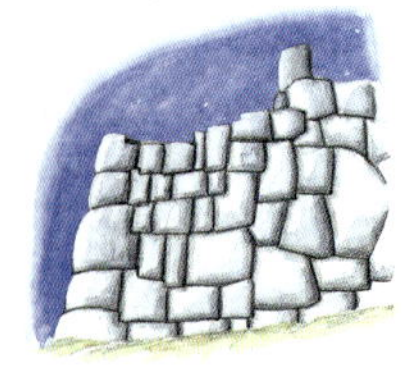

23 Sacsayhuaman, c.15th century C.E., detail of masonry. Diorite. Cuzco, Peru

elaborate, toothed construction, which is like nothing else on earth. It must surely have had a religious significance, and perhaps in some way it celebrated the shuddering power of Pachacamac. Inca culture was based on praise and fear. We know they practised human sacrifice, though probably only on very rare occasions when disaster threatened. It's possible that their gods had some relationship to, or at least shared an ancestry with the deities of the people who lived far to the north in Mexico and Guatemala. There the god Tlaloc (ill.24) lived on mountain tops and was lord of rain and streams. He owned four pitchers of water; one was good, the other three brought disease, frost and death. Tlaloc means "the pulp of the earth" from which all living things were made.

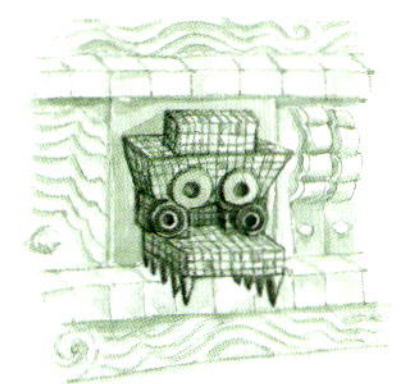

24 Tlaloc, 1–250 C.E. Painted stone. Temple of Quetzalcoatl, Teotihuacan, Mexico

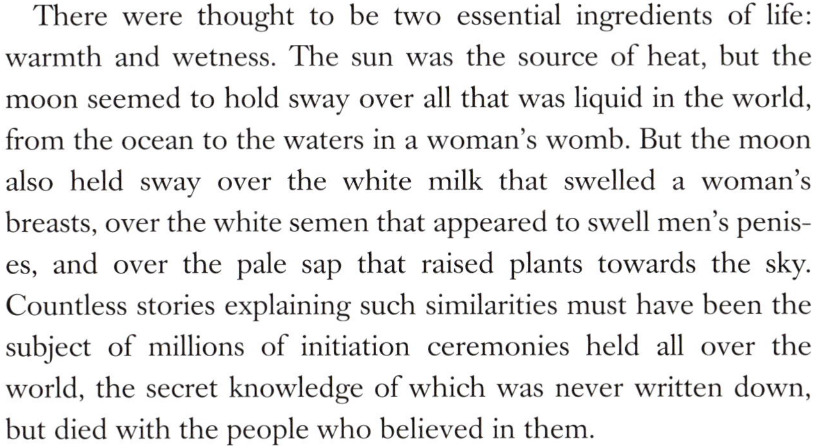

There were thought to be two essential ingredients of life: warmth and wetness. The sun was the source of heat, but the moon seemed to hold sway over all that was liquid in the world, from the ocean to the waters in a woman's womb. But the moon also held sway over the white milk that swelled a woman's breasts, over the white semen that appeared to swell men's penises, and over the pale sap that raised plants towards the sky. Countless stories explaining such similarities must have been the subject of millions of initiation ceremonies held all over the world, the secret knowledge of which was never written down, but died with the people who believed in them.

In the past, things that looked alike were assumed to *be* alike. Leonardo was fascinated by the similarity between the heart – which he was the first to dissect and draw with any accuracy – and a germinating seed (ill.25). People's world pictures, including Leonardo's, were made up of a myriad of visual echoes. The hair on people's bodies looked like grass; therefore the earth was a body with plants growing through its skin, and sap was a form of

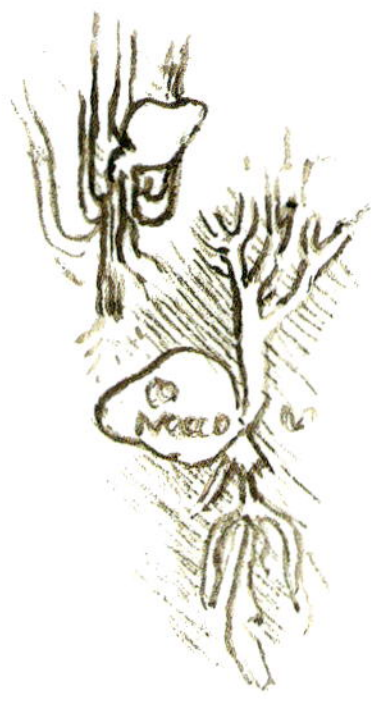

25 After Leonardo da Vinci. Cardiovascular system – a comparison between the shoots and roots of a seed and the veins and arteries of a heart, c.1506. Royal Collection, Windsor Castle

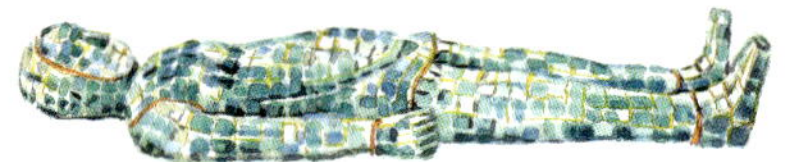

26 Jade burial suit, sewn with gold thread, western Han Dynasty, Hebei Province, Ding County. National Museum of Chinese History, Beijing

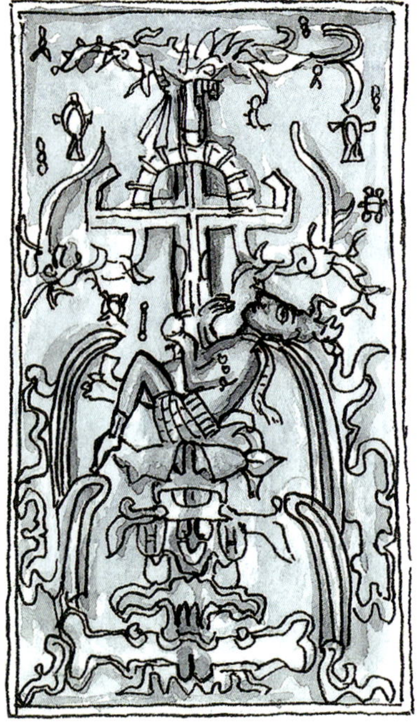

27 Pakal II's funerary slab, showing the cosmic tree, 683 C.E. National Museum of Anthropology, Mexico City

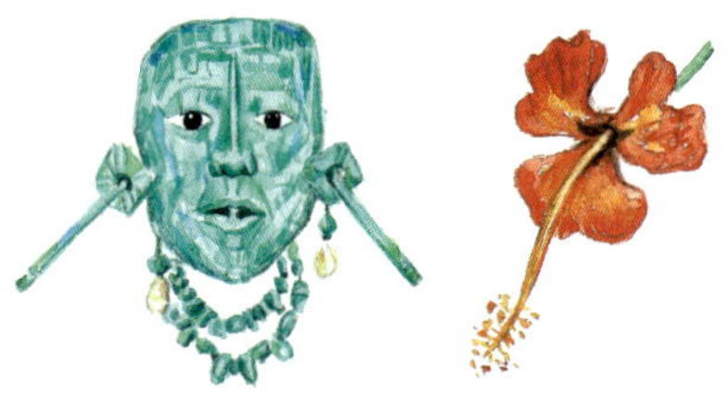

28 Pakal II's mask, 683 C.E. Jadeite, 24 x 19 cm. National Museum of Anthropology, Mexico City

29 Hibiscus flower

blood. Jade—an extremely hard but deceptively soft-looking greenish stone—was revered throughout China and the ancient cultures of Central and South America. It was like crystallised sap that was green and translucent but could last for ever. In the early years of Chinese civilisation, the nobility were buried in jade suits (ill.26) to ensure their longevity in the afterlife. In these cultures there was a direct link between vegetative and animal life. Both shared a belief in a world tree whose roots spread through all creation and whose branches reached to heaven.

The colour green appeared to have a sacred meaning for the ancient Mayan people who built their extraordinary temple complexes in the forests of what is now southern Mexico and Guatemala. Their great king, Pakal II (603–83 C.E.) was buried under a slab engraved with an image of the cosmic tree (ill.27) that would lift him to eternal life. The modern writer Erich von Daniken, who has fed our appetite for wonder by claiming that early man came from outer space, looked at this image on its side and was delighted to interpret it as an astronaut piloting a spaceship. Pakal's jade mask (ill.28), which is probably lifelike, confirms the former interpretation. The resurrected king will regenerate all living things. The earrings could suggest hibiscus flowers (ill.29) with their long stamens. Flowers were frequently used as decorations by the Maya, and it would be perfectly possible for a ruler to have flowers in his ears. But these earrings could also symbolise the flat, square world with the tree of life at its centre. The Maya collected stalactites wherever they found them in caves, and erected them at the centre of their temples (ill.30). In their new location these peculiar stone trees that grew down into the ground now grew up to heaven. If what grew down could grow up there was hope for the world.

Strange things like stalactites had to be accounted for. Around the Mediterranean, flint spear heads were believed to be Zeus' thunderbolts. Lightning flashes were thought to be the gods at work at their anvils or, if the storm was particularly fierce, fighting. Lightning is forked and flickers like a snake's tongue. So, in sympathetic magic around the world, which uses like to stimulate like, snakes were often employed in dances designed to provoke storms, and bring rain (ill.31). The zigzag snake designs found on the pottery of pre-Inca people in Peru are thought to symbolise the flow of the "soul force" throughout nature. In subtropical India, where erotic fulfilment was highly valued by society, lightning was believed to stimulate growth and sexual desire. In this picture (ill.32) a woman, sexually aroused by the storm, searches for her lover. A snake, emerging from a hole in a tree, reminds her of his absence.

One of the most haunting paintings in the world is the so-called *Tempesta* (ill.33). The Italian

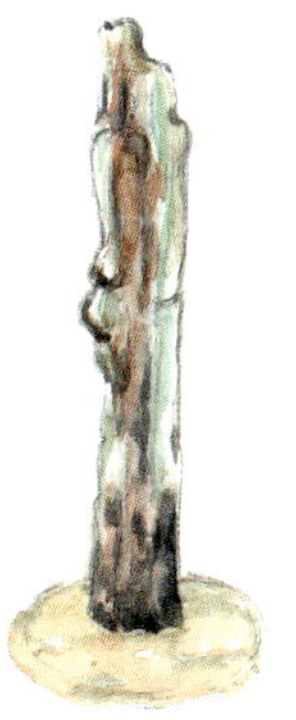

30 The Mayan World Tree, a stalactite at Yaxchilàn, erected c. 700 C.E.

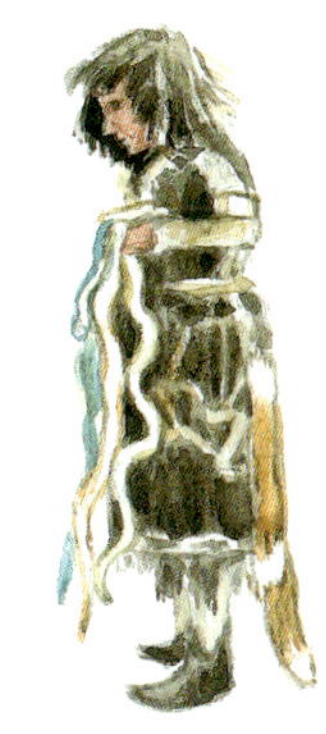

31 After Edward S. Curtis: *Picking up the Snakes*, Hopi, 1922, detail. Photograph from *The North American Indian*, vol. XII, 1922

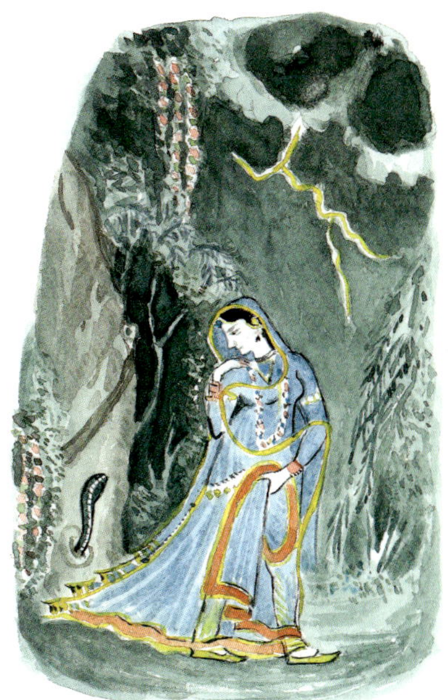

32 After *A Woman Searching for Her Lover*, 18th century C.E., detail. Kangra miniature. Chandigarh Art Gallery, India

Renaissance painter Giorgione was famous among his contemporaries for creating mysterious images. He worked in the immensely wealthy city of Venice at a time when artists were encouraged to express their own poetic imagination rather than merely illustrating the Bible or promoting the status of a powerful client. We don't know why it was painted or what it means. The chances are that it was intended as an ethereal vision of the relationship between men and women, of the transience of all things

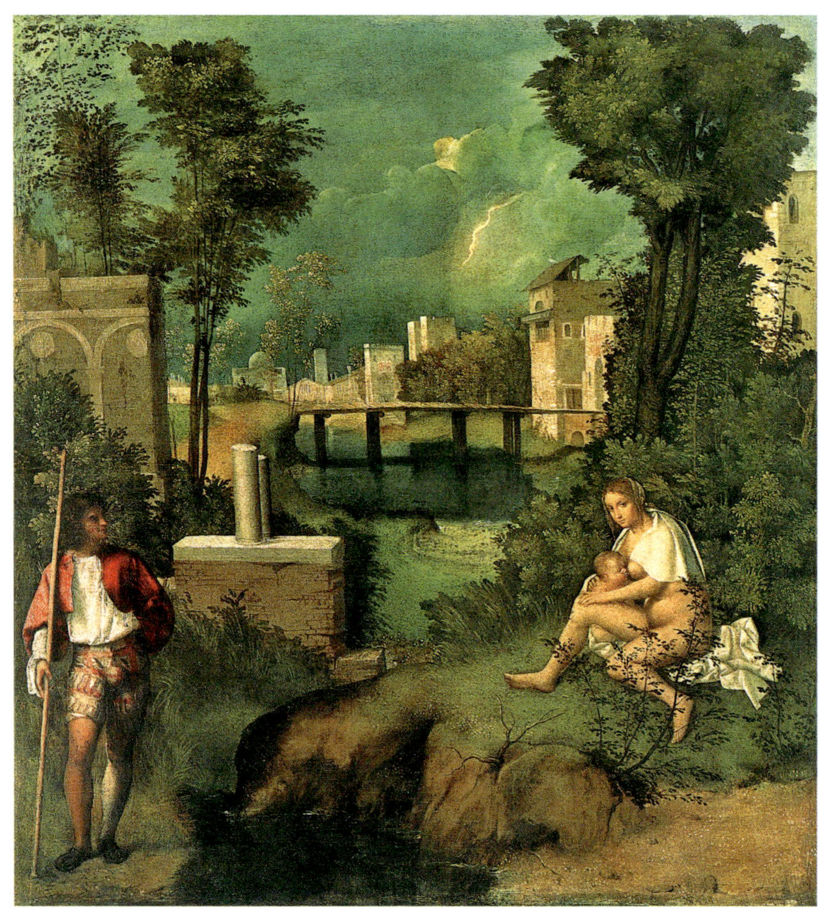

33 Giorgione. *Tempesta*, c. 1508. Accademia, Venice

and of the power, at once threatening and invigorating, of a storm.

Sex was the business of the moon, the only heavenly body to become pregnant. Buddhists, Christians and Muslims are used to sexual desire being suppressed or at least kept under wraps, but in earlier religions sexual intercourse was celebrated, as it still is today in Hinduism, the native religion of India, from which Buddhism itself sprang. Hinduism is by far the oldest major religion still practised in the world. Its origins are extremely obscure and certainly prehistoric. It had no single founder, no Christ, Buddha or Muhammad, but seems to have grown out of a plethora of nature spirits, particularly animals, rivers and mountains. At the heart of Hindu faith is the belief in a universal power from which the whole panoply of creation emanates and to which it all returns. Reincarnation is inevitable but also full of hope. If you are good in this life you will be born into a better life. Hindus believe that all animals are on their way to becoming humans—but it takes 52 million reincarnations for this transformation to be achieved!

Sex is crucial to Hinduism, because that's when the next reincarnation begins. Marriages are carefully arranged to ensure that both partners' ancestral lines are well placed to ensure a soul's auspicious return. Love-making is an act of praise to the gods and undertaken with exuberant joy. Two great texts, the Natyashastra, second century C.E., and the Kama Sutra, fourth century C.E., list the best ways to make love, according to the hour, week, month, and the weather. They suggest how to prepare for love-making, by decorating the room with sweet-smelling flowers, what to talk about and eat and what music to listen to, and how to acquire self-knowledge so as to be able to give the greatest satisfaction to your partner. They explain many ways to kiss and caress different parts of the body, always assuming that the woman's pleasure needs to be as great as the man's. For Hindus this pleasure is not merely sensual but religious, for the act of love-making celebrates the creation of the world, which began when Lord Brahma created Kama, the god of desire–for the wellspring of all new life is desire.

In the Hindu *Vedas*–religious poems–Kama is described as a youth with well-rounded calves and thighs, a narrow waist and broad chest, a ruddy, healthy complexion, black wavy hair and eyes like lotus petals. His fragrance filled the heavens and his breath was as sweet as a summer breeze. He carried a bow with arrows that were tipped with flowers–for their piercing was soft and the pain they brought bore fruit. All the gods were alarmed by Kama's birth, for they knew none of them could escape his arrows, including Lord Shiva himself. But what would happen when Shiva–who existed before creation began, who was timeless and limitless, the pure essence of joy–was struck by the flower arrows of Kama? What would be the fruit of happiness inflamed by desire?

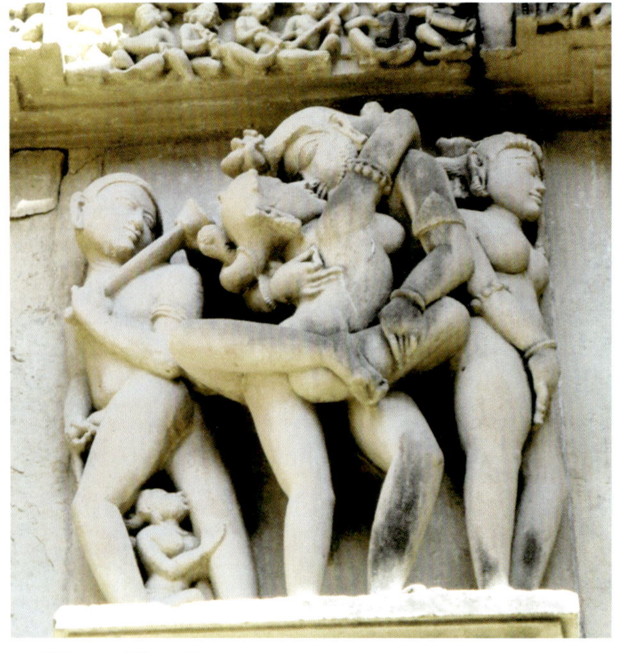

34 Shiva and Parvati, Kandariya Mahadeva Temple, 12th century C.E. Red sandstone. Khajuraho, India

The remarkable temples at Khajuraho celebrate this cosmic moment–when Shiva fell in love and married the beautiful Parvati. Her face, as the poets of the *Vedas* wrote, shone like the moon, and her breasts were firm and pointed like lotus flower buds, their dark nipples like bees hovering around them waiting for the petals to part. What would be born into the world when this lotus flower opened in response to the love of the sun? The beautifully proportioned, human-scale temples at Khajuraho, built during the eleventh and twelfth centuries C.E., are probably a reflection on earth of the celestial city that the heavenly architect, Vishvakarma, built for Shiva and Parvati's wedding. Each temple housed the heavenly beings who thronged to attend the ceremony. The temple walls are alive with details of all the activities at the festival–everyone is caught off-guard by the arrival of the heavenly couple; one nymph hasn't finished dressing and her clothes slip from her as she rushes out to catch a glimpse of Shiva. Another emerges from her bath, her wet sari and her hair clinging to her graceful body. In the central section on many of these temples are scenes of Shiva and Parvati consummating their marriage. One shows the moment their hands first touched–and their bodies started to glow. Many show them in different positions of rapturous love-making (ill.34) while their attendants, stimulated but unable to leave their posts, masturbate, as they and the world share in the first manifestations of the delights of creation.

Like most Hindu temples, those at Khajuraho are mountains in miniature–reflections of Mount Kailash, Lord Shiva's home in the Himalayas. They were solid throughout, except for a cave-like entrance carved into their base, like a tunnel leading into a womb. There the image of the god was placed directly under the temple peak. The highest point of the temple (ill.35) was capped with an image of a coconut, the divine fruit that was adopted by Hindus as a substitute for animal sacrifice about 2,250 years ago. It had two eyes in its skull, plus a third–the third all-seeing eye of Shiva–and when its shell was cracked by the priest, its blood spilled out, white and pure, like milk and semen. Beneath the

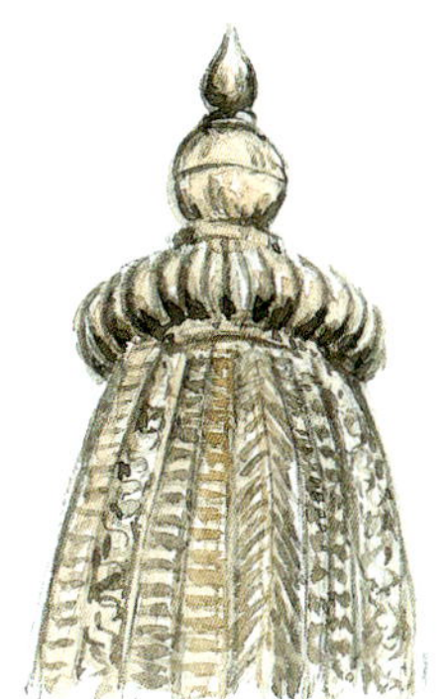

35 Finial of temple, 12th century C.E. Khajuraho, India

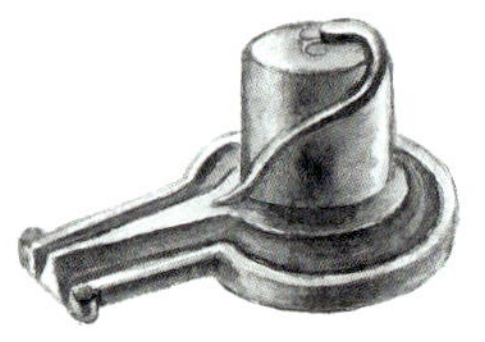

36 *Lingam* and *Yoni* Stone, India, c. 18th century C.E. British Museum, London

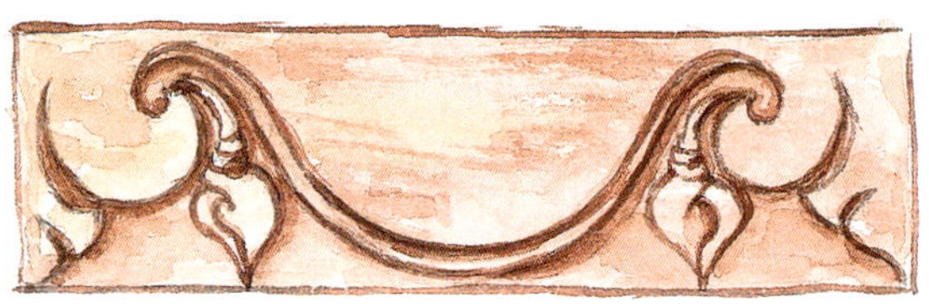

37 Conch and crescent moon, 12th century C.E. Temple lintel, Khajuraho, India

coconut was an image of a pot which held the water of the Ganges, the Hindus' holiest river of life, that was believed to have flowed directly down from heaven. It could be seen riding across the sky every night as the Milky Way. Every devout Hindu family has a pot of Ganges water in their home–it's administered as the first drink at birth and the last at death.

In many Shiva temples a pot of Ganges water hangs over the image of the god in the inner sanctum, but only when Shiva appears in his most popular form, as an erect phallus, or *lingam*. The most holy were those that were believed to have grown up out of the earth, rather than being man-made. Lingam usually stand in a *yoni*, a stylised vagina, which serves to collect the holy water dripping on the *lingam* and directs it back to Shiva's birthplace, for *yoni* always point north. In this *lingam* (ill. 36), the cobra serves as a protector but also expresses the spill of semen. The *yoni* reflects the lake in the foothills of Mount Kailash, known as the Lake of Parvati, Shiva's wife. The *lingam* is Shiva's mountain. The imagery of these temples is even more inclusive, because they almost invariably face due east, so that the pure, fresh beams of morning sunlight, not yet tainted with the corrupting emanations of the day, wake the god in the womb. A worshipper entering the sanctum has to step over a lintel carved with two conch shells and a crescent moon (ill. 37). These are symbols of purity and peace. The conch, which trapped in its coils the first sound of creation, is blown at the start of all religious pilgrimages. The appearance of the new moon is celebrated because it means that Shiva and Pavarti have returned from their absence on Mount Kailash to attend to the world's needs. Everything connects in the Hindus' sublunary world.

An erect penis is one of the most potent of all visual symbols, and certainly no less a mystery than anything else in creation. It's unlikely that there was only one giant like the one at Cerne Abbas (ill.38) in England, guarding a fort, wielding his club with an erection that proclaims his virility; this one luckily survived Victorian prudery. The supposedly more civilised Romans, who invaded Britain in 54 B.C.E., had their own god of fertility and protector of property, Priapus, whose symbol was a huge erection. When Julius Caesar eventually, by proving his brutality, earned the ultimate honour of a triumphal march through Rome, he donned a purple cloak decorated with the sun and stars, and was borne aloft through the crowded streets in a carriage pulled by four white bulls. Between its wheels swung a huge phallus, while a slave whispered in the conquering hero's ear: "Remember you're only a man". Rulers were expected to have sexual prowess. Britain, right up until the modern era, made much of male potency: Henry VIII's huge codpiece (ill.39) was central to his politics, and his row with Rome. He had to have six wives to ensure his succession.

More recent civilisations have tried to distance man from beasts and played erections down, but in many early societies they were an accepted part of public imagery. In ancient Japan, for example, any fork in a road was marked, like the fork in man, with a phallus carved in wood or stone (ill.40). These were usually erect, as a symbol of good luck. Almost all of these have now been removed. When Japan voluntarily cut itself off from modern

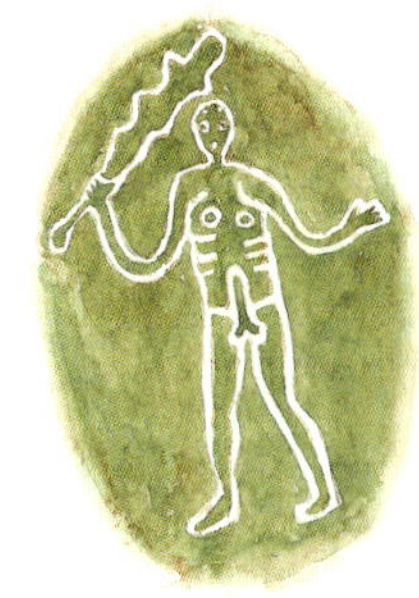

38 Cerne Abbas Giant cut into the chalk hillside, Dorset, c.1st century C.E. England

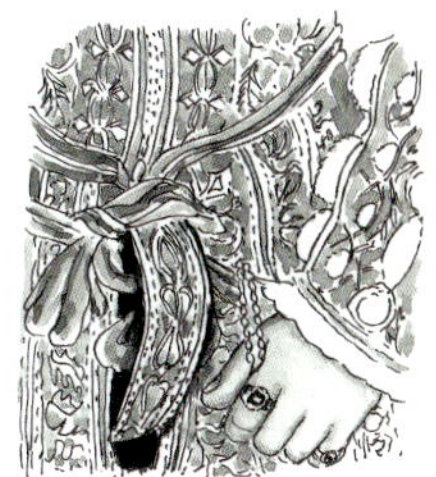

39 The codpiece of Henry VIII, detail from a cartoon for the Whitehall Palace Mural after Hans Holbein. 1537 C.E. National Portrait Gallery, London

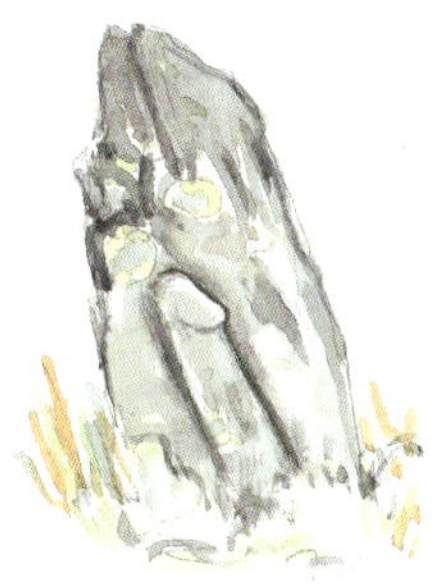

40 Phallic stone, Japan. Photographed by Phillip Rawson, c.1980

influences, it produced some of the greatest erotic art of the world (ill. 41). One of the few poetic quotes in this book of pictures by Utamaro (1753–1806) reads: "Its beak caught in the clamshell, the snipe cannot fly away this evening."

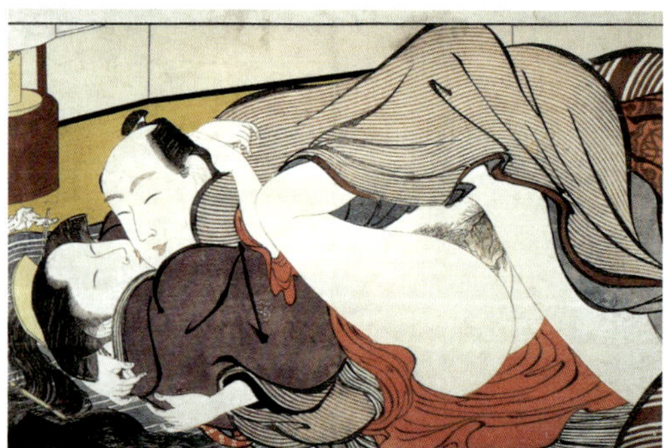

41 Kitagawa Utamaro. *Lovers beside a Standing Lantern*, 1788. Colour woodblock print, 25.5 x 37.4 cm. 3 from the book *Utamakura* (Poem of the Pillow). British Museum, London

Until very recently, visual changes at puberty, swelling breasts and menstruation, dropped testicles and body hair—alterations that appeared to be unique to humans—were regarded as highly significant events in people's lives. Under the volcanic ash that covered Pompeii, a remarkable painted room has been discovered (ill. 42) that is believed to represent a sexual initiation ceremony for a girl—here shown lifting the veil on an erect phallus whilst being flagellated, not as a punishment but as a purification, to drive out the evil spirits that could prevent her conceiving. In small-scale tribal societies around the world pubescent girls and boys were, and sometimes still are, led away in separate groups, often for months, into wild places to be initiated into tribal secrets and to learn their adult rituals. Initiates were taught the mysteries rather than just the facts of life—how everything changed, just as they were changing. The brow of this African initiation mask (ill. 43) is also its belly, the cheeks are its breasts as well as its spread thighs, its nose is its penis as well as its vulva. The six lizards that form its hair are thought to represent the cosmic forces that control our

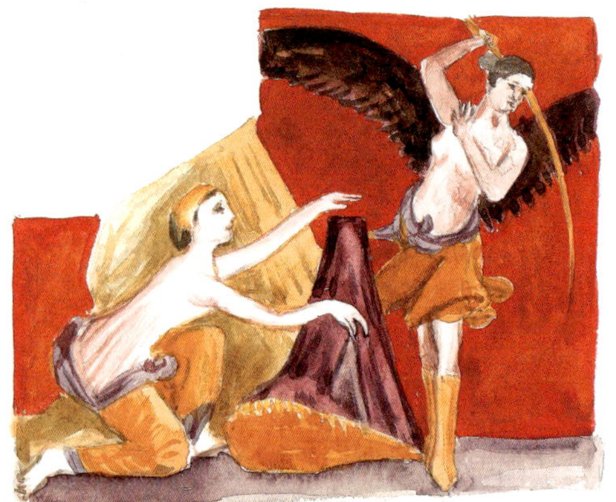

42 Detail showing girl lifting veil on phallus and being flagellated, 1st century C.E. Fresco in the Villa of the Mysteries, Pompeii, Italy

existence. The eternal cycle of this design represents the endurance of the Bamileke in the kingdom of Bamendou. It was carved from a tree believed to have been planted by Jeugman, the founder of the kingdom.

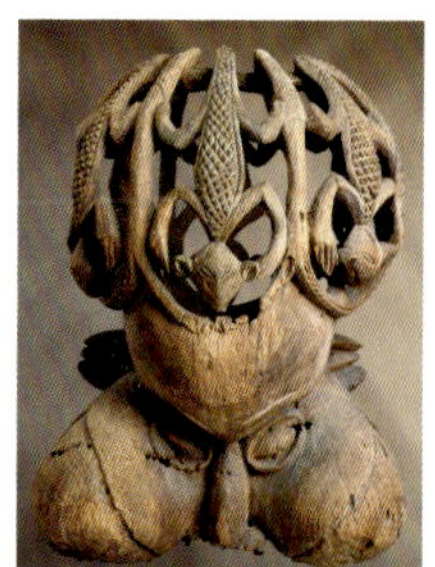

43 Royal mask of the Kah Society, Bamileke, Western Province, Cameroon. Wood. Musée Quai Branly, Paris

Possibly the earliest man-made sculpture ever found, the so-called *Venus of Willendorf* (ill. 44), could be another initiation figure. Like most surviving sculptures from very early cultures, it is very small. This Venus rests easily in the palm of your hand. She could be an image of the earth as the great mother. It's significant that the figure has no eyes. This suggests that it's not an image of a person or a goddess, but of the cosmos as a whole. The strange faceless head has been variously interpreted as being wrapped with plaited hair or, more absurdly, covered entirely with a knitted bonnet. Even more bizarrely, it has been argued that the figure is a self-portrait by a woman looking down at her body, hence the odd foreshortening. The sculptress left her head undefined because she'd never seen it—as if she'd never seen another woman or indeed her own reflection! A more logical explanation is that these starry coils represent the movement of heavenly bodies in the celestial sphere above the body of the earth. The spiritual life of the native Ainu people of Hokkaido, Japan, whose culture is thought to be extremely ancient, is governed largely by women shamans. When in a deep, meditative trance, communing with the upper world, the shaman's ancestors are believed to flicker around her head like stars. Her mind becomes the moon-mother of everything that has lived and died beneath her.

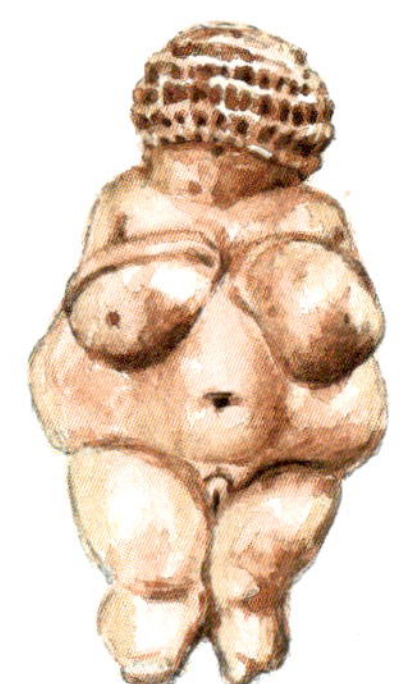

44 *Venus of Willendorf*, c. 30,000 B.C.E. Oolitic limestone. Naturhistorisches Museum, Vienna

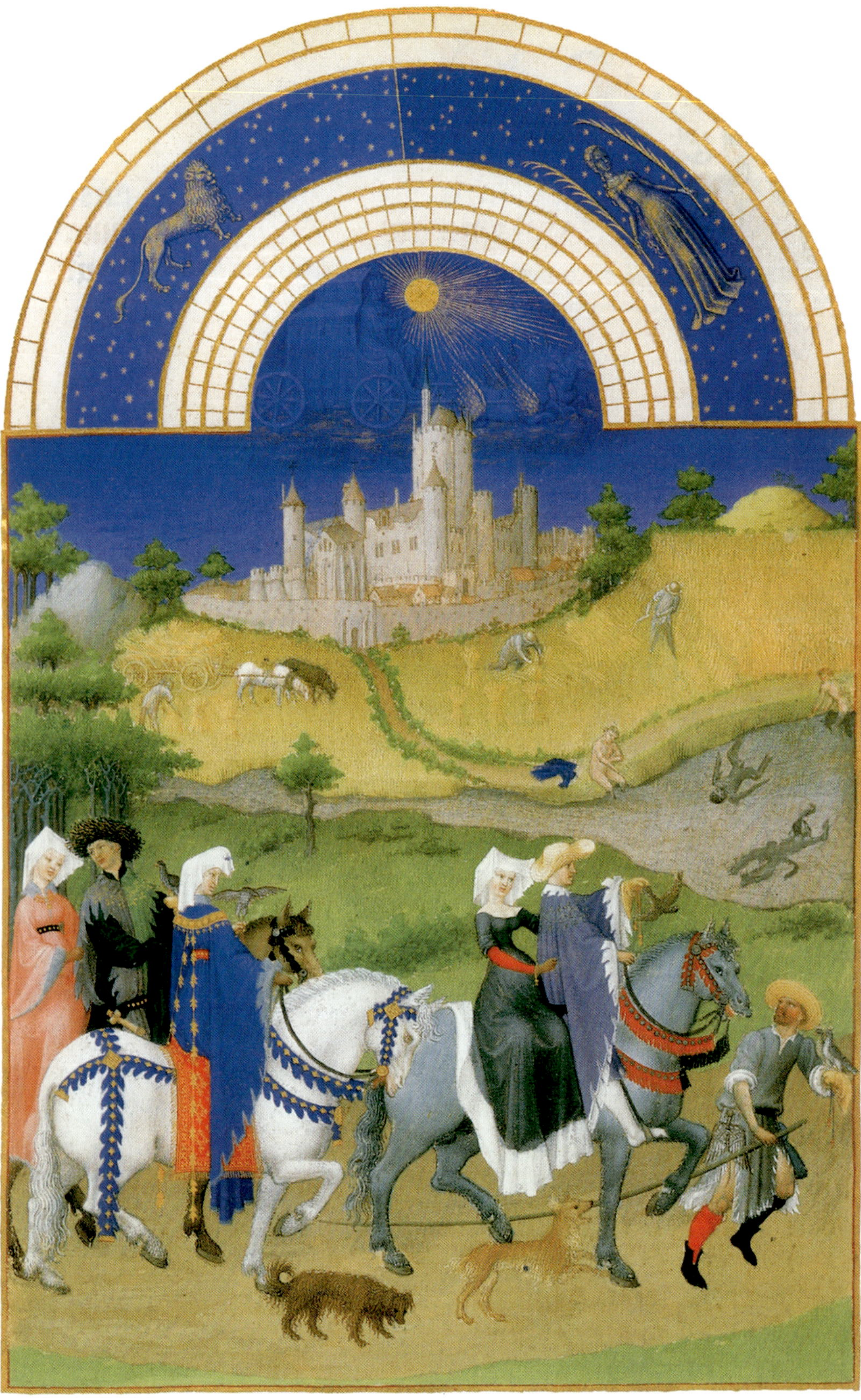

Chapter 5
Birth

Birth was one of the profoundest of all the mysteries of nature. What caused it no-one knew exactly, until spermatozoa were discovered in about 1670. Even then, most people continued to believe until a century and a half ago that small creatures—up to the size of rats—were spontaneously generated out of dust and debris. Bees were thought to reproduce without sexual congress, and the "king bee"—not then known to be in fact a queen—was thought to have no sting—a lesson for the monarchy. It was obvious that beasts and birds couldn't have appeared out of the blue, by dropping from the sky. Nor could they have climbed out of the sea, because fish don't have legs or wings. Or so most people believed, except the Hindus, who maintained that all creatures had emerged from the ocean when, at the beginning of time, the sea was churned, as the gods and demons fought each other to extract from it the poison of eternal suffering and the nectar of eternal life. Snakes and deer, tigers and men spun out from the vortex they created. But most people believed that terrestrial animals had been born on land. Lucretius thought that during "the childhood of the world" there had been a "superfluity of heat and moisture in the soil" and "there grew up wombs clinging to the earth by roots" from which all living creatures had been born.

It is probable that early mankind thought of caves as wombs. If the earth was the living mother of all creatures, and the rocks, soil and grass were her bones, flesh and hair, then caves must be her orifices, leading to internal mysteries. The earliest art we know of has been found in the caves of France and Spain. Very few caves

1 Limbourg Brothers. August, from *Les Très Riches Heures du Duc de Berry*, c.1410. 29 x 21 cm. Musée Condé, Chantilly, France

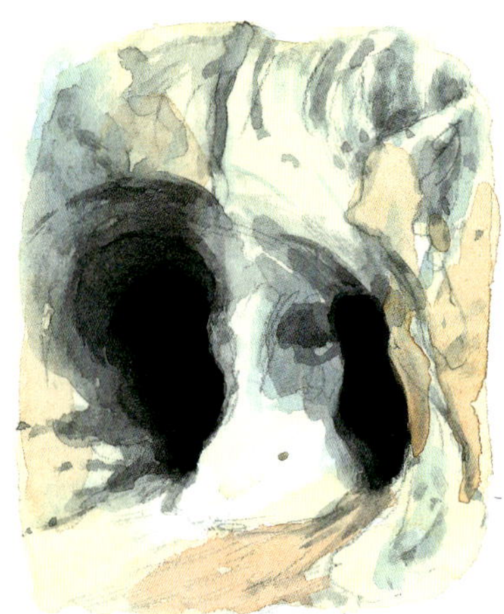

2 Original entrance to Font de Gaume cave, France, c. 25,000 B.C.E.

survive with their original entrances – in fact most were preserved only because these entrance ways collapsed. Two whose entrances have been preserved – Les Comabarelles and Font de Gaume (ill. 2) – both have twin apertures that look like the gaping eyes in a skull, or the larynx at the back of one's throat. The journeys our ancestors took into these caves, sometimes hundreds of yards deep, must have required great courage. They can have had no idea where they were going, or what dangers lurked down there. It's almost certain that they believed they were walking, and often crawling, into a living being. But they did have light to help them on their way. Human use of fire dates back to at least 500,000 B.C.E., but *Homo sapiens sapiens* was the first species of man to invent lamps. Dozens have been found deep in the caves of France. They were mostly hollowed-out stones (ill. 3) filled with animal fat, and lit using juniper wicks. Their low, guttering light must have made the bulbous, dripping walls appear to move and breathe.

The silhouettes of animals that they painted and scratched on to these bulging walls and roofs were first interpreted, in our materialistic age, as prayers for successful hunts. But they were more likely to have been pleas for birth than hopes for death. There are, after all, few images in these caves of these people's favourite food, reindeer. The images are mostly of mammoths and horses, rhinoceros and cats, bison and bears, aurochs and, very occasionally, a fish or a human being. Virtually none show hunts. The paintings and engravings range over an extraordinarily long period, from about 32,000 to 12,000 B.C.E. The paintings in Lascaux, c. 15,000 B.C.E. are about equidistant between our time and that of the earliest paintings ever found, those in the

3 Stone lamp found in Lascaux cave, France, c. 15,000 B.C.E.

Chauvet cave. Over such a vast period, it's highly probable that the way these caves were used changed in subtle ways. To make matters more complex, modern research indicates that each cave was used in several ways, possibly during the same period.

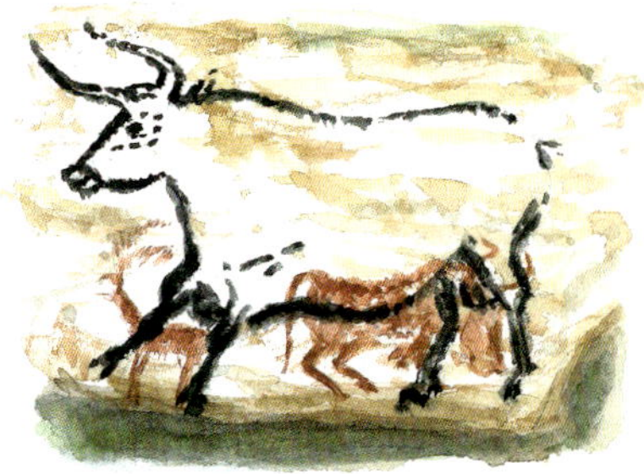

4 Hall of Bulls, Lascaux cave, France, c.15,000 B.C.E.

There appear to have been "public" areas, in rock shelters where art has been found, such as the *Venus of Laussel* (p.90, ill.3) and the extraordinary relief frieze of life-size horses, sadly much deteriorated, at Le Cap Blanc, Périgord. There were large caverns near the entrance to some caves, such as the first gallery in Lascaux, with its elaborate painted ceiling (ill.4). Inner caves were used by individuals and small groups, possibly for "spirit quests" or initiation ceremonies. Footprints made by youths tens of thousands of years ago have been preserved in some. The most inaccessible recesses were used for shamanistic rituals, for instance at the bottom of a shaft at the back of Lascaux where a drawing of a man with an erection, a bird-headed staff and a disembowelled bison have been found (ill.5). It's difficult to interpret cave art because nothing remains of the body painting, masks and dance costumes, and house and shrine decorations that most probably accompanied its making. We only have the tip of the iceberg to go on. This almost certainly represented only part of these people's world pictures, and that must have been as illogical and poetical as anyone else's.

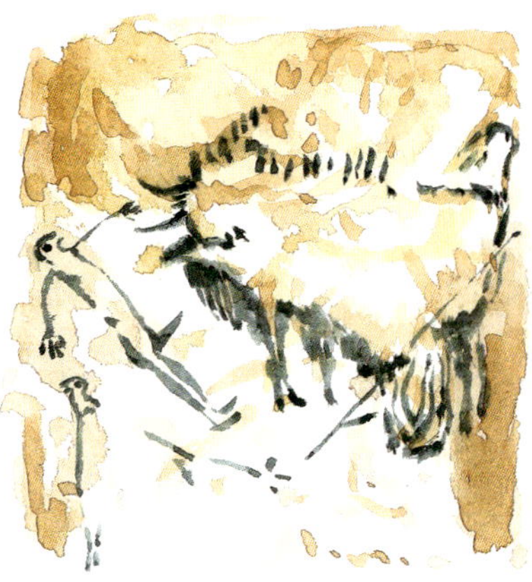

5 Shaft, Lascaux cave, France, c.15,000 B.C.E.

There are, however, unique features that are common to cave art throughout the 25,000 years of its practice, and which distinguish it from the rock art of more recent times, particularly that of

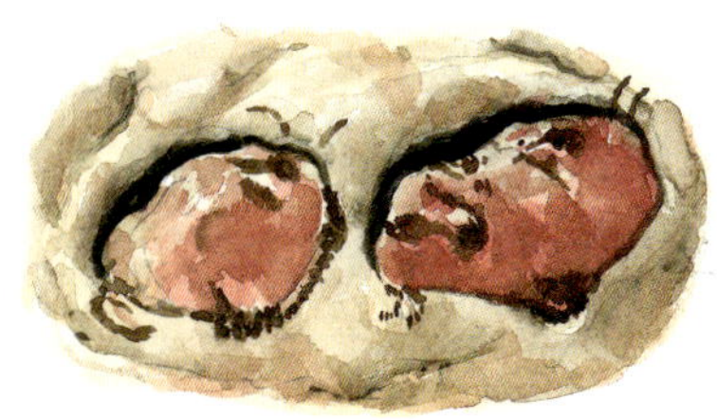

6 Bisons, Altamira cave, Spain, c. 13,000 B.C.E.

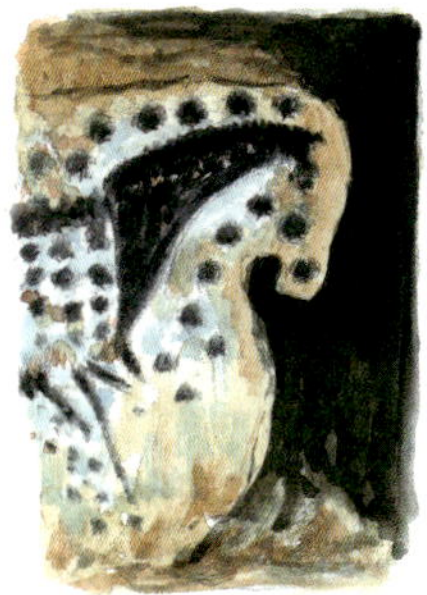

7 Detail of profile head of horse, Pech-Merle cave, France, c. 20,000 B.C.E.

the San people of southern Africa, to which it has often been compared. Later rock art usually evokes scenes of people dancing or hunting. But none of the attempts to interpret early cave paintings as pictures have been entirely convincing. It's possible that these images weren't meant to be read in this way, and many might not have been meant to be seen by humans at all. One of the remarkable features of these ancient caves—which can't be seen in illustrations, but springs vividly to life as soon as you visit them—is that many of the animal silhouettes follow the curves and edges of the rock, as if the bulging cave surface were giving birth. Some of these correspondences between rocks and beasts are startling, such as the bison in the Altamira cave painted in a foetal position on natural bosses on the roof (ill. 6), and the horse (ill. 7) at Pech-Merle delineated within a natural horse-like profile in the rock face.

It's true that many cave art images do not appear to follow any natural feature, but that is perhaps because we study these caves by modern electric lighting, and with very different thoughts in our minds. By the light of flickering lamps, any slight undulation in the surface could have inspired a vision of an animal in the mind of early man, especially in one whose imagination had been heightened by fear and sensory deprivation as well as being, quite possibly, stimulated by drugs. To imagine that something was there might have been enough to inspire a drawing. Perhaps, once imagined, it became a duty to tie the animal's image into the rock, lest it wander free and do harm. The major task these people set themselves was to help the earth bear life. This might explain why so many images are incomplete—often, for instance, they have no feet—as if they're emerging out of the rock. One wonderfully expressive line was enough to indicate a mammoth—

the rock would do the rest, and perhaps, once the process had been started, it would do so for ever more. There might easily have been a taboo about completing an outline. Perhaps that would have led to a stillbirth. Certainly none of the animals are still. Lines ripple with muscular motion, not just because these people were hunters and knew their animals intimately, but because they wished to create animals that would be alive.

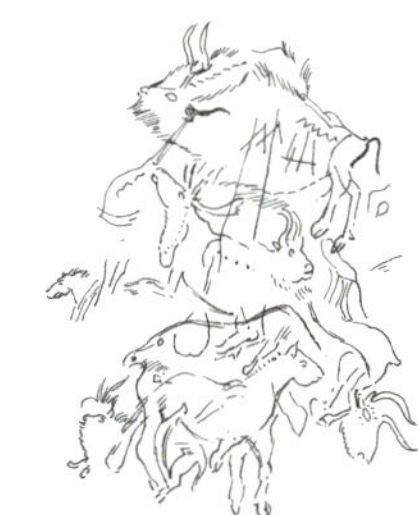

8 Engravings, Les Trois Frères cave, France, c.12,000 B.C.E.

Such an interpretation might help to explain why so many images in these caves are overlapping, some bewilderingly so (ill.8). This is confusing to people used to reading images as scenes. But if the act of making the image was what was important, rather than who looked at it afterwards, then it was logical for early man to go on drawing on the same rock surface—for why shouldn't a sacred cave give birth to many animals, just as one woman can give birth to many children? This interpretation also explains why there are no suggestions of landscapes—no plants or trees or suns or clouds—though clearly these people were skilled enough to paint such things. But image-making was perhaps a holy and highly restricted activity which was only used to bring things to life. It's possible that these caves were full not just of paintings, but also of sculptures, made out of their clay walls and floors. Remarkably preserved in one exceptionally dry corner of the Tuc d'Audoubert cave are two bison (ill.9). They have been modelled by hand—nearby one can still see the cavity where someone scooped the clay to make them.

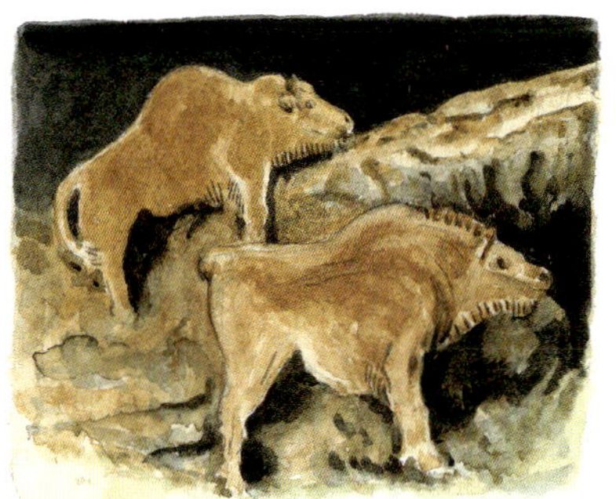

9 Pair of bison, Tuc d'Audoubert cave, France, c.15,000 B.C.E. Clay

These decorated caves are about birth, not death. They take your breath away when you enter them, not because they were created by mankind so long ago—we shouldn't after all be so surprised that our ancestors were as able as ourselves—but because the animals on their walls are so full of life. They appear to be breathing. So you hold your breath when you see them, as you do instinctively when you see a wild animal near you. Breath was probably magical to these early people. Some animal pictures have parallel lines drawn from their nostrils which are thought to indicate breath. Navajo hunters in North America would chase a deer all day till it collapsed from exhaustion. If the meat was to be used in a religious ceremony, the hunter would hold a little sacred pollen to its mouth before strangling it, to ensure that its last breath was holy. Perhaps similar rituals were performed by the people who lived and hunted above the caves in France.

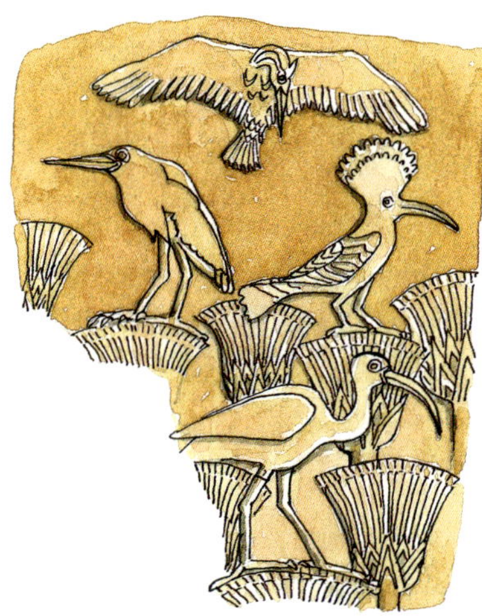

10 Birds in a Papyrus swamp, 2560–420 B.C.E. Limestone relief from Saqqara, Egypt. The Egyptian Museum, Cairo

Everything dies under the sun, as the sun does itself. But the great solace for our ancestors was that everything appeared to be reborn, just as the sun appears again at dawn. Hoopoes and herons, kingfishers and ibis (ill. 10) gave birth to hoopoes and herons, kingfishers and ibis as they had in the age of ancient Egypt, just as pigs gave birth to pigs in medieval Italy (ill. 11). And they all still do so today. The Roman orator Cicero (106–43 B.C.E.) observed that there was "such an admirable continuity and succession of things that there must be some most excellent and pre-eminent Nature that originally made and now moves, directs and governs all these stupendous works." But how did man and nature relate?

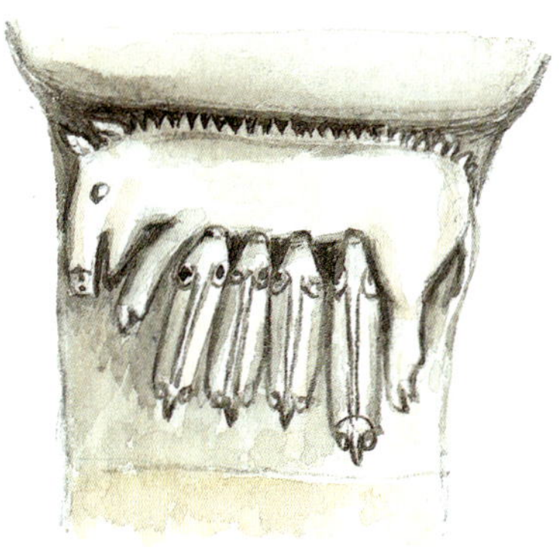

11 Column capital, 12th century. Pieve di San Pietro, Gropina, Italy

Many myths in small hunter-gatherer societies around the world tell of an age when humans and animals were not cut off from one another but could talk together, and even have sexual relationships. The discovery of evolution wouldn't have surprised them in the least, for in those times people had a lion, eagle or horse for an ancestor, as a matter of course. One of the most vivid expressions of such beliefs are the great carved totem poles (ill. 12) that stood in front of the houses of the people who lived in the redwood forests along America's north Pacific coastline. These poles were symbols of descent and ascent, showing where the house's owner had come from and where he or she would return to after death. New poles, with different configurations, were carved for newlyweds, because it wasn't just two people who were about to reproduce, but their animal progenitors as well. Elaborate feasts were held to ensure that the whale, bear and raven spirits were pleased with the marriage. Then their complex histories would be retold in songs and dances. Masks had elaborate string-pull mechanisms to show how an ancestral spirit could descend from the moon, be transformed into a bird (ill. 13) and then into a man (ill. 14).

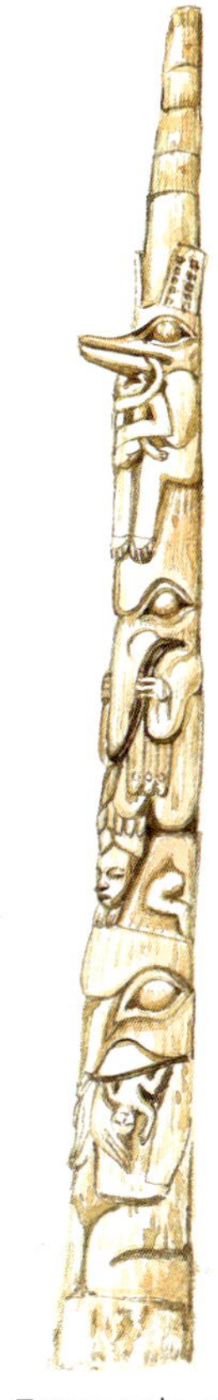

12 Totem pole outside the house of Chief Skowl, Kasaan village, 1885. Alaska

When people began to cultivate the land and live in towns, they increasingly came to see mankind and beasts as living in separate worlds. We sought a human rather than an animal ancestry, preferably including a human who was also a god. The great heads (ill. 15) on Easter Island were ancestral figures. Human beings eventually colonised this remote Pacific island in about 900 C.E.

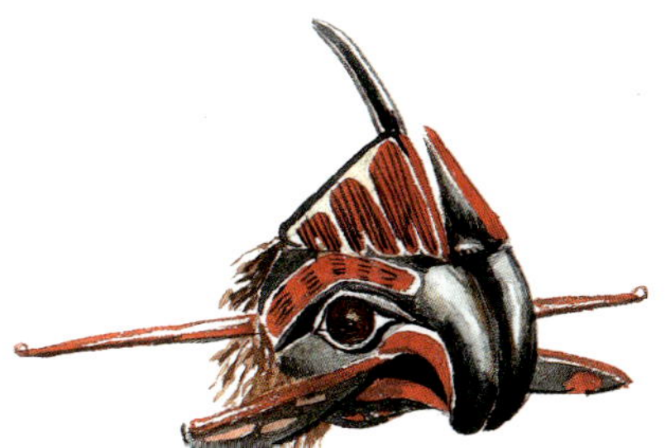

13 Thunderbird transformation mask (closed), Haida Skidegate. Canadian Museum of Civilisation, Ottawa

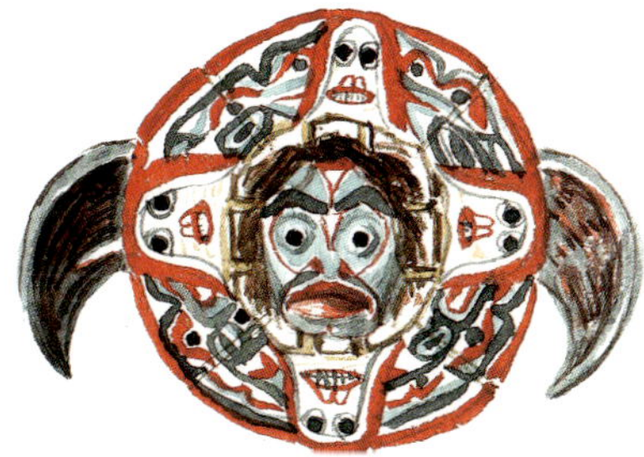

14 Thunderbird transformation mask (open), Haida Skidegate. Canadian Museum of Civilisation, Ottawa

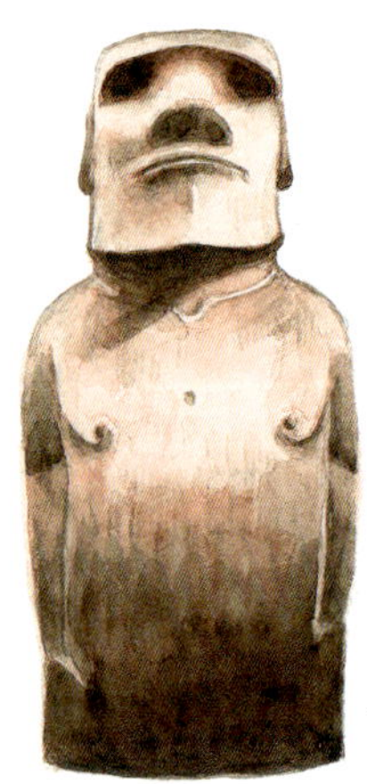

15 Easter Island Head. British Museum, London

Within a century eleven family clans had formed, all of whom claimed direct descent from their founder, the supreme creator, and they each set up statues to honour him, on sacred platforms usually ranged along the clans' territorial boundaries. Over the centuries, as competition for declining resources grew fiercer, these heads were made larger and larger. By 1700 all the trees and the once plentiful stocks of fish and birds had gone, the soil was swept away by erosion and the island's culture and society collapsed into civil war—a cautionary tale for planet earth.

Ancient and widespread beliefs in human reincarnation and ancestor-worship spring from observations of nature. The Jesse window in Chartres Cathedral (ill. 18) shows the ancestry of Jesus Christ. It's a human version of the totem pole. Both were unashamedly phallic—the tree which Jesus crowned sprang from Jesse's loins. Christ was resurrected as the leaves are reborn every spring, as the whole tree is reborn in the germinating seed. In rural China ancestors were usually buried in a dark, northeastern corner inside the house. The grain was stored above their graves, and the marriage bed was placed there, to ensure the family's continued fecundity. Confucius (551–479 B.C.E.) and all his descendants are buried in one vast sepulchral wood in Qufu, China. Nowhere else in the world can you see one family's graveyard maintained for over two thousand years.

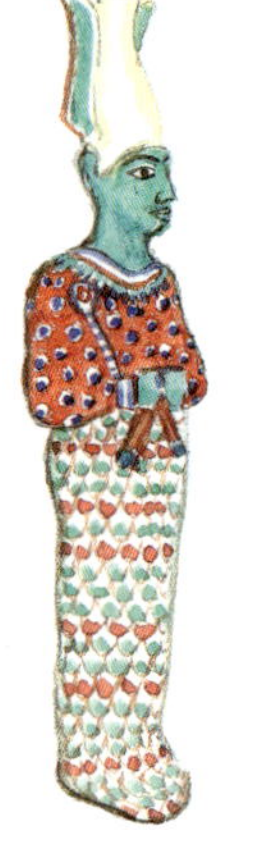

16 *Osiris*, c. 1170 B.C.E. Painted wood, British Museum, London

The belief in resurrection is very ancient. Osiris (ill. 16), the ancient fertility god of Egypt, was hacked to pieces by his jealous brother Seth, who then sprinkled bits of his body across the land. Osiris' wife gathered them up but couldn't find his penis, so she made a substitute and then breathed new life into him. Osiris sings: "I live, I die. I am Osiris. I have entered you, and have reappeared through you. I have waxed fat in you. I live, I die. I am barley. I do not perish." His green skin represents vegetation and

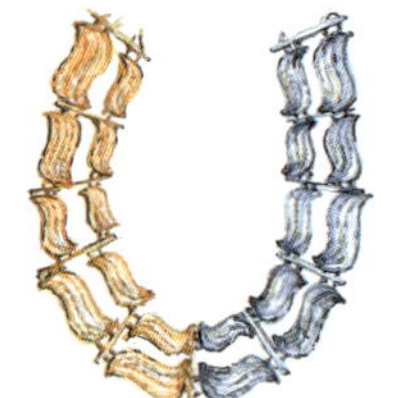

17 Peanut necklace of Lord Sipan, Moche culture. Gold and silver. Peru

rebirth. Images like this were often hollow and contained a scroll of the Book of the Dead which gave an account of the deceased's life (p. 149, ill. 28). The remarkable huge gold and silver peanut chain (ill. 17) of Lord Sipan can probably be interpreted in a similar way, though the meaning of the ancient Peruvian mythology in which peanuts played an important part is almost entirely lost. The food-giving life cycle of the peanut is equated with the cycle of the silver moon and the golden sun, though a hymn with the refrain "I am peanut. I do not perish" hasn't quite the right ring in English. Lord Sipan was found wearing this peanut necklace in his tomb.

The earliest art of mankind, from the cave paintings of Europe to the first stirrings of art in Egypt, is marked by the love it shows for nature. Our forefathers believed a harmonious order underlay all creation. When Orpheus, the son of Apollo, the Greek god of light, played his lyre and sang, all the wild animals left the forests to hear him play. As Shakespeare wrote: "Take but degree away, untune that string, and hark what discord follows." This feeling pervades the book of Genesis, even more so because the Bible taught that God had made all living creatures as they now appear. Adam in the Garden of Eden named the beasts with pride, and their forms were set forever, as if carved in ivory (ill. 19). Noah saved them from the flood; similar myths are found all over the world, and probably arose from a folk memory of the dramatic rise in sea levels after the polar caps melted at the end of the last ice age in about 12,000 B.C.E. Christian children learnt the divine order of nature as they played with their toy arks.

Our ancestors must have been amazed by the variety and minutiae of nature, yet every creature had its place and its meaning. It might seem surprising to us that Queen Ahhotep wore a necklace of golden flies (ill. 20). They probably represented her

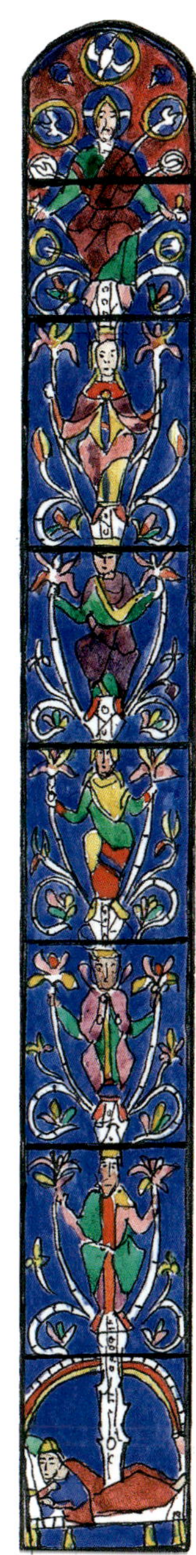

18 *Tree of Jesse*, c. 1150. Stained-glass window. Chartres Cathedral

army of soldiers who, it was believed, could swarm against her enemies with the persistence of flies. These hornets (ill.21) cannot have been merely decorative; a profounder meaning, now lost, must have merited their immortalisation in gold. One explanation could be that they are not hornets but bees, and that the brooch celebrated the collection of honey, the golden food of the gods, from the golden centres of wild flowers. A grand hierarchy was believed to flow through all creation, from the stars in heaven to the ants at your feet. Devout Jain priests in India still brush the earth in front of them with peacock feathers, symbols of the infinite diversity of nature, to make sure they don't step on any tiny creatures, for they believe that every living creature is holy. In Christian Europe, the divine order of nature came to be called the "Great Chain of Being". This great chain informed human beings how to structure their own societies. Sir Walter Raleigh (1552–1618) was voicing general wisdom when he wrote in his *History of the World*: "For that infinite wisdom of God, which hath given greater and less light to heavenly bodies, which hath created the eagle and the fly, the cedar and the shrub has also ordained kings, dukes or leaders of people, magistrates, judges, and other degrees among men."

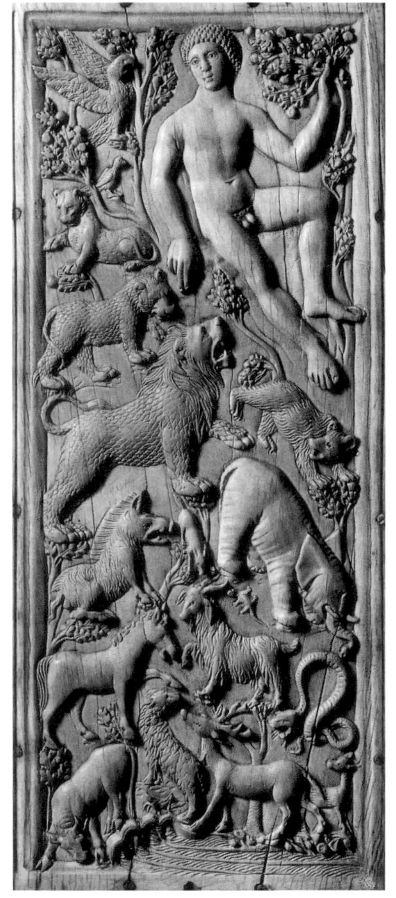

19 *Adam in the Garden of Eden Naming the Beasts*, 4th century C.E. Ivory. Museo Nazionale del Bargello, Florence

To anyone brought up in close proximity to nature–which was the vast majority of people–the social hierarchy among men appeared totally natural, even when rulers flagrantly abused their power and position, though this didn't happen nearly as often as Marxist historians like to make out. Even the *droit du seigneur* was part of the natural scheme of things. The stag was not just the monarch of the glen but also sire of the herd, and he had a right to mate with any hind he fancied. It was natural, too, that he would be deposed sooner or later by a challenger—battles among kings were not the concern of commoners. Old ideas die hard. Even in the middle of the Enlightenment in eighteenth-century England "the divinity that doth hedge a king" was believed to be manifest in nature. George Stubbs painted a large canvas (ill. 22) to celebrate a famous event involving a cheetah, presented to King George III by the governor general of Madras, which refused to attack a stag when it was introduced to one in a royal park, thus demonstrating India's subservience to the British throne.

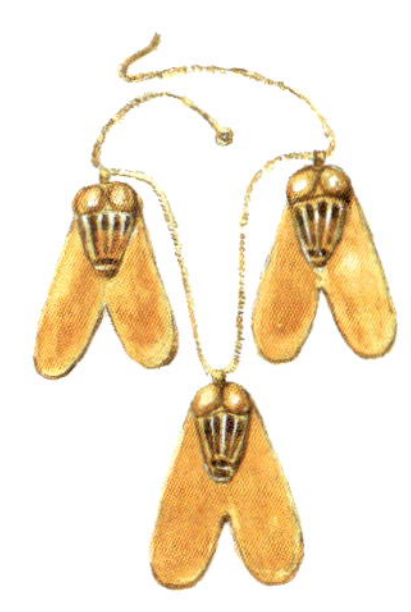

20 Chain and fly-shaped pendants, c. 1580 B.C.E. Gold, height of each fly 9 cm. The Egyptian Museum, Cairo

Just as lions had their manes, peacocks their tails, and ants no show at all, so kings had their trains, courtiers their robes and commoners merely their clothes. In this scene from a late medieval Christian book of hours (ill. 1), the aristocrats go hawking—the only type of hunting open to women—wearing inconvenient finery, while peasants wear functional garments and are even free to swim with nothing on at all. Crowns (ill. 23) gave kings added height and, when gold and jewel-encrusted, made their heads shine with the light of heaven. A curious custom developed among the Paduang people who live in the northeastern hills of Burma, the origins of which are lost in folklore. Select girls—traditionally only those born on the night of a full moon—began to wear shining brass neck-rings at puberty. These were added to as they grew, crushing their

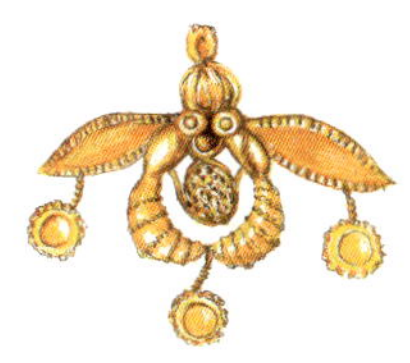

21 The hornet brooch from the cemetery at Mallia, early Minoan, c. 2000 B.C.E. Gold, 4.7 cm. Archaeological Museum, Heraklion, Crete

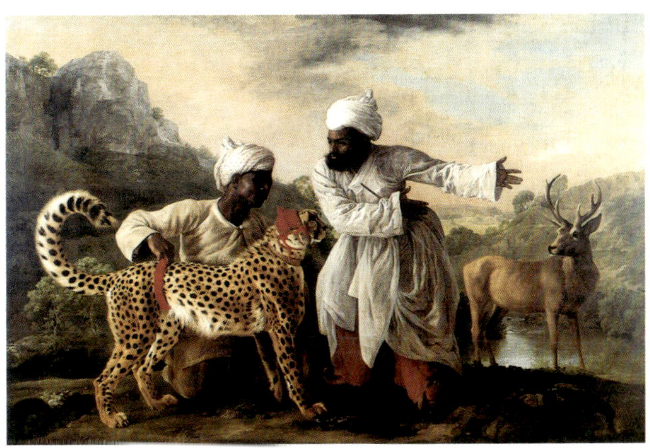

22 George Stubbs. *Cheetah and Stag with Two Indians*, 1765. Oil on canvas, 180.7 x 273 cm. Manchester City Art Galleries

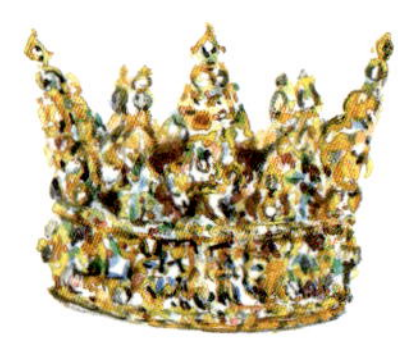

23 King Christian IV's crown made by Dirich Fyning, 1595–96. Gold, enamel, precious stones and pearls. Rosenborg Castle, Copenhagen

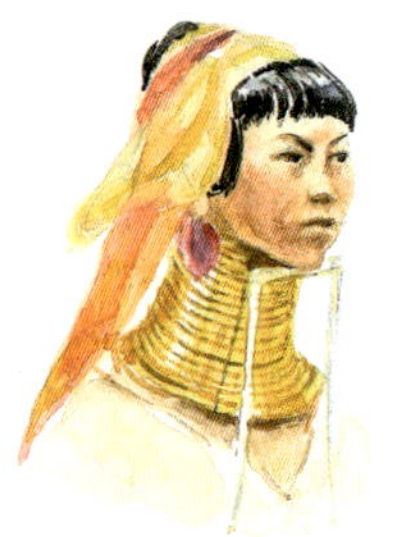

24 Paduang woman, Burma. Contemporary

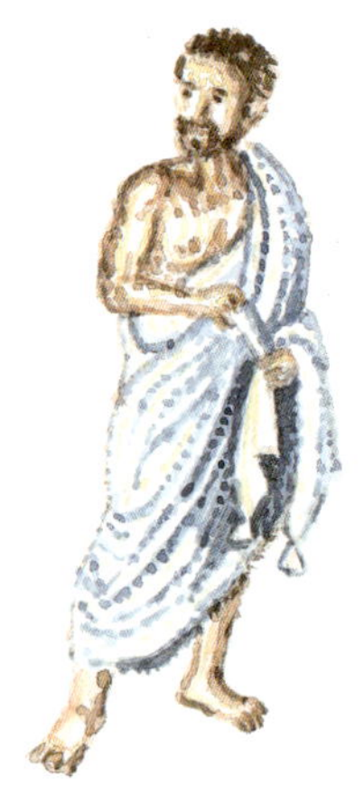

25 *Academy of Plato*, 1st century C.E., detail: Man Wearing Toga. Mosaic. Pompeii, Italy

shoulder blades and lifting their chins, so that, in time, they had necks five inches or so longer than average, their stretched and weakened vertebrae supported by as many as twenty-four coils (ill.24). This practice could relate to a local myth which tells of a beautiful long-necked dragon which was made pregnant by the wind and gave birth to the people of Paduang. The rare appearance of these elegant, gold-necked girls must have been startling to anyone who believed in the existence of higher beings. This tradition is now sustained merely to earn money from tourism; the sight has lost its wonder, and is little more than sickening.

Clothes were displays of power and position. The outstanding exception were the togas (ill.25) of the ancient Greeks and Romans. These were intentionally simple and similar, to demonstrate their wearers' belief in democracy and republicanism. Laws had to be passed forbidding flamboyant dress, for many tried to circumvent this restriction on appearance. This code of dress remained unique; it had no successor until the advent of the suits and overalls of modern capitalism and communism. The simple habits of Hindu, Buddhist and Islamic priests and many Christian monks and nuns were more indicative of a withdrawal from the world than of the idea of equality within it. We might be equal before god, and death, but in everyday life we each had our allotted role to play. The vast majority of us thought that social classes were a fact of life and we expressed our standing by the clothes we wore. The evidence for this hierarchy was all around us. It couldn't be a coincidence that the most powerful beast of all, the lion, which originally roamed widely across Africa, Europe, the Middle East and India, was golden in colour and had a mane like the sun.

It is difficult now to look at the royal lion hunts of the past without a sense of disgust, especially when we realise that the lions were trapped in a ring—as bulls are still in Spain. The halo around the Moghul emperor Shah Jahan (ill. 27), his equivalent to the lion's mane, symbolised the divine light that Islamic belief maintained was transferred to a king by god, without the assistance of man. But how could a king be so cruel just to display his power? An inscription on this Assyrian relief (ill. 26) reads: "I am Assurbanipal, King of Assyria. In my abounding, princely strength I seized a lion of the desert by his tail and at the command of the gods who are my helpers, I smashed his skull with the axe in my hands." Today we think of lions as rare creatures, but in Assurbanipal's time there are accounts of a plague of them: "The hills respond with their roaring … the villagers are mourning day and night." In the past there were many more animals than people, so our ancestors felt free to kill creatures that were killing them. It's only during the last hundred years that the tables have turned; now all of our large predators are contained or extinct. But what's even more difficult for us to appreciate is that our ancestors thought it was an honour for the *lion* to be killed by a king. That's why they rendered these beasts' deaths with such great dignity and sympathy.

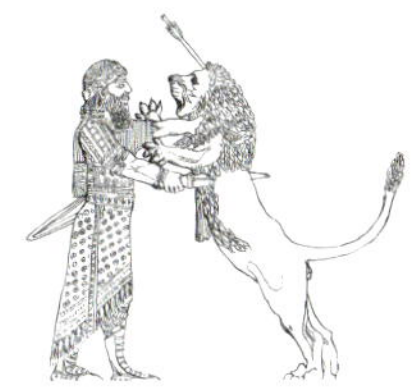

26 *The Great Lion Hunt of Assurbanipal*, 645–35 B.C.E., detail showing king killing a lion. Stone relief. British Museum, London

As lions were kings on land, so eagles were kings of the air. They were the strongest birds and could fly the highest. Their eyesight appeared godlike because they could see much further than man. There was a widespread belief that eagles were the only creatures that could gaze directly into the eye of the sun. The Aztecs thought

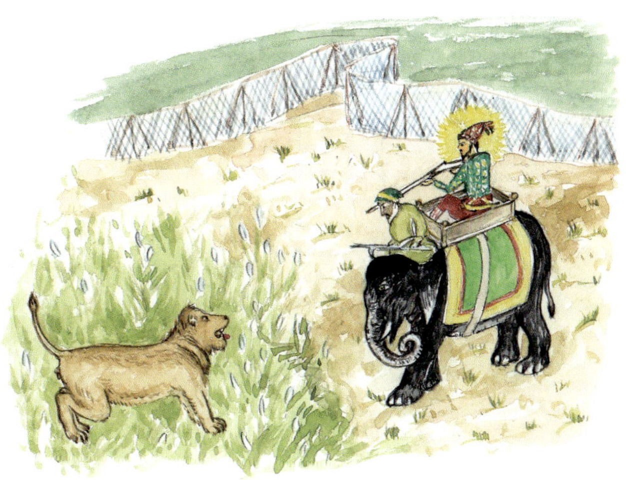

27 After *Shah Jahan Hunting Lions at Burhampur*, July 1632 (detail) C.E. Padshahnama Royal Collection, Windsor Castle

eagles actually flew right into the sun. Extraordinary life-size clay figures (ill.28) have recently been found in a buried temple in the heart of Mexico City, one of the few the Spaniards failed to destroy. They represent the elite band of soldier priests who were chosen to become "eagle warriors" so that their blood, when they were eventually sacrificed, could be flown directly to heaven. The beautifully modelled sensitive gestures of the hands on these figures don't indicate aggression or fear, but anticipation.

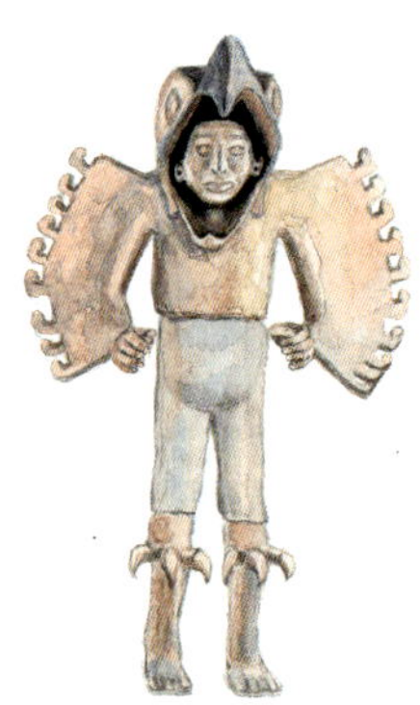

28 *Eagle Man*, Aztec, c.1440–69 C.E. Baked clay, stucco and paint, 170 x 118 x 55 cm. Museo del Templo Mayor, Mexico City

The eagle is deeply rooted in the cultural history of the American continent, and this possibly dates from the time of the earliest human settlements, about 30,000 years ago. High Hawk's ceremonial costume (ill.29) indicates his prowess in war—a human scalp dangles from the end of his war club—but his eagle headdress also signals his spiritual authority. Eagles were far-sighted, so High Hawk was much in demand to advise on auspicious dates for marriages, hunts and wars among the Brules, Native Americans who lived in the central plains. Aware of this tradition, the young United States, which advocated equality among all people while still allowing slavery in some states, used the bald eagle (ill.30) to emblazon its great seal in 1782. In doing so it was partly emulating republican Rome whose soldiers had marched, two thousand years earlier, behind the banner of the emperor's eagle.

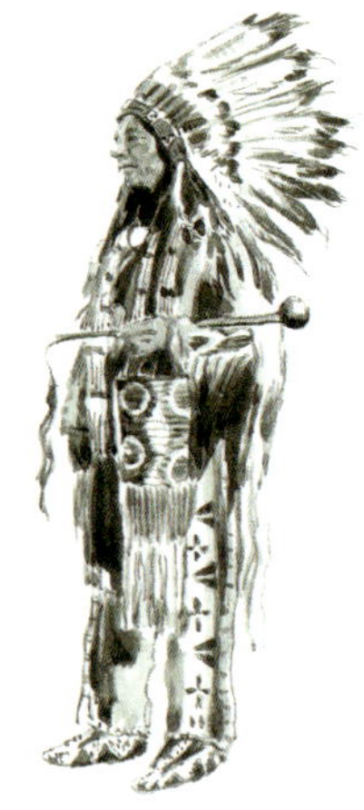

29 After Edward S. Curtis. *High Hawk*. Photograph from *The North American Indian*, vol. 3, 1908

Among the plants, trees were dominant because they reached the highest and lived the longest. The pre-eminent species depended on where you lived. In the New Hebrides Islands in the Pacific Ocean tree ferns were highly prized, and an elaborate ritual developed where a deceased man of rank was reunited with his fern tree spirit. When he died, the man's head was removed and attached to a body rebuilt out of tree fern bark and pith. The whole ensemble was carried into the jungle so that the dead

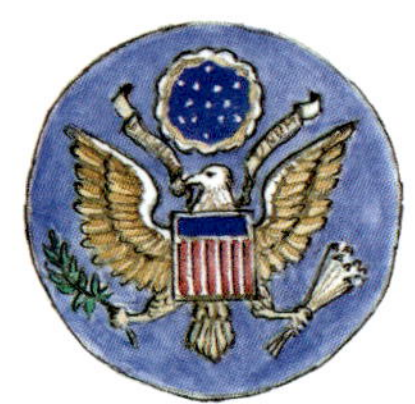

30 The American seal

man's soul could return to his ancestors. In Europe the oak was regarded as royal, on account of its great crown, girth and immense age. Oak wreaths were worn in religious processions and awarded to the winner of the musical contest at the Panathenaic games in Athens. A remarkable gold oak wreath survives, wrought with a bee and two cicadas (ill. 31). A Roman tradition held that the oak was consecrated by Jupiter, that it could resist lightning strikes and had provided the wood for Hercules' club. During the English Civil War, which witnessed the execution of King Charles I, a legend grew up that the crown prince had survived by hiding in an oak tree (ill. 32).

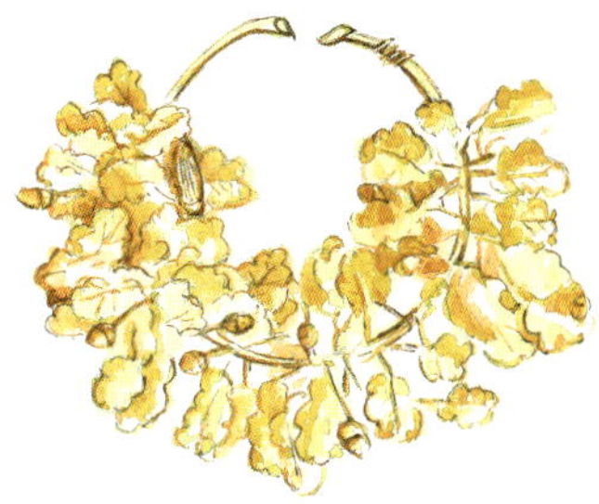

31 Gold oak wreath with a bee and two cicadas, 300 B.C.E. British Museum, London

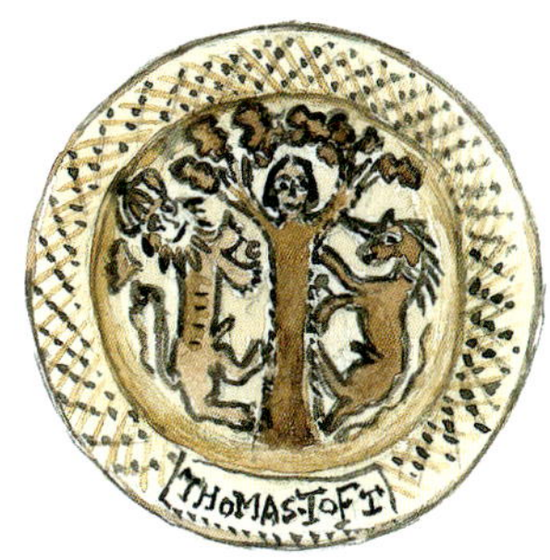

32 Thomas Toft. *Charles in the Boscobel Oak*, late 17th century. Slipware, 50 cm diameter. Manchester City Art Galleries

The sunflower had to be the highest among flowers, not just because it had a corona, like a lion's mane, that emulated the sun, but because its head turned to follow the sun's path across the heavens. It therefore had the stirrings of sensitive life, the distinction that separated animals from plants in the hierarchy of existence. The big sunflowers common in Europe today were introduced from America, but the continent had its own humbler heliotropes, whose ability to follow the sun was explained by the classical myth of Clytie, the nymph who fell in love with the sun god Apollo. He kindly turned her into a sunflower so that she could gaze at him for ever. This version of "Clytie" (ill. 33) is probably also a portrait of Antonia, the daughter of Mark Anthony and mother of the emperor Claudius.

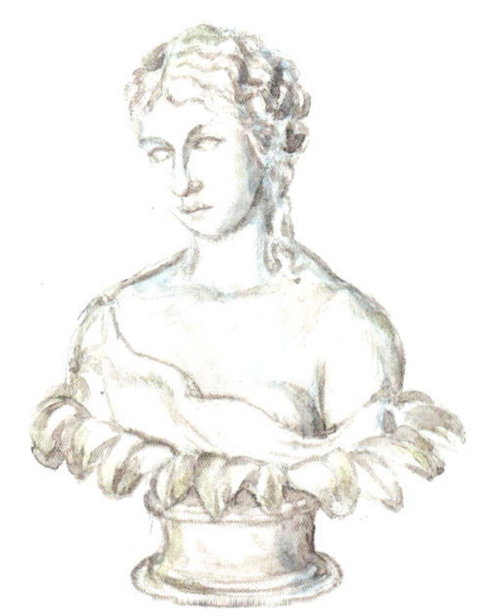

33 "Clytie", possibly a portrait of Antonia, c. 30 C.E. Height 68.5 cm. British Museum, London

If every living creature was a link in a chain of being that descended from heaven, it was logical to think that there must be some creatures which lived above us as

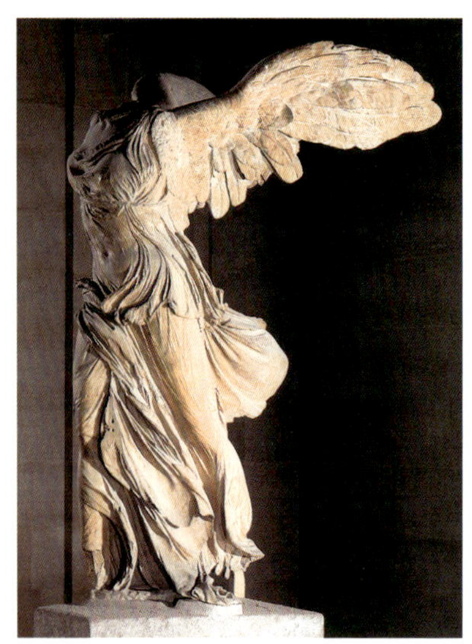

34 *Nike of Samothrace*, 250–190 B.C.E. Marble. Louvre, Paris

well as those that lived below us. One of the most popular occupants of the upper air in Greek and Roman antiquity were winged girls, the Nike (ill.34) or Victories, who swept over the battlefield in flowing robes, choosing who would win and who would lose. Christians carried out their daily tasks with the comforting thought that angels were flying just above their heads. These heavenly creatures were an amalgam of androgynous, virginal youths and birds. But just below human beings, demons (ill.35) were also snapping at their feet. These were concocted out of old men, bats' wings, cloven hooves, claws, horns, fangs and asses' ears, all that was lowly and bestial. Christians have tended to categorize animals as being of a lower order than mankind. So they naturally thought all dragons were as evil as the monster slain by St George before it could devour the virgin sent to feed it. In China, however, dragons (ill.36) were celestial creatures that appeared in the sky when an emperor was born. The fantastic kites (ill.37) of China, nowadays mostly toys, were originally manifestations of the spirits who lived in the upper realms.

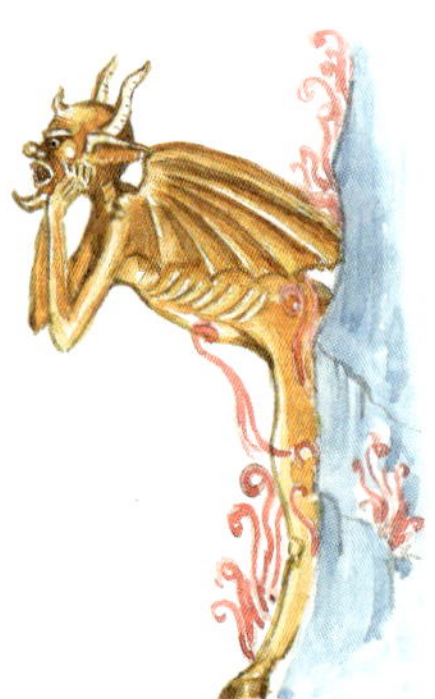

35 After Andrea da Firenze. *The Descent of Christ into Limbo*, c. 1365 C.E., detail of a devil. Fresco, Santa Maria Novella, Florence

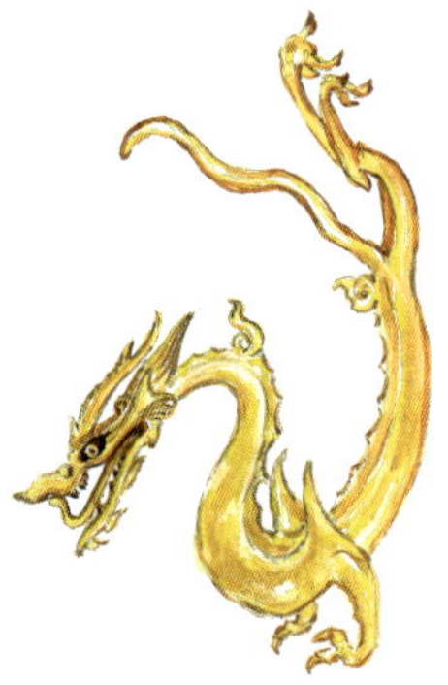

36 Gilded Dragon, Tang dynasty, from Caochang-po, Xi'an, 618–906 C.E. Gilded bronze, 34 x 28 x 10 cm. Shaanxi History Museum

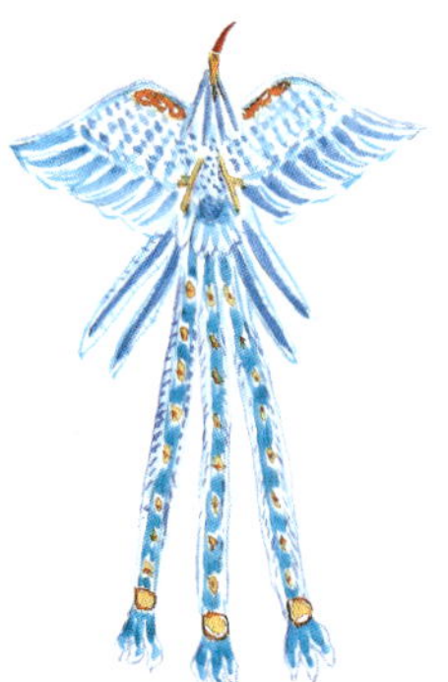

37 Phoenix Kite. Contemporary, Chinese

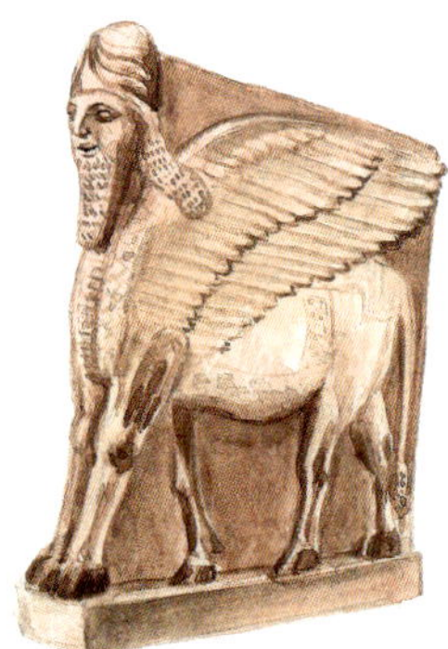

38 Winged Bull, 8th century B.C.E. Palace of Sargon II, Khorsabad, Assyria. British Museum, London

Many western commentators have assumed that the bulls (ill. 38) that guarded the entrance to the palace of Sargon II were images of his ferocious and oppressive power. They *are* powerful—no other culture carved such massive muscles—but the combination of a bull's body with an eagle's wings and a human head logically implies overpowering goodness. The delicacy and charm of these statues would have been much more apparent when they were painted—when you would have seen at once the flowers and feathers in their headdresses, and noticed the gentle smile playing about these so-called monsters' lips. These creatures were guardians, preventing misfortune entering through the door. They may be related to the eagle-winged lion gods who were believed to guard the gates of sunrise and sunset and who knew yesterday and tomorrow. The Egyptian Sphinx (p. 86, ill. 39) exudes a calm authority. It has the latent power of a lion lying in the savannah quietly surveying the scene while his pride laze and play. The Greek Sphinx, who had the head and breasts of a woman, the body of a lion and the wings of an eagle (ill. 39), certainly had the capacity to become a monster, because she ate anyone who couldn't solve her riddle. When Oedipus came along and answered her question: "What is the animal that has four feet in the morning, two at midday and three in the evening?" she threw herself off a cliff. Her life's work was over. The Greeks believed that the answer to all mysteries could be found within man himself.

Where did mankind fit on the ladder of creation? We tended to see ourselves as being the highest of the animals, but many thought we were more than that. We were part of nature, yet not part of it. Alone among the beasts, we walked upright. We perceived ourselves to be a hierarchy in miniature, standing above and to the side of the Great

39 Sphinx, archaic Greek statue found at Sparta, 6th century B.C.E. National Museum, Athens

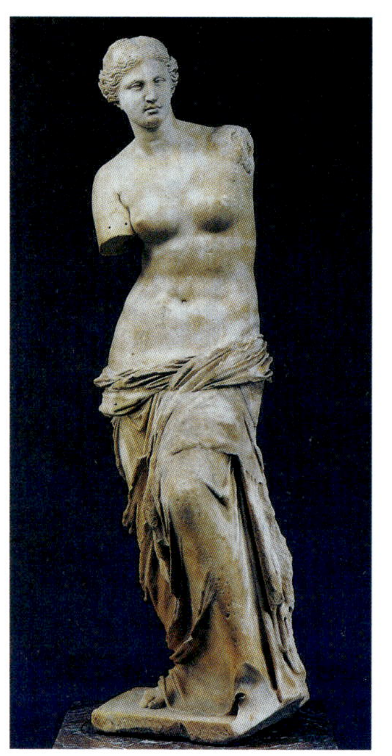

40 *Aphrodite*, "Venus de Milo", c. 350 B.C.E. Marble, 122 cm high. Roman copy of the *Aphrodite of Knidos* attributed to Praxiteles. Louvre, Paris

Chain of Being. We alone could feel the force of gravitas, with our proud bearing and straight backs. As the ancient Greek philosopher Aristotle wrote: "Man alone of all the animals is erect because his nature and his substance are divine. To think, to exercise intelligence, is the characteristic that is most godlike." This explained why the human skull was uniquely domed, like the sky. It had to be, because it contained the thoughts that can lift mankind to heaven. Below our "temple" lay our senses. Sight, until the modern era, was regarded as our highest sense, literally and physically, and not just because our eyes enabled us to reach up to the stars. Hearing came next–our ears were slightly lower than our eyes; with them we could, if we were lucky, hear the music of the spheres. Below these came the lesser senses of smell and taste, and below them, the most sensuous, least godlike of all, the sense of touch. Our arms are conveniently long for our fingers to reach our genitals, organs we have in common with animals, and which are positioned near to or share our excretory orifices. Our body, as we look down it, becomes increasingly bestial. And at the very lowest point our feet are wedded to the clay from which many believed our body had been created and to which it would return when it was no longer held upright by our godlike spirit.

Hardly surprisingly, in most creation myths around the world, human beings usually depicted themselves as being created last–

the finishing touch to the universe. They saw themselves as the link between mortality below and immortality above, with all the hopes and responsibilities that such a position brings. Some faiths, like Christianity, believed mankind to be miniature replicas of God in person. The ancient Greeks had no doubt about it. They worshipped youthful beauty (ill.40), not just as a sexual stimulant but as a manifestation of the divine form of goodness. This statue (ill.41) was probably made as a gift of thanks to the gods for winning an athletic competition. It was originally painted flesh colour and had inlaid, realistic eyes. In *Hamlet*, written in 1600, Shakespeare summed up our favoured image of ourselves: "What a piece of work is man! How noble in reason! How infinite in faculty! In form, in moving, how express and admirable! In action how like an angel! In apprehension how like a god! The beauty of the world! The paragon of animals!" Nonetheless, Prince Hamlet, as the son of an adulterous mother who has married his father's murderer, is so disillusioned with a world that has become "out of joint" that he can see nothing of merit in "this quintessence of dust". The mystery of one's birth, no matter how high one's blood, was trumped by the mystery of one's death.

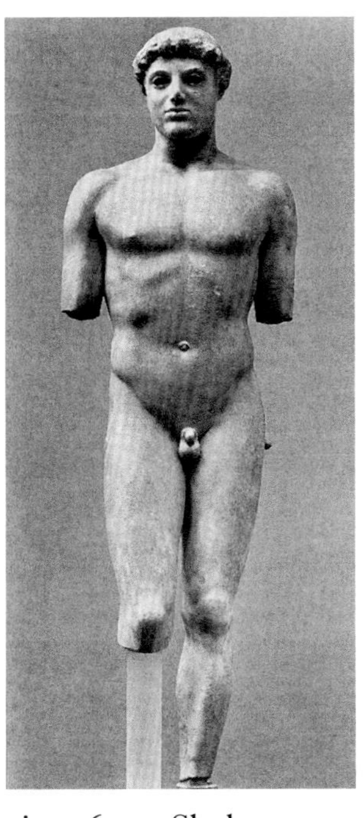

41 *Kritian Boy*, c. 480 B.C.E.. Marble. Acropolis Museum, Athens

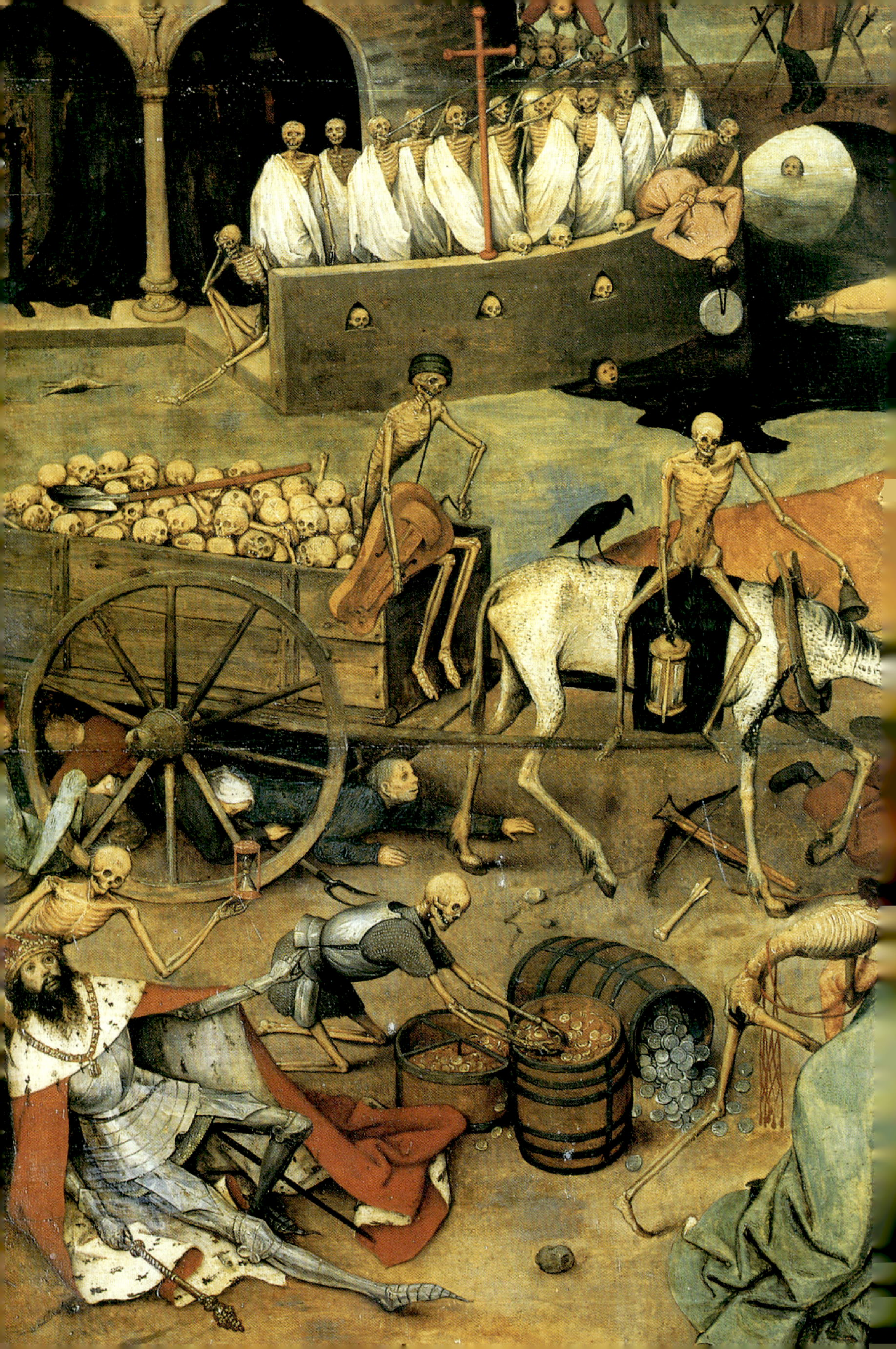

Chapter 6

Death

The experience of death today is much the same as it was hundreds of years ago for the millions of people who live in traditional rural areas (ill.2), and for people in those countries racked by war, famine and disease. But in wealthy urban communities, death has been more or less swept under the carpet. Despite violent film fantasies, this is the first era that, for many, aspires to be death-free. A dubious science called cryogenics was developed in mid-twentieth-century America, which claimed to be able to preserve a corpse until some future time when scientists would have discovered how to resuscitate it. The idealistic communist societies of the twentieth century developed the bizarre practice of embalming the bodies of their leaders, as if they were incorruptible Catholic saints. In Russia, Lenin, and in China, Mao, lie in state, their cheeks rouged, not to await their spirits' return, like the mummies of the Egyptian pharaohs, but to make it look as though they had never died, and never could die. And yet, despite all this emphasis given to life, an estimated sixty million people were exiled, imprisoned or killed in the U.S.S.R. during the Soviet era alone. Pretending death doesn't exist diminishes life. Accepting death's existence doesn't make it any easier to face, though. The theme of the three living coming across the three dead (ill.3) was regularly painted on medieval church walls as part of murals

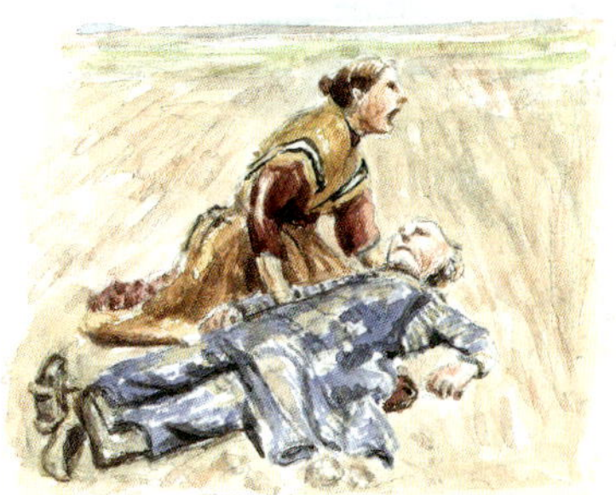

2 After H.A. Brendekilde. *Udslidt (worn-out), 1889*, detail. Oil on canvas, 207 x 270 cm. Fyns Kunstmuseum, Denmark

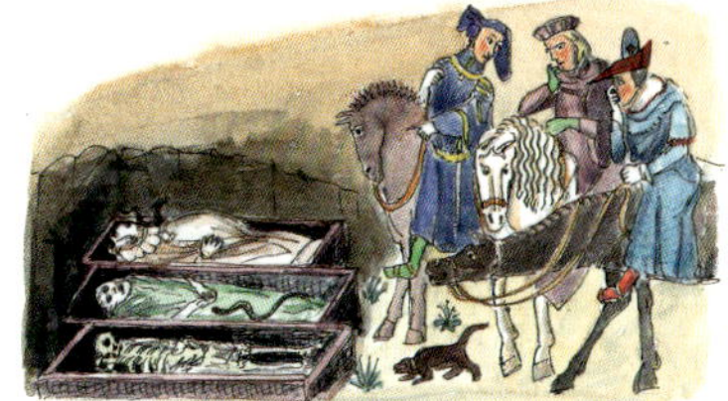

3 After Buonamico Buffalmacco (attrib.). *The Meeting of the Three Quick and the Three Dead*, early 14th century C.E., detail. Fresco. Camposanto, Pisa

1 Peter Breughel. *The Triumph of Death*, c.1562. Oil on canvas, 117 x 162 cm. Prado, Madrid

showing the Triumph of Death. It was in the interests of the Church to remind people of their mortality.

Though the evolution of self-consciousness is much debated, a strong case can be made for the idea that our species of human being is the only animal which is aware that it will die. There is no convincing evidence to suggest that our closest relatives, the Neanderthals, buried their dead or paid any particular attention to this event, though that in itself doesn't mean they were not aware of death. The few Neanderthal corpses that look as though they might have been arranged for burial could possibly have been imitations of modern man's rapidly developing funeral rites, for there is strong evidence that Neanderthals copied behaviour, such as wearing ornaments, during the period when the two species lived side by side in Europe. It's logical to think, however, that when humans became aware of death, much earlier in our history, we began to dream of finding ways in which to avoid our fate.

The early myths of the world are full of tales of heroes trying to overcome death. Maui, the endearing trickster spirit of Polynesia who had stolen fire from the gods and slowed the sun down for man's benefit (it had previously whizzed across the sky at a bewildering speed) decided to do humanity one last favour, to kill death. He found Hine-nui-te-po, the Great Mother, fast asleep and, slipping off his clothes, with his club strapped to his wrist, he began to climb into her vagina, from which all things including death were said to have emerged. Before he finally disappeared, he whispered to his friends, the birds, to keep quiet. But they couldn't help screeching with laughter. Hine awoke and crushed Maui to death between her thighs, an event recorded on many Maori coffins (ill. 4).

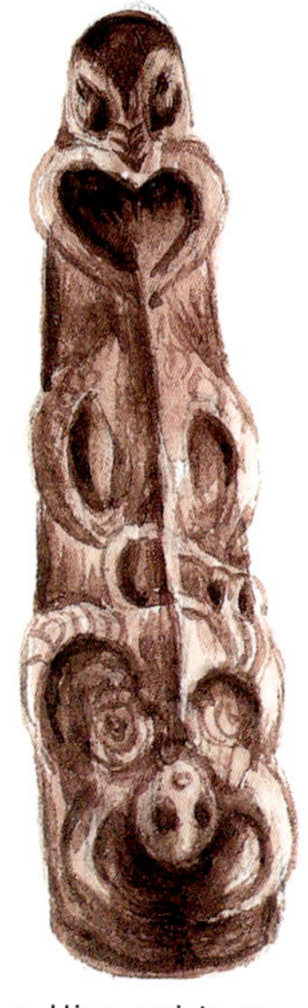

4 Hine-nui-te-po, Goddess of the underworld, from the Bay of Islands, 18th century C.E. Carved Bone Box, 102 cm. Auckland Museum, New Zealand

The first story to be written down in the world, in cuneiform script, as distinct from hieroglyphic inscriptions, dates from about

2000 B.C.E. As a spoken narrative it was almost certainly much, much older than that. It tells the tale of Gilgamesh, a king of Mesopotamia. Gilgamesh was an idle youth, picking fights with everyone and generally being a nuisance, so the gods created Enkidu, who would be strong enough to keep him in order. Enkidu lived in the forest, a wild, hairy, naked giant and a friend to all the animals – perhaps, who knows, a distant folk memory of Neanderthal man. Enkidu couldn't speak and avoided humans, but he kept freeing the animals they had caught. The townsfolk decided to set a trap for him by making a beautiful young girl stand near the pool where he came to drink. He fell in love with her and she allowed him to kiss her. The animals immediately deserted Enkidu; they smelt mankind on him. Now he had to live with humans. One day he met Gilgamesh, and they immediately fought to see who was the strongest. Neither won, but they became inseparable friends, carrying out increasingly daring raids, which finally culminated in their killing the bull of heaven (ill. 5). The gods realised that they had just doubled their trouble, so they killed Enkidu – perhaps this was a folk memory of the Neanderthals' extinction. Gilgamesh was heartbroken, and travelled to the end of the world to see if he could conquer death. The gods told him he could try, but only if he was strong enough first to conquer death's little sister, sleep. But Gilgamesh dozed off as soon as he sat down to begin the trial. He was sent back, ignominiously, to live the life of a mortal man.

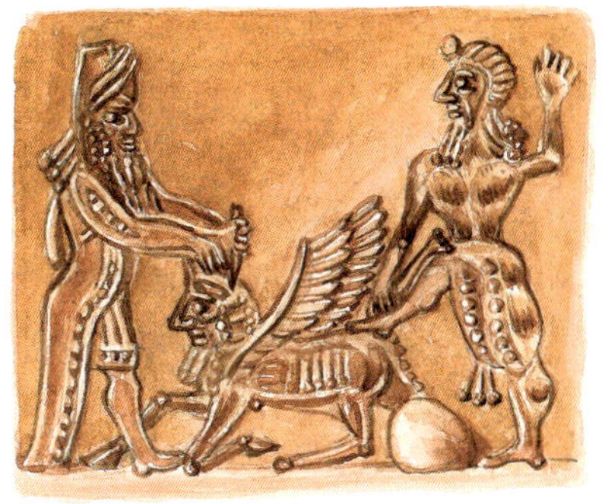

5 Gilgamesh and Enkidu killing the bull of heaven, c. 2000 B.C.E. Wax impression from a cylinder seal. British Museum, London

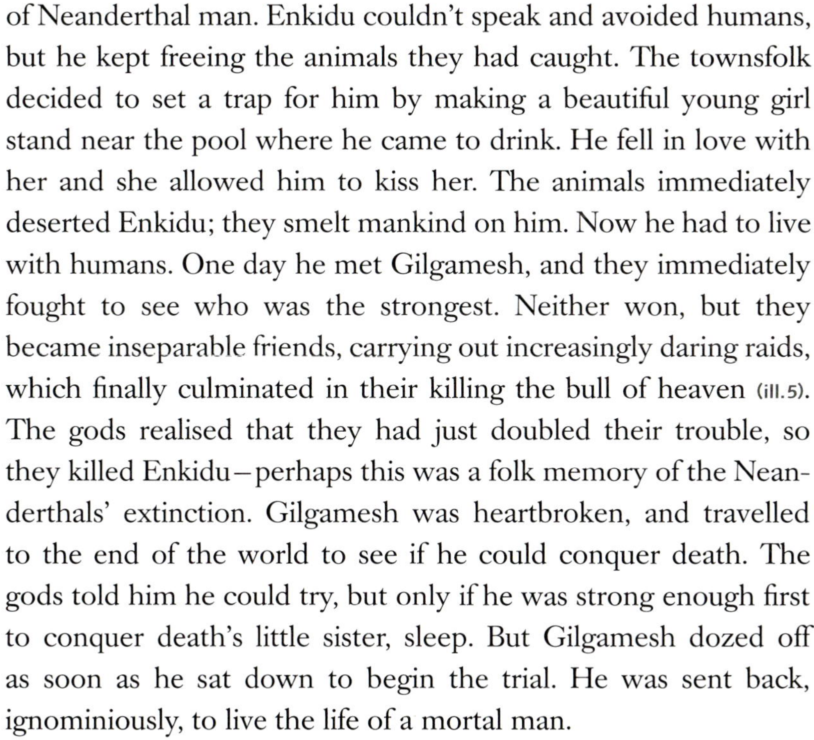

People throughout all ages and cultures have sought, and still seek, to prolong their lives. There are myths all over the world that tell of rivers of life, whose waters, once dipped into or sipped, would make a person live forever. The Chinese believed that

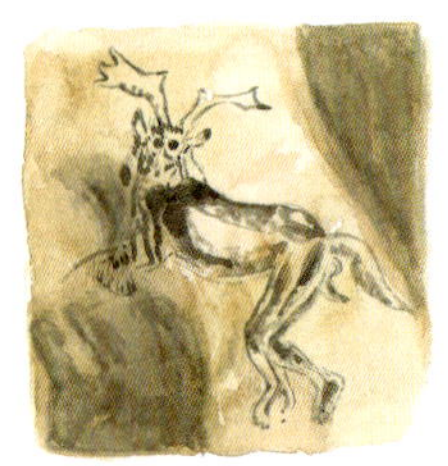

6 Shaman, c. 16000 B.C.E. Les Trois Frères cave, France

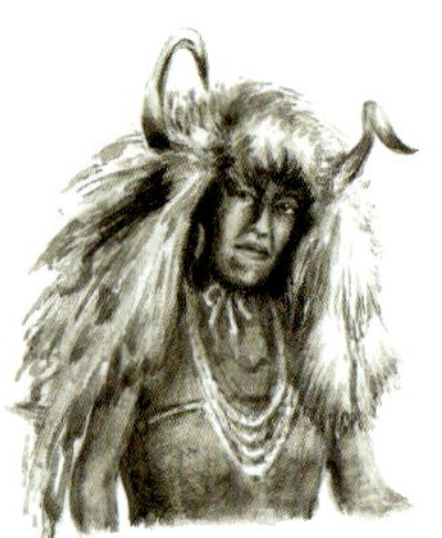

7 After Edward S. Curtis. *Sia Buffalo Dancer*, 1926, detail. Photograph from *The North American Indian*, vol. XVI, 1926

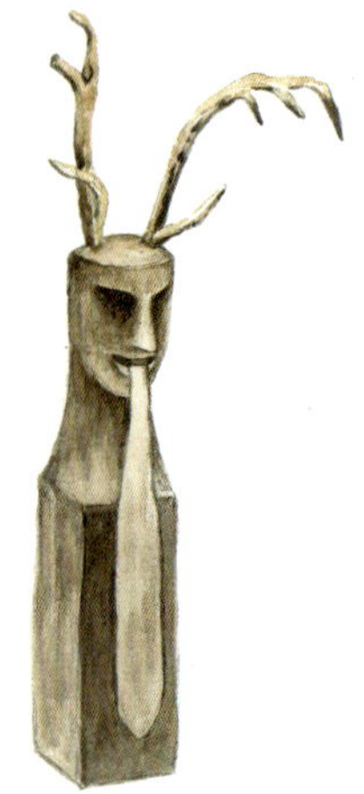

8 Shaman tomb guardian, Chinese, Changsha, Hunan Province, eastern Zhou period, 4th century B.C.E. British Museum, London

longevity came from drinking dew; all royal gardens had dew ponds to collect this magic exhalation from the morning air. The manna that kept the Israelites alive in the desert has also been explained as a type of dew. But no-one could really complain as long as they survived into maturity. It was a different matter, however, if people's lives were cut short. Their contemporaries then sought the cause for this interruption in the regular, ordered flow of existence. Premature deaths and diseases, droughts and famines, trouble with neighbours or wild animals, abnormal births or freak weather conditions were all taken to be signs that something had gone wrong, and that usually meant that a spirit had been upset. The most common response was to call a wise man or woman to discover the cause of the disturbance and take the necessary action–usually rituals and sacrifices–to heal the wrong and so restore accord and harmony.

These wise people, gifted with powers to commune with the spirits and heal the sick, are usually called shamans in Asia and medicine men in the Americas. Their practices, though they differ greatly in detail around the world, have many ingredients in common. These specially gifted people were usually selected, reputedly by the spirits, from among girls as well as boys, during initiation ceremonies held at puberty. The chosen few would then be taught the myths of their people, the complex procedures of traditional medicine and their associated rituals. They then almost always had to endure an ordeal of suffering–a period of starvation, isolation and sensory deprivation, in a forest or desert, up a mountain or down a cave or, in northern climates, in a heated sweat-lodge. During this period, which might last days or weeks, they undertook a "dream" journey that usually involved descending into the realm of the dead, where they engaged in a ritual battle with their people's traditional foes. They often suffered dismemberment or burning, but finally survived to climb the "world tree", where they made contact with the higher spirits. After this trial—which is similar to the spiritual journeys undertaken by many religious leaders, including Jesus Christ—these now gifted people would return to the world to help the living. They were able to slip back, whenever needed, into the spirit world to discover those past transgressions that had caused the current ills. They did so by dancing themselves into a trance-like state, often after taking hallucinogenic drugs. These enabled them to bridge the gulf that separated humans from other living creatures and from the spirits.

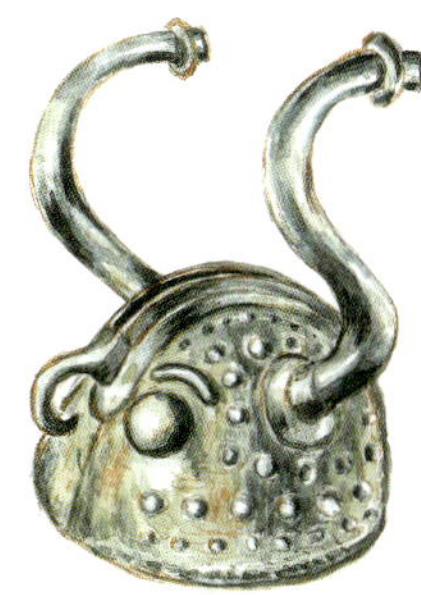

9 Bronze helmet from Vekso, Mose, Sealand, c. 750 B.C.E. National Museum of Denmark, Copenhagen

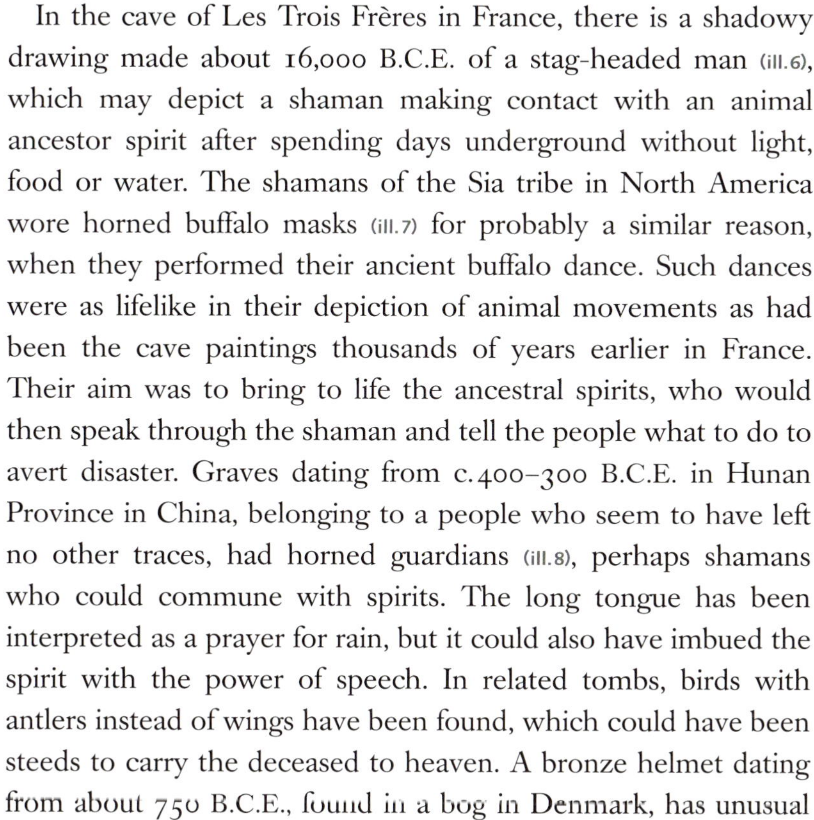

In the cave of Les Trois Frères in France, there is a shadowy drawing made about 16,000 B.C.E. of a stag-headed man (ill. 6), which may depict a shaman making contact with an animal ancestor spirit after spending days underground without light, food or water. The shamans of the Sia tribe in North America wore horned buffalo masks (ill. 7) for probably a similar reason, when they performed their ancient buffalo dance. Such dances were as lifelike in their depiction of animal movements as had been the cave paintings thousands of years earlier in France. Their aim was to bring to life the ancestral spirits, who would then speak through the shaman and tell the people what to do to avert disaster. Graves dating from c. 400–300 B.C.E. in Hunan Province in China, belonging to a people who seem to have left no other traces, had horned guardians (ill. 8), perhaps shamans who could commune with spirits. The long tongue has been interpreted as a prayer for rain, but it could also have imbued the spirit with the power of speech. In related tombs, birds with antlers instead of wings have been found, which could have been steeds to carry the deceased to heaven. A bronze helmet dating from about 750 B.C.E., found in a bog in Denmark, has unusual

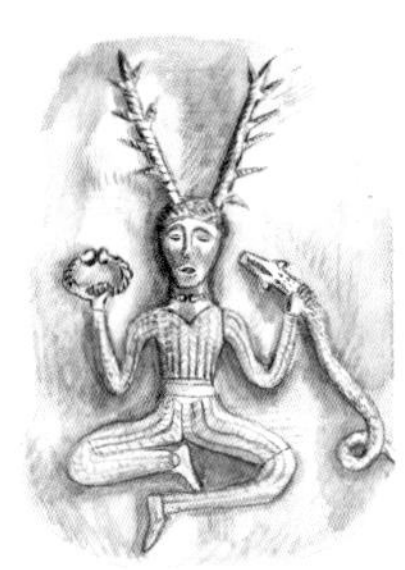

10 Stag-antlered shaman, detail of the Gundestrup cauldron, c.100 B.C.E. Silver. National Museum of Denmark, Copenhagen

hollow horns (ill.9). It is thought that these might have held feathers, thereby transforming the helmet into a bird mask, which would explain the owl-like eyes and beak-like nose. A misreading of this particular mask gave rise to the modern myth that the Vikings wore helmets with pointed horns.

The huge silver Gundestrup cauldron (ill.10) was also discovered in a bog in Denmark. It had been carefully placed there as a sacrificial object for the gods. Probably made much further east, perhaps near the Black Sea, it could have been a gift to a Danish chieftain or a spoil of war. It's one of the few relics to have survived of the elusive Celtic religions, which were practised by a great swathe of peoples across northern Europe and Asia before and, for a time, during the Christian era. Among many scenes around the cauldron's rim, most of which elude definite interpretation, is one which might show a Celtic priest practising a form of trance-inducing meditation. His right heel puts pressure on the perineum, between the scrotum and the anus, creating a sensation of heat through the body. This Celtic yogi has, in his trance, evidently made contact with, or temporarily become Cerunnas, the stag-antlered Celtic lord of animals, nature and abundance.

It was comforting to think that tragedies and disasters were the effect of bad spirits, because then people could do something about them. There was a belief among the Inuit peoples of the Arctic that humanity's sins fell like dirt into the sea and got lodged in the hair of Sedna, the fearful underwater goddess. She couldn't comb them out because she had no fingers. Her father had cut them off as she clung to his boat, when she had tried to stop him, without success, from drowning her as an offering to the bird spirit. Her fingers had then turned into seals. As more and more human sins drifted down into the sea, they got tangled in Sedna's hair and she grew more and more uncomfortable and irritable. She decided not to release any fish for men to catch until a shaman, who could readily turn into a fish, swam down to comb her hair, a task that the Inuit shaman had regularly to perform.

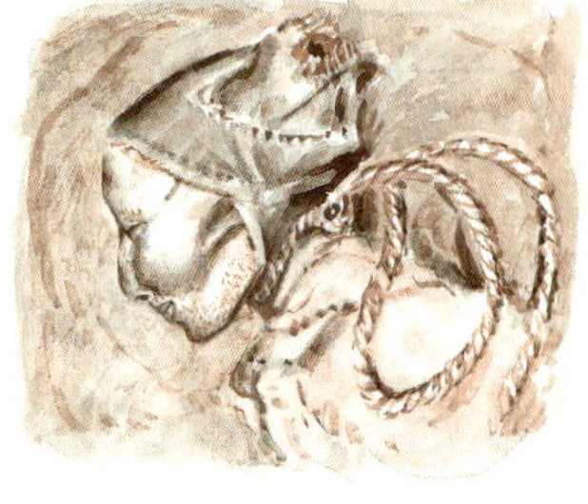

11 Tollund Man, c. 200 B.C.E., detail of face and neck. Silkeborg Museum, Denmark

If all else failed to stop a plague or a drought, it was logical to appease the angry gods or spirits with the ultimate gift of a human life. Human sacrifice seems abhorrent to us today, but it was evidently widespread in early societies around the world, though probably much more rarely practised than Christian missionaries and later sensationalist modern historians liked to make out. The people selected for sacrifice appear to have been treated with respect. It was an honour to be a messenger to the gods, and the victims were likely to be high-ranking, whether captured from another tribe, or chosen from one's own people. An angry god wouldn't be appeased with a lowly mortal. In about 200 B.C.E. an individual who has come to be known as Tollund Man (ill. 11) was shaved and his fingernails carefully manicured before he was hanged, and his body consigned to a bog in Denmark, believed by people living near it to be the entrance to the underworld. The priests officiating at this ceremony would probably have studied the twitches and jerks of the man's body as he died, because it was believed that death throes signalled the gods' intentions, as the sacrificed man crossed the threshold into the other world. That is why hearts and livers were ripped from sacrificial animals and humans while they were still hot, and read like palms—so desperate were people for signs that might give them clues to how they might end their suffering.

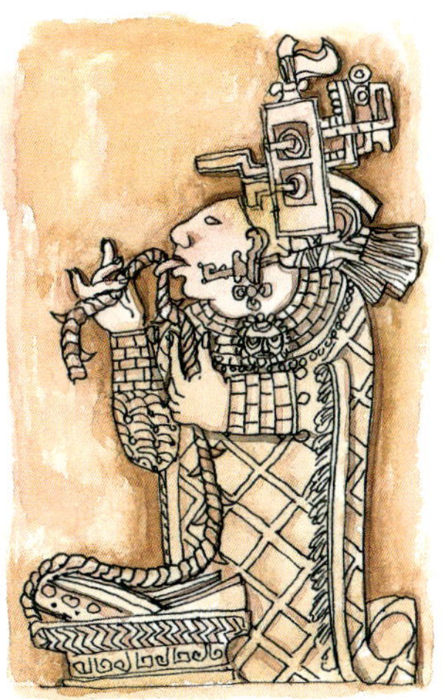

12 Lady Balam-Ix, a wife of Bird Jaguar, draws blood from her tongue, 725 C.E. Maya Lintel 17, Yaxchilán, Mexico. Limestone. British Museum, London

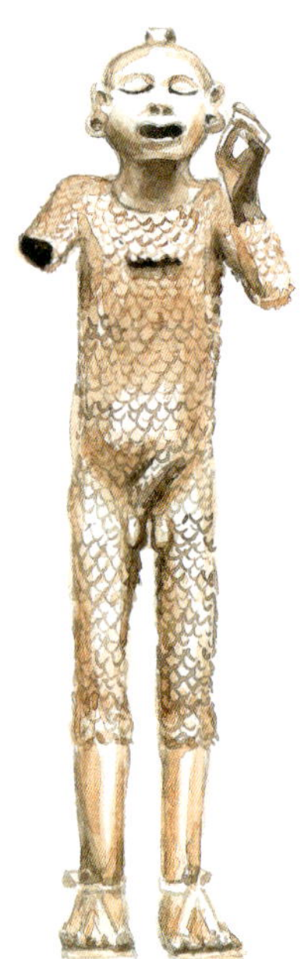

13 Xipe Totec, c.1500 C.E., Aztec. Fired clay and paint, 97 x 43 x 70 cm. Museo Regional de Puebla, Mexico

In the Mayan culture of Central America, blood-letting was the duty of aristocratic warrior priests and it was performed in temple complexes out of bounds to the uninitiated, and therefore spiritually unclean public. Holes were pierced through queens' tongues and kings' penises. In a relief from a temple at Yaxchilán in Mexico the Mayan king, Bird Jaguar, holds his stylus ready to inflict this gruesome wound on himself, while one of his wives threads a string through her lacerated tongue (ill.12) so that her royal blood can be drained down to a basket of paper quills. These would have been lit once they were saturated with blood. Priests would then have watched how the smoke rose from the basket, for it was believed that it took the form of spiritual demons, out of whose mouths tribal ancestors would emerge to tell the future of the royal family and their people. The wounds in penises and tongues were then cauterised with hot ashes. Some kings and queens survived.

In Aztec temples, the blood of nobles captured in war cascaded down the altar steps and splashed on to the broken moonstone (p.65, ill.2) at their base. This ceremony ensured that the moon and her brothers the stars would be reborn, and the rhythmic harmony of the world maintained. The priests of Xipe Totec (ill.13), the god of springtime, wore the flayed skin of a sacrificed

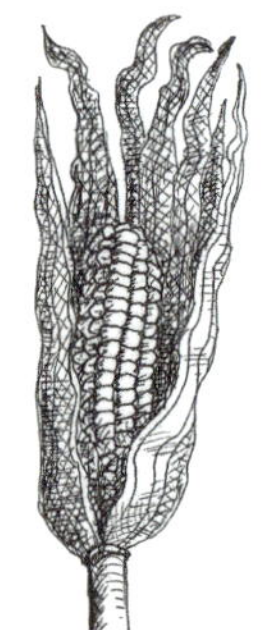

14 After G.B. Ramusio. *Maize*, 1556 C.E. Woodcut, 18.5 x 5.8 cm

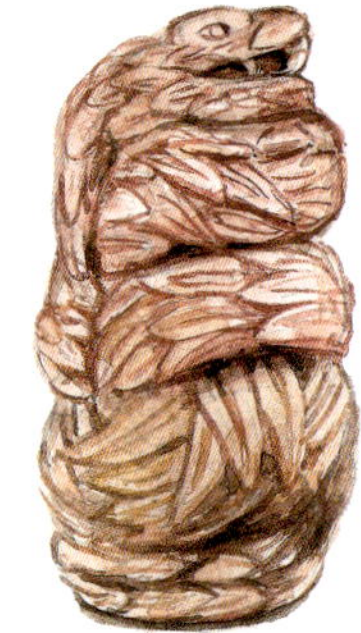

15 Quetzalcoatl stone, 15th century. 53 x 24 x 25 cm. Vatican Museums, Rome

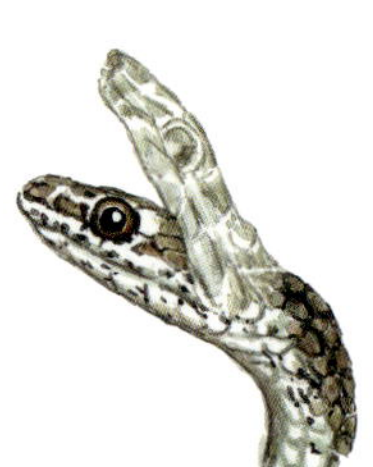

16 Snake beginning to shed its skin

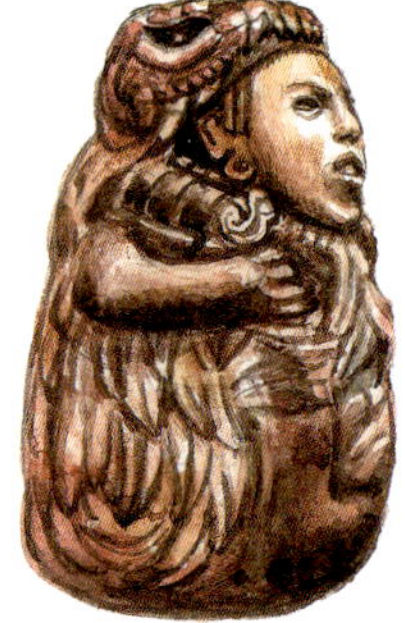

17 Quetzalcoatl in human-animal form, c.15th century. Red porphyry, 44 x 25 x 23 cm. Louvre, Paris

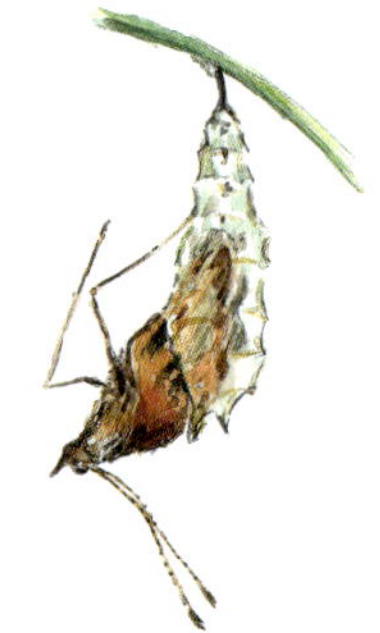

18 Butterfly emerging from its chrysalis

man for twenty days. The skin was turned inside out. The lumpy, bloody, ripped-away flesh was like the ripe, beaded corn cob breaking through its sheaf (ill. 14). There are few more vivid images of the interdependency of life and death. Quetzalcoatl (ill. 15), the ancient god of agriculture who entered the underworld and resurrected the dead, was imagined to be a serpent that had feathers instead of scales and could fly. The image comes from nature – a snake's skin can't expand, so it has to be shed to enable the snake to grow (ill. 16). The idea that a magical snake once emerged from its old skin not with a new set of scales but with an array of feathers is a beautiful image of spiritual change and rebirth. Our ancestors must have sensed that things in nature had changed and were changing, though they had no idea of the process of evolution. They attributed these changes to spiritual influences; this is why the shaman was so concerned with transformation. A remarkable image survives of a man – a spirit warrior? – emerging from Quetzalcoatl's jaws (ill. 17). It is reminiscent of a butterfly emerging from a chrysalis (ill. 18). When butterflies emerge they have small, crumpled wings. They pump body fluid into these until they inflate and flatten out, and then dry in the sun. Before they take their first flight, butterflies usually exude a bead or two of surplus fluid called meconium that is often red, like blood.

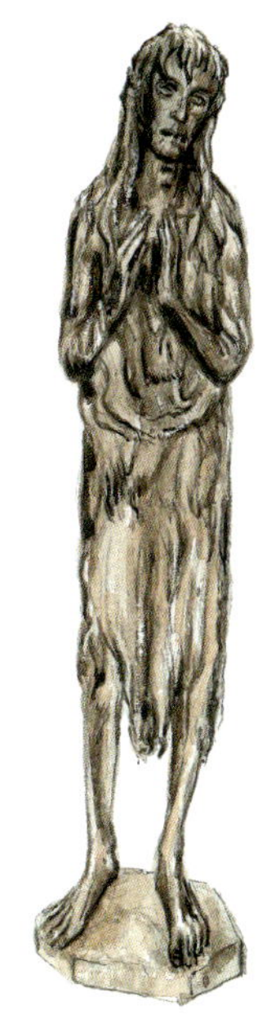

19 Donatello. *St Mary Magdalene*, c. 1453–55. Polychromed wood, 188 cm high. Museo dell'Opera del Duomo, Florence

Though Christianity is replete with similar imagery of spiritual transformation through suffering – Mary Magdalene (ill. 19), for instance, reputedly spent thirty years in the desert atoning for her prostitution – and the gruesome martyrdoms of the early saints – St Lawrence was roasted alive on a grill, St Cecelia was boiled in oil before being imperfectly beheaded, and St Bartholomew was skinned alive – nevertheless it demonised shamanism as it spread through the world. This is one reason why in western folklore devils have horns, witches can change into animals, and medicine men became known as witchdoctors. The Christian argument was that the pain in the world, including death itself, sprang from humanity's own wrongdoing and could not be blamed on spirits (cf. ill. 1, 20). Many religious practices include penitence, but it is usually more to do with purification than with absolving personal guilt. In Hinduism, Parvati, when she fell in love with Lord Shiva, realised that she would have to cleanse herself before she could be accepted as his wife. Her penance, which lasted for 60,000 years, started with her leaving all her worldly possessions and the comforts of her family and friends, to live in solitude in the forest. So complete was this penance, the Hindu poets wrote, that the whole forest became filled with the fragrance of her harmonious spirit, animals ceased to hunt one another and plants bloomed everywhere with abandon.

20 Peter Breughel. *The Triumph of Death*, c. 1562. Oil on canvas, 117 x 162 cm. Prado, Madrid

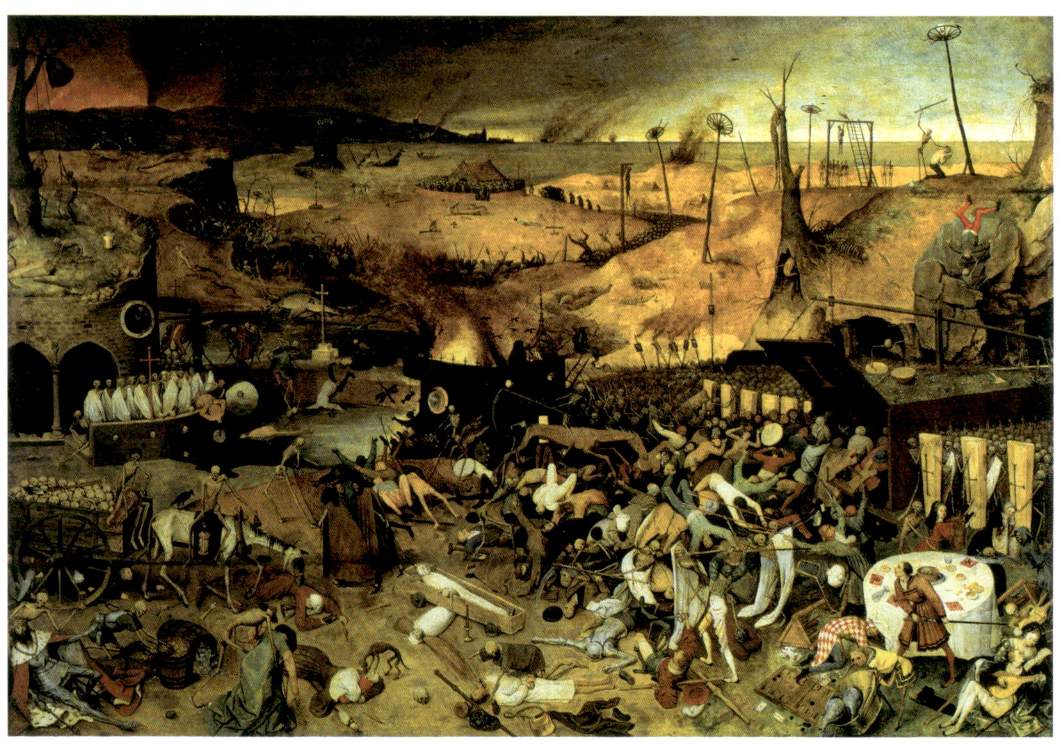

Christianity has placed a special emphasis on the Biblical creation story. In the beginning God created the Garden of Eden with all its beautiful flowers and delicious fruits. In it he placed all the animals and birds, and then Adam, moulded out of clay in God's own image, and finally Eve, fashioned from one of Adam's ribs and called "woman, because she was taken out of man". They would all have lived happily ever after, had not Eve persuaded Adam to eat the forbidden fruit of the tree of knowledge, which mysteriously contained the seeds of the awareness of good and evil. The couple instantly became conscious of their nakedness, and covered their private parts with the nearest sizable leaves, usually thought to be those of the fig, which were conveniently shaped for the purpose (ill.21). When they were accosted by God, they each tried to pass the buck (ill.23), charmingly revealing their new humanity with their guile. Having sinned, they were expelled from Eden (ill.22) to a life of labour and misery on a now-cursed earth, their days ending in the death that they themselves had released into the world.

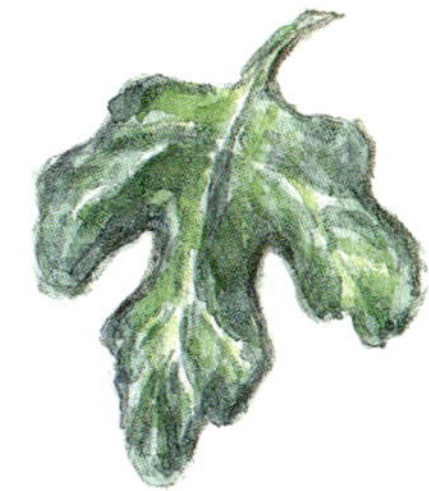

21 Fig leaf

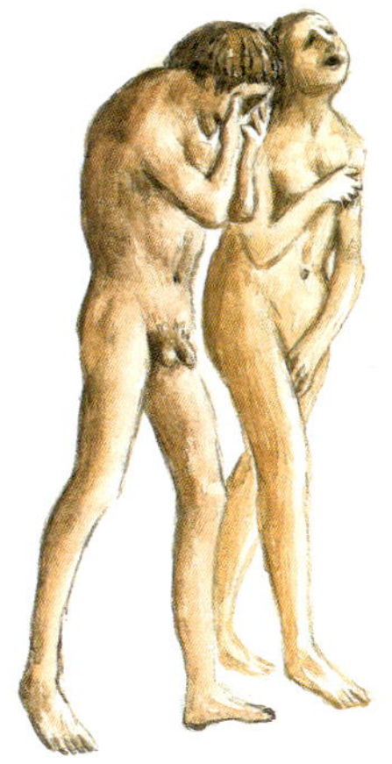

22 After Masaccio. *The Expulsion of Adam and Eve*, 1425–26, detail. Brancacci Chapel, S. Maria del Carmine, Florence

The myth of Adam and Eve is best understood as an allegory: at its simplest, of growing up and, at its subtlest, of the enigma and responsibilities of self-awareness and free will. The story took a particular hold over Christianity, much more than over its fellow religions of the Bible, Judaism and Islam, because Christians believe that death, released into the world by Adam's sin, was itself killed by God's sacrifice of his own son on the cross—an exceptional act of generosity for a god. Medieval Europe saw the history of the world vividly contained within the compact cycle of the creation, the fall and the resurrection. Though the sources for its imagery are not known for certain, there is a strong case for thinking that the

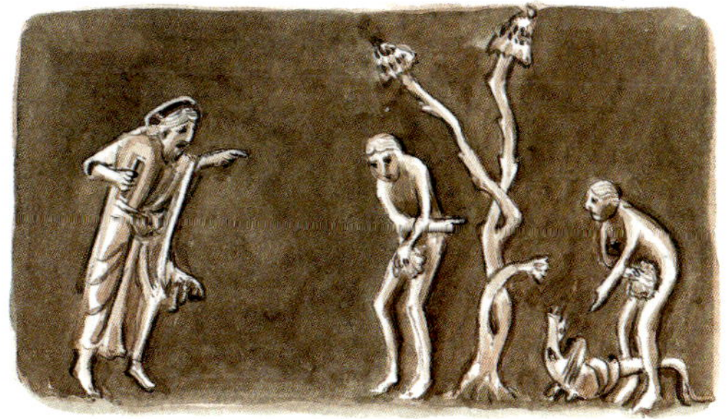

23 *Adam and Eve after the Fall*, c.1015 C.E. Bronze panel from the doors of Hildesheim Cathedral, Germany

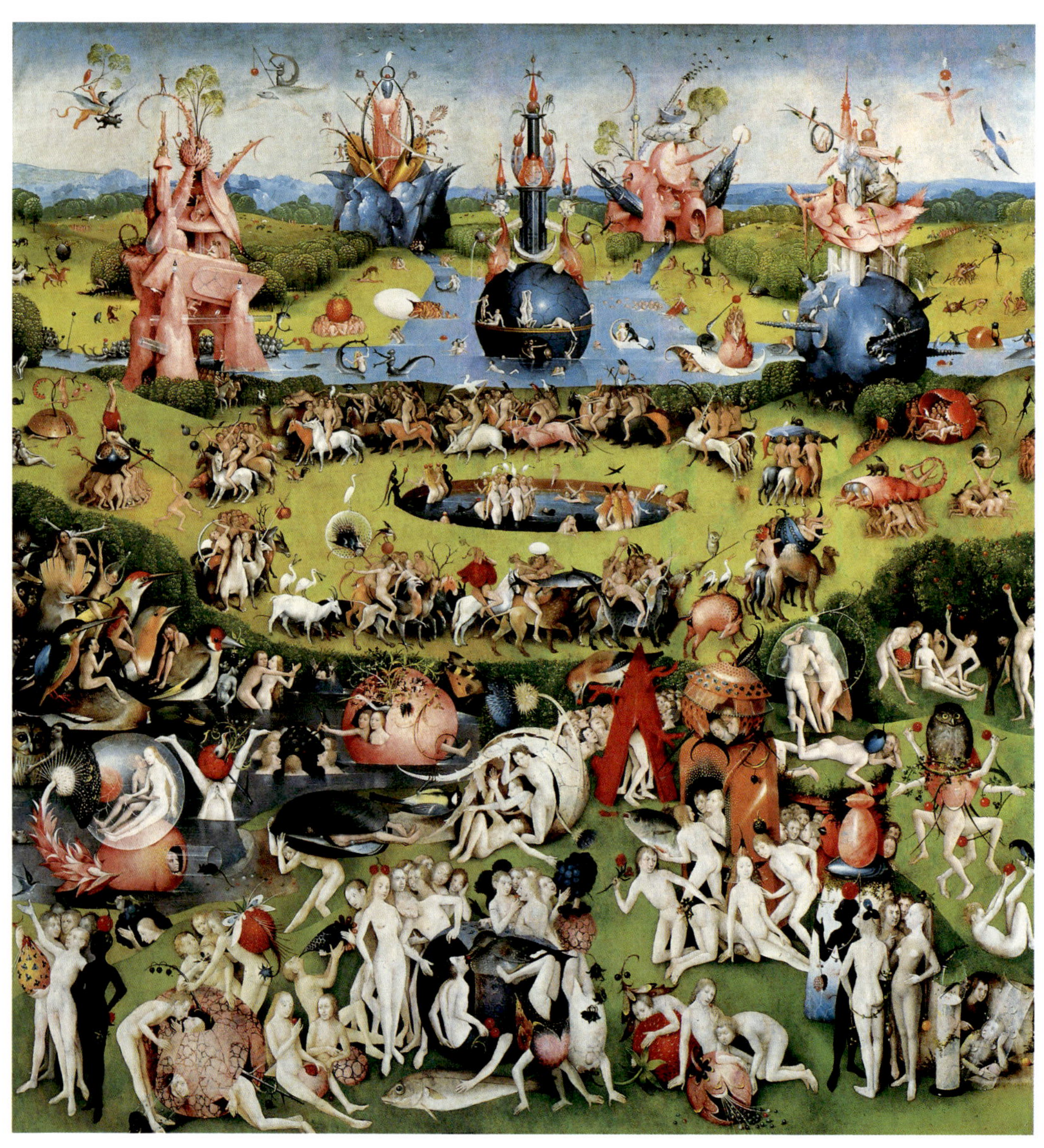

24 Hieronymus Bosch. *The Garden of Earthly Delights*, c.1505, central panel of triptych. Prado, Madrid

Flemish painter Hieronymus Bosch's picture of *The Garden of Earthly Delights* (c.1505) (ill.24) shows what the world might have looked like if mankind had not sinned, and we were all still living in the Garden of Eden. There are no children, nor is anyone old. Delights abound – it's a land of fruit and honey; no-one has to eat other living beings. In the clear, liquid world of Bosch's imagination, vividly brought to life by his precise, fluid brushstrokes, plants, animals and people grow together to create a crystalline, otherworldly planet, before extraterrestrial places were ever thought of. It's a land of contented shamans. There's no evil here; Bosch saved that for his extraordinary scenes of hell (p.214, ill.34). In this garden everyone and everything is at play; it's a country without war or death, class or race. The black lady weds the white gentleman (bottom left-hand corner) and everyone feasts on strawberries. But the world into which we were born, or, as Christianity taught, which we had made, wasn't trouble-free at all.

Christianity promises the ultimate solution. It teaches that death itself, which only came into existence when Adam and Eve sinned, began to die at the moment when God's son Jesus Christ died for man's sins. Death will finally be put to death when Christ returns for the second time, which many Christians expect daily. Effectively, Christianity has claimed special rights over death. Certainly no other religion has shown the moment of dying in such agonising detail (ill.25), but then Christians believe

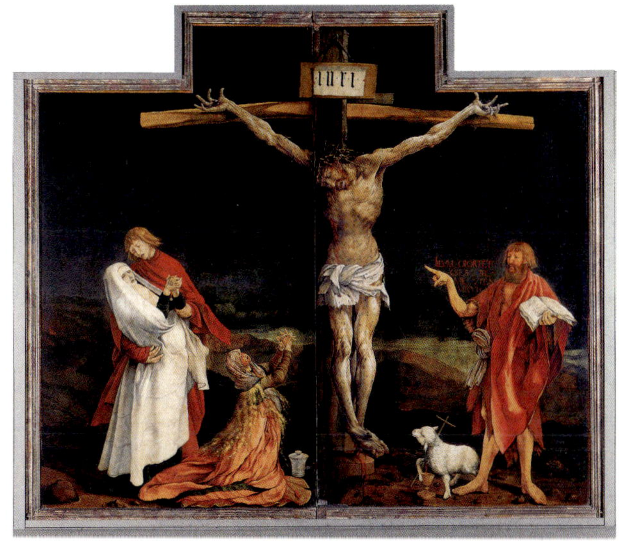

25 Matthias Grünewald. *Isenheim Altarpiece*, c.1515, exterior: Crucifixion. Unterlinden Museum, Colmar, France

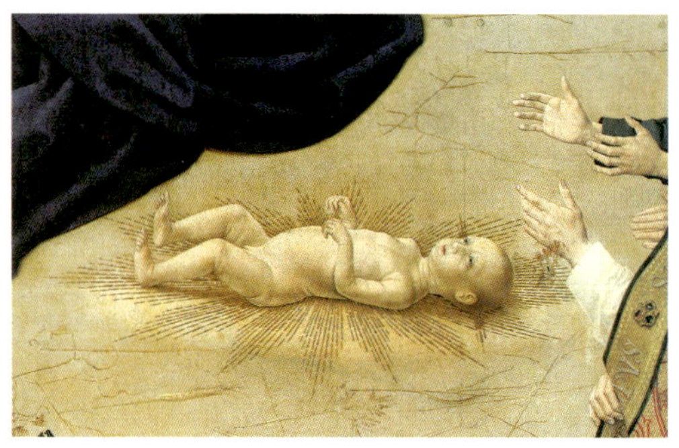

26 Hugo van der Goes. *Portinari Altarpiece*, cf. p. 6, The holy chield

that they can look death in the face, for death itself will one day die. Alone among world religions, Christianity has succeeded in enlisting the two most powerful and universal images of human life to its cause – a man in the throes of death and a newborn baby. Buddhism, influenced by Christianity, adopted the latter image; there are many paintings in Buddhist temples showing a plump baby Buddha magically able to walk the moment he is born: from his first seven footprints spring seven lotus blossoms. However, it would have been against mainstream Buddhist belief to apotheosise pain, though certain sects within Tibetan Buddhism have done so in a symbolic way. But fear of death and love of life were both harnessed, in the most vivid, visual way, to the Christian chariot.

The birth of Jesus in a stable amongst the beasts (ill. 26) – because there was no room at the inn – became one of the most evocative religious images in the world, tugging at the heartstrings of all who have felt the irresistible pull of protective love for a tiny new being – a powerful affection to associate with a god's son who was to become one's liberator from death. The whole of creation, from the beasts to the angels and from kings to shepherds paid tribute to this being of helpless innocence and eternal wisdom. The similarities between the wrinkled face of a baby and that of a wise old man must have struck our ancestors. The name of Lao Zi – the mysterious founder of Taoism in China – literally means "old child", and that's just how he is depicted in many posthumous, imaginary portraits (ill. 27). The makers of the film *E.T.* employed a similar concoction of baby and sage to create their Christ-like extraterrestrial. And Christianity adopted an-

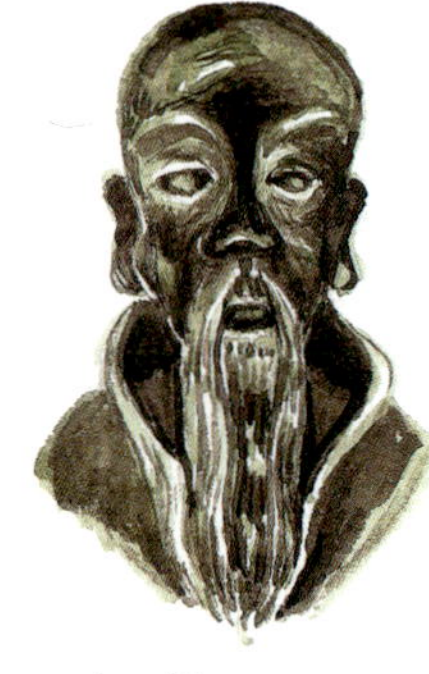

27 *Lao Zi*, c. 1700 C.E. China Qing dynasty, reign of Kangxi. Bronze. Gulbenkian Museum of Oriental Art, Durham, England

other universally heart-rending image—that of the young, fluffy, wide-eyed lamb (p. 182, ill. 1), the very creature which had most commonly been sacrificed on altars by earlier religions. The message was that Jesus Christ was a lamb that mankind had slaughtered, the innocent lamb which, Christians believe, will become our final judge on the Last Day.

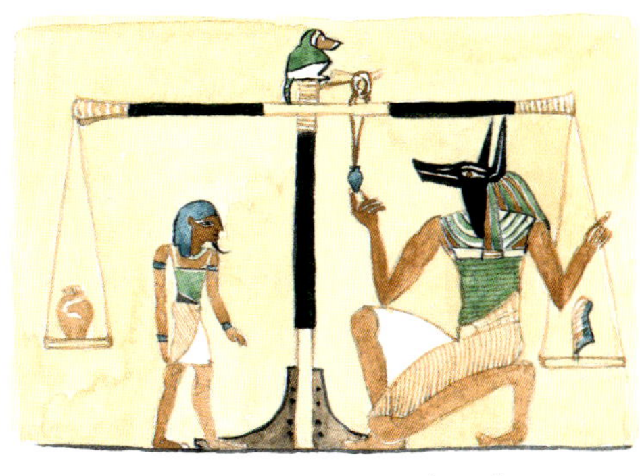

28 *The Judgement*, c. 1280 B.C.E., from the Papyrus of the Scribe Hunefer. British Museum, London

Good and evil only become apparent when you make a judgement. And judgement seemed to hold us in its grip every second of the day, even though we couldn't see the mysterious, grave force that ceaselessly tried to pull us down. There was a widespread assumption that the good would rise while the wicked would sink. So judgement found its perfect expression in the scales. This copy of the Egyptian Book of the Dead (ill. 28) was compiled in about 1280 B.C.E. for the scribe Hunefer, who had just died. Hunefer looks on while his heart is weighed against the feather of truth. What is lighter than a feather? As the Christian mystic Hildegard of Bingen (1098–1174) wrote: "A feather on the breath of God. Thus am I." Hunefer has led a good life. He has not stolen, been covetous, killed anyone, damaged a grain store, lied, trespassed, practiced usury, gossiped, committed adultery, had sex with a boy or abused a king, so he is declared Maa-Kheru—true of voice—and is presented by Horus to Osiris, the resurrected god of justice who had rid Egypt of cannibalism long before, introduced agriculture, and disarmed the whole world with his gentleness.

This image is essentially the same as Michelangelo's great vision of *The Last Judgement* (ill. 29), which he painted on the east wall of the Sistine chapel in the Vatican in Rome. The picture

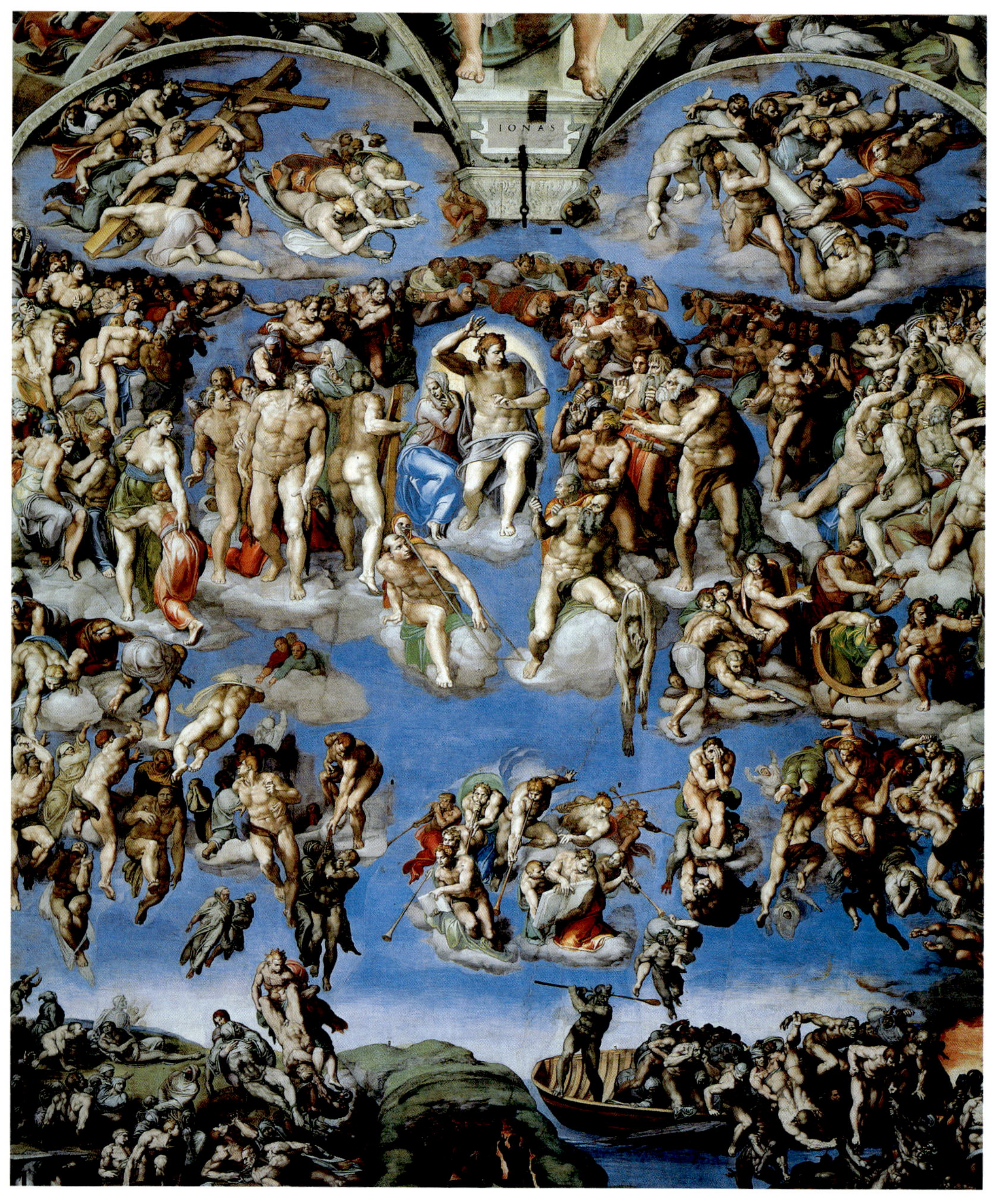

29 Michelangelo. *The Last Judgement*, 1536–1541. Fresco.
The Sistine Chapel, The Vatican, Rome

depends for its effect entirely on our awareness of gravity. Christ raises the righteous with his right hand—and simultaneously condemns the sinful to sink to eternal damnation. On the centre right, St Bartholomew holds his flayed skin to show how he was martyred for his faith. Michelangelo has painted his own face on this skin, and given St Bartholomew the features of Pietro Aretino, who had once remarked that he thought Michelangelo's nudes would look better in a bathroom than a chapel. Michelangelo might also have been making an oblique reference in this image to the mortal Marsyas who claimed to be able to play the flute better than the god Apollo. Apollo had him flayed alive for his presumption. Was Michelangelo suggesting that he could create better-looking men than Pietro Aretino? If so, he deserved his punishment because Pietro Aretino, like all men, had been made in the image of God, and how could Michelangelo claim to be a better artist than God? The deflation of the guilty before the rectitude of the righteous here acquires a whole new level of meaning in this extremely complex, devout and, to modern eyes, homoerotic image. But its overall magisterial power is based entirely on our sense of weight, and the daily awareness of the gravity of our situation. This is an awareness which most of us have almost entirely lost.

Tibetan Buddhists hang their temples with paintings of the wheel of life. The animals shown in its centre represent the mind's poisons—the pig of ignorance, the snake of anger and the cockerel of desire. These are the sources of all human suffering. Around them turns the wheel of life. It's a wheel that is held vertically. The good rise to the top and the evil fall below. Hell is the lowest region and heaven the highest, and all the interim stages of reincarnation lie in between. This is still essentially a moral vision that stems, perhaps, from the time of Buddha himself.

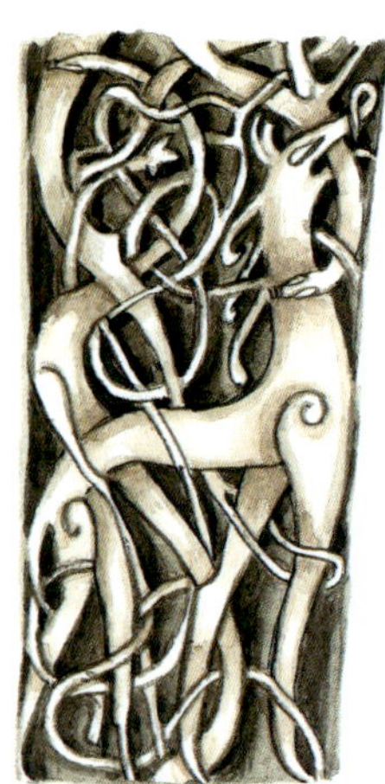

30 Keyhole Doorway, c.1050–70 C.E. Carved wood. Urnes Church, Norway

Something strange happened to humanity around 500 B.C.E. We then began to think that we were morally responsible for the world. This was the epoch of the great philosophers: Socrates in Europe, Confucius in China and Siddhartha, the founder of Buddhism, in India. These three men all advocated an aspiration towards goodness, and one way to achieve this was by not harming others. Jainism—a faith that emerged alongside Buddhism in India—logically extended this respect for life to all living creatures. The heroes of this religion died in a state of voluntary immobility, while creepers grew up their legs. They didn't move for fear of killing a little creature inadvertently. Like Buddhists, Jains are vegetarian. They teach that you must not harm any living creature except, and only if, for a good reason, yourself. The Buddha, in one of his previous lives before he achieved enlightenment, once saw a tigress with her cubs trapped and starving in a ravine. He threw himself down to feed them, and was reborn a rung higher on the ladder to nirvana.

Buddhist and Jain beliefs are based on the assumption that the natural order of life is one of suffering. Death is not wrong, merely inevitable. Humanity's sense of good and bad probably originated quite simply from the awareness that some plants and animals were nourishing whilst others were poisonous. The ancient beliefs that Buddhism and Jainism sprang from—which we now refer to under the umbrella term Hinduism—along with many other animistic and spirit-based interpretations of the world, saw life as a cycle of creation and destruction, an eternal round of day and night, summer and winter, growth and decay. All animals, including mankind, have to kill other living things in order to live, even if they are only munching leaves. One of the most widespread symbols in ancient art is of creatures devouring one another. The Vikings, the ancient native people of Scandinavia, believed that all life sprang from the world tree Yggsdrasil, whose leaves remained evergreen and whose branches flowed through all creation. This tree of life and death–made of and entwined with elegant, long-necked dragon-like creatures all biting each other–is depicted here in a carved decoration (ill.30). It was incorporated, probably with the intention of appeasing local spirits, into the side of a later Christian church in Norway, which is why it survived.

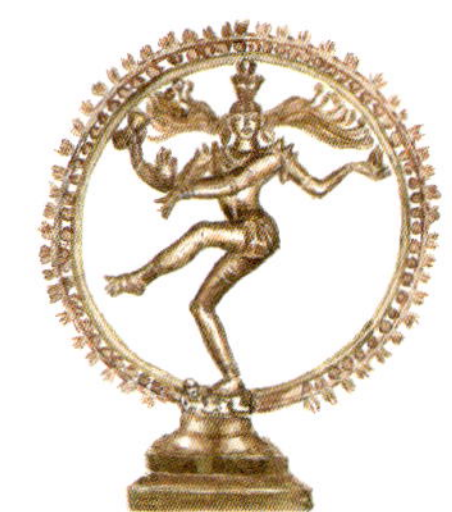

31 Shiva Natarajah, 10th century C.E. Chola period, from Tamil Nadu. Bronze, 86 x 72 x 22 cm. National Museum, Delhi

Early cultures perceived existence as a dance of life and death. The Hindu god Shiva (ill.31), one of the world's oldest continously worshipped deities, is the supreme lord of this dance. He existed before creation as eternal and infinite joy but, when he started to dance, the cycle of life and death began. In his upper right hand he holds the drum of the primal sound of creation and in his upper left hand the flame that destroys evil. He treads underfoot the dwarf of ignorance with which all his worshippers must identify, to some extent. With his hair he broke the fall of the Ganges–the holy "Milky Way" of heaven–when it fell to earth, and the goddess of the river got caught in his locks, arousing the envy of his wife, Pavarti. The eternal cycle of life and death is inevitable, but hope is possible if your deeds are good, for Shiva wipes away your sins as he prepares you for a higher incarnation. He is the destroyer not of life itself but of our inadequate perception of it. That is why his dance is so mesmerising.

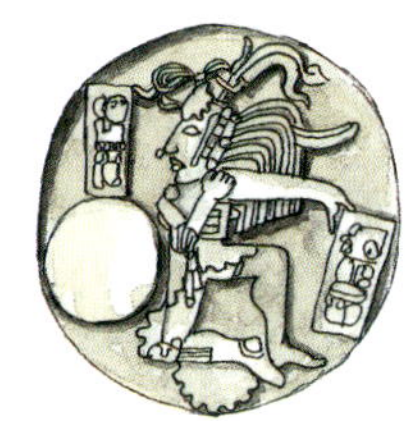

32 Mayan Ballgame Marker, ball player hitting the ball with his hip, 590 C.E. Chiapas. Stone, diameter 56 cm. National Museum of Anthropology, Mexico City

The eternal dance of life and death appears to have been reenacted in a strange religious ball-game (ill.32) performed in Mayan temples in Central America before that culture was eradicated by the Spanish in the sixteenth century. Games that incorporated an element of chance–which revealed the will of the gods–were used as forms of divination in many early societies. The Olympic games in Greece originally had a religious function that is now lost. The winner had the honour of lighting the sacrificial fire, nowadays reduced to our Olympic flame. All that remains of the Mayan ballgame are the ruins of the large courts where it was played in the temples. They are like a cross between a royal tennis court and a baseball field, with extensive seating areas for priests and royalty; ordinary people were not allowed to see this sacred ceremonial game. Unreliable accounts of the game made by Europeans who claimed to have seen it suggest that it was played very fast and with great skill. The game began, apparently, when the sun was directly overhead, at the precise second when the Mayan world tree, represented by a stalactite (p. 105, ill. 30), cast no shadow. The art of keeping a ball in the air almost certainly had cosmic and divinatory significance. The ball–claimed by the Catholic invaders to be a human head, though it was probably made of gum, perhaps with sacrificial material in it–was kept in the air by athletic warriors for hours (or for days, as some commentaries suggest, though this is difficult to comprehend) until it was dropped through a ring in the centre of the court. At that moment the signal was given for a sacrifice to be made, possibly of one of the players themselves, and this might have been a sought-after honour.

Skulls grin because death has the last laugh in our sublunary world. A haunting juxtaposition confronted our ancestors: a smile was believed to express the radiance of the soul, but just beneath the soft, curving lips lay the jagged grimace of the jaw. One of the most popular objects in the British Museum used to be a skull carved out of one piece of rock crystal (ill. 33) which was believed to be Aztec until it was discovered, recently, to be a nineteenth-century fake. But it's still a wonderful image of the ghostly, x-ray presence of a skull under every mobile face. Our predecessors felt much closer to death than many of us more fortunate souls do

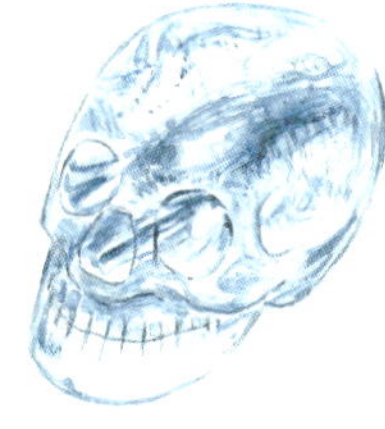

33 Rock Crystal Skull, 19th century, fake Aztec. British Museum, London

today. People's life expectancy was much shorter, children commonly died in infancy and mothers in childbirth. Plagues spread like wildfire through populated areas – the most notorious in Europe was the Black Death, which killed one in three of the population during the years 1348 to 1350. Fires and floods, wars and famine all took their toll. Death grinned because he was the conqueror – kings and mothers, gamblers and lovers were all struck down without mercy (ill.1). The German artist Hans Holbein (1497/8–1543) painted a portrait of two young ambassadors (ill.34), wearing their finest robes and surrounded by symbols of their many material, intellectual and spiritual attainments. But at their feet he painted a curious grey streak which makes no sense at first sight, but which when viewed obliquely turns into a skull. You only had to look at life from a slightly different angle to see how death ridiculed all your worldly aspirations.

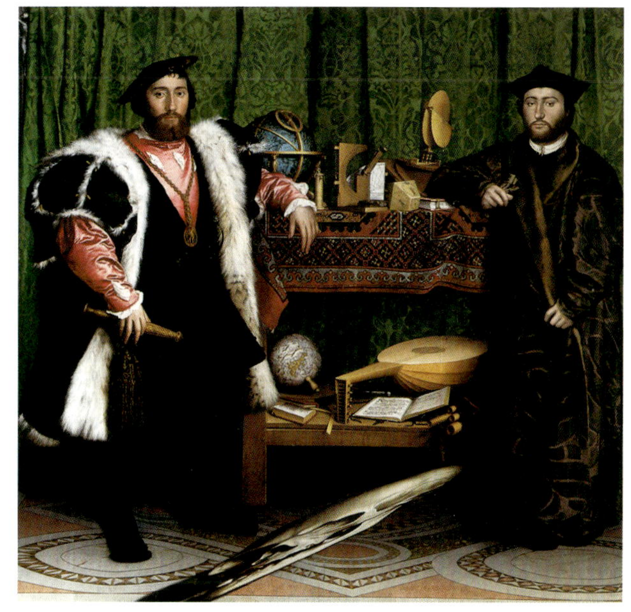

34 Hans Holbein. *The Ambassadors*, 1533. Oil on wood, 206 x 209 cm. National Gallery, London

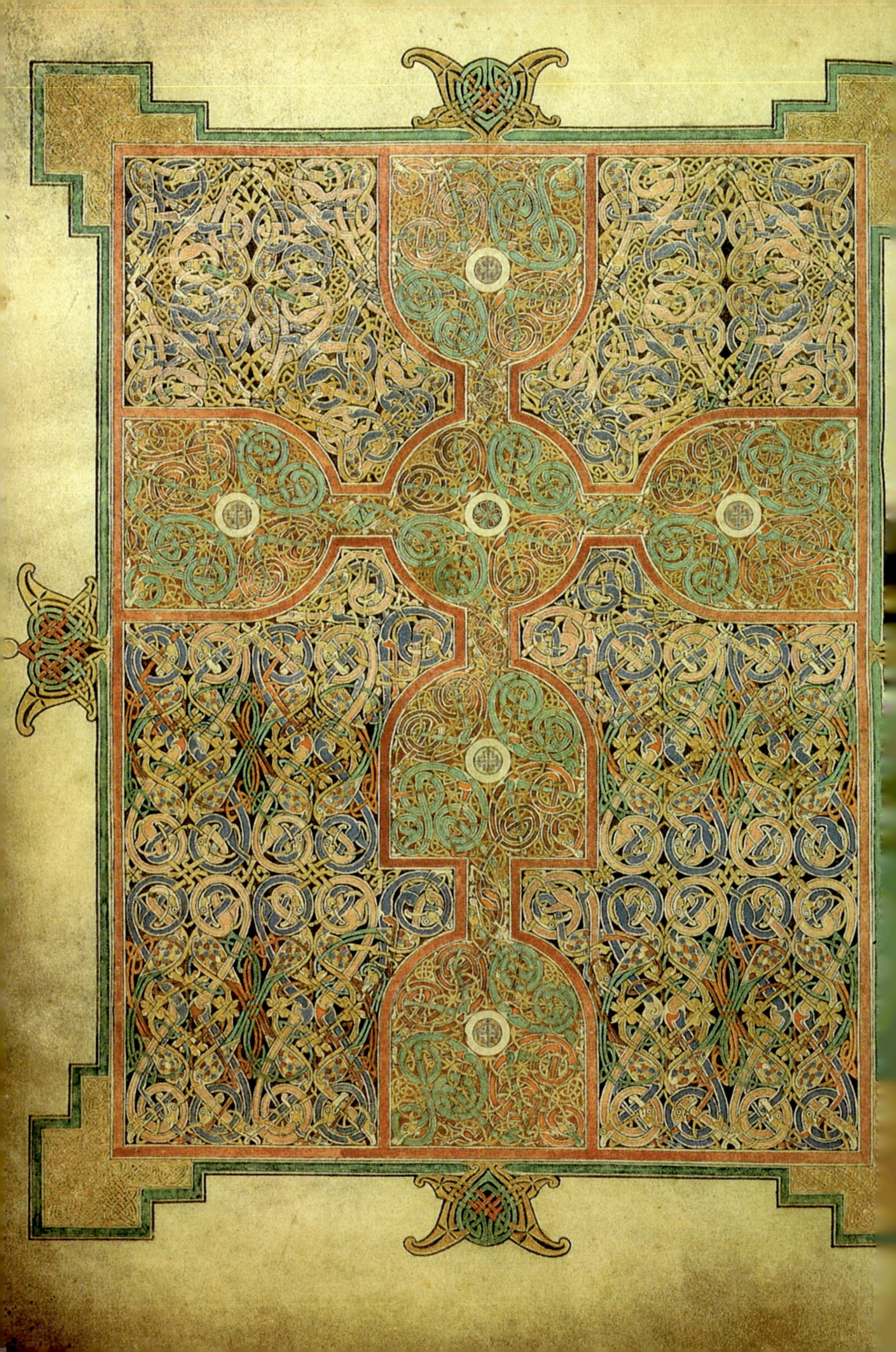

Chapter 7

Visions

Most people in the past thought that their gods could see them, and that they could, on particular occasions and in special places, see the gods. It's easy for us today to pour scorn on the worshipping of images and to maintain that people who follow such practices are just projecting their hopes and fears on to lifeless chunks of wood or plaster. But our ancestors could not conceive of a carving of the Madonna with a beatific face as just a length of painted wood any more than they could think that the moon was just a lump of light-reflecting rock. Anyone who has painted a face or sculpted a figure knows how it seems to acquire a presence of its own as soon as it is given eyes. When the great statues on Easter Island (p. 122, ill. 15) were invoked during family anniversary rituals, white coral eyes with black obsidian pupils were placed in their vacant eye sockets to awaken the ancestors and release their divine power. Making an image was a powerful, potentially dangerous process, and it had to be carefully controlled.

Many creation myths, including that in the Bible, claim that a divine being once sculpted human beings out of clay, and then breathed life into us. The gap between the forefingers of God and Adam (ill. 4) in Michelangelo's fresco on the ceiling of the Sistine Chapel in Rome has become one of the most famous artistic details in history. On a human level, the gap conveys the intensity of expectation that any lover feels when about to touch their loved one for the first time. In Michelangelo's picture, God is the lover. On another level, the gap represents the mystery that veils the origin of life. In today's animated films, we have bridged this famous

1 *The Lindisfarne Gospels*, 715–720 C.E., Cross Carpet Page introducing St Matthew's Gospel. Watercolour on vellum. British Library, London

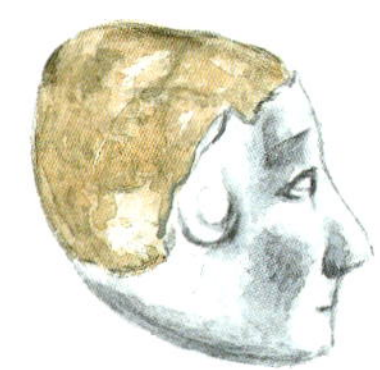

2 Skull with clay face found in the walls of Jericho, c. 7000 B.C.E.

gap with an electric spark, and we think we know its secret. But in fact scientists still don't know what triggered life in the first organic cell, from which all subsequent life eventually evolved. It's even possible that we might one day discover that that first cell was planted by some extraterrestrial intelligence. Despite all our chemical wizardry, we cannot yet create life from inanimate matter. But we can create images, and this ability is unique to us among our fellow animals. Bower birds can decorate their nests, but no creature apart from human beings can make an image of another being or of itself. It was logical to think, therefore, that our ability to make art was godlike. If that was so, then the images which we created might also be holy, or possibly demonic. What's more, we could inadvertently or intentionally mix the divine with the mundane. That was why religions were so wary of the power of images, and kept such a tight control over art.

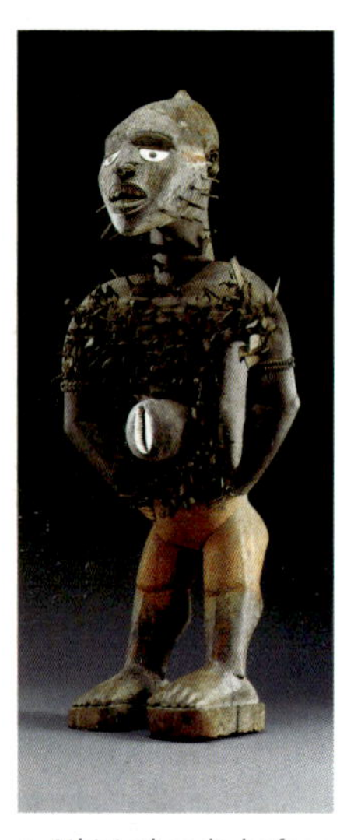

3 *Nkisi nkondi*, before 1878 C.E. Yombe, Democratic Republic of the Congo. Wood, metal, ivory, cowrie shell, height 83 cm. Detroit Institute of Arts

If art was a form of magic, could we not bring the dead back to life by painting and modelling their portraits, or at least provide a temporary resting home for their sad, displaced spirits? Such a belief might explain the strange skulls that were carefully hidden, in about 7000 B.C.E., in the foundations of the walls of Jericho – the very walls that later, according to biblical record, came tumbling down. The flesh had been remodelled on the bare bone in white plaster and their eye sockets set with white stones (ill. 2). The people of New Caledonia carved images of their relatives when they died and ended the period of mourning with the cry: "Go back now to your maternal kin in the forest. Leave us. We have loved you. We have made your portrait."

If statues were able to look, some had looks that could kill. *Nkisi nkondi* figures (ill. 3), used in the Congo in Africa, are wooden figurines that contained potent magic potions and could act in an unpredictable way. They could travel through the night and

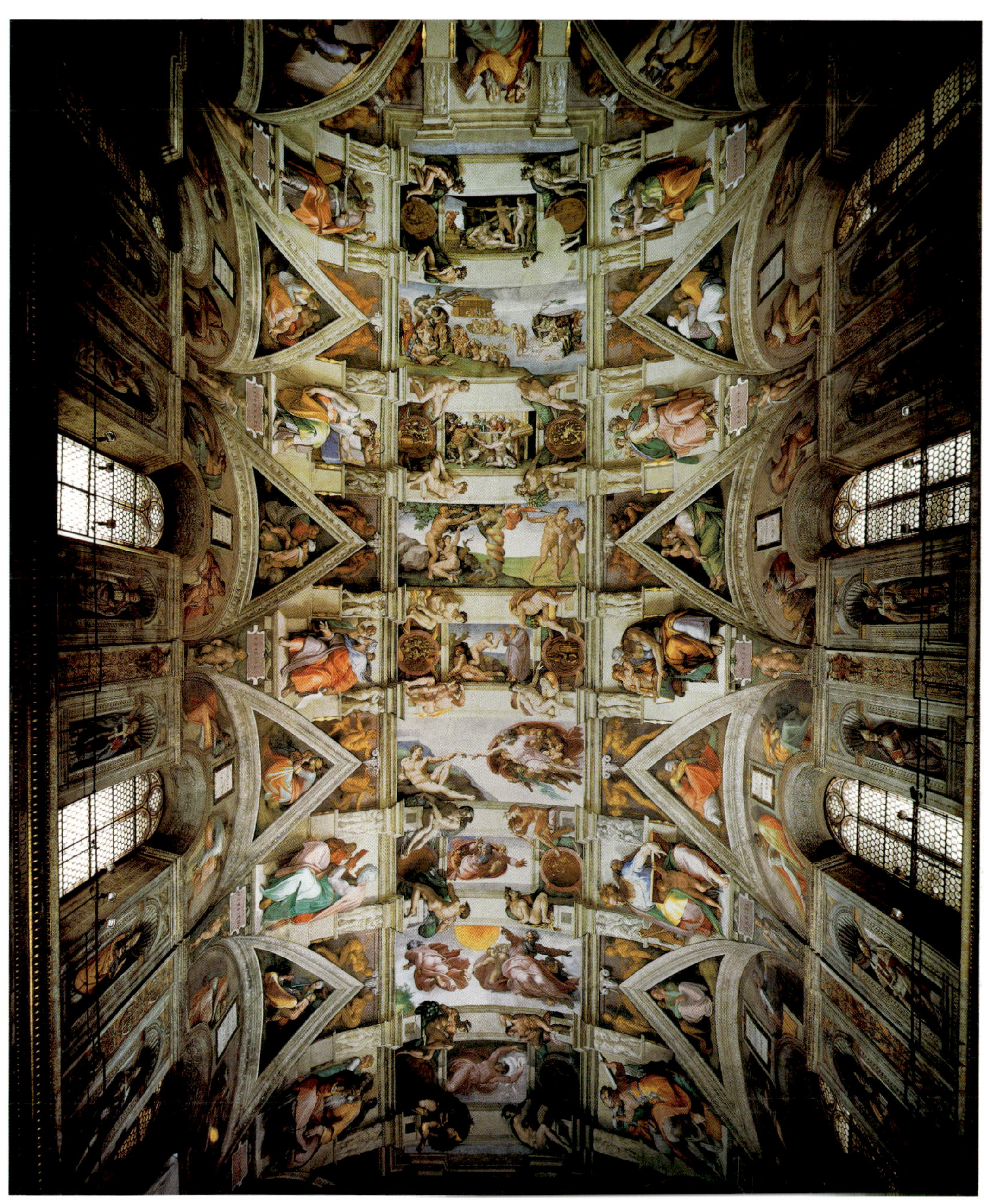

4 Michelangelo. Sistine Chapel Ceiling, 1508–10 and 1511–12, general view, including the Creation of Adam. Fresco. The Vatican, Rome

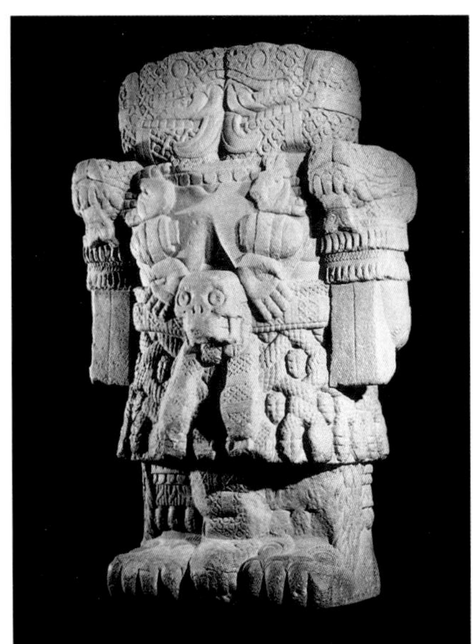

5 *Coatlicue*, 1325–1521 C.E. Aztec. 3.50 x 1.30 m. National Museum of Anthropology, Mexico City

inflict untold miseries on anyone who dared to cross their path. If you wished one to act for you, you drove a nail deep into its body, channelling all your hopes and fears to stir the statue's anger. You would usually tie a piece of clothing or hair to the nail which belonged to the person you wanted to curse, so that the *Nkisi nkondi* could quickly track its source. But they could as well protect you from potential harm. If you didn't know what was going wrong with you, or who was to blame, your prayer to the statue might be: "Lord Mutinu, if anyone is angry with me and it's a daylight matter, overlook it; but if it's witchcraft, seek it out!"

The ancient Greeks believed that there lived, in the westernmost extremities of the earth, a monster called Medusa, whose hair was made of writhing snakes. Her gaze turned anyone who met her eyes to stone. They were, as it happens, not far wrong. This huge statue – three and a half metres high – of the Aztec goddess Coatlicue (ill.5) must have struck terror into the hearts of all who were dragged before her. The full meaning of this complex image has been lost. The writhing rattlesnakes that form her head and shoulders, belt and skirt, and the skull and severed hands that hang before her breasts evoke a figure that is not just the earth mother described by the myths, but an all-encompassing embodiment of the irresistible forces of destruction and creation: a combination of Lord Shiva (p. 153, ill. 31) and the *Venus of Willendorf* (p. 113, ill. 44) on a colossal scale. Heads of snakes and rattle tails edge her dress; they evoke phalluses and corncobs. Even today, one has the feeling when one comes upon this statue – in the safety of the National Museum of Anthropology in Mexico City – that one has no right to look at her. Visitors turn away involuntarily, with a shudder. Human eyes were not meant to see such naked power. Two huge snakes, their teeth bared, clash head-on to form her massive skull. Their eyes become the two eyes that see you. Two become one as the sets of jaws lock together to create the terrible grin that completes Coatlicue's divided face. Was this a poetic insight into the force that modern scientists have discovered which binds the twin coils of DNA together when life begins? There are few more compelling and disturbing images in the world of art.

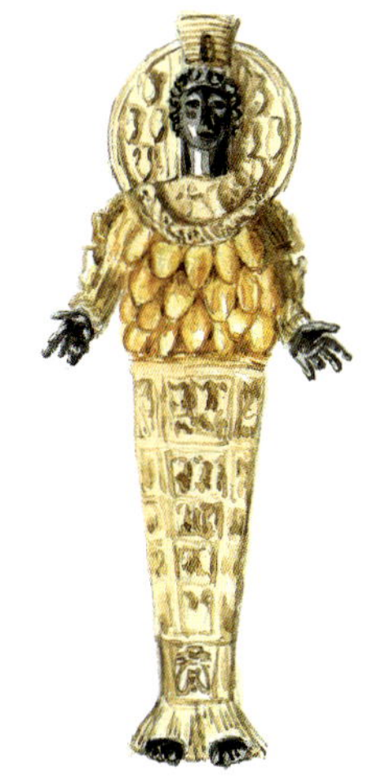

6 *Artemis of Ephesus*, c. 1st centuty C.E. Alabaster and bronze, height 2.03 m. National Archaeological Museum, Naples

Christian missionaries dismissed all such sculptures as barbaric devil worship. The Bible had long taught all its adherents not to "make unto thee any graven image, or any likeness of anything that is in heaven above, or that is in the earth beneath, or that is in the water under the earth: thou shalt not bow down thyself to them, nor serve them." In 54 C.E., St Paul preached at Ephesus that "there are no Gods which are made by hands". A certain Demetrius was not happy about this. He earned his living as a sculptor, carving images of the local deity, Artemis. She was famed for having several large breasts that hung about her chest like a huge bunch of grapes. Demetrius could carve them, if the client wished, so that they looked like a bull's testicles and also, if he went to the expense of using amber, like beads of honeydew. These additional layers of meaning greatly increased the goddess's perceived power and fertility (ill. 6). Demetrius rounded up a gang to lynch Paul, but he got wind of its approach and slipped away just in time to Macedonia.

Christianity and Islam both took their aversion to imagery from their parent faith, Judaism. The Jewish religion evolved over many centuries, as the fortunes of its followers ebbed and flowed. The Jews enjoyed periods of exceptional success and stability followed by periods of subjugation and exile. They therefore needed a transportable god who would help bind them together no matter how widely they were dispersed. Their god Jaweh was not territorial, as so many gods were in the past. Nor did he appear only in a particular temple. Nor was he embodied in an idol or in anything material that might in times of adversity have proved difficult to move. Instead he became a numinous presence that existed in everything and in particular in his chosen people, a god that was invisible but all-powerful, who loved justice and goodness and was wrathful against evil. God was the world, but at the same time he was not corporeal. This concept was confusing to many of the Jews' contemporaries, for how could anyone worship a god that you couldn't see? When the Roman general Pompey (106–48 B.C.E.) conquered Jerusalem, he tore apart the curtain masking the Holy of Holies in the temple and discovered to his amazement that it was empty. It is a concept of an invisible god that has survived unscathed into modern times partly because it was not undermined even when our understanding of the visible world changed.

Judaism and Islam remained adamant that it was not possible to make an image of God. Indeed they taught that it was sacrilegious even to make an attempt to do so. But Christianity soon began to waver, and found a pragmatic compromise. Unlike Judaism, it was a missionary religion, and wished to make converts. Buddhism, founded 500 years before Christianity, followed a similar course. At first imagery was outlawed, for it taught that infinity could not be seen. But as Buddhism was gradually transformed from a contemplative philosophy into a missionary religion, images came to be allowed as aids to worship. Some of the earliest Buddhist sculpture is to be found at the Great Stupa at Sanchi in India, which represents the Buddha's symbolic burial mound and the dome of heaven. It was erected between the third and first centuries B.C.E. In one scene showing the Buddha's miraculous walk on water his presence is indicated by a rectangular block of stone (ill.7). Five hundred years later it had become acceptable to render the Buddha as the familiar plump, smiling, pot-bellied middle-aged man sitting cross-legged on a lotus flower with his eyes half-closed, meditating. Purists argued that these images were, of course, not gods in themselves, but they rapidly acquired that status in the popular imagination. Images grew larger. They were increasingly encrusted with gold, and hung with tokens, of hope for broken limbs or gratitude for diseases caught or cured. Soon many came to be paraded through the streets, particularly in times of famine or of plague, drawing as much emotion from the crowd as any idol of old.

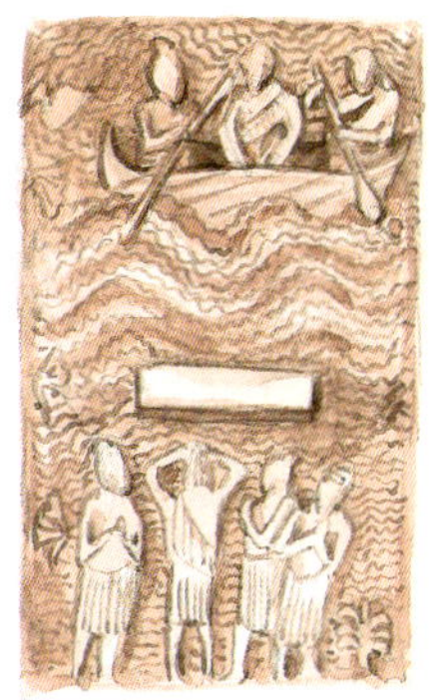

7 *The Buddha Walking on Water*, c.100 B.C.E., detail from the gateway to the Great Stupa. Stone relief. Sanchi, India

The histories of Christianity and Buddhism are marked by rising tides of image-making, followed by counter-reactions as the leaders of each religion tried to return it to its humble roots and sweep away anything that appeared to be distracting its followers from contemplating their religion's ineffable source. The Franciscan and the Dominican orders of monks, founded in 1209 and 1215 respectively, advocated the simple life. They abandoned the fancy gold-embroidered vestments of high church priests and wore instead simple habits of Dominican black and white or Franciscan brown, tied around the waist with a length of plain rope. Their early monasteries were beautifully simple, arched but undecorated constructions, though the Franciscans, at first, preferred to live under nature's vault. A similar reaction occurred in Buddhism at almost exactly the same time. Zen Buddhism emerged in China, but soon spread to Japan where it found its most refined expression. The Zen Buddhist temples in Kyoto, with their austere black and white interiors and gardens of rocks, gravel, moss and the occasional tree, were designed to stimulate spiritual contemplation. There are no images of the Buddha, vast, plump and gilded, as there were in conventional Buddhist temples: there is simply nature and a contemplative mind.

In sixteenth-century Europe, Christianity suffered another reaction against images. In 1506, Pope Julius II decided to pull down the old Church of St Peter's in Rome to build a new, vastly more splendid one. With good reason, he was determined to harness the remarkable wave of creativity that we now call the Renaissance to the cause of God. In 1508 he commissioned Michelangelo to paint a new fresco sequence on the ceiling of the Sistine Chapel in the Vatican (ill.4). Looking up at it today—unbelievably the single-handed, back-aching work of one man—it is as if the heavens have opened to reveal the whole force of God's creation. The Bible said that God had made man in his own image, therefore God and the assembled heavenly host must look like perfect human beings, and there was nothing Michelangelo enjoyed better than imaging idealised youths from every angle. The ceiling is certainly imbued with erotic passion, but it's also agitated by an all-encompassing energy that is new in art. Perhaps this was an expression of a growing presentiment not just on Michelangelo's part—that the heavens were not the eternally peaceful, static and stately hierarchy that man had so long believed, but were in fact whirling in restless motion.

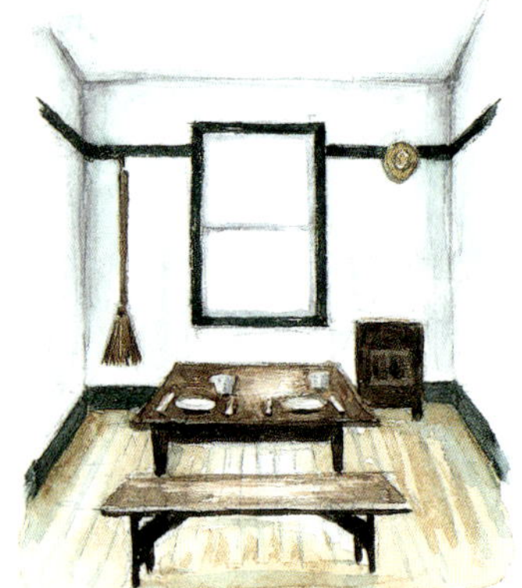

8 Dining room in house at Pleasant Hill, Harrodsburg, Kentucky

As far as the Pope was concerned, Michelangelo's achievement merely added to the Church's glory. But to raise the huge funds he needed for his new St Peter's, the Pope charged his supplicants higher taxes and sold "indulgences" to people who could afford them; these were, essentially, fast-track passports to heaven. In 1517 Martin Luther declared that mankind's salvation depended on the grace of God, not on building magnificent churches or buying favours. Protestantism subsequently spread rapidly through northern Europe, especially, of course, among those who had additional financial and political reasons to free themselves from the yoke of Rome, for faith is rarely, if ever, the sole cause of a dispute.

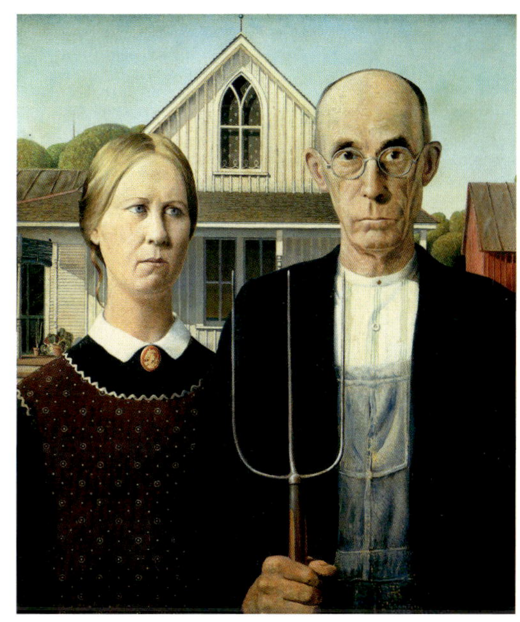

9 Grant Wood. *American Gothic*, 1930. Oil on compressed fibreboard, 74.3 x 62.4 cm. The Art Institute of Chicago

Perhaps the most beautiful visual expression of the ensuing new Puritanism appeared in America, where the pilgrim fathers, driven out of Anglican Great Britain, sought to create a Christian paradise–once they had cleared the land of the "heathens" who were inconveniently already living there. The Shakers, named after their shaman-like trance-inducing dances, developed a style of living that was entirely in keeping with their beliefs in communal property, pacifism, equality, celibacy, efficient work, and the all-knowing omnipresence of an invisible God. Father Joseph Meacham summed it up: "Plainness and simplicity is becoming to the people of God." Nothing fancy was allowed to "feed the pride and vanity of man." Mirrors could not be larger than 45 by 30 centimetres–there was no need to see anything but your face–and sexual intercourse was forbiden, which was one reason why membership declined. Everything was regulated to ensure that maximum time was spent on spiritual development (ill.8).

This puritan spirit survived in America into the twentieth century, and can be seen in this portrait of a poor farmer with his spinster daughter in Cedar Rapids, Iowa (ill 9), entitled *American*

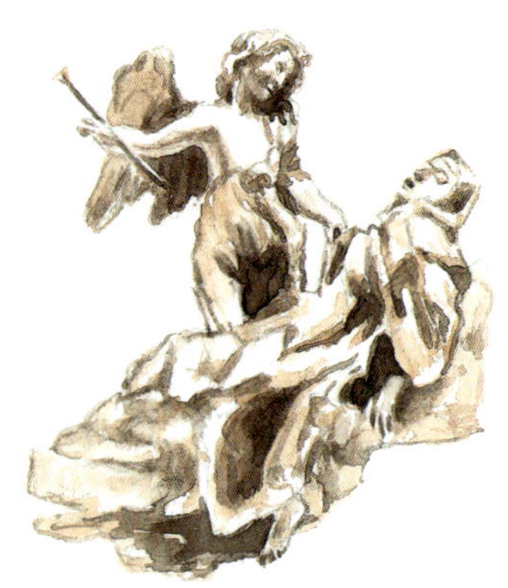

10 Gianlorenzo Bernini. *The Ecstasy of Saint Teresa*, 1651. Marble. Altar of the Cornaro Chapel, S. Maria della Vittoria, Rome

Gothic. Good, honest, hard-working people are, in themselves, the New World's Gothic churches. The three spikes of the husbandman's fork—so precisely painted and placed—represent the cathedral's spires. They symbolise the trinity of the Christian faith, and the three crosses upon which Christ, and two thieves, were crucified.

Nothing could be further from this picture of humble rectitude than this image of St Teresa of Avila (ill. 10), caught in a moment of orgasmic, spiritual ecstasy. Both are Christian, both feature spikes, but the image in the latter is quite different. St Teresa wrote in her autobiography: "I would see beside me … an angel in bodily form … not tall, but short and very beautiful, his face so aflame that he appeared to be one of the highest types of angels … In his hands I saw a long golden spear and at the end of the iron tip … a point of fire. With this he seemed to pierce my heart several times so that it penetrated to my entrails. When he drew it out, I thought he was drawing them out with it and he left me completely on fire with a great love of God. The pain was so sharp that it made me utter several moans; and so excessive was the sweetness caused by this intense pain that one can never wish to lose it." Was it possible that one could glimpse god not only in moments of quiet contemplation but also during instants of heightened passion? Christianity has had a complex, duplicitous and generally closed attitude towards sex. It developed the peculiar notion of the virgin birth, for how could the son of god have been born from a man's semen and a woman whose blooded waters fell to earth?

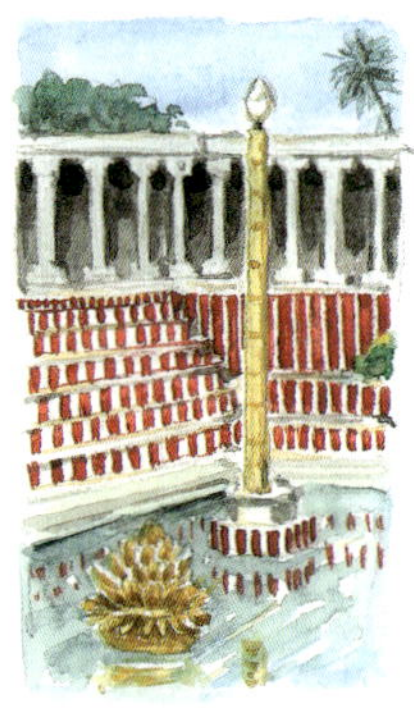

11 Painted steps leading down to the golden lotus reservoir at the Meenakshi-Sundareshwarar Temple, Madurai, southern India

Hinduism saw meaning in this conjunction however. The steps up to every shrine in the vast temple complex at Madurai in southern India and those leading down to the golden lotus reservoir are all painted with vertical stripes of red and white (ill. 11). The temple is the home of Sundareshwara, and his wife Meenakshi, southern Indian personifications of the Lord Shiva and his consort Parvati. Red in Hinduism symbolises the blood of life and the vulva, and white the ashes of death and semen. In the main shrine at Madurai, topped by a golden tower, is Shiva's symbol, the lingam: his erect penis, carved in stone, and black and glistening from the centuries of having oil poured over it. On its tip, priests often place the succulent white flowers of sweet-smelling jasmine and frangipani. Village houses in India are surrounded by flowers grown for the gods. Hindu gods love flowers; they are the beauteous display of a plant's sexual organs, without which there would be no food for people, animals or the gods. When Europeans discovered the sexual life of plants three hundred years ago, many people were deeply shocked. The white lily and the red rose, both sacred to the Virgin Mary, appeared defiled. But in India purity and sex are not in conflict, but rather confluent. In the temple at Madurai, the god and goddess live apart by day, but as soon as night falls, the god is carried through the temple in a silver palanquin and, once his feet have been washed by the high priest, he joins his wife in her bedchamber so that they can enjoy the serious business of procreation.

Since the gods enjoyed sexual relationships, some thought that sex could be a way to the gods. In certain Hindu-related Tantric sects of Buddhism (Hinduism and Buddhism, like Islam and Christianity, are closely intertwined) it was thought possible to use sexual passion as a sort of spiritual rocket fuel to shoot the soul into the heavenly realm above. Tantric priests were supplied with beautiful young virgins (ill. 12) who aroused them to an orgasmic climax which they were

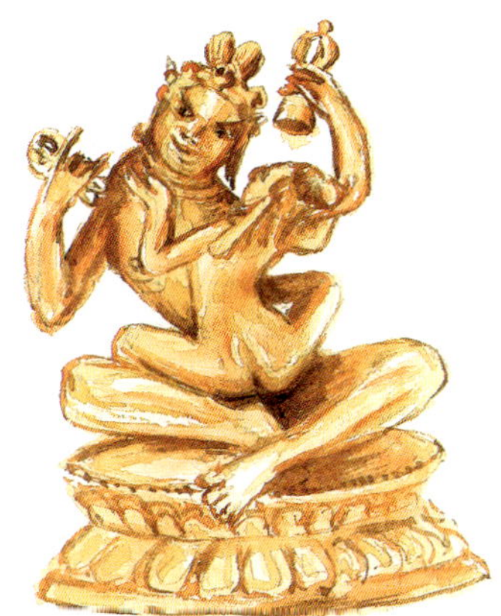

12 The Tantric Buddhist Saint Gandhapa performing ritual intercourse with a virgin, 16th century. Tibet. Gilded bronze. Gulbenkian Museum of Oriental Art, Durham, England

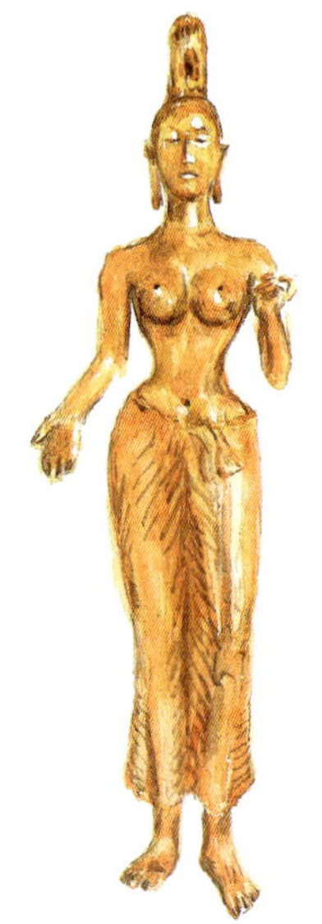

13 *Standing Tara*, 7th–8th century C.E., Sri Lanka. Cast bronze, gilded. British Museum, London

then, reputedly, able to hold and redirect to a higher cause. There was a widespread belief that men were allocated a set amount of semen at birth. Every ejaculation reduced this store and with it, its owner's lifespan. Withheld ejaculations were believed to increase longevity and push one's spiritual being up a notch or two. The ultimate union of the soul with god was conceived in Tantric teaching as an orgasmic embrace – the perfect fusion of wisdom (female) with compassion (male). In Tibetan Buddhism, Avalokitesvara is the god of compassion. He wanders the lower worlds, bringing new hope to those reincarnated as worms, and refreshing water to those roasting in the fires of hell. His helpmeet and consort, who pleads each sufferer's cause, is the beautiful, buxom Tara (ill. 13), who was born from his tears. One cannot imagine a figure more diametrically different to the Christians' discreetly robed Virgin Mary, though people pray to each for the same reason in different parts of the world – to bring them mercy.

Passion fires up the body. We think of this rising temperature nowadays only in terms of anger and desire. But in the past earthly love had a spiritual dimension, just as fire rises and aspires to heaven. Nicholas Hilliard was a miniature painter and jeweller who worked for the court of Queen Elizabeth I and was a con-

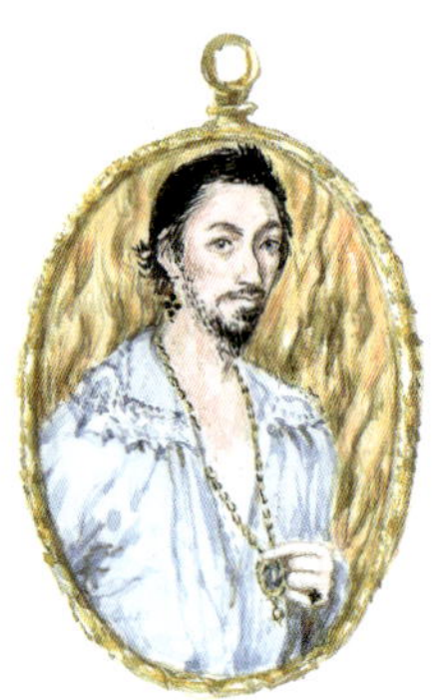

14 After Nicholas Hilliard. *Young Man against a Background of Flames*, c.1600. Victoria and Albert Museum, London

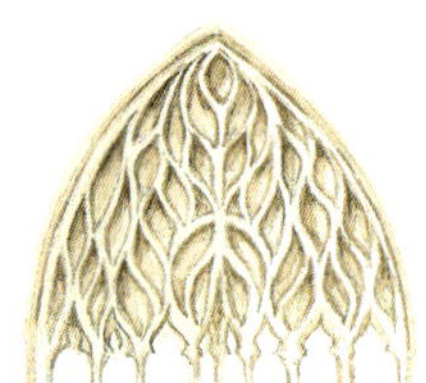

15 Flamboyant Gothic façade, c.1500. Church of the Trinity, Vendôme

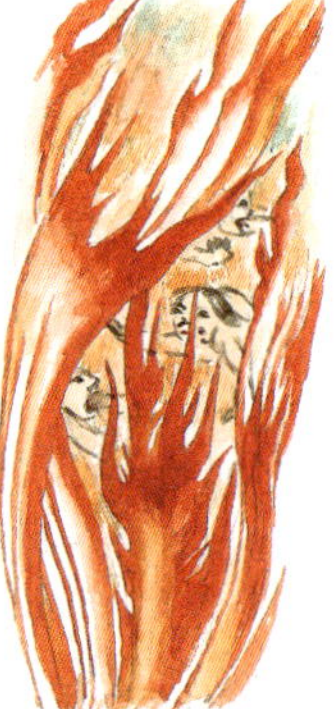

16 *Jigoku Zoshi* (Hell Scroll), 12th century C.E., Kamakuri period, detail. National Museum, Tokyo

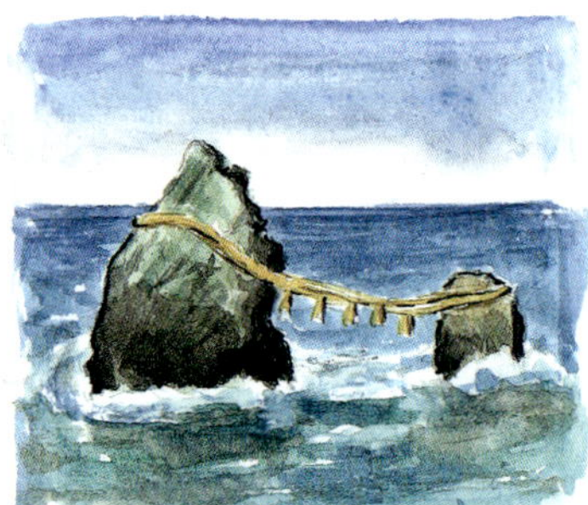

17 *Meota-iwa* ("wedded rocks"), Futamigaura Bay, Japan

temporary of Shakespeare. He painted love tokens for the rich to wear on chains around their necks. One shows an unknown young man against a background of flames (ill. 14). These do not burn him. Nor are the flames that flicker up the spires of Gothic cathedrals and break out in every lancet window arch (ill. 15) destructive. They symbolise the life-giving love of God. The flames of hell (ill. 16)—the opposite side to god's uplifting love—were life-sustaining too. They ensured that the sinful would go on suffering—in those few cultures in the West and East which maintained a belief in eternal damnation.

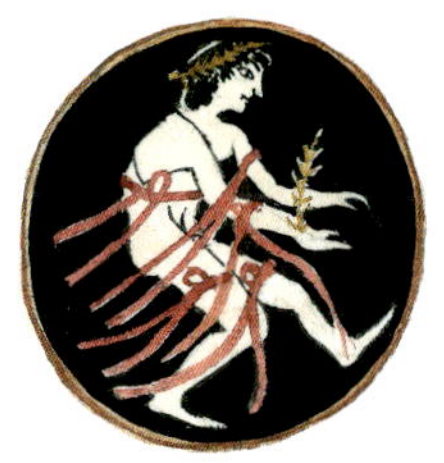

18 Drinking Cup by Oltos showing a victorious athlete garlanded with ribbons, 5th century B.C.E. Athenian. Staatliche Museen zu Berlin

Many cultures around the world, particularly in the East, have taught that the beautiful sights of nature are in themselves sources of goodness and gateways to spiritual enlightenment, while at the same time being unashamedly products of sexual congress. Shinto—the oldest religion of Japan—has, like Hinduism, no known founder, but emerged out of the ancient worship of the gods who were believed to inhabit the mountains, trees, rivers and valleys of Japan. These marriage rocks in Futamigaura Bay (ill. 17) were believed to be Izanami and Izanagi, from whose sexual union the Japanese archipelago was supposed to have been created. They are still worshipped as personifications of steadfastness in marriage. The sacred rice-straw rope through which no evil can pass—the *shimenawa*—that binds these rocks together is made of two thick strands plaited together symbolising the positive and negative threads of life to which nature owes its existence—a remarkable prefiguration of the structure of DNA.

All sacred natural sights in Japan are hung with *shimenawa*, in the same way that the Greeks bound the prize-winning attributes of athletes, such as thighs and forearms, with ribbons (ill. 18) in their worship of divine-

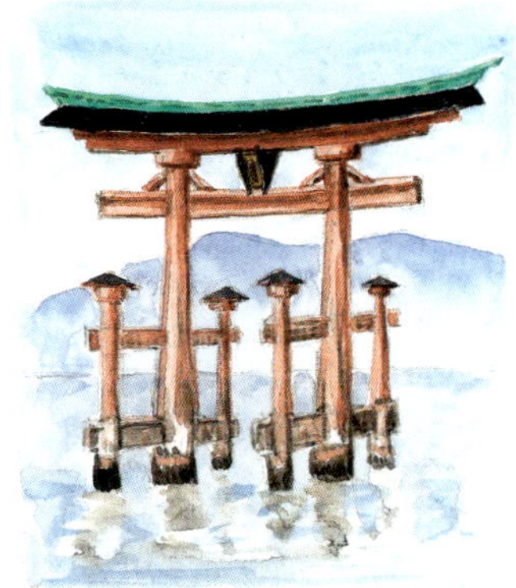

19 Torii Arch at the It-sukushima Shrine, Miya-Jima Island, Japan

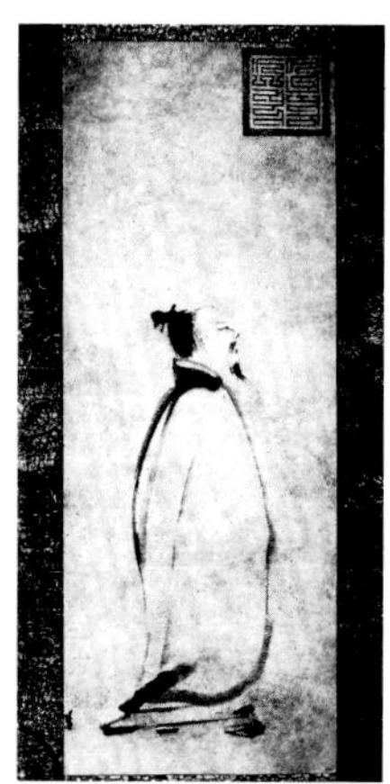

20 Liang K'ai, *Portrait of the Poet Li Bo*, early 13th century C.E. Chinese, southern Song. Ink on paper. National Museum, Tokyo

ly proportioned parts of the human body. Beauty spots in Japan are often marked with Torii arches (ill.19), indicating the presence of a gateway leading to spiritual ground. Painted red, they are also suggestive of a vulva. The ancient It-sukushima shrine is built in the tidal zone along the beach. When the tide is high, the temple and the distant Torii appear to float. A butterfly dance, performed since medieval times on an open platform hovering over this tidal scene of outstanding beauty, symbolises the rebirth of the soul into the spiritual world.

Confucius (551–479 B.C.E.) advocated humane governance based on naturalness. He loved walking through beautiful countryside. One of the oldest pieces of music in the world, "The Elegant Orchid", is attributed to him. It was composed when Confucius saw a field of flowers in a desolate valley, which he likened to his ideas of good government that the princes had not been persuaded to follow. Ever since, poets (ill.20) have wandered through China seeking inspiration from the sights of nature. Confucius advocated a practical philosophy, not a religion, although centuries later he came to be worshipped as an ancestral god, and Confucianism acquired all the trappings of a state religion.

The same fate befell Taoism, founded by Lao Zi, said to have been a contemporary of Confucius (if he existed at all) who argued that human beings are merely part of nature, and that anything we try to do that violates or dominates nature is evil. A return to nature is the only salvation—so Taoists priests are meant to live as hermits contemplating the changing seasons, though many spend their lives officiating at gilded temples. Taoism advocates that gateways to the spiritual life could be found in the humblest activities. One student spends years searching for a master. He eventually finds one who is sweeping leaves, but the master refuses to talk to him. Years later, the student

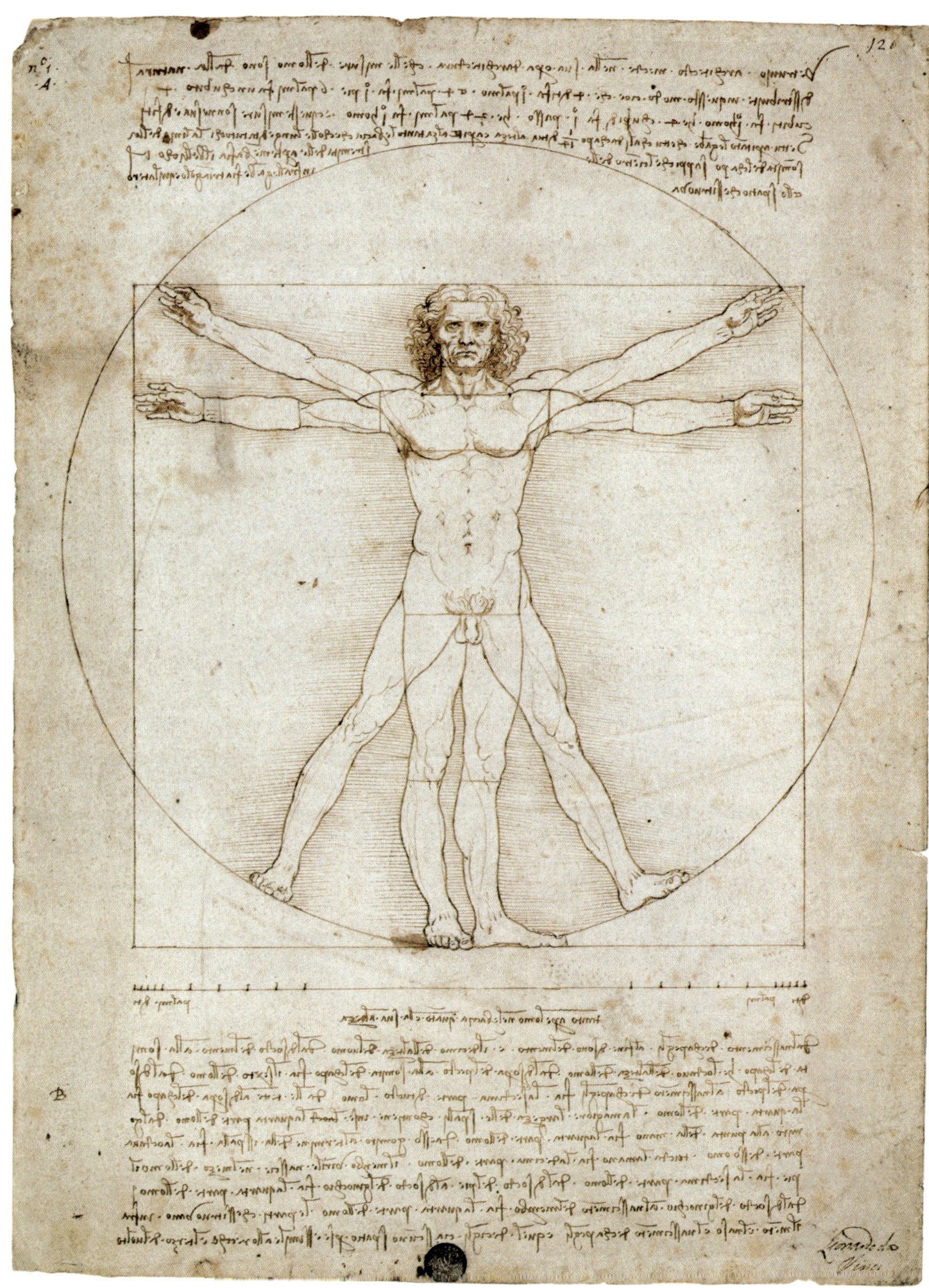

21 Leonardo da Vinci. Human Figure in a Circle, showing that the body forms a square when at rest, but a circle when dynamic, c.1485–90. 34.5 x 24.5 cm. Accademia, Venice

finds himself sweeping leaves and understands at last what his master has taught him. Another master, while instructing his students, points to the moon, and then rebukes them for looking at his finger.

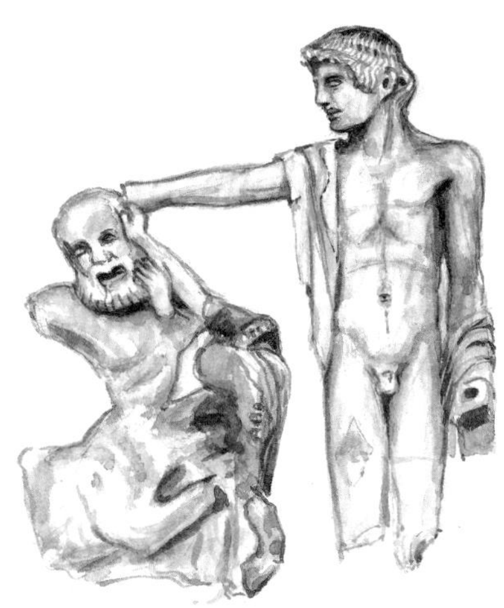

22 Apollo and Centaur 468—56 B.C.E., central motif, west pediment, Temple of Zeus. National Archaeological Museum, Olympia, Greece

The gods might be beyond our sight and comprehension, but there was a feeling their divinity could be glimpsed in the hidden order that seemed to underlie all creation. As the English poet Sir John Davies wrote in his poem *Orchestra*, in 1596: "Kind nature first doth make all things to love / Love makes them dance and in just order move." The mathematics underlying musical scales, harmonious designs and the proportions of the body—our height, for example, is exactly equal to our outstretched span from fingertip to fingertip (ill.21)—were all thought to be evidence of the marvellous handiwork of God. And it was that same divine creator who had gifted mankind alone with the particularly godlike faculty of thought. Socrates (469–399 B.C.E.), whose philosophy influenced his pupil Plato's theory that everything is a distorted shadow of its ideal, observed the fact that ordinary objects, like cheap pots or pebbles, which have little aesthetic merit individually, can reveal beautiful harmonies when arranged in a row—what he called "the form of the good".

The statues on the pediment of the Temple of Zeus at Olympia in Greece were found in pieces on the ground, and we are not sure of their original configuration. However, this group (ill.22) is interpreted as Apollo, god of reason and light, admonishing a centaur. Centaurs were half-man half-horse beings whose origins perhaps lay in a demonisation of the nomadic tribes who drove their cattle on horseback through the wilder regions of Greece.

The centaurs had been invited to a wedding where they got drunk and tried to carry off the women. The victory represented is of order over chaos, and thought over sensuality.

When the sculptures of Benin (ill.23) were pillaged by British troops in the nineteenth century and the even earlier sculptures of Ife (ill.24) were brought to the attention of European scholars, it was thought that they couldn't possibly have been created by "primitive" people in "darkest" Africa but had to have been made by Greek or Roman craftsmen, or at least copied from their work. In fact, a great school of sculpture had emerged independently along the banks of the River Niger in Africa. These were the flowers of a culture that also valued order and gracefulness as a manifestation of divinity. This is expressed in depictions of people whose beautiful proportions are emphasised by repeated striations which probably reflect painted decorations or scarification, and appear by their arrangement to draw power down from above, and perhaps lift the spirits up, as in a head held high.

Westerners, in their prejudices, tend to assume that all African sculpture is dynamic; they hear drum beats and imagine vigorous dances. But the majority of African sculpture is, in fact, symmetrical and quiet, and the eyes in the faces are, more often than not, shut. There might be tremendous energy in the forms, but the power is usually stilled. In Mali, among the Bamana people, Faro is the goddess of water and the mother of all mankind (ill.25).

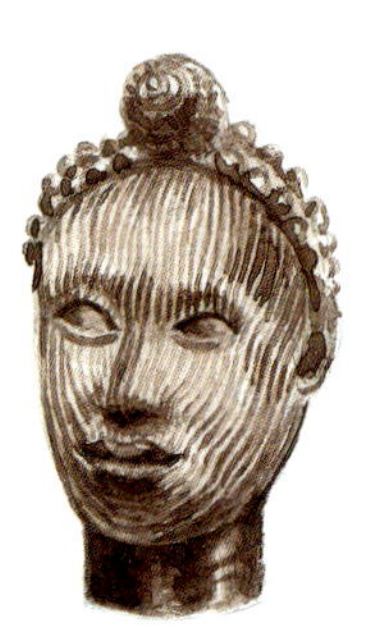

23 Crowned head of an Oni, c. 12th–15th century. Ife. Zinc and brass, 24 cm high. The National Commission for Museums and Monuments, Ife, Nigeria

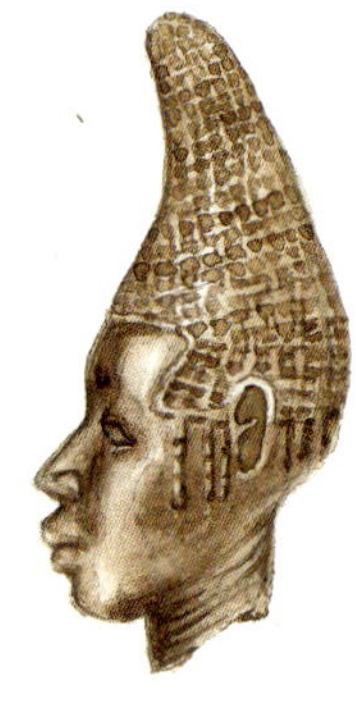

24 Head of Queen Mother, 16th century C.E., Benin. Brass, 35 cm high. National Museums and Galleries of Merseyside, Liverpool

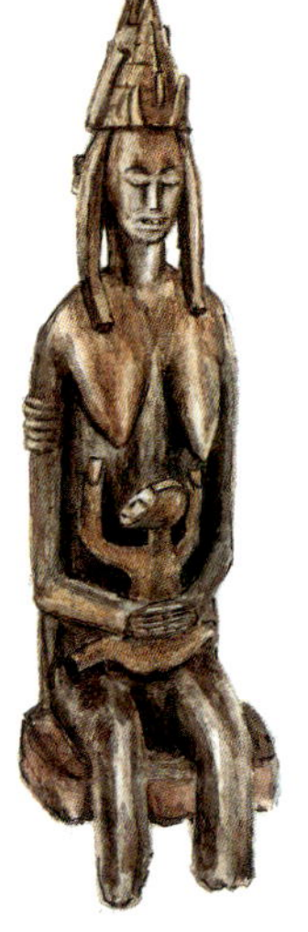

25 Mother and Child, 19th–20th century C.E., Bamana, Mali. Wood, 123.5 cm high. Metropolitan Museum of Art, New York

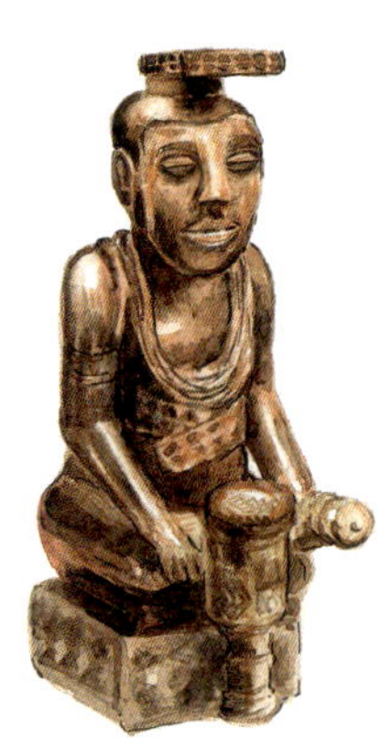

26 Ndop Figure of a King, 18th–19th century C.E. Kuba (Bushoong), Nshyeeng. Democratic Republic of the Congo. Royal Museum for Central Africa, Tervuren, Belgium

She appears in thunder and lightning, which is perhaps illustrated here on her peaked celestial hat, and is shown either as pregnant or holding a child, who is always male. The goddess appeared on many occasions during the ritual life of the Bamana, particularly during initiations in the sacred grove at night when hymns calling for "Yeelen! Yeelen" (Light! Light!) were sung in her honour. She could lead mankind along the spiritual path at the end of which waits Matigi, the master and creator of all things. Her closed eyes indicate that she has already begun to take her followers on that journey.

The Kuba people of the Congo carved statues of their kings at coronations. These figures maintained their presence when they were away from the court, and embodied their spirits when they died. In this sculpture (ill.26) a Kuba king is shown sitting cross-legged on a dais, with the drum and sword symbolic of his power. His eyes are closed and his expression composed, showing that he is performing his main function, which is to keep in close contact with the spirit world in order to ensure that everything is harmonious below, on earth. Closed eyes usually indicate higher thoughts. The Buddha is almost invariably depicted with his eyes nearly shut—he is aware of this world only enough to help lift followers on to a higher plane. Sufi mystics—adherents of a sect of Islam which developed in the ninth century C.E. and which includes the whirling dervishes—always dance with their eyes shut, so that they can make direct contact with Allah.

If a better, spiritual world did exist apart from our own, the problem then was how to get there. To use Scottish historian Ninian Smart's brilliant analogy, developed for his pioneering comparative studies of religion: some believed that you were saved by god reaching down—you didn't have to work for your salvation; you were just like a kitten carried out of danger by its mother. Others taught that you were saved by reaching up—you had to work for your own salvation, like a young monkey clinging to its mother. And there were some who thought that god would meet you halfway. But what they all agreed on was that mankind's noblest ambition was to quit this mortal coil. The Buddha (c. 563-c. 483 B.C.E.) taught that the way to escape the inevitable suffering of life and achieve spiritual elevation is not through self-sacrifice, but by seeking the Middle Way through the Four Divine Dwelling Places—friendliness, compassion, sympathy and equanimity. So one could rise, through several reincarnations, to that state of being when one's spirit is at one with all creation, the blissful state of nirvana. Myths accrued about the Buddha—including one which said that, like Jesus, he was not born of man. His mother dreamed that she was impregnated by a white elephant, and subsequently lost all desire for sex, which amounts to a virgin birth of sorts. In time the Buddha's spiritual journey came to be symbolised by the lotus (ill. 27) whose roots are stuck in the muddy waters of materialism but whose flower unfolds as a bowl of light in the heavenly air above the waterline. The symmetry of the lotus is like that of the butterfly, with its perfectly matched, abstract-patterned wings. From out of the twisted root or the lumbering caterpillar a divine beauty is born (ill. 28).

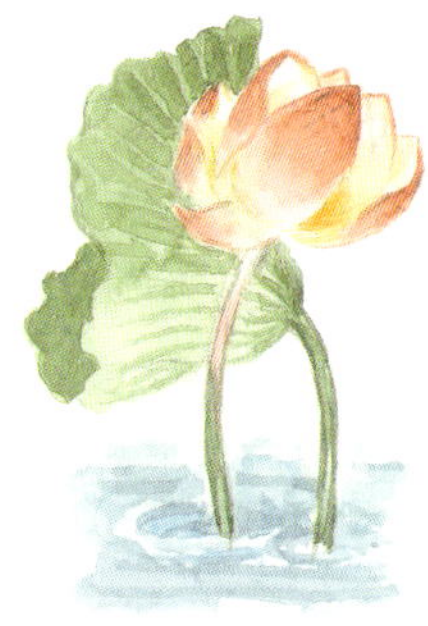

27 Lotus flower

On a vast, high, barren plateau at Nazca in southern Peru there are traces of the prayers of people who eked out a desperate living there one and a half thousand years ago. Rain hardly ever falls there, and because of this their prayers have survived. These people depended almost entirely on water reaching them in underground rivulets from the distant Andes. But when these waters failed, the people left the dry creeks and climbed up on to the high plateau to draw pictures for the gods. They removed the dark stones that littered the flat surface to reveal the paler dusty

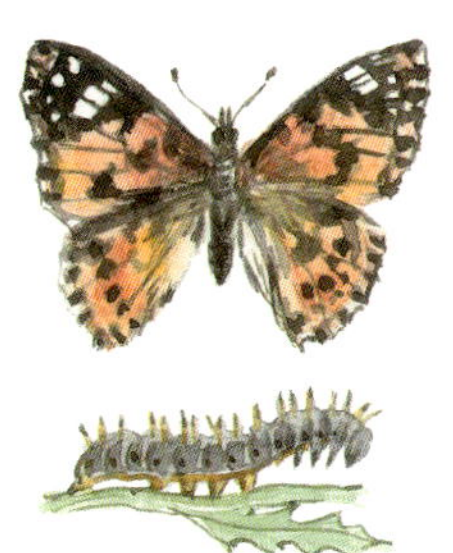

28 Painted lady butterfly with its caterpillar

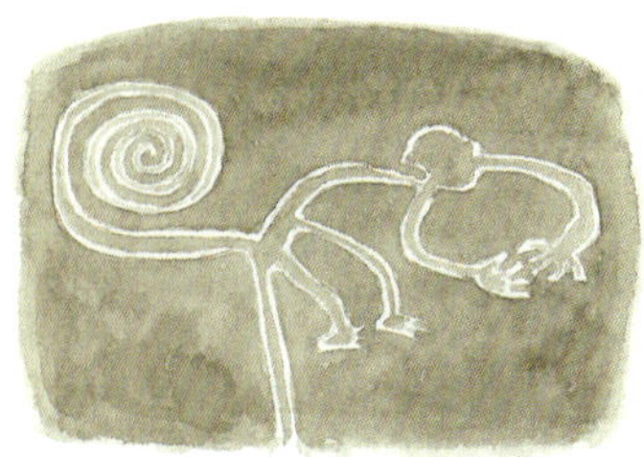

29 Spider monkey, 200–700 C.E. Traced in a single line 1.5 kilometres long. Earth drawing. Nazca, Peru

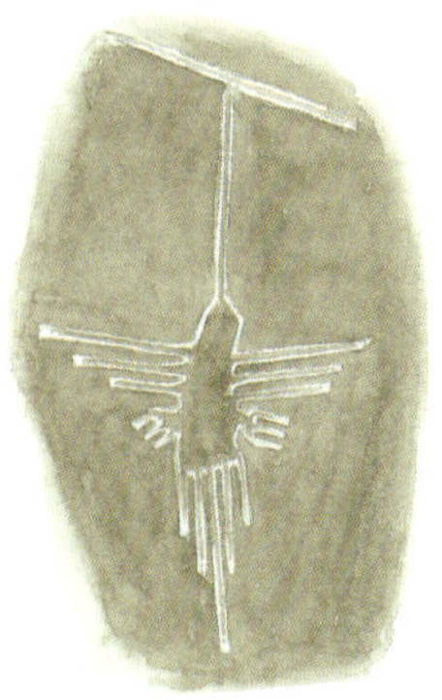

30 Hummingbird, 200–700 C.E. Earth drawing. Nazca, Peru

rock beneath, making patterns of straight lines and highly stylised drawings of animals on such a colossal scale that they only make sense when seen from the air. Several of the straight lines point towards distant mountain peaks, and the drawing, always traced by single, continuous lines, depict creatures from the rain forest such as the monkey (ill.29) and the hummingbird (ill.30). It is believed that these lines formed ceremonial paths trodden repeatedly by people as they prayed for rain to fall in the distant mountains. The patterns were writ large to be seen by the gods. The monkey could have represented a constellation that included the Great Bear, which appeared above the horizon just as the rainy season was due to start far to the east. The Nazca lines are a remarkable, fragile survival of rituals that must have been much more widespread; obsessive processions made by desperate people at the mercy of the elements, and not able to live elsewhere because hostile tribes fiercely defended their more fertile territories.

The belief in the power of ceremonial procession seems to be deeply rooted in the human psyche, because it is found in so many ages and cultures around the world. At Chartres Cathedral in France there is a remarkable, huge labyrinth mapped out in tiles on the floor (ill.31). It used to have a bronze plaque in its centre showing Theseus and the Minotaur, an unusually explicit echo of a pre-Christian tradition. Pilgrims would drag themselves around this labyrinth on their knees, in a ritual which symbolised the soul's journey to the heavenly Jerusalem, of which the church around them was a jewelled representation. This journey first took them near to god – as children supposedly were – and then further and further away, until, after a brief second childhood, they faced their maker at the end. The concept of life as a continuous thread is very ancient; many believed that it was necessary to retrace its length if you were seeking what had gone wrong in the past and what you had to do to put things right in the future. This mask of Humbaba (ill. 32), the Assyrian god of death, is a model made out clay to show how the god's face could appear in the intestine of a sheep when it was removed after sacrifice. Intestines and livers were widely used for fortune-telling.

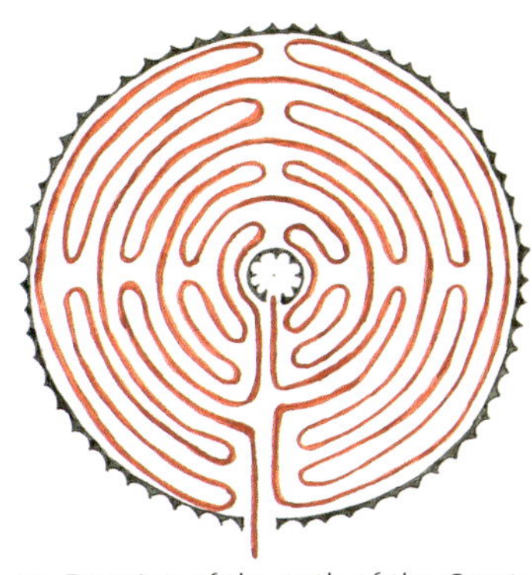

31 Drawing of the path of the Great Labyrinth on the floor of Chartres Cathedral, c. 1200. 12.89 m diameter

The continuous thread had long been a key symbol of the ancient Celtic and Viking cultures of northern Europe when Christian settlers, with typical pragmatic skill, found a way of marrying their imagery with the symbolism of the earlier faiths. A cross emerges out of the extraordinarily complex interlocking tracery on the four pages that introduced the gospels in the Lindisfarne New Testament (ill. 1). These illuminations were painted on vellum by one monk over a period of five years, between 715 and 720 C.E., during the hours he had left between eight daily services and his other monastic labours. These almost abstract pages—now known as cross-carpets—preceded each gospel, and prepared the reader for entry on to holy ground.

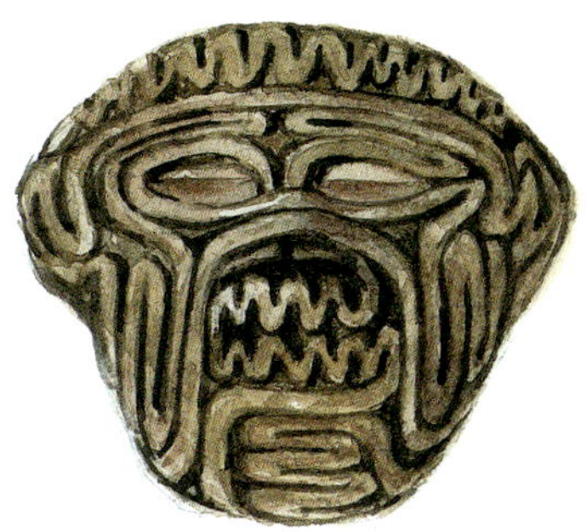

32 The face of Humbaba, c. 1700 B.C.E., Mesopotamia. Clay. British Museum, London

They served the same function as the abstract, patterned carpets which Muslims unroll five times a day on which to say their prayers to Allah, facing Mecca. The rugs represent the temporary presence of a sacred place on earth. The holy carpets of Islam—one of the greatest artistic expressions of this faith—were intended to open "sky windows" on to heaven. They are not supposed to remain under one's feet, but to lift one on to a higher plane—magic carpets indeed. The Koran explains the immanence and transcendence of God in these terms: "God is the Light of the heavens and the earth; the likeness of His Light is a niche wherein is a lamp–the lamp in a glass, the glass as it were a glittering star." The Ardabil Carpet (ill.33)–one of the largest in the world, and one of a pair–is an image of this text. It has two lamps, one larger than the other, but it's designed so that the larger lamp looks the same size as the smaller one when viewed from the further edge, as the worshipper bows to pray towards Mecca. This optical illusion has the extraordinary effect of making the further lamp appear to float, magically, in a field of flowers bathed in light. The carpet was designed by Maqsud of Kashan and woven in wool and silk from 1539 to 1540 C.E. It has a signature and the inscription "Other than thy threshold I have not a refuge in the world."

The Nazca lines, the Lindisfarne Gospels and the Ardabil Carpet are all abstractions based on repeated movements. Repetition is a key ingredient of prayer. Hindu temple mounds represent the tiers upon tiers of reincarnations by which souls ascend to heaven. The topmost finial stands directly over the inner sanctum in its base, which contains the holy phallus–the lingam also known as the Adavallan, "one who dances well". The repeated abstract decorations on their sides (ill.34) represent the phallus and the vulva and the conch, together with the Sanskrit sign for Om, the primal sound of all creation. Most religions have sophisticated abstract symbols that enable

33 Maqsud of Kashan. *Ardabil Carpet*, 1539–40. C.E., Iran. Wool and silk. Detail of the central medallion showing the two lamps of heaven. Los Angeles County Museum

them to communicate the presence of a greater power beyond that which can be expressed through human, animal or divine forms. K'awiil (ill.35) was an elusive Mayan "spirit of spirits"—represented by an almost abstract head that appears out of, and disappears into, a breathing cloud of smoke and flowers, associated with blood sacrifice and burgeoning maize.

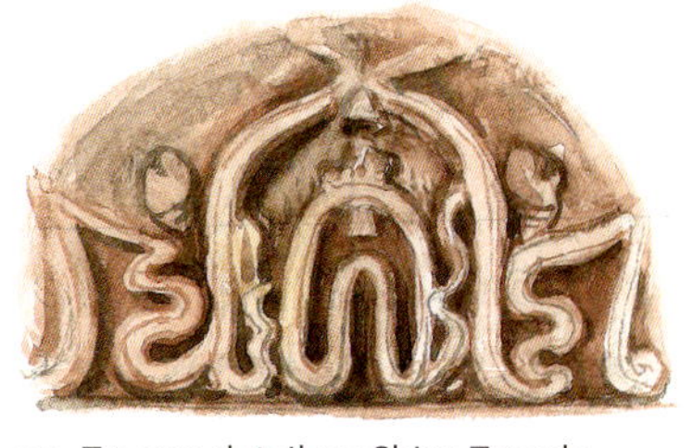

34 Tracery detail on Shiva Temple Mounts, 8th century C.E. Sandstone. Bubaneshwar, Orissa, India

Islamic religious architecture is entirely abstract. The only decorations allowed, apart from stylised, intertwined flowers, are quotations from the Koran, which is believed to be the word of god as revealed to the prophet Muhammad. Arabic, with its beautiful cursive scripts so well adapted to expression in masonry, is seen as the language created by god and the language of heaven, so it cannot be translated into any baser tongue. The citadel and palace of the Alhambra in Granada—the spiritual and secular centre of the Nasid Dynasty in Spain—was designed by Ibn al-Khatib (born 1313) and Ibn Zamrak (1333–1393), two poets who were also administrators. (The two roles were not considered separate in that civilised state.) The Alhambra as a whole, with its sequences of halls and sunny courtyards, gateways and shaded cloisters, window seats and viewpoints, arbours and hanging gardens, threaded through, inside and out, with water channels and cooling fountains, is best thought of as a three-dimensional visual poem in praise of Allah's beneficence. The sultan held court under domes dripping with *muqarnas* (ill.36)—tier upon tier of blue and white painted honeycombed domes, once side-lit by stained-glass windows, suggesting both the infinite ascendancy of god in heaven and the starlight that descends from above to fire the goodness in the soul.

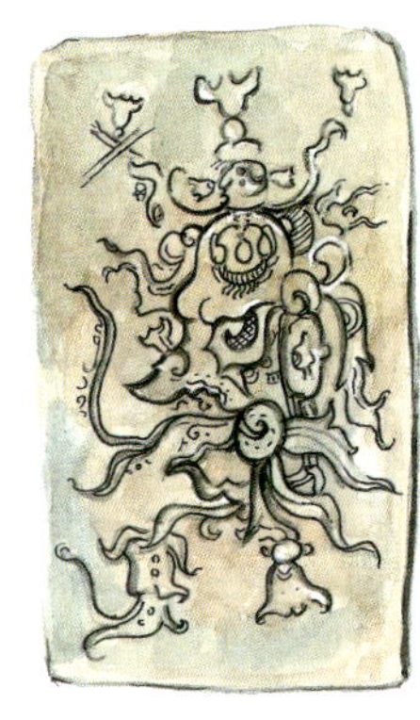

35 Profile of a head that representing K'awiil. Palenque, Chiapas. Limestone, 27.4 x 19.8 cm. National Museum of Anthropology, Mexico City

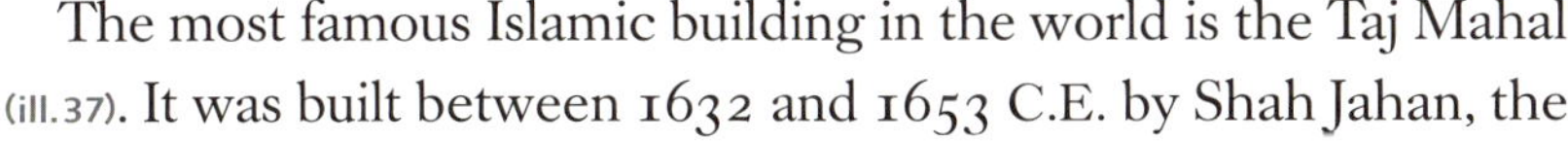

The most famous Islamic building in the world is the Taj Mahal (ill.37). It was built between 1632 and 1653 C.E. by Shah Jahan, the

fifth Mughal emperor in India, as a tomb for his beloved wife, Mumtaz-Mahal, who died while giving birth to her fourteenth child. It is a waiting chamber for her body to rest in until Allah appears on the day of judgement, seated on his throne floating above the gardens of paradise. As pilgrims approach, it is at first

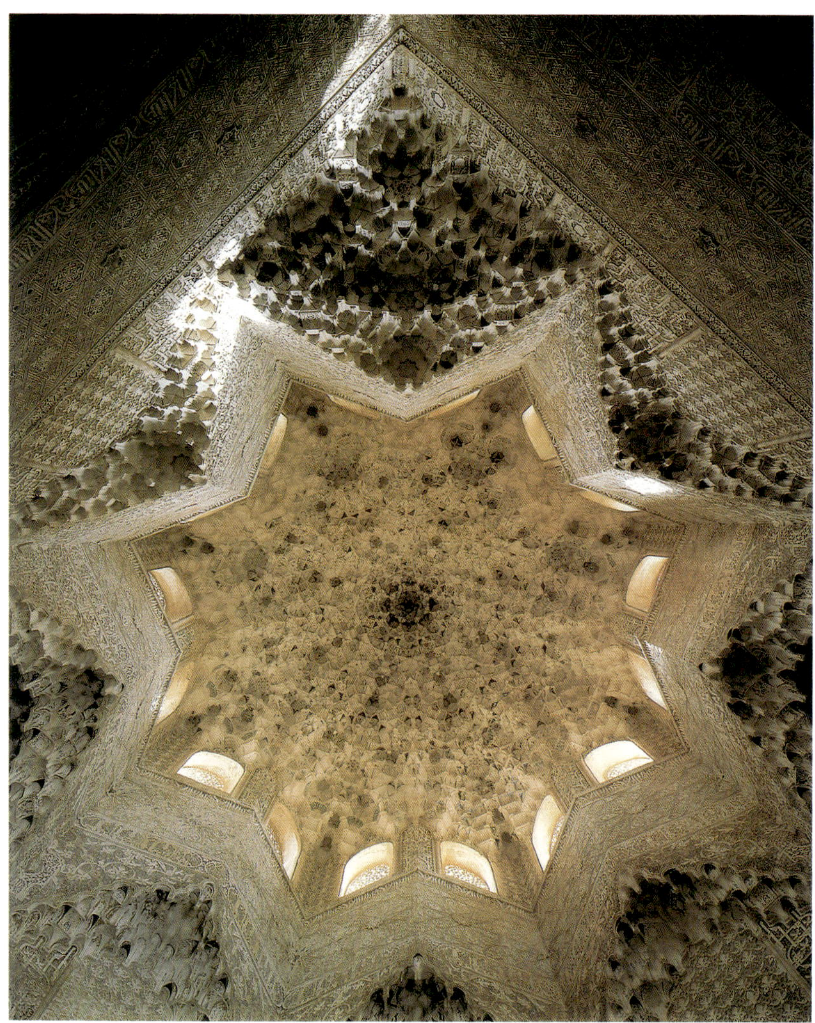

36 *The Star Ceiling*, c.1350 C.E. Hall of the Abencerrages, Alhambra, Granada, Spain. photograph by Francisco Fernandez

hidden from sight by a huge gateway of red sandstone and white marble. Only on passing under its star-cobwebbed arch (ill.38) can one appreciate the Taj in its full splendour—a colossal, shimmering mirage hovering on the far horizon beyond the avenue of fountains. The sight of it must have been overwhelming when the gardens were full of flowers, their colours picked up by the gems and semi-precious stones—amethysts, amber, lapis lazuli and malachite—that were originally set into the floral decorations on the tomb's white marble walls.

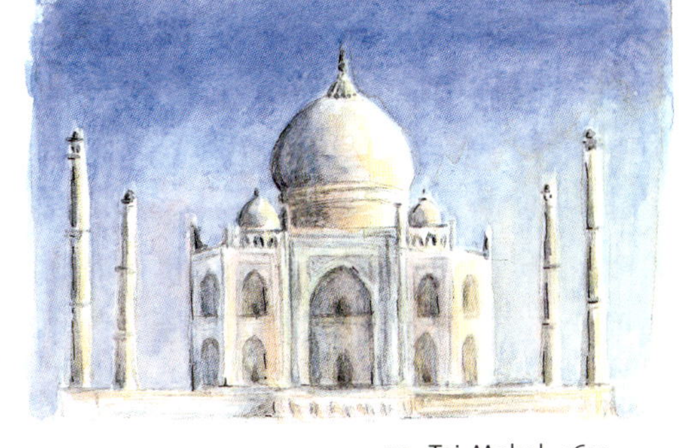

37 Taj Mahal, 1632–53 C.E. Agra, India

Despite the familiarity of its image, the Taj Mahal is breath-taking when seen in reality. This is partly due to its size—one gasps at seeing such a huge building appear so light and weightless. And there is the subtler effect of the shadowy cavities of the arches beneath the great swelling dome; it looks as though the building itself is breathing in and holding its breath, and the visitor, involuntarily, breathes in too. The dome itself has been compared by the poet Rabindranath Tagore to "an eternal teardrop descending from heaven on the cheek of time." But it could also be a drop of divine semen, for it was written in the Koran: "Man destroys himself: how stubbornly he denies the truth! How often does he consider out of what substance God creates him? Out of a drop of semen he creates him, and then determines his nature and then makes it easy for him to go through life; and in the end he causes him to die and brings him to the grave; and then, if it be his will, he shall raise him again to life." The Taj Mahal celebrates the divine seed that swells into a bud which will eventually, if it has led a pure life, flower in heaven. It is a vision, not of Allah, but of the soul waiting for Allah to appear.

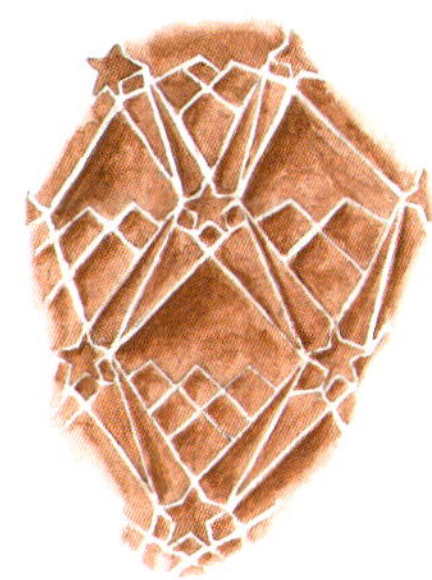

38 Star-ceiling in the apse of the gateway leading to the Taj Mahal, 1632–53 C.E. White marble tracery on red sandstone. Agra, India

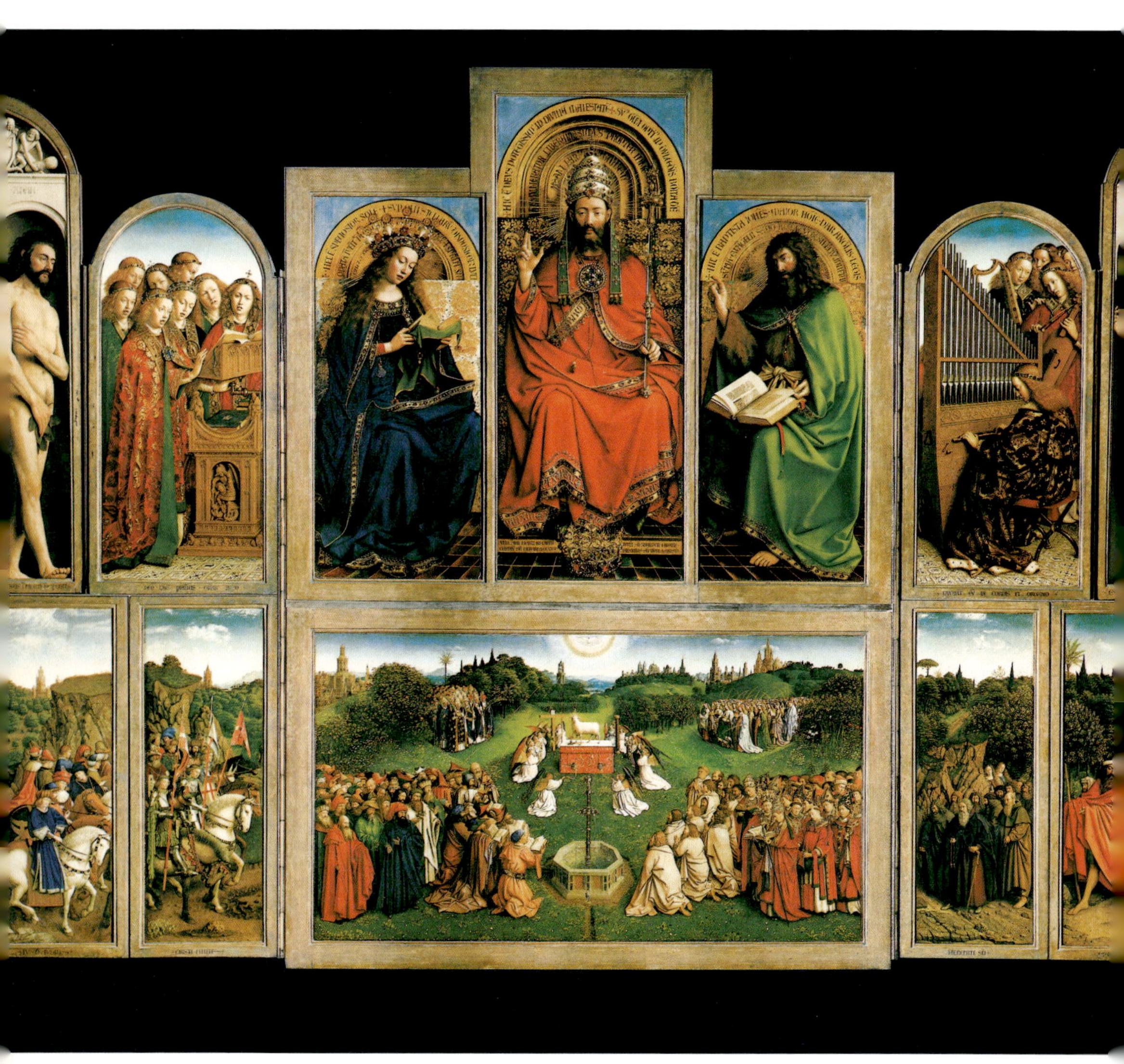

Chapter 8

The Age of Light

In this book I have so far looked at luminous bodies in heaven and solid ones below, at the transience but repeated reappearance of all things, at the grim face of death and those rare glimpses of delight which might indicate the existence of a secret and discreet divinity, in an attempt to discern what such sights could have meant to people in the past. I have swept from culture to culture and age to age, like an enthusiastic lepidopterist identifying butterflies in a virgin meadow, fearful of damaging the delicate balance that gives pattern, poise and buoyancy to their wings. I have tried to capture, without killing, fleeting imaginative thoughts, and have acted on the bold and unprovable assumption that the sculptor who modelled the dragon chasing a pearl on the wall of the Forbidden City (p. 94 f., ill. 8), the mason who chiselled the asymmetrical boulders used in the zigzag construction of Sacsayhuaman (p. 102, ill. 23), and the artist Giorgione, who painted the *Tempesta* (p. 106, ill. 33) would all have understood what the others were trying to express, once they had got over their initial surprise that such totally different religious beliefs could exist, and would have settled down to exchange views about what each felt when they looked at lightning in a storm.

What justifies this free-floating, culture-skipping, ahistorical approach is that the Peruvian chiseller, the Chinese modeller and the Italian painter saw their worlds in a similar way—not as a sequence of events in time, but as the manifestation, continuously unfolding in the present, of eternal truths. It is the difference between standing on a riverbank watching the waters flow by,

1 Hubert and Jan van Eyck.
The Ghent Altarpiece, 1432.
Cathedral of S. Bavon, Ghent, Belgium

and swimming underwater in the river with the waters continuously streaming towards you or away from you. On the bank, you feel detached, an observer, but you can become intensely aware of time passing. In the river, you feel part of everything; though you are aware of change, you feel it mostly as an ongoing and vivid affirmation of your current experience. In the swim, you cannot see where things are coming from or going to, but on the bank you have an overview of the river's journey from horizon to horizon. This chapter is the first to abandon the thematic approach and to look at the passage of time. It gives an account of our transition from swimming in the river to standing on the riverbank, when our modern, chronological view of the universe began to form before our eyes, and when so much that we had taken for granted disappeared, just as dreams do when we awake.

The clock started ticking for Christians with the birth of Christ. Judaism and Islam are both alert to time passing, for they maintain that salvation for the faithful will happen some time in the future, though neither specifies a date. Nor does Christianity, but its followers believe that the process of salvation started with the birth of Christ and will therefore end at a specific time in the future when Christ comes again. There was a widespread belief among early Christians that the world, which had taken God six days to create, had already endured for six thousand years by the year that came to be known by Christians as 1 A.D. – Anno Domini, the year of our Lord. Christ's birth and death signalled the beginning of the end of an era of human suffering and toil. His triumphant return, which early Christians believed was imminent, would herald the start of a glorious seventh day of creation – in fact a further thousand years of earthly bliss which would be enjoyed by all the faithful. This would continue until the Last Day when everyone would be judged, and confined to an eternity of either paradise or damnation. Ideas of a glorious millennium were soon dismissed as heretical by the emerging church–as the date of Christ's birth receded–but Christians remained committed to a second coming on earth. This made them intensely aware of time passing.

Every second leads Christians closer to the moment when Chris will, without warning, arrive in their midst and judge them. There was widespread fear and alarm that this would happen in 1000 C.E., and again in 1500 C.E., though by 2000 C.E. the sense of anticipation had rather lost its edge. Christianity is exceptional in seeing time, as if from a riverbank, as a straight line hurtling by from an invisible future and rapidly receding into an irretrievable past. Judaism and Islam have less punishing schedules; they are closer to older faiths which viewed time as cyclical and reiterative, something to be stilled, not chased. Buddhists go further and teach that time is not just a distraction but a pernicious tendril that ties us to the world. One of the aims of meditation is to lift the mind beyond its reach, focusing thoughts on the still point at the centre of the turning world, which some identify with the navel. But Christians have seen it as their duty to stay alert in this world, keeping their lamps trimmed, like the seven wise virgins, ready for the earthly reappearance of their spiritual groom. The first great Christian theologian, St Augustine (353–430 C.E.)–a convert, interestingly, from Manichaeanism, a religion which bravely attempted to combine the teachings of the Buddha, Zarathustra and Jesus–argued that "the infidel seeks to undermine our simple faith by dragging us from the straight road and compelling us to walk with him on the wheel". Christianity believed that God's creation had a beginning, a middle and an end. So it sowed the seeds for our modern, historical way of looking at the world.

Christians soon had their own historians to record their spiritual progress; one of the first, the Venerable Bede (673–735 C.E.), compiled the great *Ecclesiastical History of the British Nation.* But it was not until the eighteenth century that a historian looked at Christianity itself within the wider course of general history, as if standing in detachment on the riverbank. On 15 October 1764—he was mindful of dates—Edward Gibbon stood on the Capitoline Hill in the centre of Rome and decided to write the story of how the Roman empire—arguably the greatest empire the world had yet seen—had come to lie in ruins around his feet. He laid down his pen on 27 June 1787, having surveyed a great sweep of history, from Rome at its height to the dominion of Christianity, from the rise of Muhammad to the Crusades, from the urban wars in medieval Italy to the emergence of Protestantism. He did so with a tender yet surgically precise understanding of human motivation, expressed in mellifluous, ironical prose. He called it *The History of the Decline and Fall of the Roman Empire* because, from where he was standing, in Enlightenment Europe, the most important thing that had been lost during one and a half millennia of history was the orderly, humane civilization of Rome, with its originally tolerant attitude towards all religions and creeds. He attributed this decline to several causes, among which Christianity was only one. But he was in no doubt that it was the subsequent "darker ages" that had left the ruins at his feet.

Daylight was, of course, no darker then than it is today, although television reconstructions of the period following the fall of the Roman empire invariably show scenes shrouded by night, with a moon floating between threatening clouds, and a huddle of men with torches lowering a corpse into a mist-filled grave. But it's only in recent times that this period has been depicted as a darkening; to Christians at the time it was a period

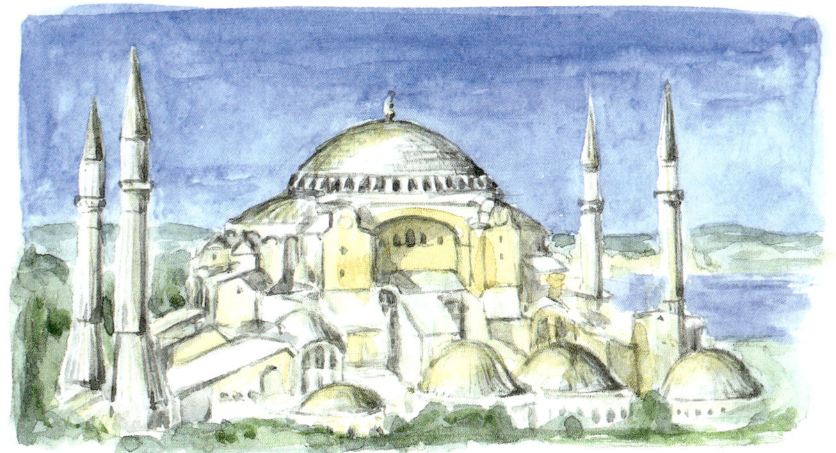

2 Exterior of Hagia Sophia, originally The Church of S. Sophia, 537 C.E. Istanbul

of increasing spiritual enlightenment. The emperor Constantine (285–337 C.E.) made Christianity the official religion and moved his capital from Rome to a small town on the Bosporus called Byzantium. The new 'Holy' Roman Empire—which survived for much longer than its unholy predecessor—was formally established on 11 May 330 C.E. Byzantium was renamed Constantinople and was vastly expanded. (It later became Islamic Istanbul.) Its great church, S. Sophia, was built by the emperor Justinian in 532–37 C.E. (ill. 2)—the minarets were added when it was turned into a mosque in 1453 C.E. It was a magnificent demonstration of the confidence of the new religion, an example of great Roman public architecture adapted for the services of the church, and one of a handful of imperial monuments, like the Pantheon in Rome, that religion saved from falling into ruin.

S. Sophia had very small windows, but it was not dark inside. One has the impression from many early Christian churches today that they had gloomy interiors, and this has helped give credence to the existence of the Dark Ages. The truth is that churches nowadays are much more parsimonious with their

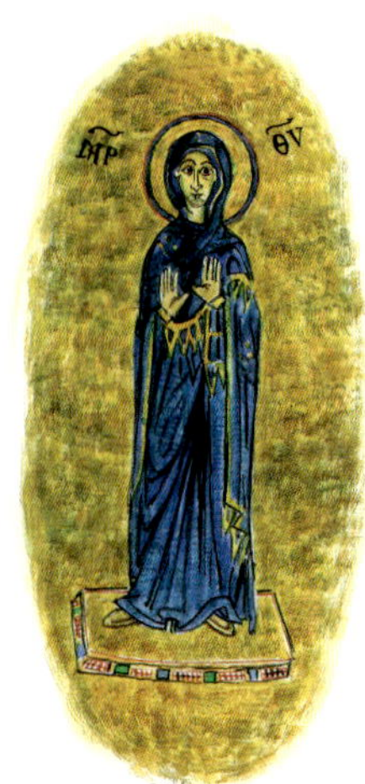

3 Virgin praying, 12th century C.E. Apse mosaic. Basilica dei Santi Maria e Donato, Murano, Italy

lighting. St Mark's Basilica in Venice, which contains some of the greatest Christian mosaics, is drab to the point of being dispiriting—a naked window, which originally contained muted glass, sends a beam of annihilating bright light into the centre while the rest is buried in shadow. The basilicas at nearby Ravenna, which predate St Mark's by nearly five hundred years, have also largely lost the sheets of honey-coloured alabaster that blocked their little windows, so that now their brilliant mosaics are emblazoned with daylight. The light in these interiors was originally more subdued, but no less powerful in effect. Contemporary accounts of these early churches describe literally thousands of lamps and candles lighting up the interiors, walls, floors and ceilings—and with good reason, for they were covered all over in glistening, golden and multicoloured mosaics. The tradition continued until the twelfth century, as in this apse mosaic in Murano near Venice (ill. 3). The idea was that worshippers left the light of the world outside—the brilliant Mediterranean sunshine—to enter a much more glorious, glowing, spiritual world inside. It was written in the Bible that the city of God "had no need of the sun, neither of the moon, to shine in it: for the glory of God did lighten it, and the Lamb *is* the light thereof". Hubert and Jan van Eyck painted a literal rendition of this divine light (ill. 1, 4). The history of Christianity in art can be told in terms of Christians' increasing ambition, which rose to its zenith in the fifteenth century, to depict God's light in the world.

4 Hubert and Jan van Eyck. *The Ghent Altarpiece*, cf. p. 182

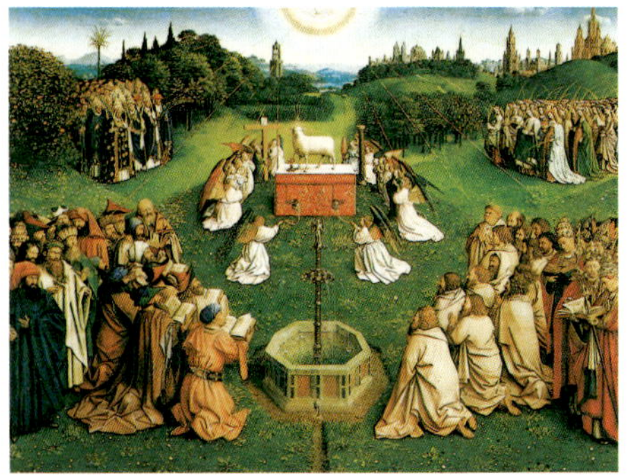

There were early disputes among Christians as to whether this was possible, and Gibbon saw these doubts rumbling on throughout the Christian era. He was particularly interested in the Paulicans, an obscure sect that emerged in the seventh century, which denied that Christ had ever had a physical presence in life or indeed on the cross. They believed that Christ's celestial spirit had, as Gibbon put it, "passed through the Virgin's body like water through a pipe". Their ideas, he believed, influenced the thinking of Luther and Calvin. The Roman Catholic Church, however, upheld the appearance of God on earth, and the manifestation of his flesh and blood in bread and wine. It had little option but to do so, for the new Islamic faith, which began to attract adherents rapidly from the seventh century onwards, taught that Jesus was no more than an inspired prophet whose testimony, at the Last Judgement, would condemn both Jews, who denied him, and Christians, who believed he was the son of God. Christianity, exceptionally amongst the world's great religions, taught that God had once appeared in this world and would appear in it again. And, increasingly, it came to believe that God could be glimpsed in the world he had created. As St Augustine (353–430 C.E.) had written: "Thanks be to you, oh Lord, for all that we see."

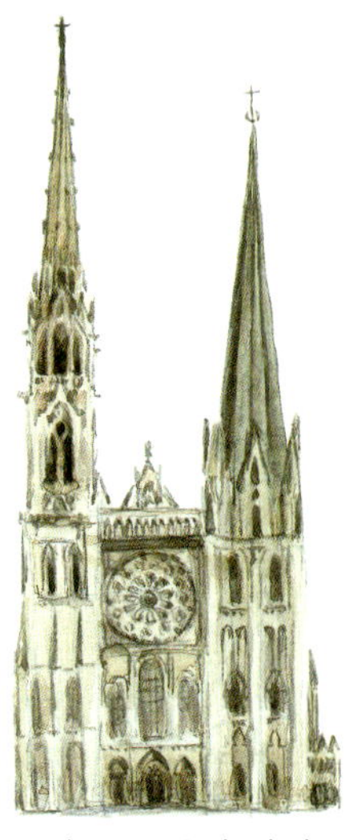

5 Chartres Cathedral
13th century, France

The development of Christian art and architecture from Byzantine (ill. 2) to Romanesque and Gothic (ill. 5) can be understood as a process of letting everyday light seep into the inner, spiritual world. The golden mosaics were superseded by murals suffused with daylight. Walking into the Arena Chapel in Padua (p. 203, ill. 20), the masterpiece of Giotto (1266/7–1337), one is bowled over by the blue which fills the vault and pours down its sides. It's as if the golden light that encases the Virgin had been condensed into the stars that decorate the ceiling, and her blue robe had expanded to become the sky that envelops and comforts us all by day.

In northern Europe, the transformation of spiritual light was more gradual. Religious beings kept their ethereal quality, but their luminous glow had its source in natural light shining

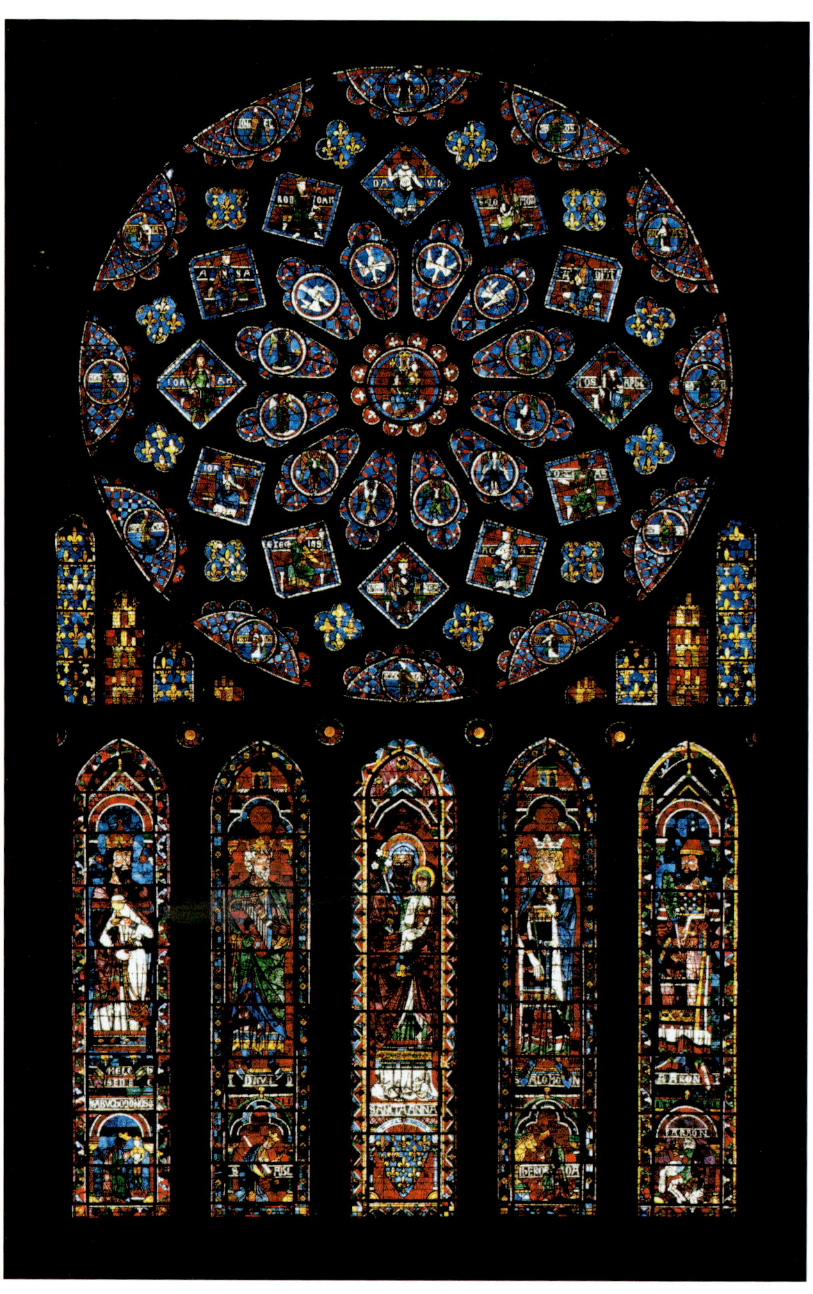

6 The north rose window,
Chartres Cathedral, c. 1230 C.E. France

through stained-glass windows, where the blues also became radiant (ill.6). The Gothic cathedrals of France, Germany and England emerged out of and in part owed their greatness to a culture that had worshipped spirits in forest glades. Christian leaders were adept at harnessing native traditions to their cause. The spires, branching pillars (ill.7) and tall, tracery windows of Gothic cathedrals are manifest evidence of Christianity emerging out of Celtic mysticism. But they also indicate Christianity turning its attention to the divinely created world.

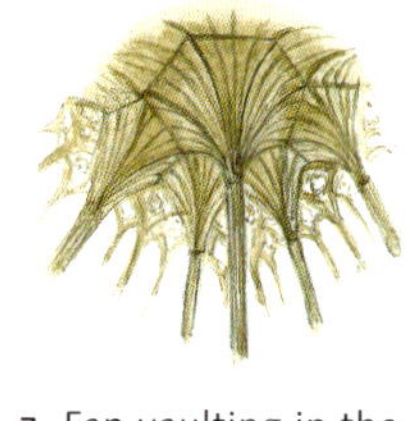

7 Fan vaulting in the Chapter House, c.1310 C.E. Wells Cathedral, England

Stained glass had been known to the Romans, and was used in Islamic architecture, but it only flowered as an art form in its own right with the Christians. One of the best places to see medieval stained glass is in Chartres Cathedral in France (ill.6) where 152 of the original 186 windows survive. There are few more uplifting experiences than seeing the fragmentary beams of rainbow light while listening to the cascading notes of the organ in the soaring interior. Chartres Cathedral burnt down in 1194, but its most treasured relic, the Virgin's cloak, was left unscathed. This was taken as a sign that Mary, the cathedral's patron, had had the church burnt down so that the people of the town could build an even more magnificent one in her honour. New designs were drawn up at once, and work started on the site only a couple of months after the charred timbers had cooled; one of the greatest works of art in the world arose from this remarkably short planning process. The Virgin was at that time known as the Rose of Heaven, and this was perhaps the reason why so much attention was given to the positioning and the design of the rose windows in Chartres. One interpretation of the different sizes of the spires (ill.5) is that the taller one represents the sun and the shorter one the moon. If this is correct, then the rose of heaven can be seen to flower between them.

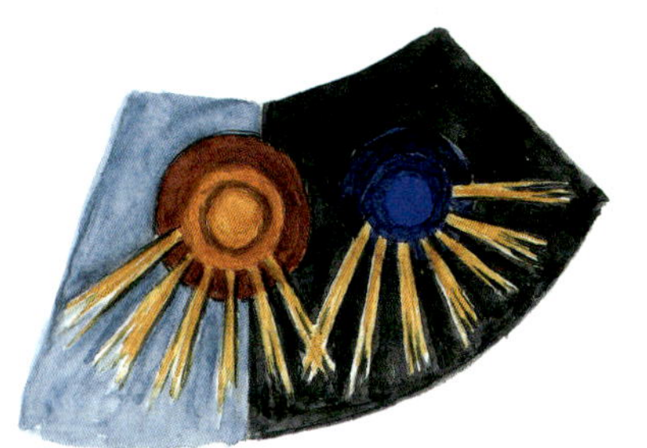

8 Detail showing God dividing the light from the darkness, c.1220 C.E. Creation mosaic. St Mark's, Venice

The light in the great Gothic cathedrals was most like that of dusk, when some colours, particularly blues and purples, appear to glow more strongly, just as people's souls were believed to shine more brightly as they approached their end. As Christians looked about them, they began increasingly to catch glimpses of God in his creation. A beautiful sequence of golden mosaics in the porch of the basilica of St Mark's in Venice tells the history of this creation, beginning with God dividing the light from the darkness (ill.8). Light is symbolised by a sphere of purplish red and darkness by a sphere of deep blue. These are the colours that mysteriously merge into darkness at the fringes on either side of the rainbow, and it's possible that their symbolic use derived from that phenomenon. Darkness was not thought to be totally black, but to have its own peculiar light. Anyone who has looked up into a night sky not yellowed by light pollution is aware of the beautiful, intangible effulgence of deep space. The blue of the Virgin's cloak (ill.3) is often interpreted as a spiritual reflection of the royal purple worn by Roman emperors. It was worthy of her because ultramarine, whose name indicates its origins from "beyond the sea", was the most expensive of all pigments. It was ground, with some difficulty, from lapis lazuli brought to Europe from the distant East. Contracts for paintings often specified that the ultramarine had to be made from the first grinding, because this alone provided the hint of purple that was so treasured. This supports the theory that the Virgin's cloak was an emulation of the rainbow's emerging rim, a blue light coming out of the darkness, as befits the bearer of Christ.

The mechanics of the rainbow were not understood until the seventeenth century. Before then, its mysterious appearance

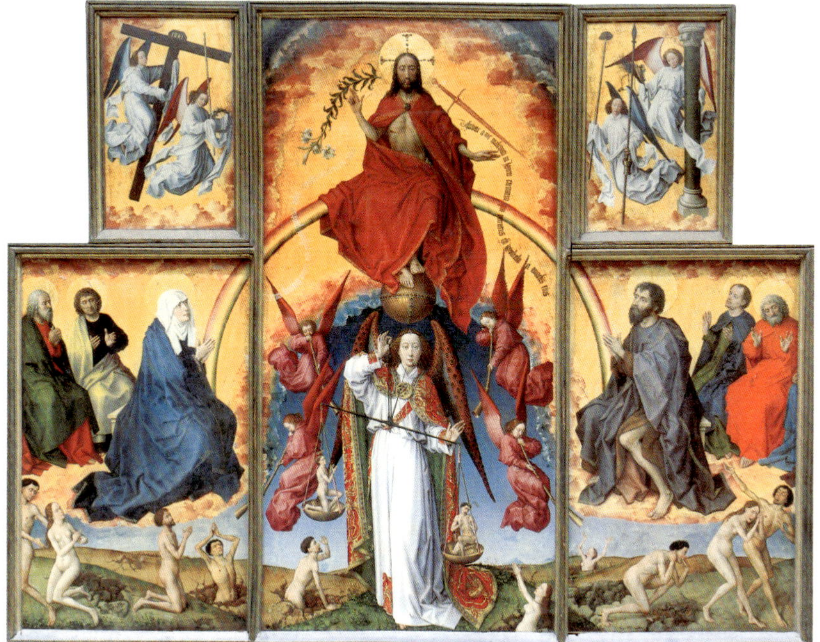

9 Rogier van der Weyden. *The Last Judgement*, c.1442–51, detail of central panel showing Christ seated on a rainbow above St Michael with peacock wings. Hospices de Beaune, France

made it holy. After the Flood, God declared: "I do set my bow in a cloud, and it shall be for a token of a covenant between me and the earth. And it shall come to pass, when I bring a cloud over the earth, that the bow shall be seen in the cloud." The implication is that God gives Christians hope–not, incidentally, a pot of gold–while they endure the misery of their fallen state. And it was believed that, on the Day of Judgement, Christ would appear seated on a rainbow, accompanied by angels with peacocks' wings (ill.9). Their flashes of iridescence would herald the end of all suffering.

Christianity was not unique in seeing religious significance in iridescence. Birds' feathers were, in many cultures, as precious as gold–their transient brilliance complemented the permanence of that noble metal. The headdress of the Aztec emperor Montezu-

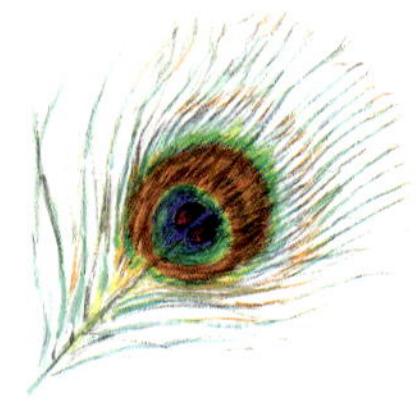

10 Peacock's tail feather

ma was made from the long tail feathers of the now nearly extinct quetzal bird, which flies through the rain forest like a flicker of luminescent green lightning. The tiara of the empress of China flashed with kingfishers' feathers – symbolic of her rebirth in heaven as the phoenix consort to the imperial, golden dragon. The peacock, now the national bird of India, struck wonder wherever it was seen. It became a symbol of immortality because it shed and renewed its tail feathers (ill. 10) every year. "How could anyone who sees the Peacock not be amazed at the gold interwoven with sapphire, at the purple and emerald green feathers, at the composition of the colours of many patterns, all mingling together but not confused with one another? ... Oh, whence comes the beautiful peacock?" – so wrote a Byzantine priest in the seventh century C.E. Gnosticism – an esoteric movement springing from Judaic and Christian mysticism that greatly influenced alchemy – taught that the radiance of the peacock emerging from a single white egg was a symbol of the ultimate mystery, God's creation of the many from the one.

The alchemists of the Middle Ages were proto-scientists whose experiments were governed by their assumption that nature had been divinely created for mankind's benefit. They believed that the source of life would eventually be found in chemistry – and up to a point science has proved them right, though it has yet to develop an elixir which you can drink to make yourself immortal. Modern science has shown that the alchemists' endless quest for a means of turning lead into gold was futile, despite the remarkably similar properties of these two metals. Had they, instead, tried to make diamonds out of coal their credibility might be higher today, but such an idea would have seemed absurd, given the totally different appearance of these two forms of the same element. Martin Luther, the Protestant reformer and possibly a friend of the artist Grünewald, wrote: "Alchemy – the philosophy of the ancients – appeals to me very much … its allegories are quite beautiful … such as the resurrection of the dead on the last day… For just as fire in a furnace draws out the best in matter, and releases spirit … so God will separate the justified from the godless as if in a fire at the Last Judgement." He could be describing Grünewald's painting of the resurrection of Christ; the aura around him is derived from the halo that appears in metal when it's heated to a high temperature (ill. 11).

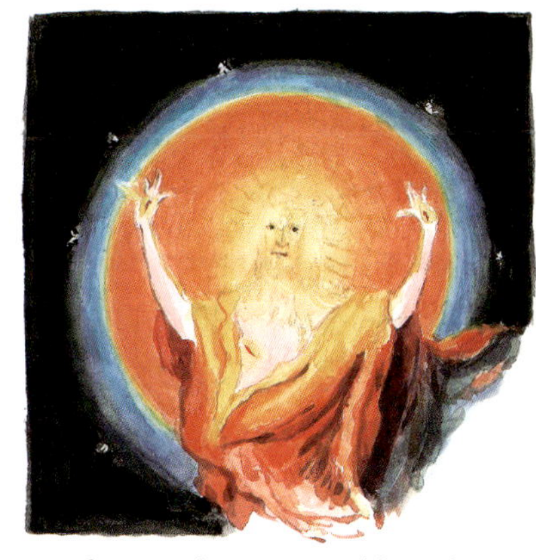

11 After Matthias Grünewald. *Isenheim Altarpiece*, c. 1515, Resurrection, detail of the risen Christ. Colmar, France

The adherents of most religions around the world have treasured precious jewels found in rocks, believing that their radiance had to have a divine origin. In Hindu belief, the Great Mother's island is built on a bank of gemstones. In Inuit legends, the northern lights were, at the beginning of time, trapped in rocks until they were released by an ancient warrior's sword – but some were left behind, and this accounted for the presence of jewels in the earth. For Christians, jewels were fragments fallen from the walls of heaven (ill. 12) which they imagined to be constructed of topaz and sapphire, diamond and amethyst. Stained glass was the perfect medium in which to rebuild, symbolically, the walls of heaven which mankind had destroyed on earth. These are described in the last book of the New Testament, Revelation. In 1150, the abbess Hildegard of Bingen wrote a beautiful song commemorating the re-founding of her abbey, St Rupert's: "Your windows, Jerusalem, are wondrously adorned with topaz and sapphire. As you blaze in the windows, O Rupert, you are revealed even to those whose faith is lukewarm – just as the valley cannot hide the mountain – crowned with roses, lilies and purple in a true revelation."

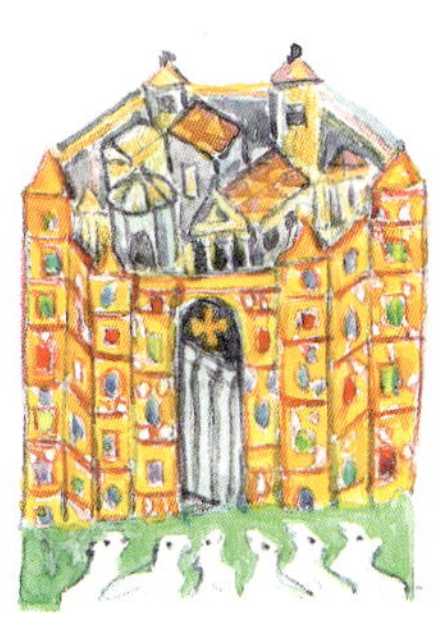

12 Jerusalem, 5th century C.E., detail. Mosaic. S. Maria Maggiore, Rome

Hildegard's praise, which seems to modern ears surprisingly sensuous, was in fact strictly orthodox. Five hundred years earlier, the bishop of Marseilles had zealously destroyed images of saints because the Bible said that graven images should not be worshipped. But Pope Gregory wrote to him to say that, although it was right not to worship images, it was useful to use them to educate the ignorant: "For the unlettered, the heathen especially, a picture takes the place of a book." Christianity, unlike Judaism and Islam, started to use images as illustrations of divinity, though these images were not in themselves divine. The history of the whole of Western art until recent times is based on this licence given to artists by the church. The confluence of streams which created the movement of art that culminated in the Renaissance was threefold: the ambition to depict Jesus as vividly as possible, as if he were living in the world; the desire to recreate the world as it was when Jesus lived, at the time of the Romans; and the duty to render as faithfully as possible the divinity present in God's creation. This led to a focus of attention on appearances that has never been equalled. But the more that artists, and later scientists, looked at the world, the more they discovered evidence that did not fit with the biblical explanation of creation. Little did Pope Gregory realise, when he gave artists the freedom to depict the world as they saw it, that he was opening floodgates that would in time rock Christianity to its very foundations.

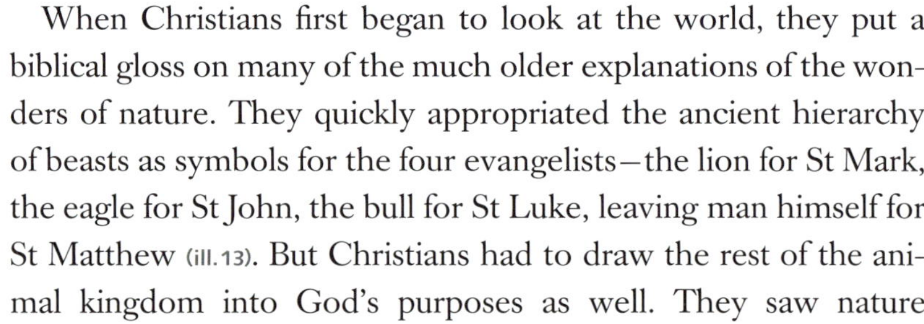

When Christians first began to look at the world, they put a biblical gloss on many of the much older explanations of the wonders of nature. They quickly appropriated the ancient hierarchy of beasts as symbols for the four evangelists–the lion for St Mark, the eagle for St John, the bull for St Luke, leaving man himself for St Matthew (ill.13). But Christians had to draw the rest of the animal kingdom into God's purposes as well. They saw nature

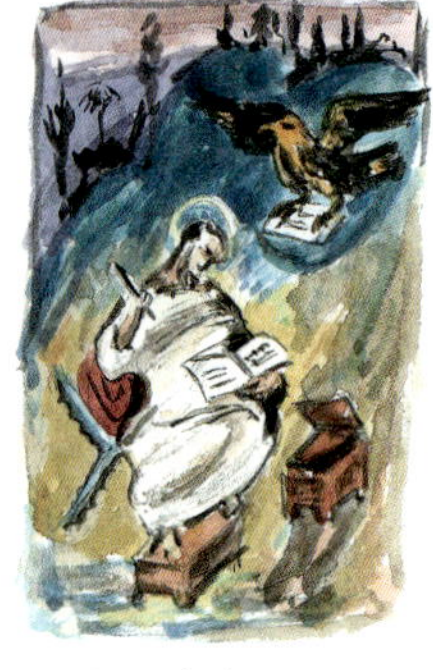

13 Detail showing St John the Evangelist with his eagle, early 9th century, Rheims, detail from the Gospels, Codex Aureus. Cathedral Treasury, Aachen

through the eyes of faith as shamans had done. Christian bestiaries were not based on observations of nature, but rather told stories of exotic creatures which most people had never seen in the wild. The pelican was believed to feed its young with the blood from its breast–symbolising Christ's sacrifice. Lion cubs were thought to be born dead. The lioness, symbolising the Virgin, watched over them for three days until the lion, symbolising Christ, arrived and breathed life into them. Even familiar creatures were treated fancifully. It was believed that hedgehogs shook vines, presumably with their little front paws, and speared the fallen grapes by rolling them on to their spines. What they did with them then was a mystery. But that didn't matter, because this practice had demonstrated that devils would always try to rob men of the fruits of their spiritual labours.

Wherever they lived, people assumed that their world was centred on the source of their spiritual power. Christians looked to Jerusalem, Muslims to Mecca, and the Chinese to Beijing. It was perfectly logical to think that life would become increasingly strange the further it was from this central source of divine beneficence. Travellers to far-flung lands confirmed this by bringing back evidence of strange beasts and wild people. Fantastic tales abounded of monstrous men with, for example, heads of birds and cloven hooves (ill.14). These tales were based on half-truths and understandable fears, and were the logical extension of a world picture totally different from our own. People who actually lived near the edge of the world took advantage of their position. Scandinavian fishermen developed a lucrative sideline in late medieval times by supplying unicorn horns to southern Europeans, without of course letting on that they were actually the tusks of narwhals. They were not at all amused when Ole Wurm, a Danish physician and antiquarian and the founder

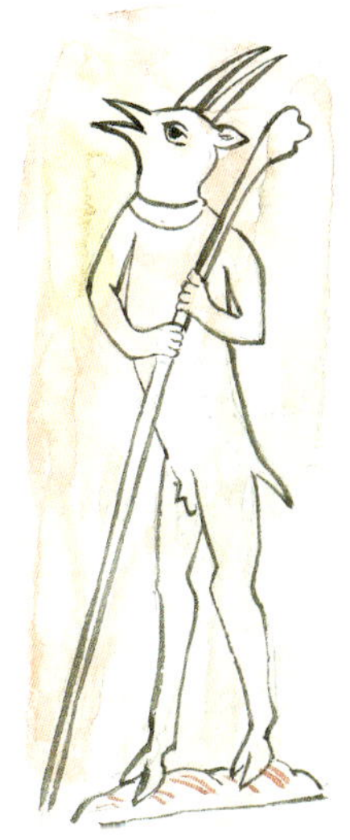

14 Detail of weird beasts and men at the edge of the Mappa Mundi, c.1300. 158 x 133 cm. Hereford Cathedral, England

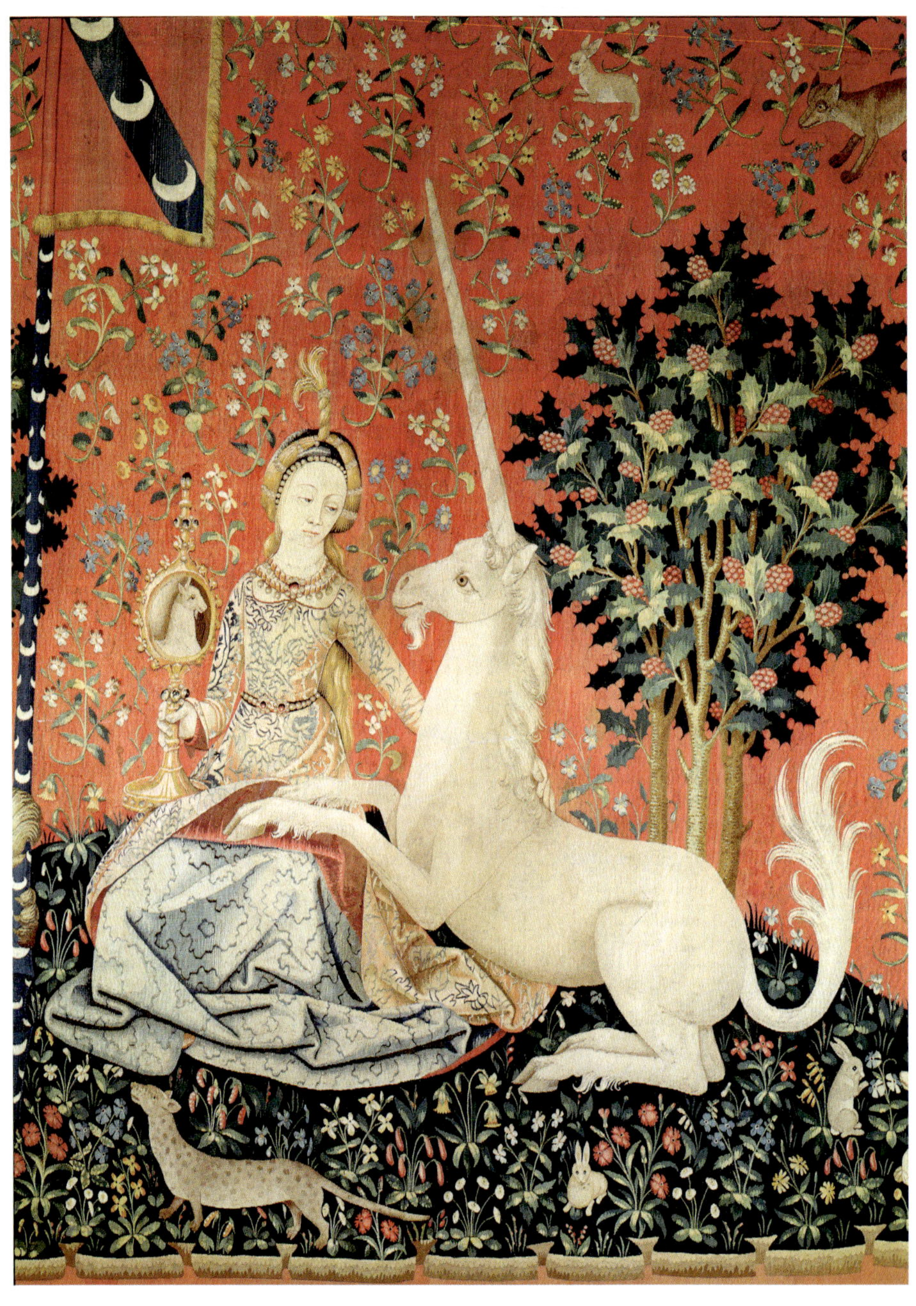

15 The Lady with the Unicorn – Sight, late 15th century. Tapestry. *Musée de Cluny*, Paris

of one of the first museum collections, told the world the truth in the seventeenth century.

The unicorn had come to be regarded in medieval Europe as a symbol of chastity. The story went that it was so fleet of foot that it could not be shot or trapped. However, it would willingly leave the forest to lay its horn in a virgin's lap. In Christian mythology, the unicorn was then caught and slain by sinful men, as was Christ, who had been born to Mary. Though obviously phallic, the unicorn's elegant white horn symbolised the triumph of grace – the word and sword of God – over bestial desire. In this late fifteenth century tapestry (ill. 15), one of a set of five which pertain in some way to the five senses, a unicorn looks at its reflection in a mirror. The message could be that virtue can recognise itself by sight, or in other words, that it's your own goodness that enables you to see goodness in yourself and others.

Strange things came out of the sea too. In almost all mythologies the sea was believed to lap all round and under the earth, and many of them make reference to a time when the sea flooded over the earth. The presence of petrified seashells on the top of mountains was convincing evidence of the Flood. No-one in the world knew what fossils were until the eighteenth century, nor did anyone have any idea how old the world really was. In China fossils were collected as "dragon bones" and ground down for traditional medicine. Thousands of dinosaur bones must have been lost in this way. In India, fossil ammonites (ill. 16) were thought to be lethal knife-wheels thrown by Vishnu – their spiral form representing the celestial order of the cosmos.

Pearl-lipped spiral conch shells, of different types, are found all over the world. They have fascinated generations of humans partly because of their origin, deep in the bottomless ocean, through which they appeared to have imbibed their wave-like beauty.

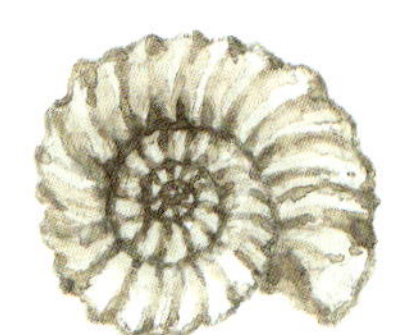

16 Fossil ammonite, Lower Cretaceous, from Devizes, Wiltshire. Natural History Museum, London

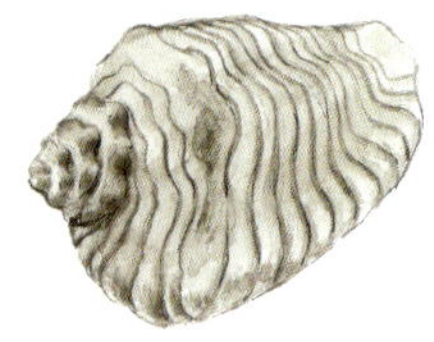

17 Queen Conch, c.1500, Aztec, from Templo Mayor. Stone and traces of stucco and blue paint, 105 x 75.5 cm. National Museum of Anthropology, Mexico City

They also have a likeness to female genitalia, which seemed only natural, for the tides and the menstrual cycle were believed to be linked. One of these shells was found in the bottom of the shaft, the most sacred part, of the caves at Lascaux in France. It had been brought 200 kilometres from the Atlantic coast, tinted with red ochre, the colour of sunsets and blood, and punctured to be used as a pendant. The conch shell became the cornucopia, pouring forth plenty into the world. It was also the Greek sea god Triton's "wreathed horn" and, when blown, became an icon of the wind. Conch trumpets heralded the start of prosperous journeys in Buddhist China. In Hinduism, their sound was the primal murmur of all creation. Children everywhere hold them to their ears to listen to the distant roar of the sea. Huge, beautiful sculptures of them (ill. 17) have been found in key positions in Aztec temples.

The other wonderfully shaped shell was the scallop. Even in the earthiness of Roman mythology, the scallop maintains its purity. Saturn, so the story went, was so incensed at his father Uranus's continual philandering that he cut off his genitals and

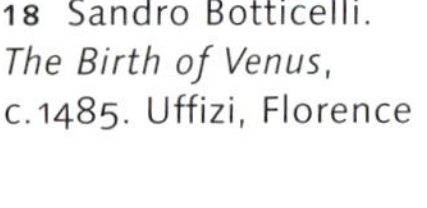

18 Sandro Botticelli. *The Birth of Venus*, c.1485. Uffizi, Florence

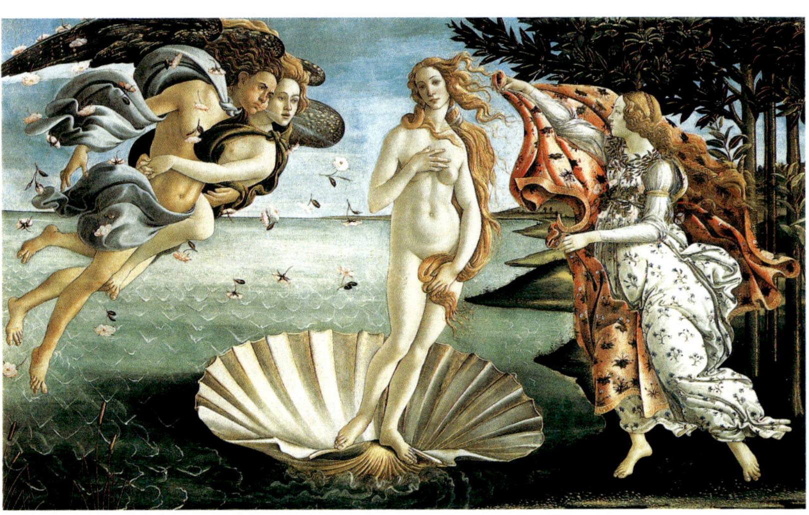

threw them in the sea. From the churning waters Venus, the evening star and goddess of love, was born. She was blown to land on a scallop by Zephyr and Aura, the cold and warm winds, and welcomed by Hora, the goddess of summer. As soon as Venus stepped ashore—legend has it on Cyprus—the barren landscape burst into bloom. Botticelli's *The Birth of Venus* (ill. 18) was commissioned by the Medici, the family of Florentine bankers who, a decade later, funded Amerigo Vespucci's voyage to the New World that would come to be named after him. Christians saw it as their duty to go forth and spread the gospel of Christ to all mankind—and if any wealth accrued in the process, so much the better for God's purpose. Christianity had always been good at harnessing other beliefs to its cause, especially if they drew crowds. Christian pilgrims wore scallop badges (p. 72, ill. 14) on their journey back from the end of the earth. The classical Venus was born in a scallop shell. The pagan goddess of love could comfortably be regarded by Christians as a prefiguration of the Virgin, who was born to bring Christ's love into this world. Venus, being a pagan, had one great advantage: she went around naked—which is not a crowd-pulling strategy that the Virgin could have adopted.

From its earliest beginnings Christian art is full of antique borrowings, but these didn't override its Christian purpose. Gibbon was right to see the Roman empire as overshadowing the whole of European history until his own times. But this wasn't just the shadow cast by republicanism and humanism. Jesus himself had lived in Roman times. There was therefore a profoundly Christian purpose behind the study of antique remains. They gave artists a glimpse of what their God might have looked like, and might have worn, when he walked on earth. This led to early attempts at historical reconstructions, such as those by Masaccio

(1401–1428?). In the Brancacci Chapel in Florence (ill. 19) he painted a scene showing Jesus telling St Peter that he will find the tax that has to be paid to the Romans in the mouth of a fish. Peter finds it – in the scene in the background – and Jesus and his disciples are able "to render unto Caesar what is Caesar's". Few artists have ever been able to combine such grandeur with such simplicity. The scene could have been carved on a monumental Roman sarcophagus, yet it is full of Christian humility.

This painting is included in most art history books about the Renaissance, a period of exuberant experiments in art and culture generally considered to have lasted from the fourteenth century to the early decades of the sixteenth century, centred in Italy and northern Europe. But the name "Renaissance" has the wrong emphasis. The era was given this name three hundred years later by scholars of the late Enlightenment who wanted to represent this period of great art as the beginning of the "rebirth" of their objective, non-religious way of looking. They saw it as the age that rediscovered the humanism of ancient Greece and Rome which had flourished two millennia before, but which had been

19 Masaccio. *The Tribute Money*, 1425/26. Fresco. Brancacci Chapel, S. Maria del Carmine, Florence

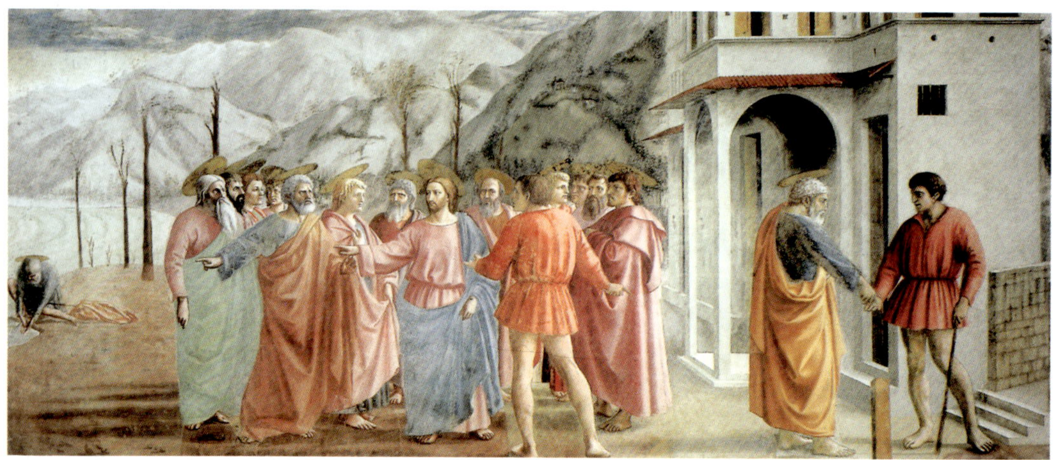

overshadowed during the "dark" ages of Christian domination. This rebirth was shown to lead directly, after the heroic struggle of a few brave individuals, to their own glorious, superstition-free scientific age. But this is a story told with hindsight. Our modern age didn't really start until the seventeenth century, when Galileo turned his telescope on the moon.

Renaissance artists painted a world that was still steeped in mystery. After all, the earth was not proved to be spherical until Magellan's ship sailed round it in 1522. Even then it was still thought to be fixed at the centre of a universe, embraced in the arms of God. What did happen during the Renaissance, though, was a shift in viewpoint. People stopped looking up to heaven to see God, but began to believe that they could see him as they looked around them. The theory of mathematical perspective was reputedly discovered by Brunelleschi (1337–1446), the architect of genius who finally worked out how to build a dome that would span the walls of Florence's unfinished cathedral. Perspectival laws had been understood in ancient Greece and Rome, and were used to decorate interiors of villas with wonderfully elaborate architectural illusions that appeared to extend the living space, like sets of receding mirrors. Their purpose seems to have been decorative and pleasurable. In late medieval Europe it was spiritual. Giotto (c. 1267–1337) was possibly the first Christian artist to depict God as if he were walking among us, unrecognised (ill. 20). In *The Betrayal of Christ*, Judas shows the Roman soldiers which figure Christ is by kissing him. Both Jesus and Judas stand on the same level. The eyes of goodness gaze into those of evil, and

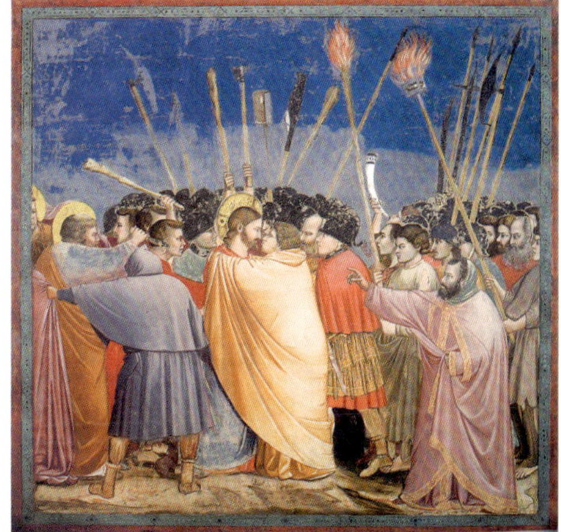

20 Giotto. *The Betrayal of Christ*, c. 1306–13. Fresco. Arena Chapel, Padua, Italy

bystanders whose faith is lukewarm are left free, in Giotto's generous art, to contemplate for themselves the significance of this intense and ultimate confrontation.

Many Renaissance artists were inspired by the teaching of St Francis of Assisi (1181/2–1226) who preached—on one occasion actually to some birds—that wild animals were not to be despised and ignored, but were God's own humble creatures and worthy companions for the poor followers of Christ. In one early painting by Giovanni Bellini (c. 1430–1516) (ill. 21), St Francis is shown receiving the stigmata—the marks of the crucifixion, and insignia of his saintliness—at night, for it was believed that on this occasion God's rays had lit up the world as if it had been day. Only the rabbits are out and about in Bellini's landscape, while a

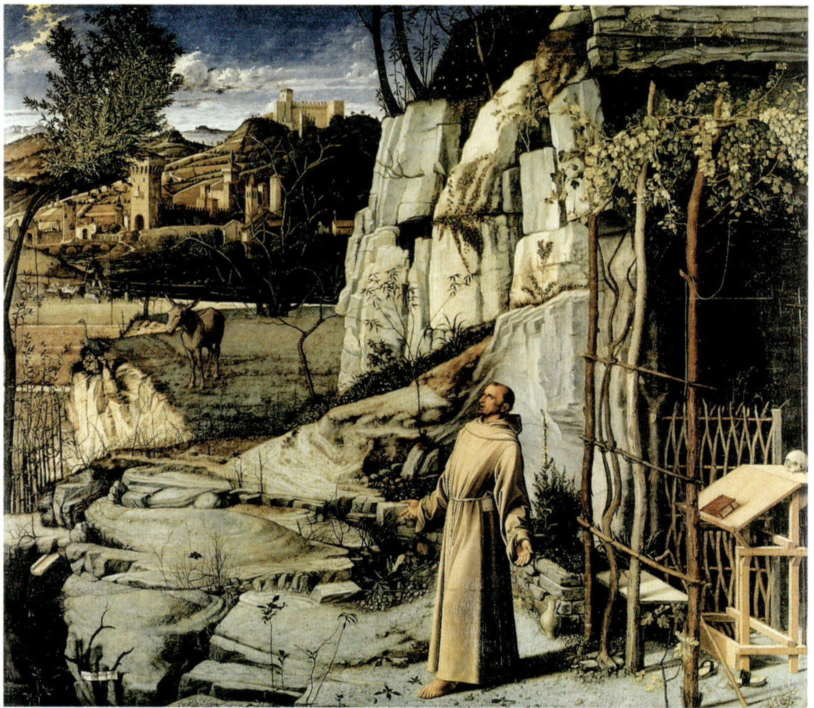

21 Giovanni Bellini. *St Francis Receiving the Stigmata*. c.1475 C.E. Frick Collection, New York

solitary shepherd guards his flock. Hinduism, and its offshoots Jainism and Buddhism, have long advocated that one should love one's fellow creatures. Fifteen hundred years before St Francis, the Buddha preached his first sermon in a deer park, and the deer joined the congregation. But the art which these religions produced was not primarily representational, because their ultimate spiritual goal was to leave this world. Christianity, alone among the major religions, encouraged naturalism in art. As late as the sixteenth century, the theologian Sebastian Franck could write, "As the light from the sun overflows the whole earth, but is not of this earth, and yet makes all things verdant, so God dwells in everything and everything dwells in him."

This is the elusive luminosity that pervades the pictures of the van Eyck brothers. Very little is known about them except that they worked between 1420 and 1440 in and around Ghent in Belgium, and that their main production was the vast altarpiece for that city's cathedral, one of the largest medieval panel paintings to have survived (ill. 1). Many artists have painted minutely, but what is remarkable when one sees the van Eycks' pictures in actuality is the extraordinary clarity of the light in them. Every blade of grass, and every eyelash, has been painted as if bathed in three-dimensional lucidity. Eyes, like jewels, are painted as curved lenses with an inner light of their own. This clarity is, of course, in the mind's eye.

The *Ghent Altarpiece* is a hymn to the whole of creation illuminated by the love of God. It's a literal illustration of a passage from the Book of Revelation: "And he showed me a pure river of the water of life, clear as crystal, proceeding out of the Throne of God and of the Lamb." This divine river of life doesn't just play in the fountain, but bathes the whole world in its glorious and glorifying light.

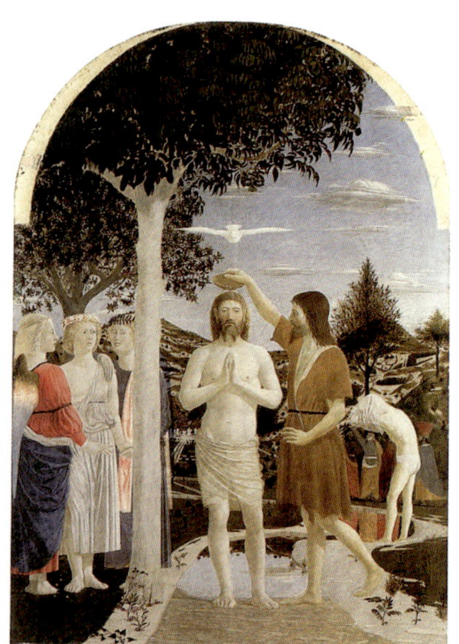

22 Piero della Francesca. *The Baptism of Christ*, c.1440. Oil on panel, 167 x 116 cm. National Gallery, London

Christian painting, right from its early tentative beginnings in the Roman empire, through to its crescendo in the fifteenth century, cannot be conceived of as a product of the Dark Ages, but rather as a revelation of light. The painter Piero della Francesca (c. 1415–1492) worked with great care to ensure that every movement, colour and shape in his pictures was complemented by another, so that the whole design would create a sense of harmony, not of fixed symmetry but of quiet stillness. His real goal in creating this scene of suspense was to fill it with light. The white dove of the Holy Spirit appears above Jesus just at the moment when the crystal baptismal waters fall upon him, heralding the start of his mission (ill.22). One highlight catches its downward-pointed beak and another illuminates the drop of water about to fall on Jesus' head. The world holds its breath; its sins have begun to clear away, for at that moment the light in the world has become more lucid. In Piero's art this light is still fresh; in that of Perugino and Raphael it turns sweet. It was difficult to harmonise the light of God with the light of day.

As soon as artists began to turn their searchlights on to the world around them, hoping to see God in his creation, they discovered realities that we can all recognise. This is the other glory of Christian art: its freshness of observation that was not, at least at first, in conflict with its religious purpose. The portrait statues of the founders (ill.23) in the choir of Naumburg Cathedral in Germany are a very early example. Their faces are uncannily modern, though they were carved and painted in about 1260. Two hundred and forty years later, in the year in which many thought Christ would come again, Albrecht Dürer (1471–1528) turned

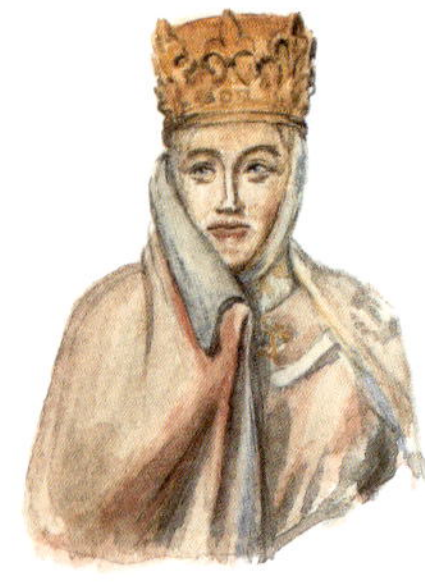

23 Uta, c.1260 C.E., detail of statue from the Founders Series in the Choir of Naumburg Cathedral. Painted stone. Naumburg, Germany

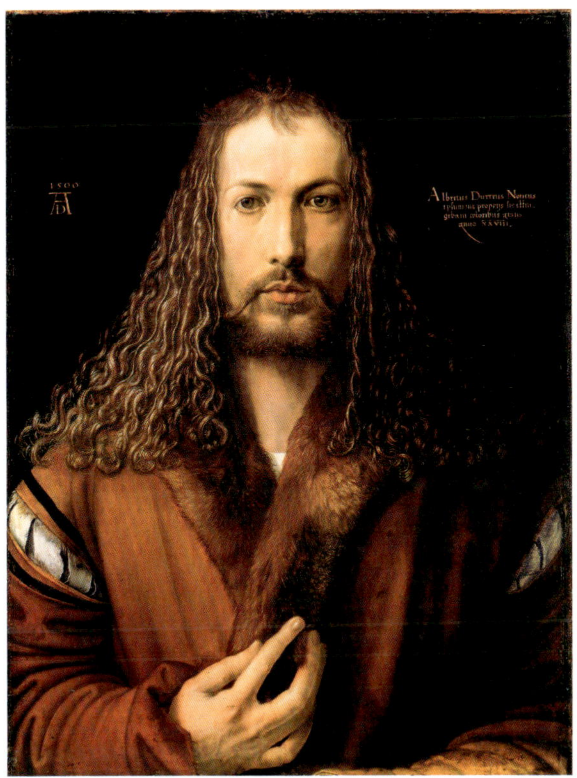

24 Albrecht Dürer. *Self-portrait*, 1500. Oil on panel, 67.1 x 48.7 cm. Alte Pinakothek, Munich

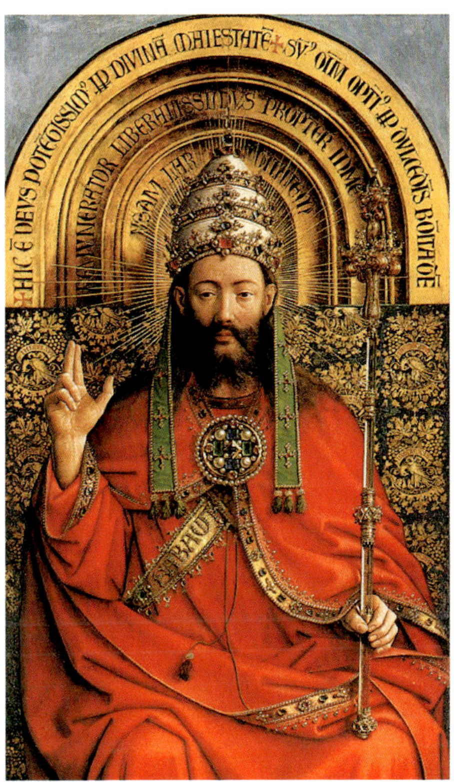

25 Hubert and Jan van Eyck. *The Ghent Altarpiece*, cf. p. 178, detail of God

the searchlight on himself (ill.24). There is a significant similarity between the van Eycks' depiction of God (ill.25) and Dürer's self-portrait. The similarity lies in the regal clarity of the gaze, the full-frontal, unhesitating confidence, and, of course, the human features.

It strikes us today as overweening arrogance to depict oneself as God, or as Dürer perhaps intended in this case, as his son, Jesus Christ. Dürer, indeed, had a great deal to boast about–his talents were extrolled by his contemporaries across Europe. Moreover his prints, which he produced by the hundred, earned him a breadth of popularity that perhaps no artist had ever enjoyed before. But this self-portrait is not a display of self-love, lavished with consummate skill, but a profound enquiry into human nature. By looking at oneself, Christians believed, one could see God, for God had made man in his own image. Even more poignantly, one could see Jesus, whom God had sent to earth as the Son of Man to become flesh, and by suffering, to cleanse humanity of its sins. Dürer's painting can be read as a response to the warning in St John's Gospel: "He was in the world, and the world was made by him, and the world knew him not." It's not an image of arrogance, but one of profound humility. The painting encapsulated, with vivid precision, the fusion of divine and earthly appearances that had troubled Christian theologians for so long, but on which so much of their faith hung. It was a fusion that would soon be torn asunder.

The man who began the process, but got nowhere near to finishing it, was Leonardo da Vinci (1452–1519). We tend to categorise Leonardo as the first modern scientist, and rather unfairly blame him for failing to take his insights to their logical conclusion. It's true that Columbus "discovered" the New World during his lifetime, but it was to be a hundred years before Galileo looked at the moon, and three centuries before Darwin finally worked out why living things look the way they do. Leonardo was a conventional, though certainly not devout, Christian. He wrote in his notebooks that "the painter is transformed into the likeness of the mind of God"—which seems to us an arrogant claim for any artist, even one as great as Leonardo. But this was a common view of the craft of painting during the Renaissance. It was not an art as we understand the term today. Painting then was an act of praise for God's creation. Leonardo believed that seeing was our noblest sense. Painting was pre-eminent among human activities because it combined the noble act of seeing with the noble act of thinking, which was in itself the ability that distinguished mankind from the beasts. What was remarkable about Leonardo was not just his ability to see but his capacity to think. He didn't just want to praise nature's beauty, he wanted to understand it. This wasn't because he was against religion – though he appeared increasingly to doubt conventional faith – but because, like so many of the great figures of the Renaissance, he was down-to-earth. He argued strongly against those who thought that life's span was too brief to spend it studying nature but, instead, wanted, "to comprehend the mind of God in which the universe is included". He thought he could find enough wonderful revelations of God's handiwork just by looking around him.

Leonardo's close examination of the world, which we can now admire so much, was essentially done in private. His sketchbooks are full of exquisitely shaded drawings which are annotated with immaculate notes written in a delicate hand in mirror writing, to hide their meaning from prying eyes. His contemporaries barely knew anything about them. Like many notes taken for personal use, they are an extraordinary jumble – a study of a horse next to the workings of a sluice, a sketch of a grotesque old man next to one showing the progressive growth of a leaf, a design for a battering ram next to the portrait of an angelic youth. In part they are a direct by-product of his work. He willingly turned his hand to any project his noble patrons wanted him to pursue, and they were often fickle – a new castle, a water pumping system, a colossal equestrian statue, a mechanical lion for a masque whose jaws opened to reveal a mouth full of flowers. It has become standard to criticise Leonardo, as indeed some of his contemporaries did also, for being too interested in everything to get anything done. But his grapeshot approach becomes understandable when one realises that he was only an initiator of a continuing effort to understand why things look like they do. The trouble for Leonardo was that the more he looked, the more incomprehensible everything became.

His agenda was hugely ambitious: to understand the order of the whole of creation. He looked everywhere – at swirling water (ill.26) and curling plants (ill.27). Why did they look alike? His searching eye led him to examine inner causes. So he dissected corpses, with the nervous approval of the church. He was the first person ever to draw with any accuracy the workings of the human body, those parts which God had designed so that we should never see them. His anatomical studies reveal a strange mixture of brilliant original observation and wishful thinking. He

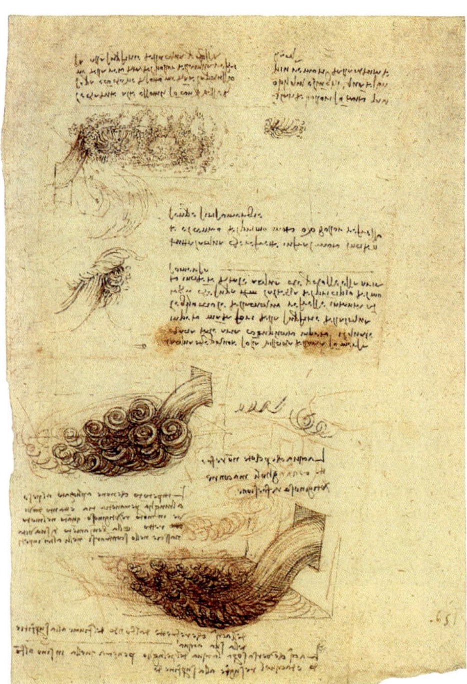

26 Leonardo da Vinci. Study of swirling water, c.1507–09, detail from a whole sheet. Pen and ink, 29 x 20.2 cm. Royal Library, Windsor Castle

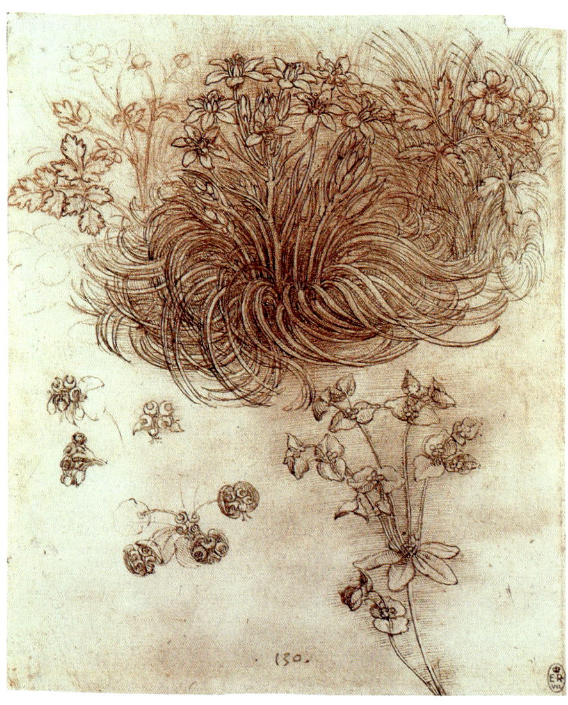

27 Leonardo da Vinci. A Star of Bethlehem, c.1505–08, detail from a whole sheet. Chalk and pen and ink, 19.8 x 16 cm. Royal Library, Windsor Castle

cut up an eye to see how it worked – "cook the whole eye in white of egg and then slice it", he advised – but he ended up thinking that it was like an onion (ill. 28). He sectionalised sexual intercourse (ill. 29) but added a tube linking the penis with the spine at the sacrum – the axial bone, once thought to be sacred, where the vertical backbone locks our heavenly connections to the earthly body which operates on the horizontal plane. This was not because he saw this tube, but because he believed it had to exist. Pregnancy couldn't result from the mixing of bodily fluids alone – there had to be spiritual juice in there too.

It's often remarked that Leonardo would have got further with his scientific enquires if he had spent less time painting. But this misses the key point: his studies were made in order to help him paint. His ambition, which no-one had aspired to before, was to depict the soul of the world. He was primarily an artist, not a scientist. His earliest biographer, Vasari, wrote that his "personal beauty could not be exaggerated – his every movement was grace itself … he possessed great strength combined with dexterity … he could sing and improvise divinely on the lyre." He was an animal lover – he bought caged birds in order to set them free – and a vegetarian – he never ate anything that had blood. Filled with a love of creation, he needed to find a way of expressing the sense of wonder and mystery he had for all that he saw around him.

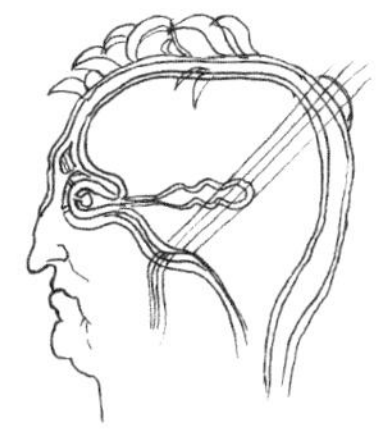

28 After Leonardo da Vinci. Section of a man's head showing the Anatomy of the Eye compared to an onion, c. 1489–90. Red chalk and pen and ink. Royal Library, Windsor Castle

Mystery was all-important. And so was mist. Leonardo didn't use such brilliant colours in his art as the earlier Italian painters had done, for he argued "in them there is no cause for wonder except their beauty" and when you admired them you were "giving credit to the manufacturer of pigments not the painter". The artist needn't just paint light but could paint darkness too, in his attempt to express the meaning of the whole of creation. So he created his famous sfumato technique, a method of painting the

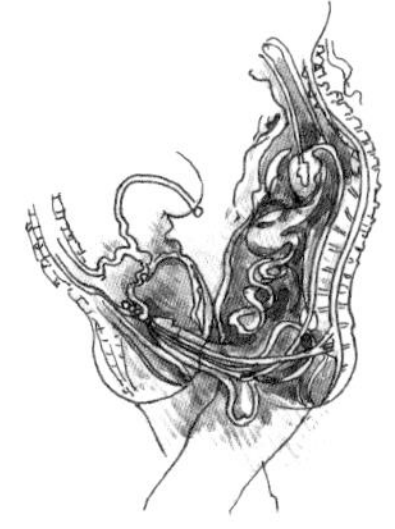

29 After Leonardo da Vinci. Coition of hemisected man and woman, c. 1492–93. Royal Library, Windsor Castle

mysterious confluence of light and shade, as evanescent an effect as warm breath visible for a moment in cold air. The mechanics of this were not understood. When they were, the steam engine was invented, long after Leonardo dreamed of machines not powered by man alone.

The ancient Greeks thought that mist was the turning point between the warmth of life and the chill of death—and they proved it with an experiment. If you blow on your hand through pursed lips, your breath is cold; open your lips and your breath is warm. These are the two winds that blow Venus (ill. 18) to her birth on land. Sir Philip Sydney (1554–1586) wrote that, "when moisture and heat unite, life is conceived". It is probable that Leonardo knew all such theories. We only have a partial view of his extraordinary, encyclopaedic mind; perhaps as many as a third of his notebooks have been lost. But we do know that Leonardo was fascinated by mist and smoke. His sketchbooks are littered with observations of their effects as they changed colour against different backgrounds, of the sun's rays falling on warm vapour evaporating into "minute atoms rendered luminous against the darkness of the fiery sphere", and of the azure sky turning

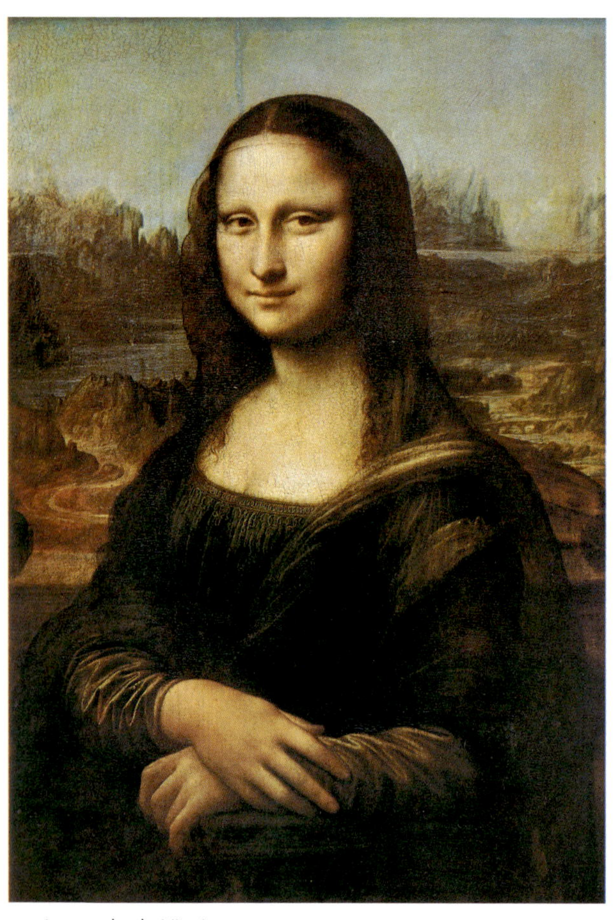

30 Leonardo da Vinci. *Mona Lisa*, c. 1503. Oil on panel. Louvre, Paris

white at the horizon, and of blue shadows on white cloth in sunlight, and of purple haze on distant mountains. Human beings are bathed in mist and their life is a mystery. It is out of mist, too, that the *Mona Lisa* emerges.

The *Mona Lisa* (ill.30) is Leonardo's attempt to paint the soul. He apparently worked on it for many years, and kept the painting with him until he died, which suggests that it might not have been a commission, or if it was, that it went on long past its sell-by date. Writing in 1568, Vasari stated it to be a portrait of the wife of a certain Francesco del Giocondo, but added that she looked "divine rather than human". He described what's still there under the layers of discoloured recent varnish, which the Louvre stubbornly refuses to remove: "The eyes had that lustre and watery sheen always seen in life. … The nostrils, rosy and tender, seemed to be alive. … The opening of the mouth seemed not to be coloured but living flesh." Leonardo created a woman who appears to breathe, and to smile–a smile that appears to know both joy and sorrow, birth and death.

The smile has a long history in art: the antique smile of early Greek statues (ill.31) that seems to be knowing but not arrogant; the otherworldly, slow, contemplative smile of the Buddha (ill.32); the gentle, caring smile of the Virgin Mary (ill.33). Marcus Aurelius

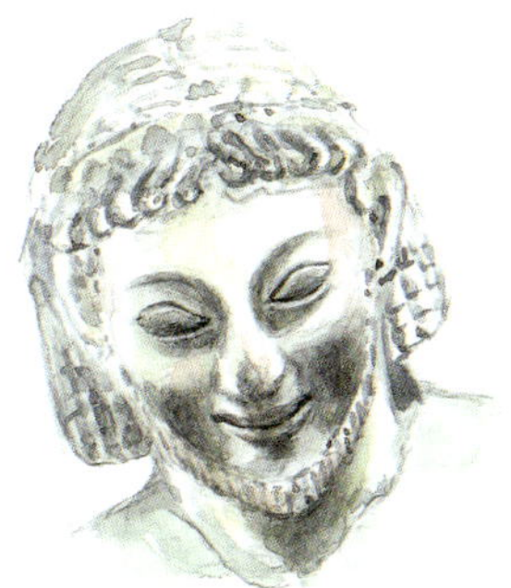

31 Head of a Horseman, called the Rampin Rider, c. 550 B.C.E., Athens. Marble, 27 cm high. Louvre, Paris

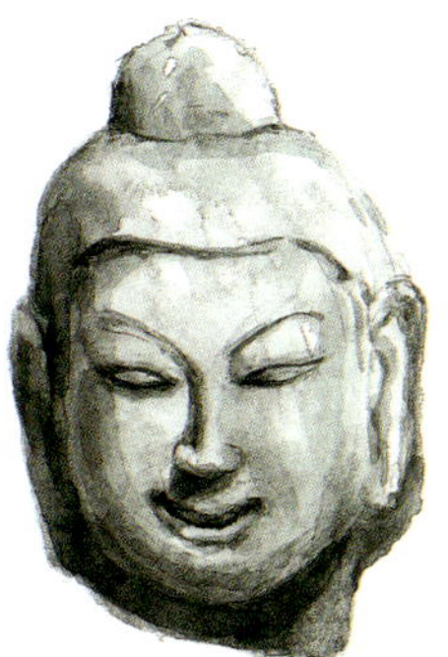

32 Head of a Buddha, 4th century C.E., Yung Kang Temple, northern China. Stone, 46.5 cm high. National Museum, Tokyo

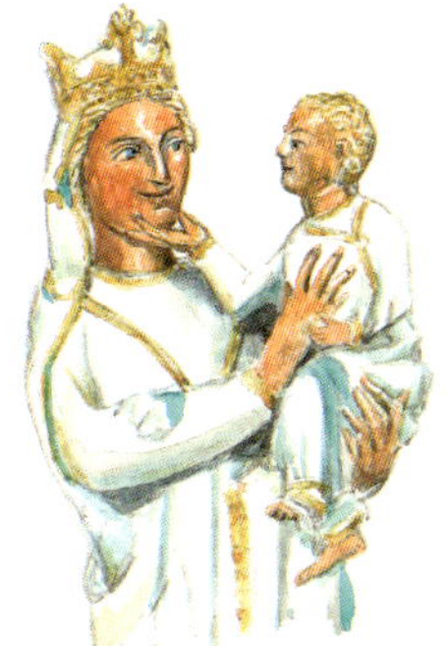

33 Virgin and Child, c. 1250–60 C.E. Marble. Toledo Cathedral, Spain

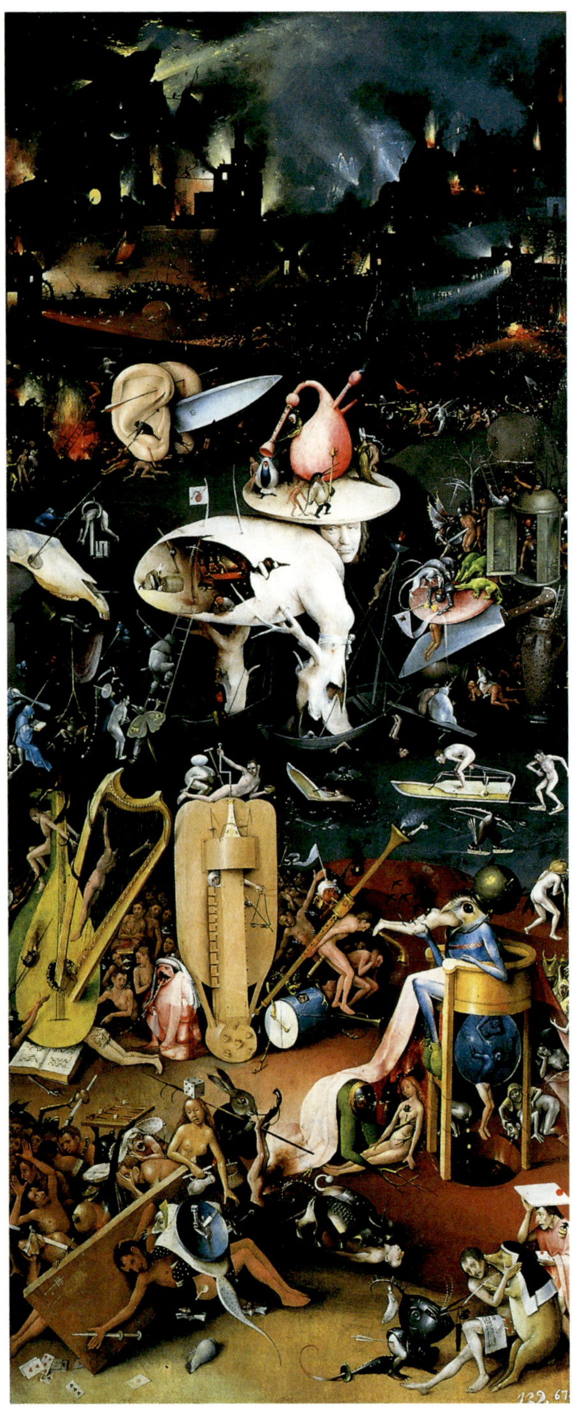

34 Hieronymus Bosch. *The Garden of Earthly Delights*, c.1505 C.E. Hell panel of the triptych. Prado, Madrid

(121–80 C.E.), the most respected and magnanimous of Roman emperors, whose equestrian portrait is the only antique sculpture to survive complete in Rome, wrote in his *Meditations* that "the soul defines the face". Dante (1265–1321) added, "What is a smile if not the flashing out of the soul's delight?" The *Mona Lisa*'s smile has become so famous not just because it expresses the mystery of conscious existence, though such an extraordinary achievement would be enough in itself. It has come to haunt our collective imagination because it is so equivocal. Is this Mother Nature—which the Mona Lisa seems so calmly to embody—smiling? And if so, is she smiling at us?

Both Leonardo and Dürer had premonitions that the world was turning dark. They became haunted by deluges. Five years before his death, Leonardo's notebooks are filled with sketches of tempests crashing down from the sky and torrents tearing away mountains. Dürer described how "in the year 1525, between Wednesday and Thursday after Whit Sunday during the night ... many great waters fell down from heaven. The first struck the earth about four miles away from me with a terrific force... I was so frightened I awoke and my whole body trembled ... God turn all things to the best." These mental storms were, in part, prob-≤ably generated by a widespread expectation that the world would end in the year 1500. Major floods in Germany in the early 1500s were thought to presage the apocalypse. The extraordinary art of Hieronymus Bosch (ill.34) is best explained in the context of millennial panic. He gloriously pokes fun at our little pink, weedy bodies, and our desires and fantasies, in ways that touch a nerve with everyone. His art looks medieval, even shamanistic, yet it is a product of the Renaissance, demonstrating that the common world picture of this period was much closer to that of the cave artist than it is to our own. But everything was about to change.

Dürer sensed it in his print *Melancholia* (ill. 35). This extremely complex image eludes definitive interpretation, but its pensiveness is new in art. The melancholic was known from medieval times as someone suffering from what we today would call depression, a world-weariness and lack of energy that was then attributed to an excess of "black bile" in the body. Dürer, who was well-read in Latin authors, appears to be eliding this with the ancient classical tradition that defined the melancholic as a man of intellect. Were world-weariness and the search for understanding becoming the same? The planet Saturn, the god of mathematics—represented by the polyhedron and the sphere—is shown in descent. The instruments of applied mathematics—the saw, plane, hammer, and melting pot—lie idle, while the angel twiddles the compass in her hand. She seems to be meditating on the pointlessness of creating or of searching for an understanding of anything in this world. A similar gloom cast its shadow over Leonardo's last years. He wandered through King Francis I's palace at Amboise, in France, pasting fake wings on to lizards to create pet dragons and inflating a ram's guts to fill a room, like a proto-installation artist. His notebooks increasingly echo with the refrain: "Tell me if anything was ever done." It was slowly dawning on him—and it was a dark thought—that "nature is full of an

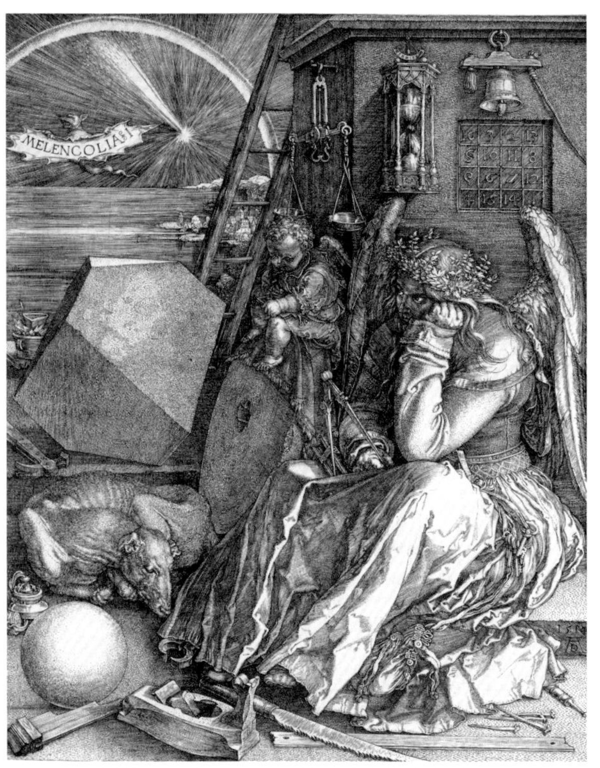

35 Albrecht Dürer. *Melancholia*, 1514. Engraving, 23.9 x 16.8 cm. The British Museum, London

infinity of operations which have never been part of our experience". The wonderful sights of nature might not, after all, have been made for us to look at. Darkness began to flood through Christian art. The twin beams that the Renaissance had shone on nature—to reveal life as it was, and God's place in it—began to diverge, and a shadow fell between them.

It had long been difficult to reconcile the idea of heaven on earth with the realities of late medieval life. Natural disasters such as plagues, famines, fires and floods were bad enough, but these were made much worse by human behaviour, the endless warfare between cities and within cities that Gibbon had identified as being one of the chief causes of the lingering decline of the Roman empire. In the 1440s, Brother Giovanni da Fiesole, who was so devout that they called him Fra Angelico, was able to paint radiant visions of Christ's time on earth for peaceful contemplation in the cells of the convent of San Marco in Florence, but artists who became increasingly dependent on the fortunes and favours of belligerent and scheming aristocrats, merchants and bankers had a tougher time conjuring up images of peace on earth, or even getting paid. Even the gentle Leonardo had to spend a great deal of his time designing ever larger weapons of destruction. As the leading ministers of the faith grew more blatantly corrupt, it became increasingly difficult to fuse reality and divinity into a single vision. The church soon gave up the struggle and decided to bludgeon its earthly adherents with visions of heaven. The Baroque period was the last great attempt by the Catholic Church to create a gesamtkunstwerk that it hoped would be as popular as its Gothic cathedrals had been in the past.

There was one artist of genius, however, who did not abandon Christianity's long-treasured ambition to reveal divinity in ordinary life, and express in visual terms the doctrine of the "Real

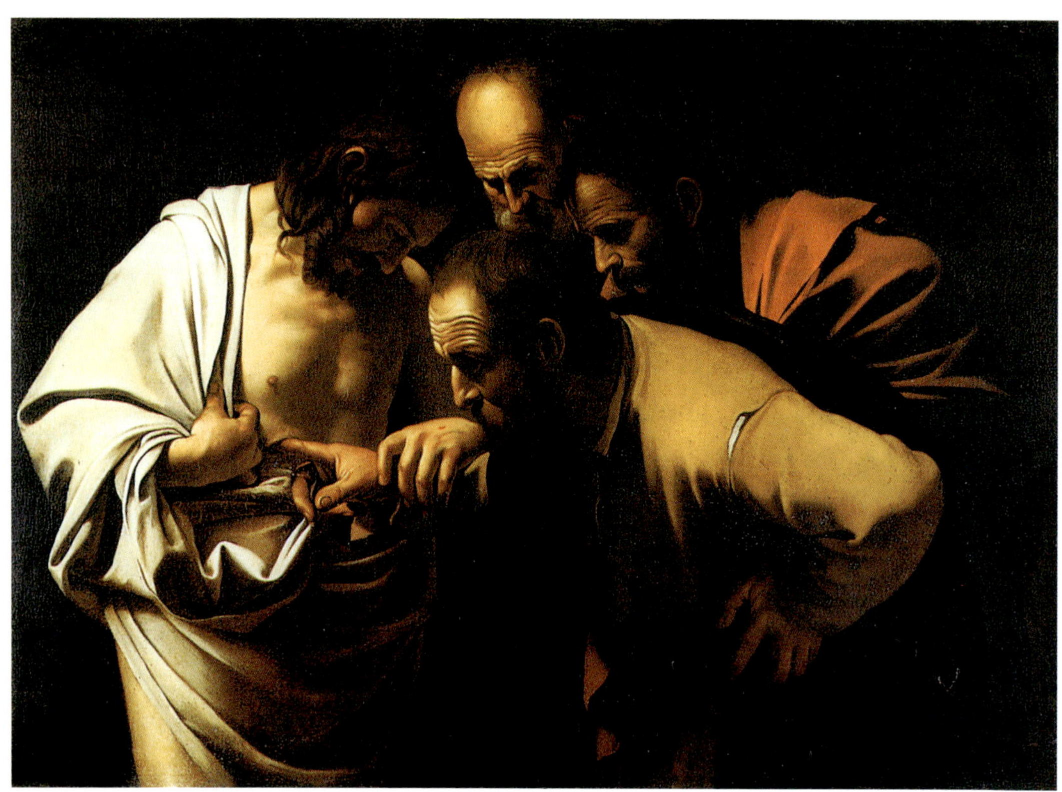

36 Michelangelo Merisi da Caravaggio. *Doubting Thomas*, 1602–03. Oil on canvas, 107 x 146 cm. Stiftung Schlösser und Gärten, Sanssouci, Potsdam

Presence". High and mighty clerics objected to the sweaty headcloths, grubby feet and weathered, peasant faces in the paintings of Caravaggio (1573–1610), but his vividly naturalistic depictions of biblical scenes always found ready buyers. His *Doubting Thomas* (ill. 36) is a literal rendition of the words of Christ as recorded by St John: "Reach hither thy hand, and thrust it into my side, and be not faithless but believing." The appearance of Christ follows a convention, as do the lines on St Thomas' brow. Leonardo was probably expressing general opinion when he noted that "men who have strongly marked horizontal lines on their foreheads are full of sorrow, whether secret or admitted".

What is fresh is that Caravaggio has tried to envisage the scene in unflinching detail, as if the event were happening just before him; the fold of skin above the wound catches the light as it is raised by St Thomas's probing finger.

A century earlier such a scene would have been suffused in the glow of God's light in the world. But that light, which had been the glory of late medieval and Renaissance art, had faded. Now spiritual reality was revealed by a beacon in the darkness. Caravaggio's own life was symbolic of the gulf that had widened between the sacred and the profane. He painted the most devout pictures of his age, but his life was spent brawling in taverns and fleeing from a murder charge. Few expected a consistency between heaven and earth. St Thomas couldn't believe with his eyes that the crucified Christ had really returned in the flesh, until he touched his wound. He was the perfect saint for the period. Caravaggio died just as Galileo turned his doubting eye on the moon and saw, through his telescope, that it was not a manifestation of the Virgin Mary in her undefiled purity, as the Catholic Church maintained, but a lump of solid rock.

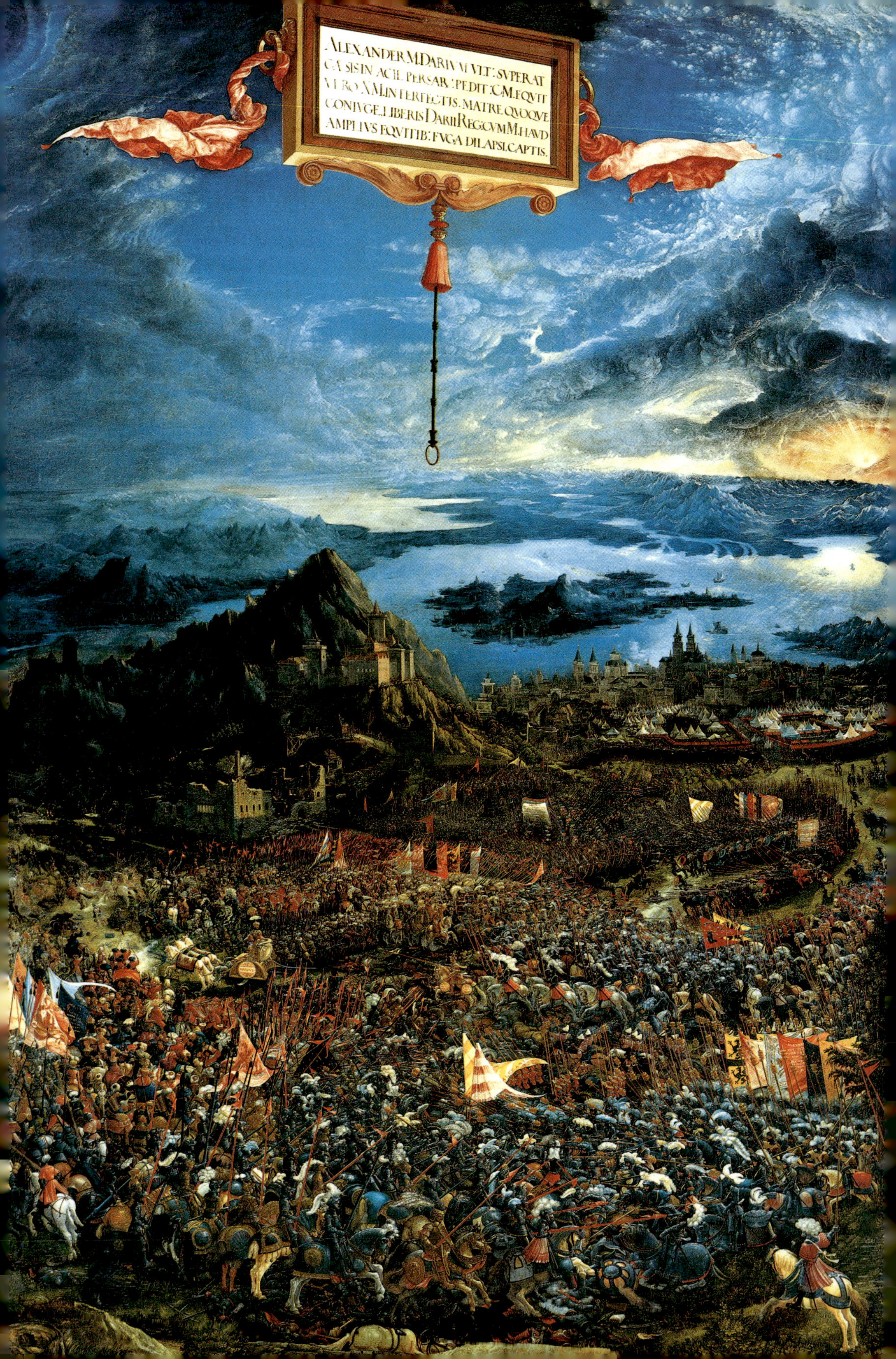
ALEXANDER M. DARIVM VLT: SVPERAT
CAESIS IN ACIE PERSAR: PEDIT: C M. EQVIT
VERO X M. INTERFECTIS. MATRE QVOQVE
CONIVGE. LIBERIS DARII REG. CVM M. HAVD
AMPLIVS EQVITIB: FVGA DILAPSI. CAPTIS.

Chapter 9

The Age of Darkness

It's human to question. Most infants go through an exhausting phase of endlessly asking "why?" Writing in 1779 James Boswell described how his little daughter suddenly announced: "I do not believe there is a God." He continued: "Said I, 'It's He who makes the sun shine'… said she, 'It shines only on good days.' It was a strange and alarming thing for her mother and me to hear our little angel talk so." His daughter, surely, soon learnt how to be an angel. Her reasoning was entirely spontaneous and natural, but it had in fact a distinguished, though suppressed history of its own. Aristotle (384–322 B.C.E.) had made the same observation, when he noted that "the rain does not fall to make the corn grow, any more than it falls to spoil the corn." Boswell was a highly educated man, but although he lived in the middle of the Enlightenment his world picture was still essentially medieval, in that he believed that God had made the sun to shine on us.

You could question what you saw if it helped you to spin thread more quickly, to shoot an arrow more accurately or to breed a larger grain of corn, but the idea that the principles governing these practical advances could explain the circulation of the stars was too disturbing for most people to countenance. So science was kept firmly in its place, as a tool for living, not for thinking. It is often thought that art followed technological advance: when Stone Age people had had enough to eat, they picked up their brushes; art was a product of wonder mixed with ease. But if that was so, why then did they paint in terrifying caves deep underground? The truth is that art, like religion, was the product of

1 Albrecht Altdorfer. *The Battle of Alexander and Darius*, 1529. Oil on canvas. Alte Pinakothek, Munich

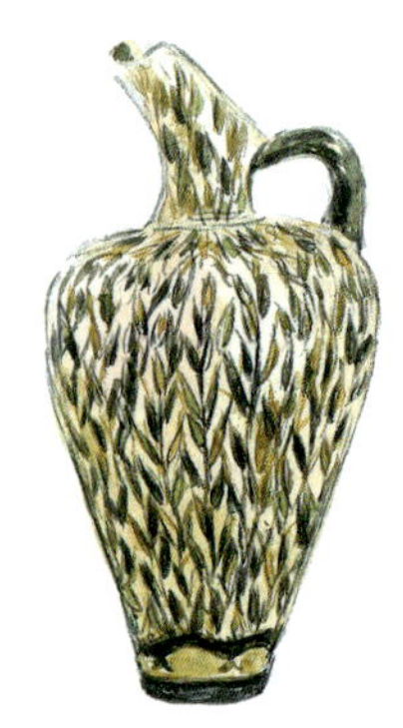

2 Flask decorated with corn, c.1500 B.C.E., Palaikastro. Museum of Heraklion, Crete

wonder mixed with fear–the fear, ultimately, of death. Far from being a product of luxury, art was a necessity for living. If this ancestral image wasn't worshipped, or that picture wasn't painted, where would the next child come from, or the next antelope? The truth is that it wasn't art but science–pure science that is, not technology–that was the product of wonder mixed with ease. Only if you weren't afraid of the sun would you dare to try to find out where it went to at night.

Aristotle wrote in his *Metaphysics*: "Men were first led to study science, as they are today, by wonder. They felt wonder about the behaviour of the moon, the phenomena of the sun, and the origination of the universe. Now he who is perplexed and wonders believes himself to be ignorant. Hence even the lover of myths is, in a sense, a scientist, for myth is a tissue of wonders. Thus if they took to science to escape ignorance, it is patent that they were pursuing science for the sake of knowledge itself, and not for any utilitarian applications... That is why the mathematical arts were first put together in Egypt, for in that country the priestly caste were indulged with leisure." The ancient Egyptians might have theorised about mathematics–they certainly used it in their technology and mythology–but it was the ancient Greeks who, as far as we know, first theorised about the universe as a whole.

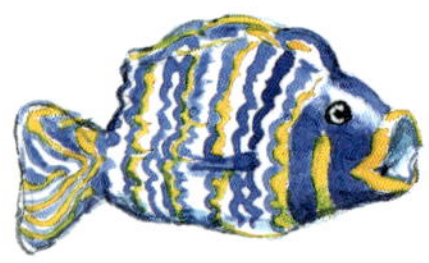

3 Fish bottle used for scented oils, 1353–36 B.C.E., Armana, Egypt. Glass, 7 x 14 cm. British Museum, London

One senses that there was a growing feeling of well-being from about 2000 B.C.E. among the people who lived around the Mediterranean. A flask exuberantly decorated with sprouting corn, fired in Crete around 1500 B.C.E. (ill. 2), and a scent bottle formed in the shape of a fish (ill. 3) with coloured bands of glass for scales, blown in Egypt about 1340 B.C.E., are fragmentary survivals that evoke an age when the sea's emerald waters teemed with delicacies for the table, and the cows, hives and vines flowed with milk and honey and dark red wine. An exquisite Greek cup

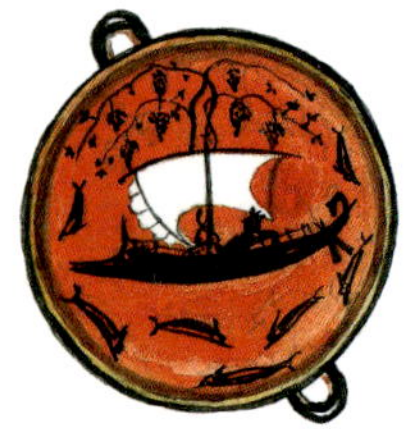

4 Dionysus on a ship, 6th century B.C.E., Athenian cup from Vulci (Etruria) signed by potter Exekias. Staatliche Antikensammlungen, Munich

(ill. 4), made in the sixth century B.C.E. and signed by the potter Exekias, illustrates a story told about the god Dionysus. One day some pirates captured him without knowing who he was; disgruntled, the god relieved himself against the ship's mast and it immediately grew into a vine bearing grapes. The terrified crew jumped into the sea and were turned into dolphins. Everything, even a god's irritation, enhanced nature's fecundity. At the Villa Imperiale in Sicily are some of the finest surviving Roman mosaics. They cascade down the sun-drenched hillside, decorating the floors of a sequence of hot and cold baths. One, seventy metres long, depicts a big game hunt in a land of exuberant plenty. Pleasures abound. Glowing under the limpid waters, ladies play ball games in their bikinis (ill. 5).

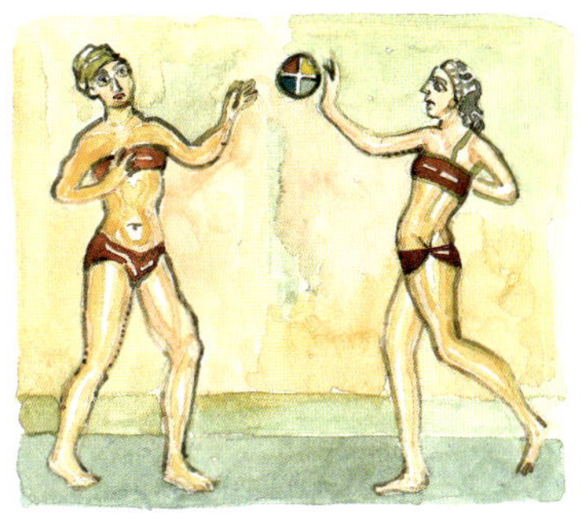

5 Room of the Maidens, 4th century C.E. Mosaic. Villa Imperiale, Piazza Armerina, Sicily

The ancient Greeks even appeared to be at ease with death, although average life expectancy was much shorter then than now. In a cemetery in Athens, a number of gravestones have been found which depict families saying goodbye to their departed. In one (ill. 6) a daughter bids farewell to her deceased mother while her father stands lovingly by. There is nothing like these gravestones anywhere else in the world. Death is only a handshake away, a tender goodbye. One of the very few paintings of ancient Greece to survive was found in a small, stone-box coffin in provincial southern Italy. It's now known as the Tomb of the Diver (480–470 B.C.E.). The underside of the lid (ill. 7) shows the dead occupant diving, naked, into the sea. This was almost certainly symbolic of the soul entering the spiritual world. But the afterlife, in this delightful age, was not characterised by either eternal suffering or eternal thanksgiving. It was thought simply to be a continuation, for eternity, of what one enjoyed doing when one was alive. The paintings on the coffin walls show what the

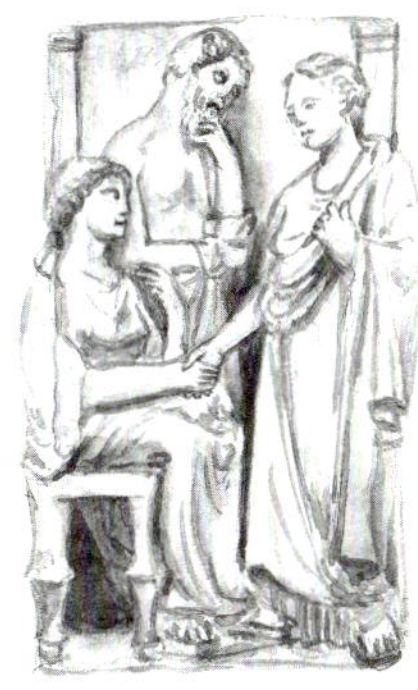

6 Grave stele, c. 400 B.C.E., found at Kerameikos, Athens. 148 cm. National Archaeological Museum, Athens

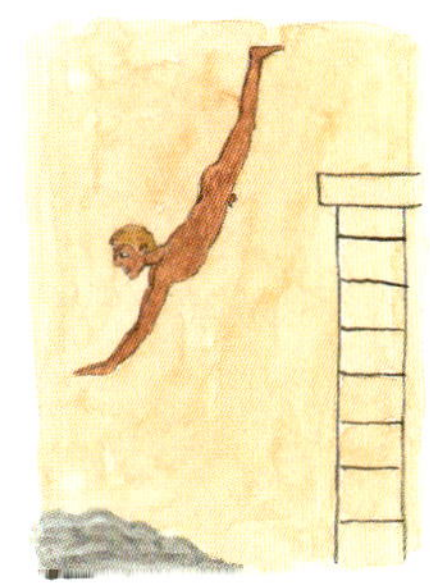

7 Ceiling fresco showing a diver, 480–470 B.C.E., Greek. The Tomb of the Diver, National Archaeological Museum, Paestum

deceased liked doing best: lying on a daybed at a *symposium*–a drinking party–while fondling his boyfriend, and playing *kottabos*–the game of aiming the dregs of your wine at a cup floating in water–while a naked youth danced to the accompaniment of a flute.

Defeating sickness most probably provided science with its first successes in its long battle against religions, superstitions and philosophies. Drugs, knives and needles could cure more effectively than the shaman's chants, even if the means by which they did so were not yet understood. Manuals dating from four thousand years ago exist in China, Sumeria and Egypt describing the workings of the human body, the preservation of the health of chorus women and how to avoid sickness during childbirth. But it was the Greek Hippocratic doctors in c. 450 B.C.E. who first tried to separate medicine from superstition. One wrote of the mysterious affliction of epilepsy that "it is no more divine than any other disease. Men think it divine merely because they do not understand it." The classical age was the first to study illness fearlessly and with sympathy. The oldest surviving botanically accurate study of a plant (ill. 8) was probably copied from an earlier edition of a herbal compiled by Dioscorides, a Roman army doctor whose book was in turn almost certainly based on a much older work now lost. The blackberry, it tells us, was good for strengthening gums, restraining the flux of women and preventing mouth ulcers and diarrhoea.

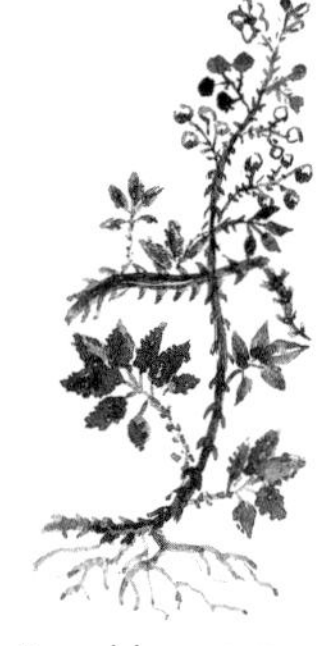

8 Bramble, 512 C.E. After the Codex of Dioscorides. Watercolour drawing. National Library, Vienna

The Greeks looked at the world with inquisitiveness free from fear. Aristotle, probably the first true scientist, rejected Plato's idea that the soul exists separately from the body. He believed instead that divinity manifested itself in the material universe, which he studied with relish, writing 170 books, of which only 30 survive, on everything from physics to zoology, biology to botany, chemistry to history. He thought that the world was a sphere, albeit one fixed at the centre of the universe, that time extended infinitely into the past and the future, and that species were fixed for all time. Heraclides of Pontus (388–310 B.C.E.) proposed that it was the earth, not the heavens, which turned, and cast its shadow on the moon; and Aristarchus of Samos (c. 310-c. 230 B.C.E.) worked out that the planets, including ours, revolved around the sun. Eratosthenes (c. 276–194 B.C.E.) calculated the circumference of the earth purely by observing the changing direction and length of a shadow cast by a stick standing in sunlight; he was only fifty miles out. But these remarkable insights remained theories known only to a few, even in Greece. What practical use were they to a farmer suffering from a drought? He'd be better off praying to Zeus. Christianity and Islam became the dominant religions in Europe and western Asia without altering the common man's world picture.

Pure science remained dormant for a thousand years. Chinese scholars were fascinated by natural phenomena, but their advances were essentially technical rather than theoretical: they invented the compass, acupuncture, gunpowder and printing. There was no state religion in China but the system operated as if there were, for all scholars were appointed by a government headed by an emperor who assumed that the world was flat and that his job was to officiate at its centre to maintain harmony, prosperity and peace. Buddhism, the dominant religion in China, didn't encourage the development of science quite simply because one was supposed to spend all one's time aspiring to leave this world, not looking at it. A new scientific age began to dawn in 1404 C.E., when the third Ming emperor, Zhu Di, employed over two thousand scholars to gather together all the wisdom of the world. He sent vast fleets of ships to the "four corners"–not to conquer other nations, but to learn about their cultures and trade with them. Chinese ships reached Australia, Africa and America (but not Europe) by 1424, seventy years before Columbus sailed across the Atlantic in the service of Spain.

It's almost certain but not yet proven that Chinese scholars had, by this time, worked out that the world was spherical. (The Chinese fleets could have sailed to the four corners and back without going around the world.) If they had, this knowledge remained secret; it was not the view of the common people, nor the official view of the imperial court, nor, apparently, that of god in heaven. Two months after the ships had set sail, on 9 May 1421, lightning struck the Forbidden City. A fireball danced down the Imperial Way destroying, one after the other, the Halls of Great Harmony, Central Harmony and Preserving Harmony. The emperor's throne was burnt to a crisp. Zhu Di issued an edict to his people, saying how distressed and confused he was by this heavenly fury, for he thought he had done nothing wrong. He had not offended his ancestors nor acted tyrannically. So he addressed an open letter to his people, asking that if they knew of anything improper, they should "lay these out, hiding nothing, so that we may try to reform ourselves and regain Heaven's favour". Conservative forces in China blamed the emperor's explorations. The fleets hadn't come back with anything worth learning or trading. Soon all "foreign trips" were cancelled, and all records of their journeys destroyed. China turned in on itself. It closed its borders to the outside world, and burnt a strip of land thirty miles wide along its coast to deter anyone from wanting to look in, or out.

The idea that the world was a sphere had never been entirely lost in scholastic circles in Europe and western Asia, for copies of

Greek texts were preserved in the libraries of Islamic and Christian monasteries, though they were carefully guarded by imams and priests. By 1400, however, the Church's missionary zeal and desire for wealth encouraged scholars to pore over these ancient texts to discover new lands to convert and conquer. Islamic expansion was mainly by land. Christians ventured across the sea. The *Geographia* of Ptolemy (c. 90–168 C.E.) – which demonstrated the principles of latitude and longitude based on the earth as a globe – caused a sensation in Europe when it was translated from Greek into Latin in 1409. The reason why it took Columbus such a long time to raise the funds for his journey in 1492 was not because educated people then thought the world was flat, but because they agreed with the ancient Greeks that it was much bigger than Columbus thought. They were right. When Columbus "discovered" the Americas – where millions of people were already living – he thought, wrongly, that he'd reached India.

Soon explorers set off from Europe in every direction. In 1522 Ferdinand Magellan's ship became the first to circumnavigate the world. The earth began to look much bigger, on the one hand, but at the same time, it appeared to get much smaller. *The Battle of Alexander and Darius* by Albrecht Altdorfer (c. 1480–1538) (ill. 1) is perhaps the first attempt to express humanity's new world picture, with planet earth conceived as a massive curved sphere, the diminutive sun and moon spinning round it, and mankind – even the great heroes of ancient times – reduced to battling ants.

The earth was believed to be a sphere, but it was fixed in space. Mankind might be small, but we were still standing – some of us, admittedly, upside down – at the centre of the universe. Nothing had fundamentally altered – until Copernicus (1473–1543) revived the Greek idea that the earth revolved around the sun. Legend has it that he was shown the first copy of his revolution-

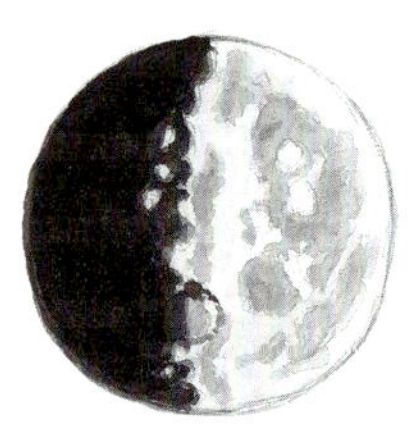

9 After Galileo Galilei. *Light and Shade on the Surface of the Moon*, 1610, original telescopic drawing for *Siderius Nuncius* (Venice, 1610). National Library, Florence

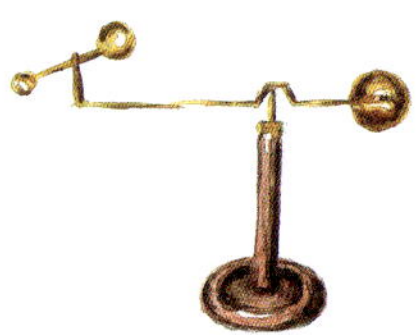

10 G. Adams (the younger). Electric orrery, showing how the moon rotates around the earth while both rotate around the sun, c.1765. Science Museum, London

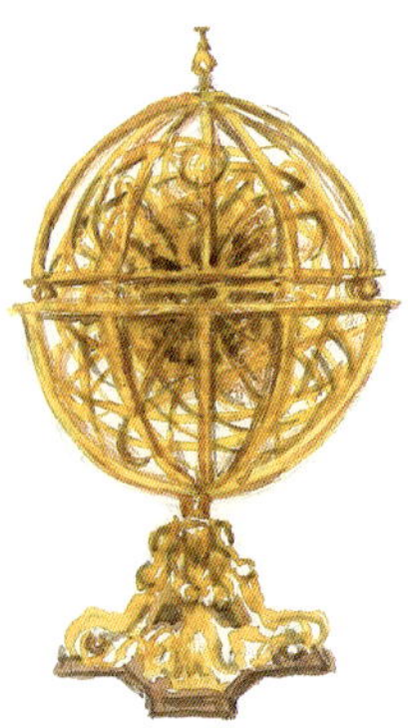

11 Antonio Santucci. Armillary sphere, 1588–93 C.E. Museum of the History of Science, Florence

ary book *De Revolutionibus* on his deathbed. He didn't live to face the consequences, but then there might have been none, because his idea was only a theory—no different from other interpretations of the mysteries of the universe.

Our modern world picture was born in December 1609, when Galileo trained his telescope on the moon. The instrument had been invented the year before in Holland, but Galileo made a more powerful version for himself. That night he watched, for the first time in history, the shadows of mountains lengthening on the surface of the moon. He made sketches of them in watercolour (ill.9), which was the only way he had to record them. He then observed the moons of Jupiter in orbit, and discovered spots on the sun. Spots! How could the sun have been impure? The heavens Galileo discovered were a wondrous sight—full of myriads of stars, planets and satellites, all spinning around each other—just as the earth was spinning around the sun.

Over a century later, when his theories began to be widely accepted, an educational model, called an orrery (ill.10), was made to show how the solar system worked. We have come a long way from the sun chariot model made by people in Denmark two thousand years earlier (p.67, ill.4). But Galileo's discovery was also a long way from the new model of the universe which had recently been accepted by the church, as exemplified by the armillary sphere (ill.11), in which the earth was a fixed globe surrounded by rotating heavenly hosts. How could the Roman Catholic Church abandon the world view they'd just grown used to, and accept one that was so totally different, and apparently nonsensical? They'd had enough trouble with Protestant rebellions in the north. Understandably, they chose to maintain the status quo. "Nothing moves above the moon", the Jesuits argued, even though they now accepted that the sun, moon and stars travelled around the earth. In 1633, his inquisitors showed Galileo the instruments of torture that they proposed to use on him and he renounced his "suspicions", as he was told to call them.

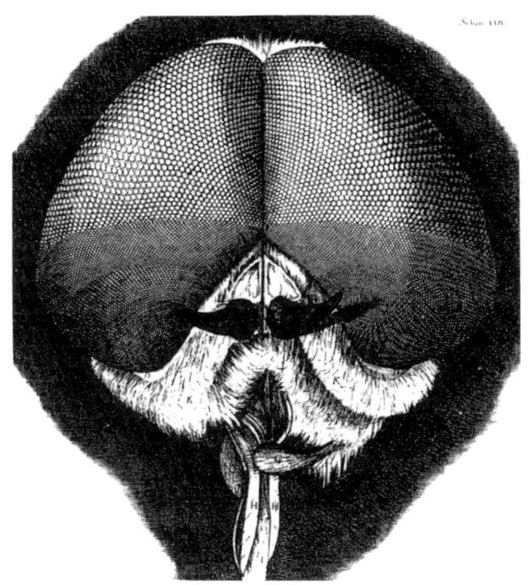

12 Robert Hooke. *The Eye of a Fly*, 1665, from *Micrographia*. Natural History Museum, London

Science, however, had had its major breakthrough. It had found a way of gathering evidence from a world beyond our sight. In about 1624, Galileo used the principles of the telescope to develop a microscope. It was perfected by the Dutch, and used by the English scientist Robert Hooke to create his great illustrated book of the wonders of nature that were too small to see, such as the structure of a fly's eye (ill.12). Hooke's *Micrographia* (1665) was the world's first scientific bestseller. People were amazed to see creatures in drops of water that no-one had imagined existed. And the pope could do nothing about it, for these wonders of nature moved under the moon.

What's surprising is that it took so long to invent these comparatively simple visual aids. We had had eyeglasses since at least 1300 C.E., but, apart from isolated proposals by Roger Bacon (1214–92) and Leonardo which remained theoretical, no-one had actually put lenses together to magnify the specks in heaven and on earth. We were not supposed to see beyond the natural range of our God-given vision, and it never occurred to anyone that there was anything there to see.

Science was gaining in confidence. The French philosopher René Descartes (1596–1650) argued that it was a disgrace to human thought that we'd discovered the telescope by chance and not on purpose. He reasoned, with Jesuitical skill, that we can question everything except our ability to question, which was a gift from God. "I think therefore I am" is the first true philosophical proposition. He believed that people would in time be able to "explain the nature of the clouds in such a way that we will no longer have any occasion to wonder at anything that can be seen of them." It distressed him that he couldn't do so yet. He considered it was his God-given right to examine everything he could see, but he kept on the right side of the Church by arguing that he did not expect to discover God by doing so, because God had banned us, for our sins, into a world of dark obscurity.

Blaise Pascal (1623–62), the brilliant mathematician and physicist, found that the more he studied the operations of nature, the darker everything became. He wrote: "When I see the blind and wretched state of man, and survey the whole universe in its dumbness and man left to himself with no light, as though lost in this corner of the universe, without knowing who put him here, what he has come to do, what will become of him when he dies, incapable of knowing anything, I am moved to terror." He interpreted this terror as fear of God, and became an even more devout Catholic, but one totally opposed to the reactionary world picture upheld by the Jesuits. The scientific examinations by the Jewish philosopher Baruch Spinoza (1632–77) led him to the conclusion that all religions are "a tissue of meaningless mysteries". He was excommunicated from his synagogue in 1656. While the sentence was read out – "Let him be accursed by day and night … and raze out his name from under the sky" – the lights of the synagogue were put out one by one, eventually leaving the congregation in total darkness. This was a sym-

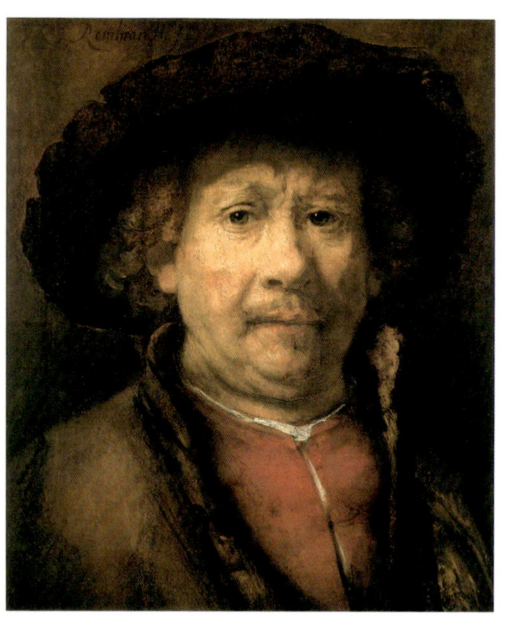

13 Rembrandt. *Self-portrait*, c.1665. Oil on canvas. Kunsthistorisches Museum, Vienna

bolic act: it typifies how the era of scientific discovery that we now call the Enlightenment led to a gradual but sustained darkening of religious belief and thought.

The sixteenth and seventeenth centuries saw religious belief battling with scientific reason, against a background of increasing gloom—the shadow play that Leonardo had, in his art, instinctively predicted. This was the age of *chiaroscuro*—the struggle between light and shade—a period unique in the history of world art. *Chiaroscuro* rolls its drums in the art of Caravaggio (p. 218, ill. 36), as sensual passion marches defiantly side by side with religious fervour. It glows through fingers held to a candle in the haunting, prayerful pictures of Georges de la Tour. But it finds its most profound expression in the paintings of Rembrandt (1609–69), Spinoza's contemporary and fellow Dutchman, as he looked at the world and himself with increasing doubt and foreboding. As he grew older he became increasingly religious, eventually joining the Mennonites, a strict Protestant sect that favoured simplicity, poverty and the direct appeal to God. He was obsessed with the look in his face, but not because of vanity. He painted and drew over a hundred self-portraits during his lifetime, and they tell a story of increasing introspection. The later ones (ill. 13) are a world apart from Dürer's confident self-examination (p. 207, ill. 24). It's as if *Melancholia* (p. 216, ill. 35) has cast her shadow over Rembrandt's spirit. He seemed to be asking, over and over again, whether God really had made mankind in his own image—and, if not, who was he?

The same tension between science and religion can be seen in the paintings of Velázquez (1599–1660), but without Rembrandt's introspection. In 1623 Velázquez became the court painter of Spain, and had to spend most of his time producing royal portraits. Standing in front of *Las Meninas* (ill. 14) is a very different experience from looking at a reproduction of it in a book. The painting is life-size; it is as though an opening has been punched through the wall into the next room. Looking at the picture, you have the sensation that you are standing where the king and queen, who are reflected in the silver mirror at the back, are posing for their portraits. Velázquez is painting you. *Las Meninas* are the maids of honour attending the Infanta who has come, with a court dwarf, to watch her parents–you–being painted. It is as though you have been lifted bodily into the picture and can inhale the subdued atmosphere created by Velázquez and feel the embrace of his gentle brushstrokes. This is a unique and very modern conceit–to treat the viewer as equal to the king and queen while showing the royal couple at the same time at the back, as if through a glass, darkly. This painting is a great requiem for the passing of the old order, when kings and queens were believed to be on a different plane from other people, as the sun was different from other stars. A gentleman climbs the stairs at the rear, glancing into the shadowy room where the old order still holds sway. One senses that he is leaving to enter a world lit by a more brilliant, modern, scientific light. The new view of the world that emerged during the Enlightenment didn't just challenge religious belief; it undermined the accepted social order. In the world reflected in the scientist's mirror, any one of us could be a king or queen.

14 Diego Velázquez. *Las Meninas*, c.1656. Oil on canvas. Prado, Madrid

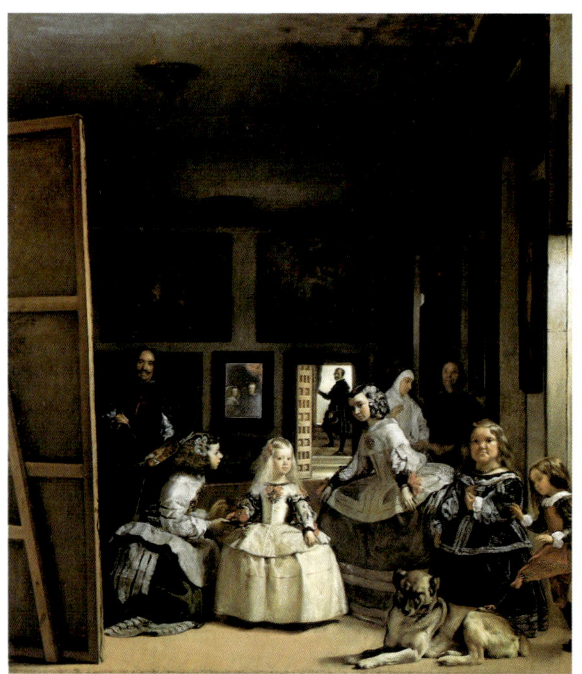

Kings, naturally enough, were reluctant to relinquish the divineness of their right and their light. Copernicus had maintained that his solar-centred universe was more harmonious than the previous earth-centred one because "the lamp [is] now hung in the centre ... where it can light up everything at the same time ... in this most beautiful temple." His book *De Revolutionibus* (published 1543) could easily have been used to justify Louis XIV of France's claim to be the Sun King, *le Roi Soleil.* His palace at Versailles (1676–1708) is the last great sun temple on earth. But *De Revolutionibus* actually contained the seeds of thought that would justify the eventual overthrow of the French aristocracy in the Revolution of 1789.

The political upheavals that accompanied the Enlightenment had complex social, economic and political causes, but they were given legitimacy by a dramatically changing world picture. If revolutions were the organising principle of the heavens, they could govern man's life too. If there was no hierarchy of heavenly bodies, why should a man bow down before a king? Sir Isaac Newton (1642–1727) looked at an apple on a tree in his orchard and wondered why it always fell when dislodged, when the moon, which reason now argued was much bigger and heavier, stayed up. His understanding of how the laws of gravity hold everything in the heavens and on earth in place, and even govern the rhythm of the tides, dispelled once and for all the idea of up and down that had dominated human thinking till then. The republican ideals of the Greeks and early Romans began to gain favour with a public who increasingly came to see themselves as the victims of a self-interested, exploitative aristocracy. There was a growing sense that all men were born equal, and had equal rights, as Thomas Paine put it in his seminal *The Rights of Man* (1791–92). Even slaves (ill. 15) were our equals—which they hadn't been in Greece and Rome.

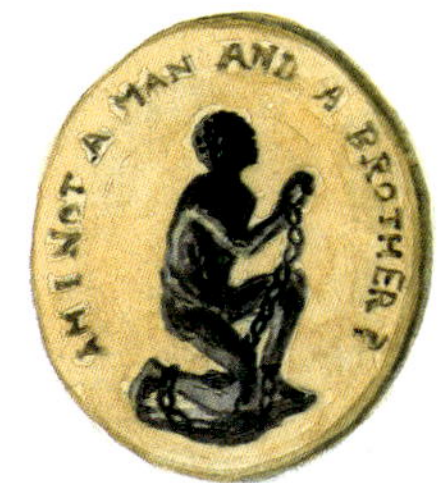

15 Josiah Wedgwood. Anti-slavery cameo "Am I not a man and a brother?", 1791. Ceramic

Mankind's changing world picture exposed the plight of ordinary people. On the canvases of the Spanish artist Goya (1746–1828), the whole scope of human nature is portrayed. Though there are kings, aristocrats, and a whole kaleidoscope of royal hangers-on, Goya treats everyone as an individual human being. *The Third of May, 1808* (ill. 16) is one of the world's first, and still among the most moving, depictions of man's inhumanity to man. It doesn't show men sacrificing themselves or being sacrificed for a cause that's "higher" in some way than their own life. It just shows soldiers doing what they're told, and their victims' sheer terror. Goya spent the last years of his life away from the Spanish

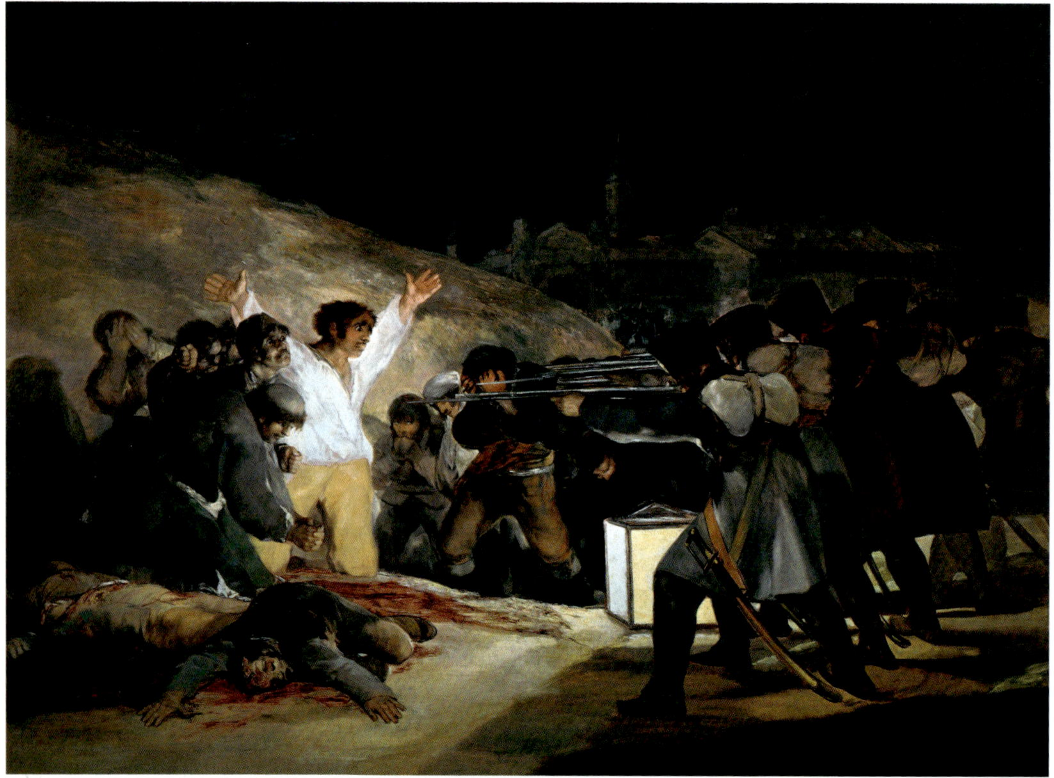

16 Goya. *The Third of May, 1808*. Oil on canvas. Prado, Madrid

court where he had earned fame and fortune, in voluntary isolation, designing prints of the horrors of war, many inscribed "this is how it is", and painting strange, dark images of nightmares (ill.17) on the walls of his home. People flee in panic as a giant looms over the world. He is only a man like one of us, but he is a monster nevertheless. There was a darkness in human nature that wasn't the blackness of the devil–the other side of good–but sprang from something much more terrifying. The Enlightenment opened our eyes not just to the inhumanity of nature but to our own.

The new scientists had discovered that even light was dark. Dissections, much more accurate than those Leonardo had performed, revealed that the eye worked like any other lens. Seeing was no longer thought to be the consequence of an emission from the eye, but became an entirely passive reception, and, most confusingly, it was discovered that the eye itself saw everything upside down. Descartes wrote in *La Dioptique* (1637) that he thought light was "a movement, very rapid and lively, which passes towards our eyes through

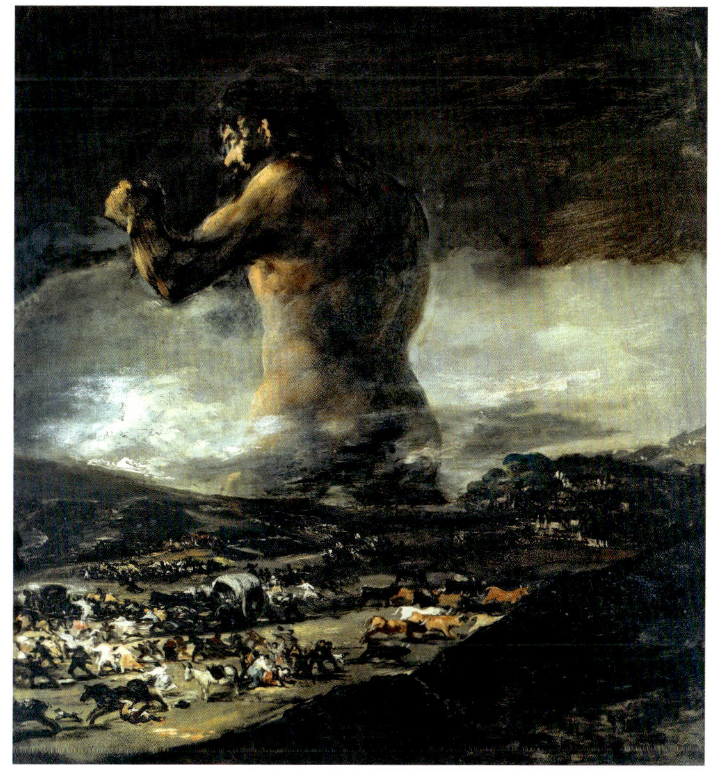

17 Goya. *The Giant*, c.1821–23. Oil on canvas. Prado, Madrid

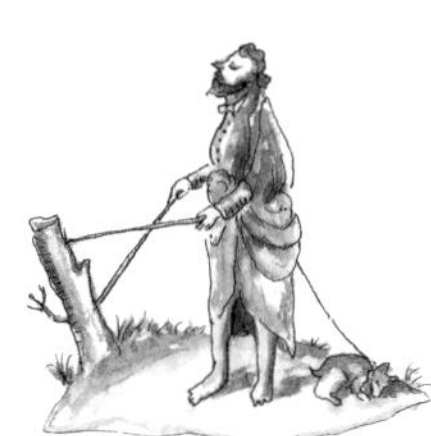

18 After Claude Nicole Le Cat. The optics of the eye and its relationship to a blind man feeling with two sticks, 1750, illustration to Descartes' *A Physical Essay on the Senses*. Wellcome Institute Library, London

the medium of the air, and other transparent bodies, in the same manner that the movement or resistance of the bodies that this blind man encounters is transmitted to his hand through the medium of his stick." (ill. 18). Descartes still thought sight "the noblest of the senses", but it's an irony of the Enlightenment that seeing came to be compared to the tactile perception of someone who was blind.

Denis Diderot (1713–84) took Descartes' line of reasoning–that God had made the world but was distant from us–to its logical conclusion. He didn't deny that God existed but argued that he was so distant he was irrelevant. Why, if he had made the world for our visual benefit, had he created people who couldn't see it? Before the Enlightenment, blindness had been regarded as a punishment or a gift from god, depending on your belief. To some, blind people were an object of legitimate ridicule and laughter. Hindus and Christian Protestants, however, both regarded blindness as a divine infliction–it helped one focus on one's inner spiritual life. But everywhere blindness was believed to be an unalterable fact of fate. Diderot, however, argued in his *Letter on the Blind for the Use of Those Who See* (1749) that creation was not ordained by God, that the sense of touch was just as important as that of sight, and that, therefore, the blind could and should be taught to read. The essay landed him, albeit briefly, in jail. The idea was so radical that it was not until 1829 that Louis Braille, blind from the age of three, invented a form of writing blind people could read.

Seeing was no longer a gift you received when you first opened your eyes; it was a skill that had to be learned, like any other. People today still fondly believe that a person who has been blind from birth will instantly see if they regain their sight. Light will pour on to their retinas, it's true, but their brains will not have developed the means of coping with this flood of new information. Many blind people who regain the use of their eyes become extremely depressed, because it's too late for them to learn to see; they feel safer walking with their eyes closed with the help of a stick.

The Enlightenment saw not just the end of seeing as we'd understood it, but the end of light itself. As Voltaire (1694–1778) put it, people thought that "light exists in the air" until Newton worked out that "it comes from the sun in six and a half minutes". Newton discovered the mechanics of the spectrum, and made rainbows appear at will. Newton was a Christian and was convinced that the principles he discovered in the universe "could only proceed from the counsel and dominion of an intelligent and powerful Being"—but what they had to teach us he was not in a position to say. The German writer Goethe (1749–1832) fought back. Surely the wonderful rainbow couldn't just be a physical phenomenon. It must have something to teach us. He devoted years of his life to studying colour, an undertaking that he thought just as important as his poetry. He conducted experiments which showed that colours could, in certain circumstances, be created out of the marriage of light and dark, and this, he believed, demonstrated the existence of a moral order in creation, though he became increasingly sceptical of all religious explanations of nature.

The scientific searchlight illuminated not just the movements of the stars, but the interior workings of our bodies. When veins and arteries were first charted in the sixteenth century, their striking similarity to river estuaries suggested that they must work in a similar way. The minute channels that linked the two systems were too small to be seen, so blood was thought to ebb and flow through the body like the tide. News of the fact that it circulated, which William Harvey discovered in 1628, took Europe by storm. Not only were the heavens going round, but so was the blood in our bodies. To some, this proved that God's creation was more wonderful than anyone had imagined. The Swedish botanist Carolus Linnaeus (1707–78) believed he was doing God's work when he invented the Latin nomenclature we still use for all living things. It was said of him that "God created and Linnaeus classified". He sent specimen hunters to the far reaches–no longer corners–of the world to help him realise his self-appointed ambition, to complete the task Adam had begun by naming all the beasts and flowers of the field.

The trouble was that the more closely scientists like Linnaeus examined the world, the more confusing things became. It had been assumed that a species–the word derives from the Latin *specere*, meaning to look at–was a group of living things that looked alike. But as groups of animals came to be classified, it was found that appearances could be superficial–porpoises might look like fish on the outside, but when Edward Tyson dissected one in 1680 it was found to be more like a squashed-up dog inside. A better way of defining a species was not by what it looked like, internally or externally, but by whether it bred true. Linnaeus developed a way of identifying plants by numbering and measuring their sexual parts, rather than recording their "look" as a whole. So the Enlightenment, with its inspection of life's innards, further undermined the God-given order of the visual world.

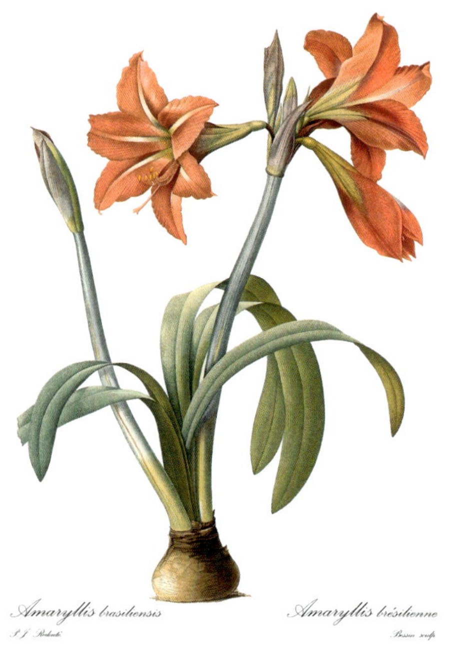

19 Pierre Joseph Redouté. *Amaryllis Josephine*, 1802–16, illustration for *Les Liliaces*. Watercolour on vellum

This new clinical way of looking found its first manifestation in art. It can be seen in the art of Pierre Joseph Redouté (1759–1840) (ill. 19) who was employed to record, in minute detail, the distinguishing features of all the lilies in the French empress Josephine's garden, because they could not be preserved by pressing in a herbarium. The cool beauty of the animals in George Stubbs's paintings (p. 125, ill. 22) springs from the years he spent dissecting them and studying their anatomy. This detached way of seeing spread around the Western-influenced world. The intellectually inquisitive emperor Jehangir of India was so fascinated at seeing the courtier Inayat Khan dying as a result of his debauchery that he ordered an artist to record the event, in minute detail, as Khan's hand shook with its last tremor (ill. 20).

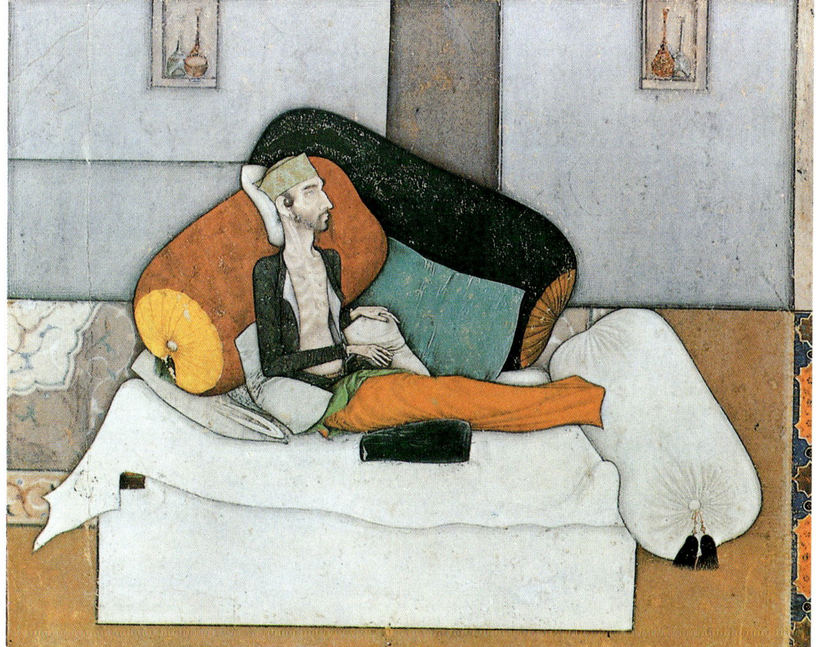

20 *The Death of Inayat Khan*, c. 1618 C.E., 23 x 19.5 cm. Bodleian Library, Oxford

One French scientist, however, rejected this cold approach. The Comte de Buffon (1707–88) despised Linnaeus for reducing nature to lists of man-made categories. He developed the radical idea that nature had a life of its own, independent from mankind. Inspired amateur naturalists toured the world, discovering and recording the behaviour of wildlife. A few artists took up this cause, most notably John James Audubon (1785–1851). He set himself the task of drawing all the birds of America (ill. 21) not just to identify species, but to praise their very existence. He travelled the length and breadth of the continent, shooting specimens—there were no binoculars then to enable people to observe them at a distance. His designs capture the wild paradise that Columbus described in his journal on first landing in the New World: "The singing of little birds is such that one would never desire to depart hence. There are flocks of parrots that obscure the sun, and other birds, large and small, of so many kinds, different from ours, that it's wonderful." Though they were drawn from dead specimens, Audubon painted his birds as he had seen them living. He was, however, criticised for his depiction of a rattlesnake attacking a nest of mocking-birds, because other naturalists had observed, rightly, that rattlesnakes do not climb trees.

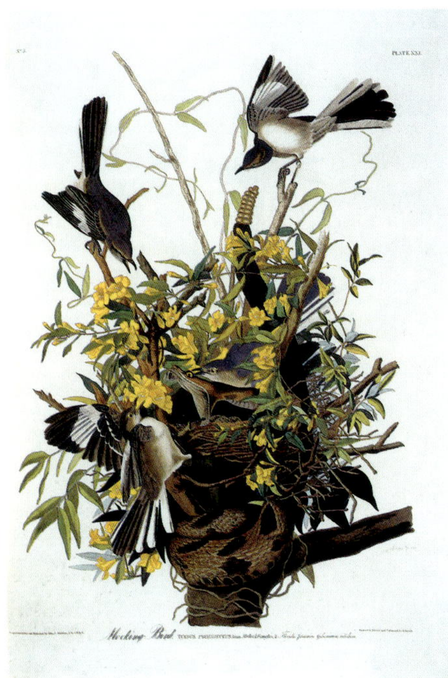

21 John James Audubon. *Rattlesnake Attacking a Nest of Mocking-birds*, from *Birds of America*, 1827–38

As more and more animals were discovered around the world, there was a growing problem with the idea of the ark. It was written in the Bible that a pair of every living creature on the earth had been taken into the Ark during the Flood—but how could they all have got in? In 1675, Athanasius Kircher, a Jesuit polymath who tried to summarise all human knowledge—"there is nothing more beautiful than knowing everything," he said—made the last attempt to depict a ship capable of containing pairs of all the animals then known to mankind, a huge floating box with layers upon layers of animals and special areas for food supplies and bedding. It looks remarkably like a modern container vessel (ill.22). In 1654, after a lifetime's study of biblical sources, Archbishop Ussher dated the Creation to 26 October 4004 before Christ, at precisely nine in the morning. The Comte de Buffon responded cleverly by arguing that nature had been created over seven aeons, not days, and had vastly changed in the process, thereby opening the door to the alarming notion that some animals, even if created by God, might have become extinct. The discovery of huge fossils proved his point. How could such monsters (the word dinosaurs didn't exist then) have been saved in the ark? The great foundation stone of biblical belief—that God had made the world as it now appears—had been breached.

Slowly but inexorably nature was being stripped of its divinity. Everyone felt it. The painter Delacroix wrote: "I have a horror of the common run of scientists … they elbow one another in the antechamber where nature hides her secrets." The romantics—as they came to be called, rather disparagingly, for turning their back on reality—mourned the severing of our emotional ties with nature, which had been such an inspiration to mankind until then. Mourning usually takes the form of looking back. The German architect Karl Friedrich Schinkel (1781–1841) painted an imaginary scene showing a

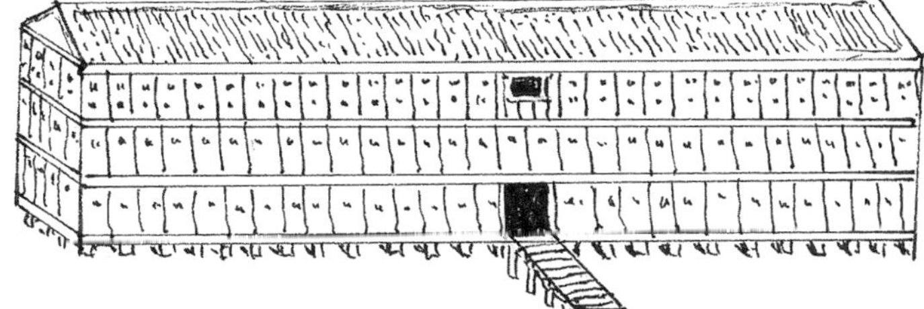

22 Athanasius Kircher. *Noah's Ark*, 1675

medieval city with its cathedral being built. There was a spate of actually finishing uncompleted Gothic cathedrals at that time, such as those in Milan and Cologne. For Caspar David Friedrich (1774–1840) the scallop-like rosy rays of dawn (ill.23) could symbolise a young girl's new life. Or they could be the last rays of the setting sun, symbolising her life after death. Or perhaps the picture symbolises both. Friedrich did not clarify his meaning, but was one of the last artists to depict the sights of nature as signs from God.

J.M.W. Turner (1775–1851) painted sunsets as if he was seeing them for the first and last time, which, in a real way, he was. Though they were no longer religious symbols, Turner's sunsets were still imbued with moral significance. He was scandalised by the activities of the crews of slave ships (ill.24), who threw the

23 Caspar David Friedrich. *Woman in Front of Setting Sun*, c.1818. Oil on canvas, 22 x 30 cm. Museum Folkwang, Essen

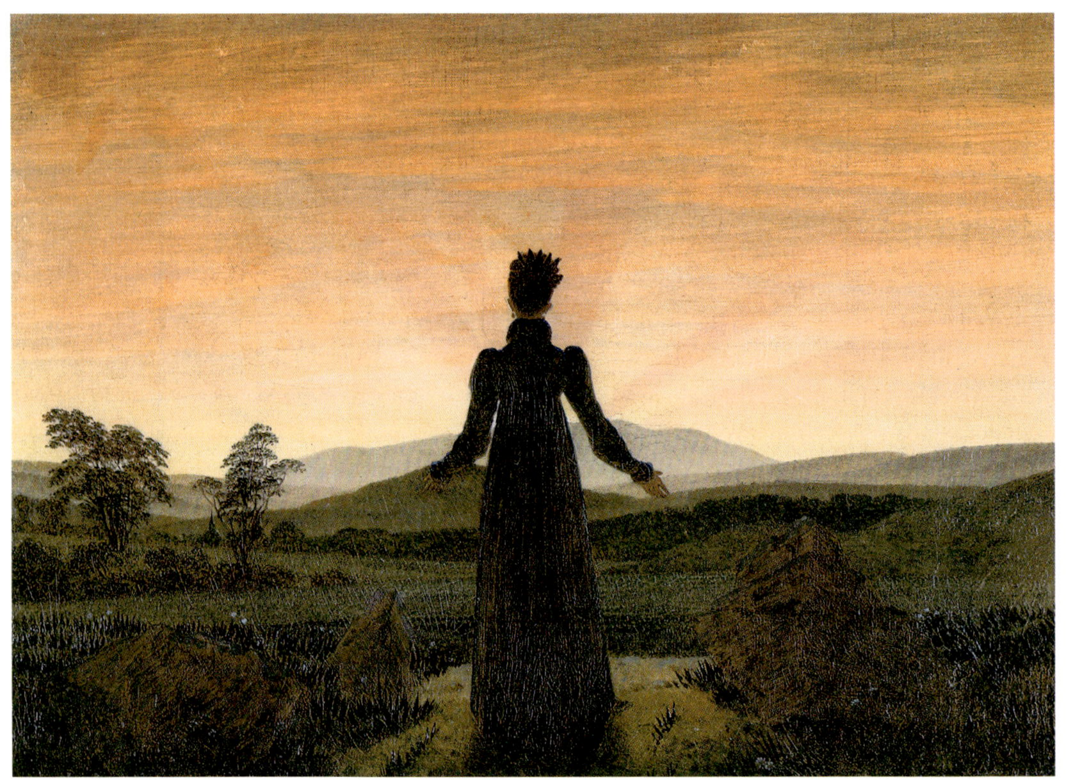

dying overboard, because insurance could be claimed for slaves lost at sea but not for those who died from malnutrition and disease. But Turner also saw his sunsets freshly and scientifically, as phenomenal conflagrations of refracted light. They are so well observed that you can sense the sun actually sinking as the colours in the sky change. This awareness of time passing due to the turning of the earth was new in art. Turner's contemporary, the poet William Wordsworth (1770–1850) described a similar sensation when he wrote: "The solitary cliffs wheeled by us, as if the earth had rolled with visible motion her diurnal round." There was a sense of loss here, but also a new excitement. Turner was as interested as most people were in the remarkable demonstrations of electricity by Michael Faraday (1791–1867) at the Royal Institution in London in the 1830s. His fondness for using

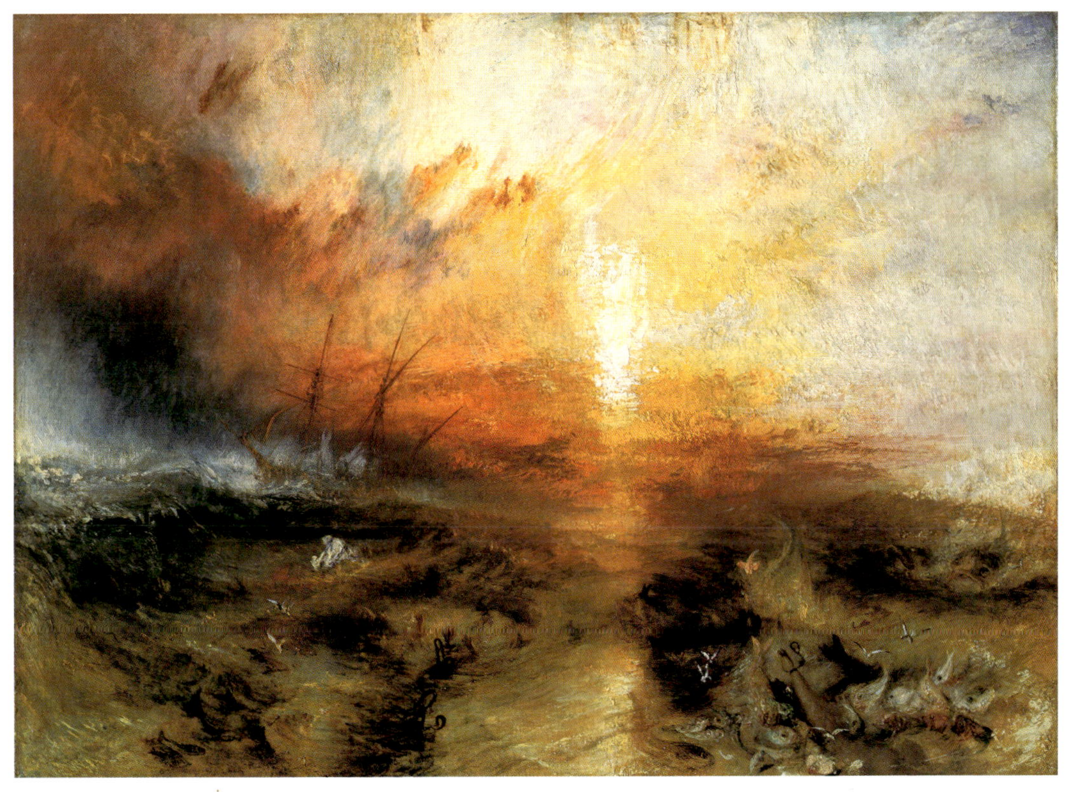

24 J.M.W. Turner. *Slavers Throwing Overboard the Dead and Dying*, 1840. Oil on canvas. Museum of Fine Arts, Boston

vortices in his painting could in part have sprung from his observations of magnetised iron filings. John Constable (1776–1837) felt this excitement too. As a devout Christian, he remained convinced that any study of nature would lead him closer to God. Hc followed with intense interest the new study of climatology; few artists have ever painted clouds more convincingly or luminously (p.97, ill.13).

In 1502, Dürer had painted a clump of grass (ill.25) with the utter conviction that every blade in it was created by God. Three hundred years later the poet Goethe could still write: "When I lie in tall grass … and become conscious of the thousand varieties of little plants … and countless little worms… I feel the presence of the Almighty who created us in His image." But Charles Darwin (1809–82) dedicated his life to understanding the play of forces that determine "the kinds and proportions of each plant in a square yard of turf". He wondered why the world looked as it did and came to the conclusion that "nature cares nothing for appearances, except in so far as they may be useful to any being". Like many amateur naturalists, he travelled the world, collecting specimens of strange creatures. When he landed on the Galapagos Islands in 1835, it was the smallness of the differ-

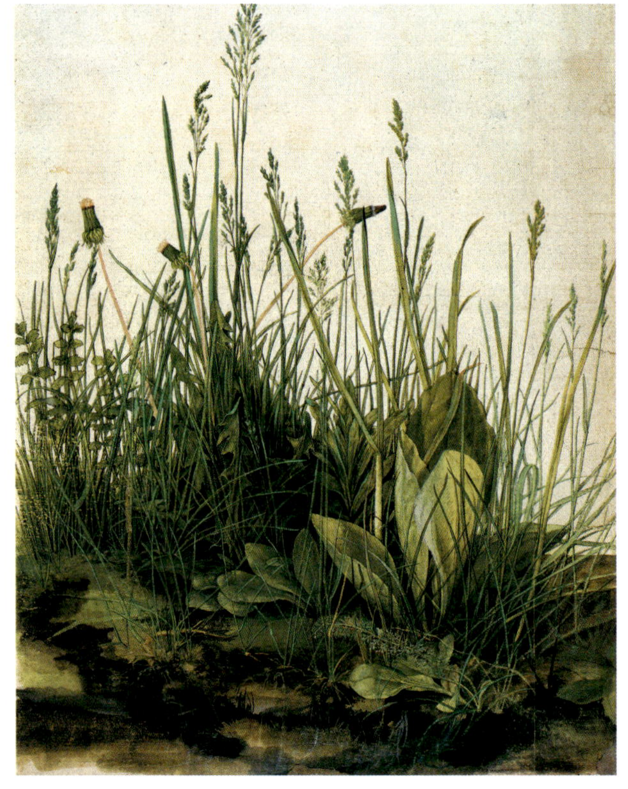

25 Albrecht Dürer. *A Piece of Lawn*, 1502. Watercolour. Albertina, Vienna

ences between the creatures living there that surprised him. The giant tortoises on different islands had slightly different shells. The little black finches that hopped about at his feet looked alike, except that they had differently shaped beaks (ill.26). It was only later, when he got home, that he realised that these beaks varied because the finches ate different food. One finch had a big beak for cracking large nuts, another had a long thin beak for holding twigs to poke insects out of holes (it is one of the very few tool-using animals in the world) and yet another had a sharp little pointed beak for stabbing blue-footed boobies to drink their blood. Darwin sensed that on the Galapagos he was near to solving the mystery that had eluded all scientists: how species had appeared on earth.

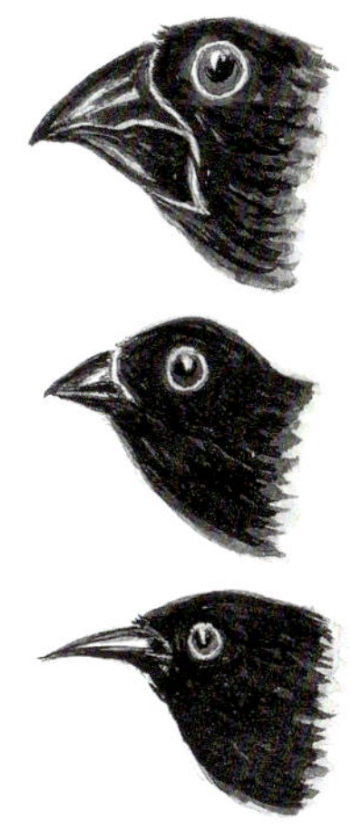

26 Darwin's finches

Until then, people the world over believed that lions had always given birth to lions, ants to ants and humans to humans, as every child in the Christian West knew who had a toy ark (ill.27). Hindus today might claim that they always understood evolution because they believed that it took twenty-three million reincarnations for an animal to become a human being. But in truth they thought that types of creatures stayed in their places. It was the soul that rose; the worm didn't become the man. Darwin's great insight was to realise that no offspring is exactly the same as its parents, and that tiny differences could give an individual an advantage if times got hard. It might be that one bird was born with a slightly longer beak or claw or better camouflage, but any of these could be crucial to its survival. The beings that survive are the fittest – the most suited, that is, not the

27 Toy ark

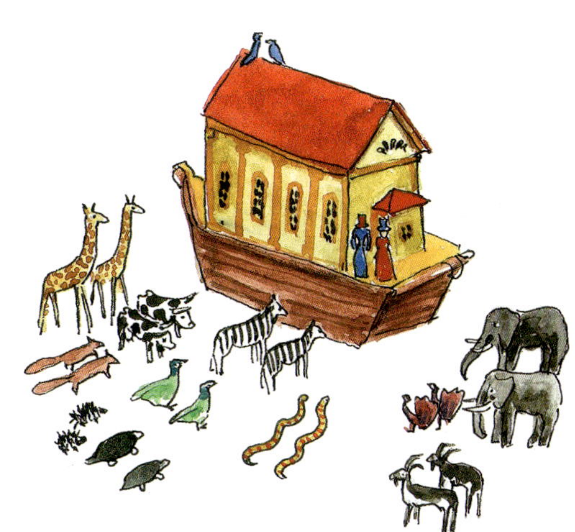

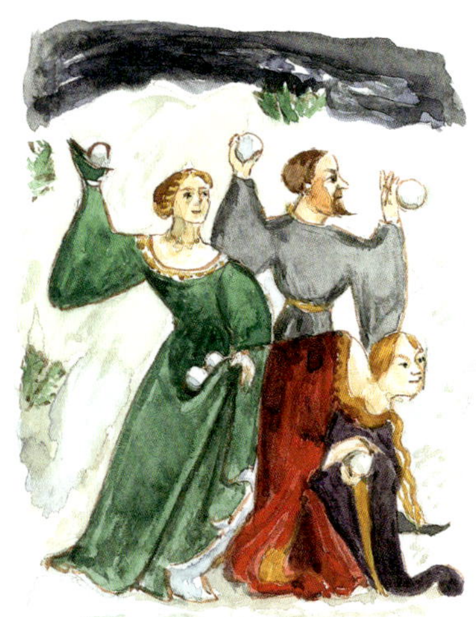

28 After Maestro Venceslao, attr. Month of January, detail. Fresco. Castello del Buonconsiglio, Trento, Italy

strongest–to their changing environment. So the whole panoply of life has evolved higgledy-piggledy, through the "clumsy, wasteful, blundering and horribly cruel work of nature" over countless millennia. "Our ancestor," Darwin wrote, "was an animal which breathed water, had a swim bladder, a great swimming tail, an imperfect skull, and was, undoubtedly, an hermaphrodite." Once one accepts that species might pass into each other, blindly, by chance and not by intent, then, as Darwin wrote, "it's absurd to talk of one animal being higher than another", and "man, wonderful man ... with his divine face turned towards heaven" collapses into nature's melting pot. This had huge implications for how mankind saw the world.

It affected, for one thing, how we dressed. It used to be natural in all societies for the ruling classes to wear clothes that expressed their status. At the end of a long passageway in the Castello del Buonconsiglio in Trento, northern Italy, is a little tower room decorated with fifteenth-century frescoes showing the months of the year. Everyone is dressed according to his or her station. In the month of January (ill.28), noble ladies and gentlemen in flowing, multicoloured robes with great long hanging sleeves, expressions of pleasure on their faces, throw snowballs at each other outside the castle walls, while servants dressed in livery go about their daily tasks, ankle-deep in snow. Today princes and generals, politicians and managers are indistinguishable. In capitalist Japan and communist Russia, the suit and the overall ruled. In China, the hierarchical depiction of court life disappeared with the last emperor, and artists were brought down to earth to depict the People building the New China, with eternal smiles on their faces – though the reality was very different. At first sight this painting by Chang Chin-feng (ill. 29) looks as though it shows another jolly snow scene. In fact the commune's militia women are being taught how to throw hand-grenades.

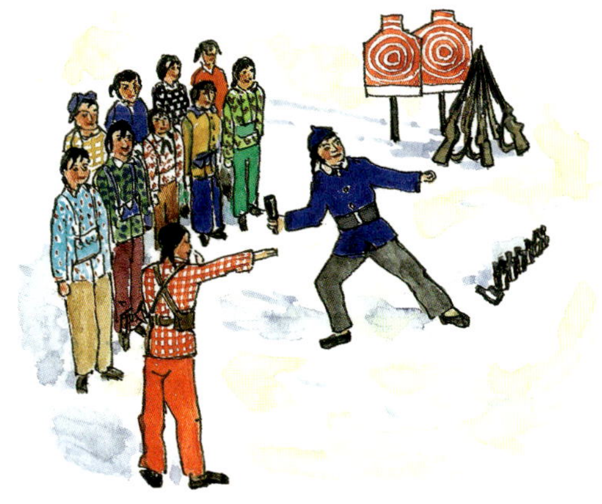

29 After Chang Chin-feng, *How Bright and Brave they Look*, c. 1970, detail of commune militia women learning to throw hand-grenades. Gouache, 57 x 81 cm

This uniformity of appearance was partly a product of the perception of Karl Marx (1818–83) and others, that the upper classes exploited those beneath them. Marx wrote that "Darwin's book is very important and serves as the basis in the natural sciences for the class struggle in history." Marx's friend and close associate Friedrich Engels (1820–95) commented, using an outdated hierarchical comparison, that Marx, with "his lion-like head and jet black mane", was destined to "pull down to earth the spacious tent of heaven up on high". Communism was based on the belief that all human beings were equal and that no-one was automatically "above" another, and that God had not made mankind, but mankind had made God. They dreamt of creating a new society. If the world was always changing then people could make a better world for themselves, a world without classes and without private property in which everyone would work for the benefit of everyone "with a willing hand, a ready mind and a joyous heart".

Communists believed that capitalism was the great evil because it forced labourers to work longer hours than necessary for a subsistence wage, and then cashed in on their additional output which it effectively got free. Its profits were therefore made by selling commodities at their "real" value and not, as one would expect, by adding a surcharge. "This," wrote Marx, "seems a paradox and contrary to everyday observation," but "it's also a

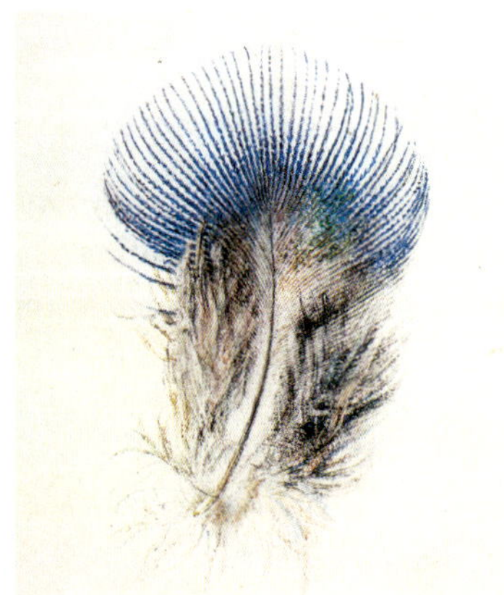

30 John Ruskin. *A Peacock's Breast Feather*, 1875. Watercolour. Sheffield City Art Galleries and Museums Trust (Collection of the Guild of St George)

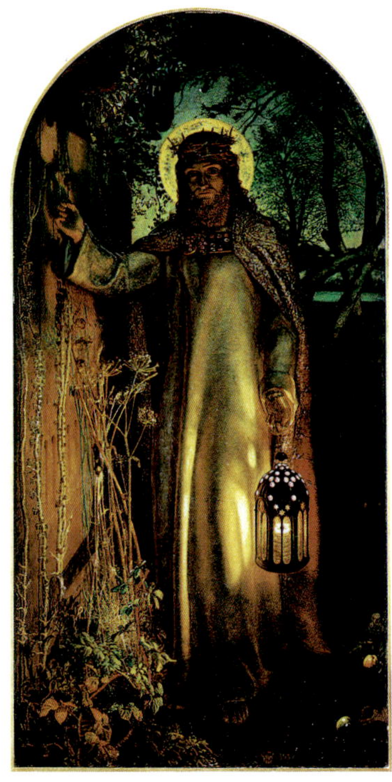

31 William Holman Hunt. *The Light of the World*, 1854. Oil on canvas. Keble College, Oxford

paradox that the earth moves round the sun, and that water consists of two highly inflammable gasses. Scientific truth is always a paradox." Communism, he argued, would be built on scientific principles. The subject of Marx's doctoral thesis had been two Greek philosophers: Democritus, who argued that everything was the product of the mechanical operation of atoms, so neither death nor the gods were to be feared; and Epicurus, who advocated that people should live in self-help communes. Like Darwin, Marx dismissed all notions of a hierarchy in nature. The first chain the workers had to throw away was the Great Chain of Being. The next were those of economic exploitation and religion. Science increasingly came to be associated with atheism.

One of the best-known writers to resist this emerging materialist view of the world was the British art critic, social commentator and artist, John Ruskin (1819–1900). He painted a peacock's breast feather (ill.30) with a delicacy that makes one hold one's breath, in order to demonstrate the harmonious balance within God's creation. For a bird's feather, he argued, is exactly half-way, in form, between the scale of a fish and the fur of an animal. Ruskin could not believe, as Darwin did, that the splendour of the peacock's plumage had evolved purely to interest peahens. He had a personal reason for doing so; he was tragically attracted to pubescent girls, and could not admit that the delicate beauty he saw in them had a sexual purpose. How could that be, when he saw the same beauty in high cloud, a moss agate or a wild rose? He wrote beautifully about Turner's sunsets, Gothic architecture and the Alps, and he advocated a social order in harmony with nature. He was one of the first to warn against the growing threat of pollution. His writings had a huge influence in their day and thereafter on thinkers as widespread as William Morris and Proust, Tolstoy and Gandhi, and he inspired a group of young artists who called themselves the Pre-Raphaelites, in their attempt to revive the way of looking at the era before Raphael, which showed nature glowing in God's light.

Two of the most popular paintings of the second half of the nineteenth century were William Holman Hunt's *The Light of the World* (1854) (ill.31), and Jean François Millet's *The Angelus* (1854–59) (ill.32). Both were painted just before the publication of

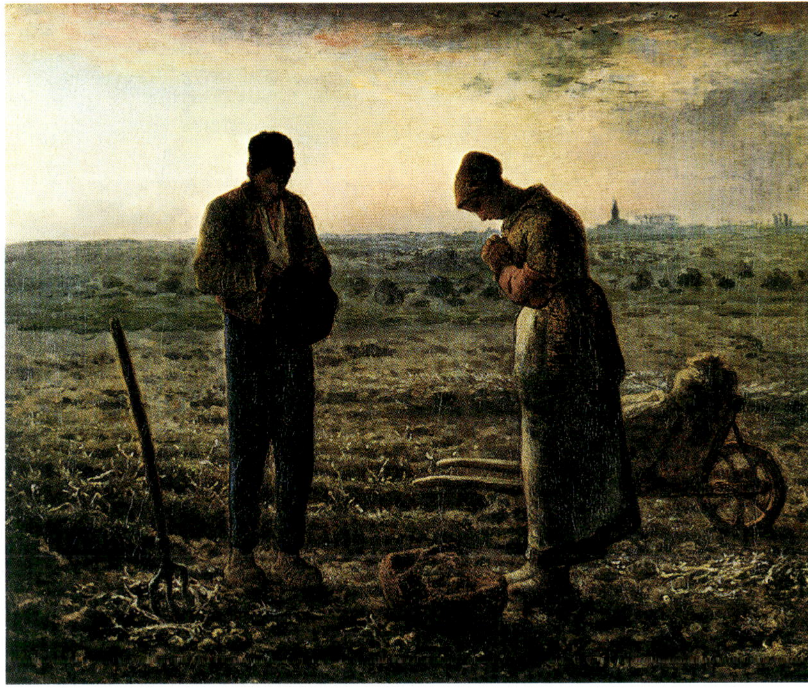

32 Jean François Millet. *The Angelus*, 1854–59. Oil on canvas. Louvre, Paris

Darwin's *The Origin of Species* in 1859. Their immense appeal sprang from people's reluctance to give up their religious interpretation of nature and accept the modern scientific view of the world. The universe Darwin saw was no longer lit by God's light. But in Hunt's painting Christ still walks on earth with his lantern in his hand—and knocks at the door of a soul which is increasingly becoming choked with the weeds of materialism. In Millet's painting, peasants have stopped their work in the fields at sunset, as they had been doing for thousands of years. The fields have fallen silent as the sun sinks beneath the horizon. Farmers bow their heads and pray for the dead, and for their own souls. When the picture was first shown in Paris, crowds gathered round it with tears in their eyes. They were weeping not just as a reaction to the mournful beauty of the scene, but also for the passing of a whole way of life, in which the beautiful sights of nature were reflections of human fate.

The Impressionists thought such paintings to be cloyed with sentiment. They were excited by the freshness of the new scientific way of looking, particularly the discovery that the colours we see are actually mixed *inside* the eye, which led to the brilliant "dot" paintings of Georges Seurat (1859–91) and eventually, nearly a century later, to the Op Art of Victor Vasarely and Bridget Riley in the 1960s. The Impressionists took Turner's work (ill. 24) and stripped it of its moral message. The painting of a sunrise by Claude Monet (1840–1926) (ill. 33)—the picture that gave the Impressionist movement its name—shows no trace of good or evil. The pictures of Monet, Sisley, Pissarro and Renoir, the later works of Manet and the early works of van Gogh and Cézanne burst on to the world like sunshine falling on a spring meadow after winter storms. Their canvases captured what the newly invented camera could not: fleeting atmospheric effects in full colour, sunlight sparkling under racing clouds. Monet was the most monumental; he painted series of cathedrals, haystacks, trees, bridges and water lilies from the same viewpoint but at different times of the day, in mist, under cloud or in bright daylight. Monet was a poet of colour and a magician of light; he celebrated a pantheistic vision of the world. Cézanne famously commented, when he was beginning to try to see lasting forms beyond fleeting appearances: "Monet is no more than an eye – but, my God, what an eye." The issue was whether visual delight in nature was enough.

This is a major theme in Tolstoy's novel *Anna Karenina*, which was written in Russia between 1874 and 1876, at the same time that the Impressionists were beginning to paint in France. One of the book's main characters, Levin, is wracked by his inability to accept the modern notion that "this whole world of ours is noth-

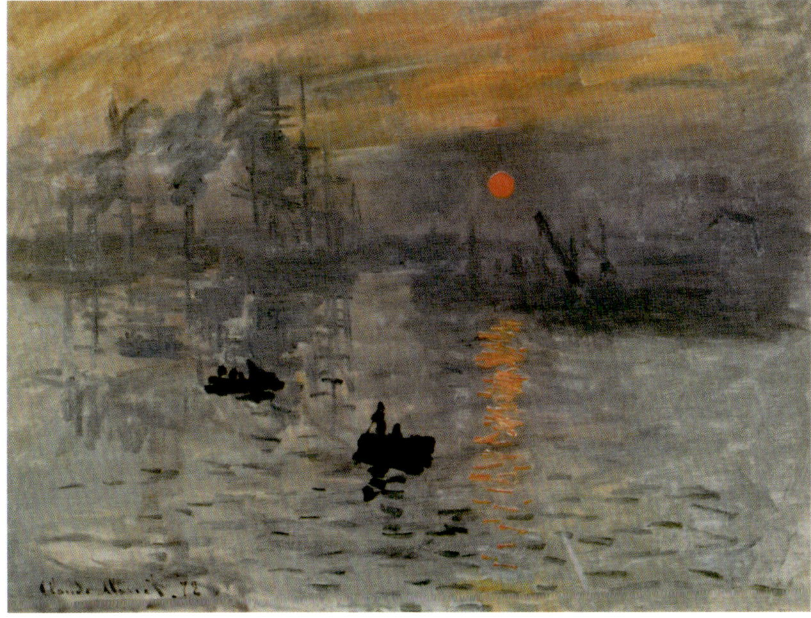

33 Claude Monet. *Impression: Sunrise*, 1872. Oil on canvas, 48 x 63 cm. Musée Marmottan, Paris

ing but a speck of mildew, which has grown up on a tiny planet". He is at a loss when a priest asks him: "What will you reply to your children when they ask you who made all the lovely things in the world–the earth, the water, the sun, the flowers and the grass–will you answer 'I don't know'?" His resolution of this problem ends the novel. Lying on his back in a forest glade, contemplating the tiny living things around him, Levin muses: "In the body of this grass and of this beetle a transformation of matter takes place in conformity with certain physical, chemical and physiological laws. And in all of us, including these aspens and the clouds and the misty patches in the sky, evolution is proceeding. Evolution from what? Into what? An unending evolution and struggle?" Then looking up into the cloudless sky he asks himself: "Do I not know that that is infinite space, and not a rounded vault? But however much I screw up my eyes and strain my sight I cannot see it except as round and circumscribed, and in spite of my knowing about infinite space I am incontestably right when I see a firm blue vault, far more right than when I strain my eyes to see beyond it."

Then Levin has his revelation. He suddenly perceives that this split between the world he can see and the world that science tells him exists is the same as the split between a moral vision of the world, which only comes into view after a leap of faith, and a materialistic one, which is based on personal interest. "Do I not know that it's not the stars that are moving? … But seeing the stars change place and not being able to picture to myself the revolution of the earth, I am right in saying that the stars move … just as I am right to found my conclusions on that understanding of goodness and evil which was and always will be alike for all men." His happiness floods back as he realises that the beautiful world that he sees and loves and lives within is a moral vision overlying the world revealed by science, which appeared to him to be dark and amoral, and which would be all that he would see if he had no faith. It was a tenuous hold on the value of appearances.

One painter, however, still believed passionately that the sights of nature were signals from God. Vincent van Gogh (1853–90) never intended to become an artist—he dedicated himself to a devout Christian life. He gave away all his possessions, wore a second-hand coat and sackcloth shirts, and slept on the ground. He helped poor miners in Belgium, sufferers from typhus fever, and an alcoholic prostitute with a destitute family. He only began to paint and draw when he was twenty-seven; but, as he did so, it was like a door slowly opening, letting light flood into his profound mind and heart. He had found his language, a way of revealing his deepest feelings to himself and to others. We owe his oeuvre—one of the greatest in the history of art—to a rising crescendo of activity that lasted just ten years. He hardly exhibited during his lifetime, but when he did he was soon recognised as a genius. Shortly after this first critical success, he committed suicide. His pictures rapidly became immensely popular, not just because they were masterpieces of world art, but because van Gogh was one of the last great artists to paint nature as a revelation of God's love.

Van Gogh interpreted the sights of the world as a Taoist, Hindu or Shinto priest might do; for him, everything was symbolic. The healthy white flesh inside the dark potatoes that come out of the earth *was* the goodness glowing in the eyes of the peasants who tilled the soil. This was the subject of one of his first dark paintings, *The Potato Eaters.* He soon left Holland and went to Paris where his palette flowered in the sunlight of Impressionism. But he was soon discontented with mere enjoyment, and went to live in the poor countryside in the south of France, where he rented a

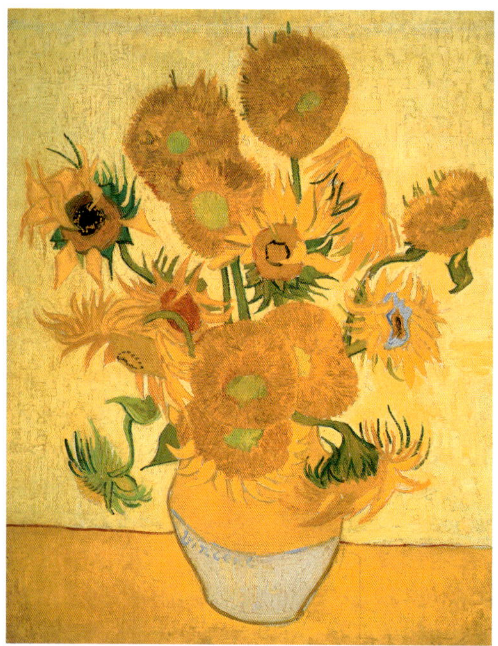

34 Vincent van Gogh. *Sunflowers*, 1889. Oil on canvas. Vincent van Gogh Foundation, Amsterdam

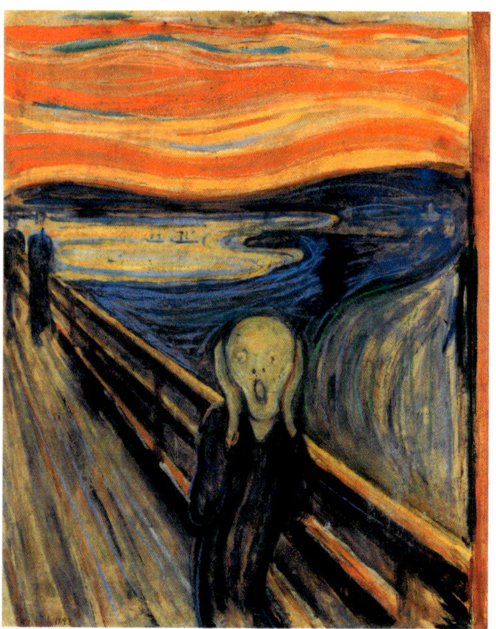

35 Edvard Munch. *The Scream*, 1893. Oil on board. National Gallery, Oslo

house, which he painted bright yellow, in the hope of establishing a community of artists dedicated to living, as the "simple Japanese" did, "in nature, as if they were flowers". Only Gauguin responded to his invitations, and van Gogh hung pictures of sunflowers (ill.34) around the house for his arrival. He wrote in a letter that the pictures looked like "Gothic rose windows". Sunflowers, for van Gogh, were "the opposite and yet the equivalent" of cypresses. Their black flaming branches, reaching up to heaven, were, for him, images of death (p.278, ill.33), while sunflowers were radiant images of life. Van Gogh's art is the last, wonderful, world-illuminating flare in a line of spiritual visions that date back, through the art of the ancient Egyptians, to the very earliest imagery of mankind. But it was the end of a way of seeing.

Edvard Munch painted the last sunset (ill.35). In late 1883 or early 1884, he was taking an evening walk along the Mosseveien road by the harbour in Oslo when an extraordinary conflagration lit up the evening, as if the sky had been on fire. The effect was caused by the detritus from the eruption of the Indonesian volcano Krakatoa, which had by then just reached Norway. But Munch didn't just record a freak event. It took him nearly ten years to mull over the emotional impact of the scene. It had for him a much wider and deeper meaning. He wrote: "One evening I was walking along a path ... the sun was setting and the clouds turning blood red. I sensed a scream passing through nature... I painted the clouds as actual blood. The colours shrieked." The divine robes in which nature had until then been dressed were finally rent asunder.

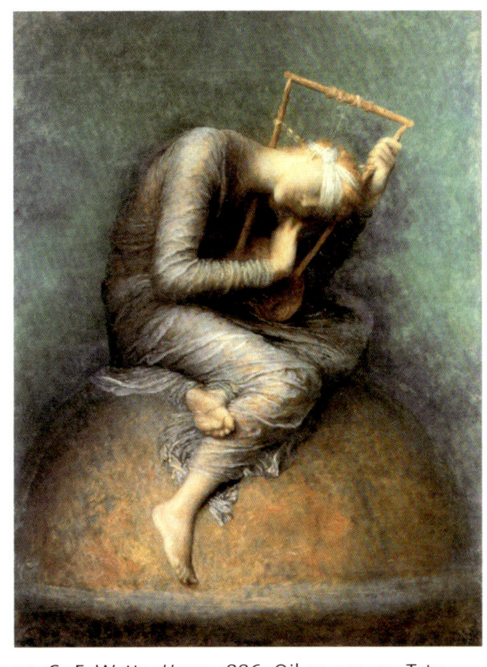

36 G. F. Watts, *Hope*, 1886. Oil on canvas. Tate Gallery, London

By the end of the nineteenth century, science had so stripped nature of its mystery that it presented no sights on which people could pin their faith. G.F. Watts' painting *Hope* (1886) (ill.36) summed up humanity's new predicament: blindfolded, sitting on a planet that is little more than a barren lump of rock, surrounded by an effusion of endless space, playing a lyre, all of whose strings are broken, save one–perhaps a symbol of the poor wretch's soul–which alone emits a sound that she can barely hear. How far our vision of the world had changed from that revealed in the *Mona Lisa*! But Watts' painting became, at the end of the nineteenth century, almost as popular as Leonardo's. Reproductions of it sold all over the world, especially in Islamic countries. Iran adopted it as its official postage stamp, and as recently as 1967 the Egyptian government issued reproductions of it to their troops to hearten them after their defeat in the war with Israel. Our hope resides where Buddhists, Jews and Muslims have long maintained it does, in a divinity which we cannot see.

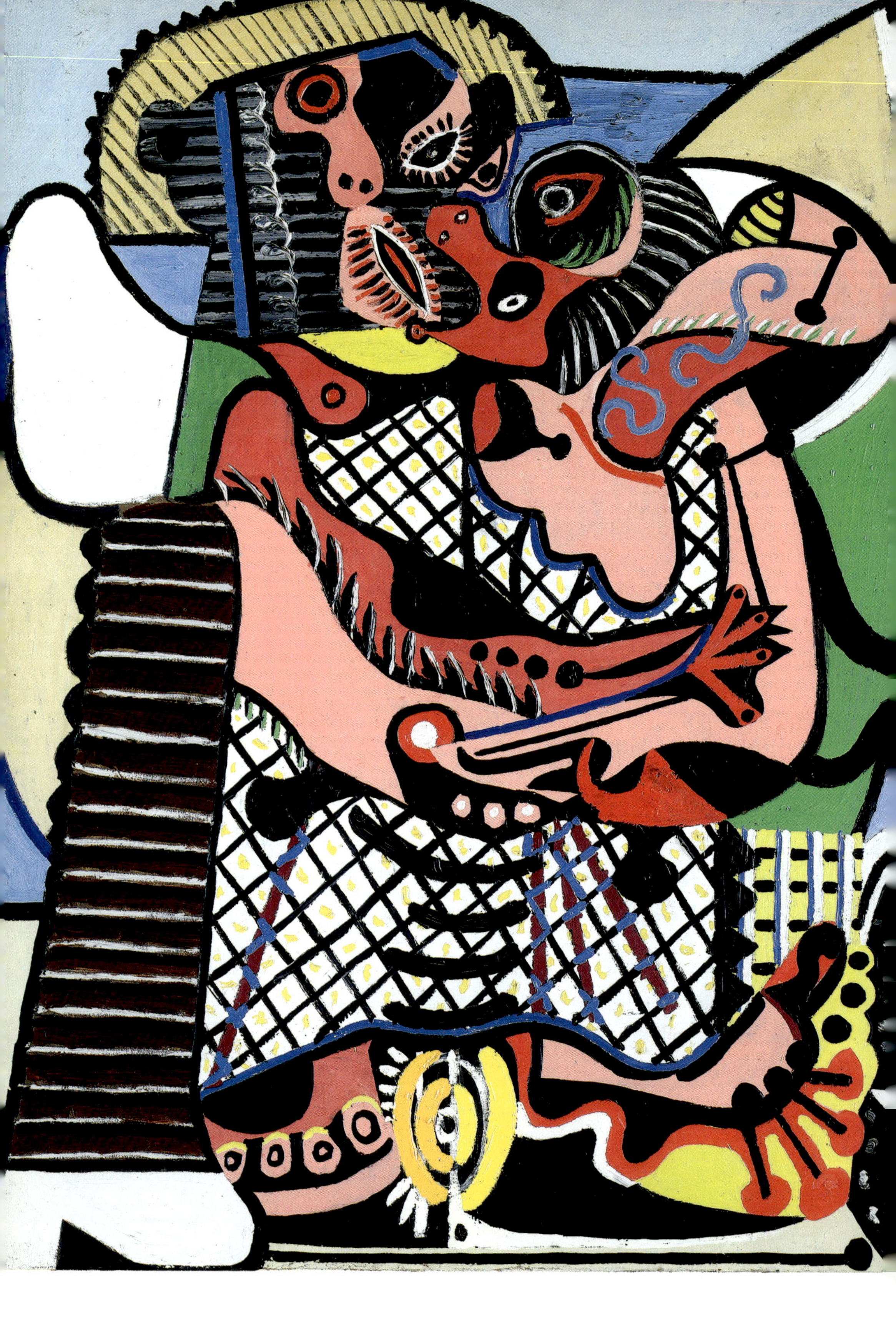

Chapter 10

Out of Sight

Our current world picture took shape during the early years of the twentieth century. By then, neither artists nor scientists were interested in limiting themselves to the world they could see. Both were beginning to feel their way towards truths that they believed were out of sight. Between 1907 and 1913, Ernest Rutherford (1871–1937) and Niels Bohr (1885–1962) actually tracked the atoms that Democritus had imagined over two thousand years earlier. Rutherford compared the atom to a fly in a cathedral—the tiny nucleus was the fly, surrounded by even tinier orbiting electrons, which formed the cathedral walls—such was the immensity of the miniature world within us. Between 1905 and 1916 Albert Einstein (1879–1955) developed the theory of relativity, which provided a mathematical model showing how matter diminishes in size and mass as it approaches the speed of light. He wrote: "The creative principle resides in mathematics. In a certain sense, therefore, I hold it true that pure thought can grasp reality, as the ancients dreamed." The world that we could see appeared mundane in comparison with the world that existed out of sight, which we could only hope to picture in our mind's eye.

Mandarins, the scholars who administered China for 2,000 years, loved to see the macrocosm reflected in the microcosm. They read the essential forces of life in the eroded rocks (ill.2) that decorated the elaborate gardens in which they relaxed, taking a rest from their official duties. Many of these rocks were specially made by lowering suitably soft boulders into the turbulent,

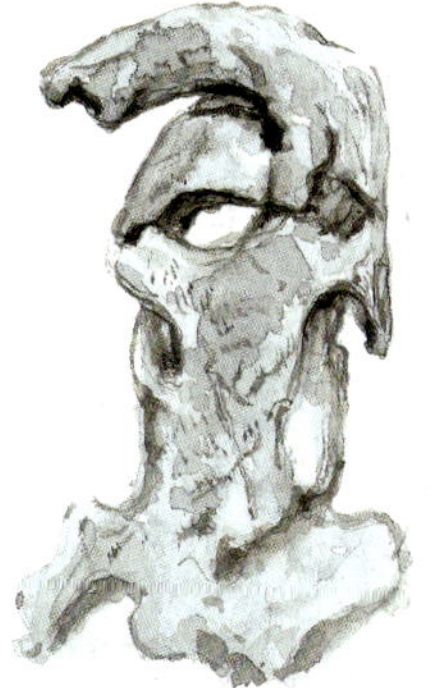

2 Wangshi Yuan (Master of the Nets Garden). Eroded rock, 1140 C.E., restored 1770 C.E. Suzhou, China

1 Pablo Picasso. *The Kiss*, 1925. Oil on canvas, 130 x 97 cm. Musée Picasso, Paris

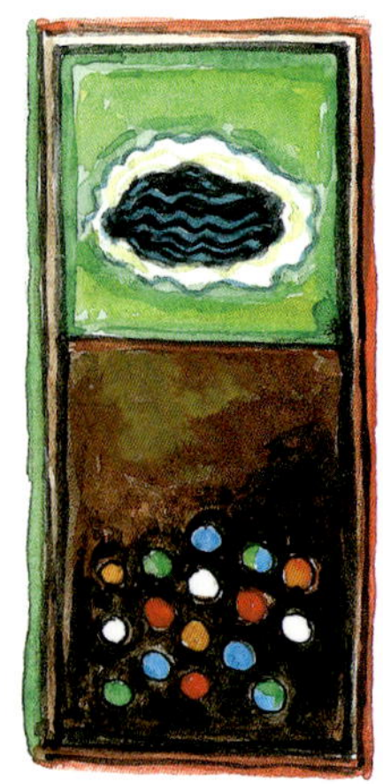

3 After *The Separation of Atoms from the Waters of Non-entity*, Jain, Rajasthan, 18th century. Gouache on paper, 26 x 10 cm. Ajit Mookerjee Collection, New Delhi

pebble-strewn waters of Lake T'ai. All the experiences of life—from political turmoil to eras of peace, from dragon-storm battles to tender love making—could be read into their contorted forms, in the same way as pictures were seen in clouds by poets in Europe. Many philosophies and the more mystical religions often described the hidden forces of existence in abstract terms, but they rarely depicted them as such. Exceptionally, a few Jain watercolours exist that tried to make visible the invisible, such as this painting from eighteenth-century Rajasthan, which illustrates the separation of atoms from the waters of non-entity (ill. 3). Buddhist initiates, to help them meditate, were advised to start by thinking of a blue flower, and then to think only of the blue.

Spiritualism enjoyed a revival in the West in the late nineteenth century, when the Russian-born Madame Blavatsky and her successor Annie Besant attempted with their theosophy to get close to the ineffable source of all world religions, from ancient Egyptian to Islam, from Buddhism to Christianity. Blavatsky used abstraction to convey her meaning. She compared "a beam of blue light, like a pencil of rays, that shot upward towards the sky" to "a thought of living devotion to the Christ in the mind of a Christian". Such writings profoundly influenced artists like Kandinsky and Mondrian, who tried to express their own spiritualism through abstraction. Wassily Kandinsky (1866–1944) began his career painting fairy-tale

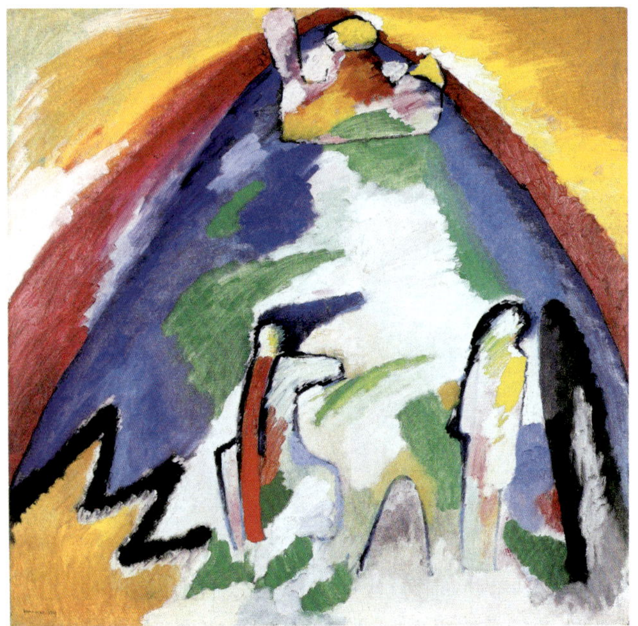

4 Wassily Kandinsky. *Mountain*, 1909. Oil on canvas, 109 x 109 cm. Municipal Gallery, Munich

scenes of princesses in flowing dresses, being carried off by knights in shining armour riding through dappled forests in the starlight. He then produced a series of miniature mountain landscapes that capture, with exceptional intensity, the glowing colours of dusk. Next, he tried to draw the colours and shapes out of what he called an "inner necessity". These increasingly took an abstract form (ill. 4).

Kandinsky commented in 1912 that "in many ways art resembles religion. The development of art does not consist of new discoveries which supersede old truths and dismiss them as aberrations (as is apparently the case with science). Its development lies in sudden revelations like flashes of lightning … that throw a brilliant light upon new perspectives and truths which are basically no more than organic developments of earlier wisdom… Would the New Testament have been possible without the Old?" He described how, when beginning to paint, he prepared his studio and his mind as if he was anticipating the arrival of an honoured guest. He believed that every colour and line had its own spiritual character. "The deeper the blue," he wrote, "the more it draws one into infinity, awakens in one the longing for the pure and, finally, for the supernatural." The Blue Rider became the symbol of the group of artists that formed around him in Munich – the knight has returned, though he is no longer saving damsels, but lancing the dragon of modern scientific materialism.

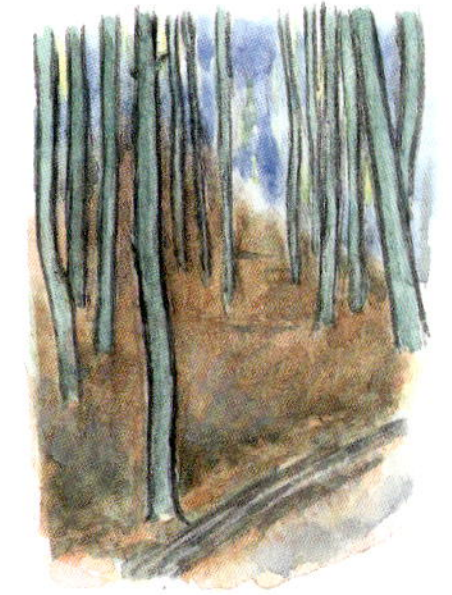

5 After Piet Mondrian. *Wood with Beech Trees*, c. 1899, detail. Watercolour and gouache on paper, 45.5 x 57 cm. Gemeentemuseum, The Hague

Piet Mondrian (1872–1944) also began searching for a spiritual source of life. He started painting light through trees (ill. 5), and later simplified these to branches in space. But then he reduced this imagery further, to create compositions constructed entirely out of horizontal and vertical lines of force which, when crossed, occasionally generate colour (ill. 6). They are, essentially, expressions of our sense of breadth and gravity as interpreted spiritually

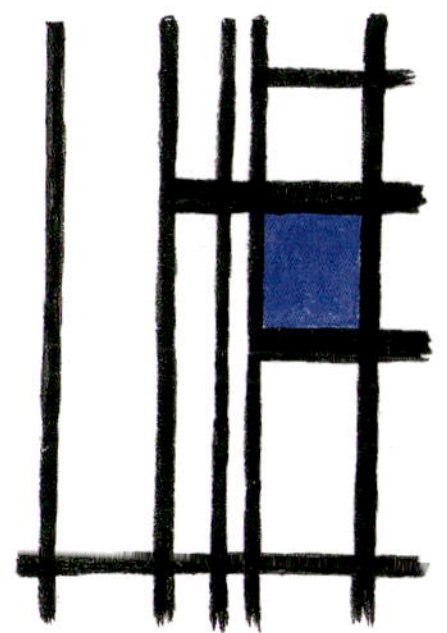

6 Piet Mondrian. *Composition 12 with Small Blue Square*, 1936–42, detail. National Gallery of Canada, Ottawa

by Madame Blavatsky. When visiting the studio of the British abstract artist Ben Nicholson, which had just one window in its pure white space, Mondrian commented, "Too much nature for me." Appearances had become a distraction from the essence of experience.

Henri Matisse (1869–1954) was too much in love with the sights of the world–particularly flowers, and light through windows, and radiant fabrics, and full-bosomed naked women–to want to deprive himself of the pleasure of looking at them. Yet he was an artist of his time for, as he stated in his *Notes of a Painter* (1908), his aim was to discover the "essential character" of things beneath their superficial appearance, in order to create "an art of balance, purity and serenity". He discovered this essence in light and space. Both fill his work with their presence, like a numinous

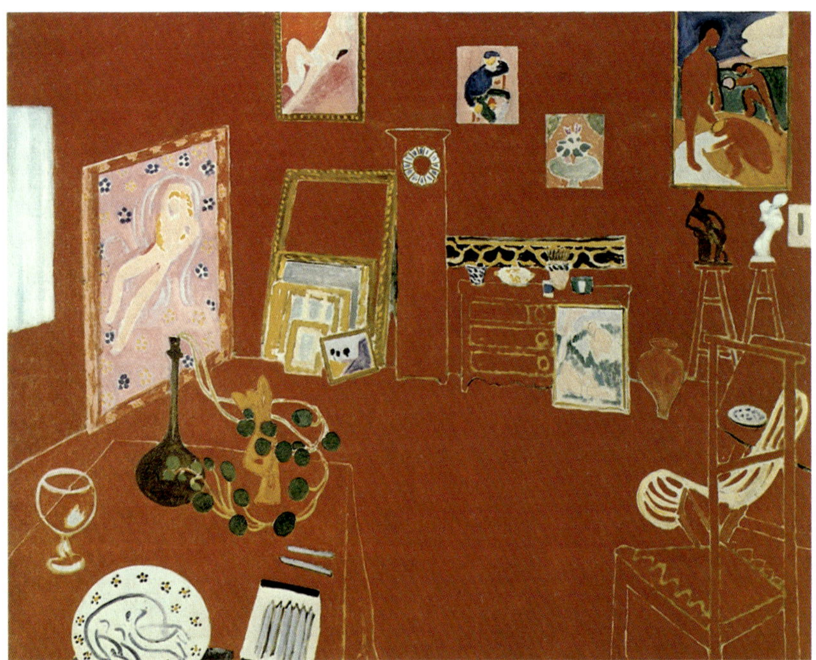

7 Henri Matisse. *The Red Studio*, 1911. Oil on canvas, 181 x 219 cm. The Museum of Modern Art, New York

ancient Mediterranean god. In Matisse's art, light and space become one; and both are coloured. The colour is the joy. In *The Red Studio* (ill.7) the glowing red *is* the space that floods through everything. The only things of substance are the works of art themselves, but these are windows on to another world, like luminous thought-clouds suspended in a room in the artist's mind. The picture looks as though it's a purely imaginative creation, but it is actually a distillation of a real scene. Matisse drew from nature all his life. He was *the* master of appearances, who gave them the most intense sensuality. Matisse's art springs from what he could see; Picasso's art from what he could not.

Many people still find it difficult to come to terms with the art of Picasso. They instinctively react against an artist who puts eyes, mouths and vaginas in places where they don't belong (ill.1). It's natural to think in that way if you still believe that looks are important, and, in some way, god-given. But that is a very western, Christian perspective. Traditional cultures in Africa, the Americas, Asia and Australia were the world's first "abstract" artists; they altered appearances at will (p.113, ill.43), though they originally did so to create images of gods, not ornaments for living rooms. We like living in a world of visual ease; we hide the body parts we prefer not to display, just as our skins veil the innards which many people believed we were never meant to see.

Those who criticise modern art for its apparent lack of skill are usually still hankering after the faithful representation of nature. For them "a child of five could do it" is generally a derogatory phrase, yet Baudelaire defined genius as "nothing more, nor less, than childhood recaptured at will". This is not far from Jesus' "Suffer the little children to come unto me … for of such is the kingdom of heaven." Children's art is crudely expressive, not

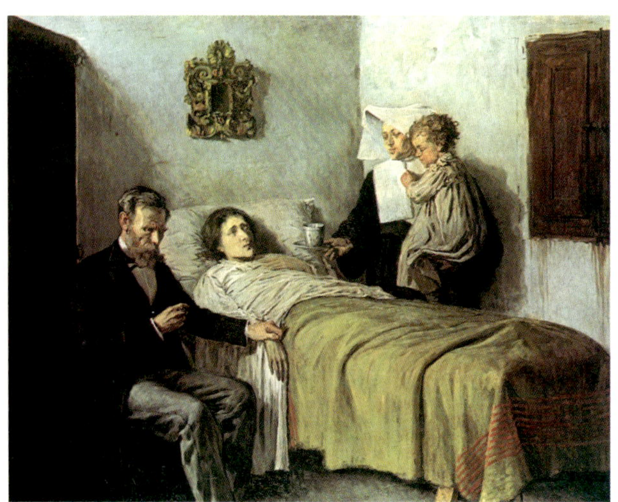

8 Pablo Picasso. *Scientific and Religious Care*, 1897. Oil on canvas. Museu Picasso, Barcelona

9 Pablo Picasso. *Les Demoiselles d'Avignon*, 1907. Oil on canvas. The Museum of Modern Art, New York

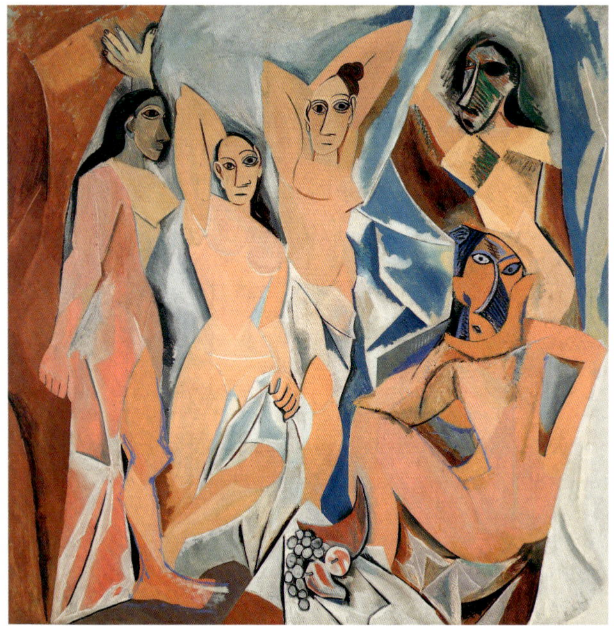

politely representative. Many people still find it hard to accept that artists can now play any visual games they want to, but that's just the result of the freedom that Picasso, Matisse, Kandinsky, Mondrian and other pioneering artists of the early twentieth century carved out for them.

Picasso was prodigiously gifted—even when only sixteen he could paint anything he chose to, and he liked to tackle ambitious themes (ill.8)—his father posed for the doctor in this composition. But Picasso wasn't satisfied with painting what things looked like. He wanted to show what things felt like. So he roamed the world of art, like a lone lion, devouring anything that interested him. With an intense sense of purpose, he created a new language of art that swept aside the great tradition of praising nature, and established, instead, a means by which he could give visual form to his inner feelings. One huge canvas, *Les Demoiselles d'Avignon* (ill.9)

(1907), served as his crucible. Into it he poured, in a fury of instinct, a whole host of images that dogged his thoughts from a huge gamut of sources: the charged energy of the devoutly Christian El Greco (ill. 10); the distortions of an African mask designed to counteract epilepsy and smallpox – though he had no idea of the functions of such images at that time (ill. 11); Cézanne's attempt to build monumental figures in space (ill. 12); and his own love of classically beautiful women (ill. 13).

The ostensible subject matter of the painting is a scene in a brothel, which the poet Baudelaire had called "the perfect image of savagery in the midst of civilisation". Picasso was a regular user of brothels, though he lived in dread of venereal disease. He had just visited the ethnography museum in Paris, and instinctively realised that African sculptures weren't art as Europeans understood the word, but were "weapons … to help people avoid coming under the influence of spirits… Spirits, the unconscious … emotion – they're all the same thing. I understood why I was a painter … all alone in that awful museum. *Les Demoiselles d'Avignon* must have come to me that very day." The picture remained in Picasso's studio for twenty years; he knew that he'd never managed to make it cohere as a whole. But in it he had, single-

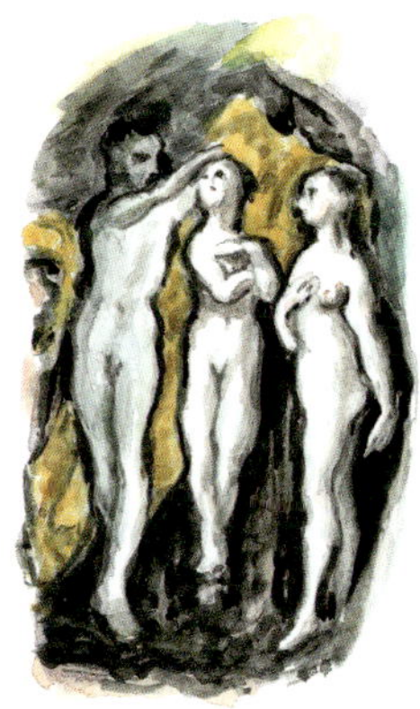

10 After El Greco. *Apocalyptic Vision*, 1608–14, detail. Oil on canvas, 224.8 x 199.4 cm. Metropolitan Museum of Art, New York

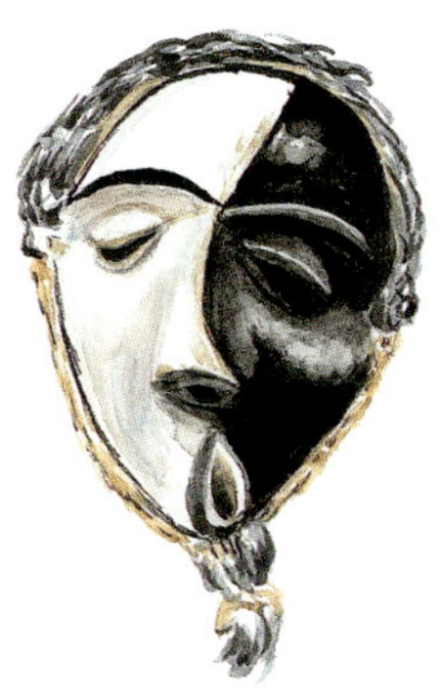

11 Mbuya (Sickness) mask, Pende, Democratic Republic of Congo. Royal Museum for Central Africa, Tervuren, Belgium

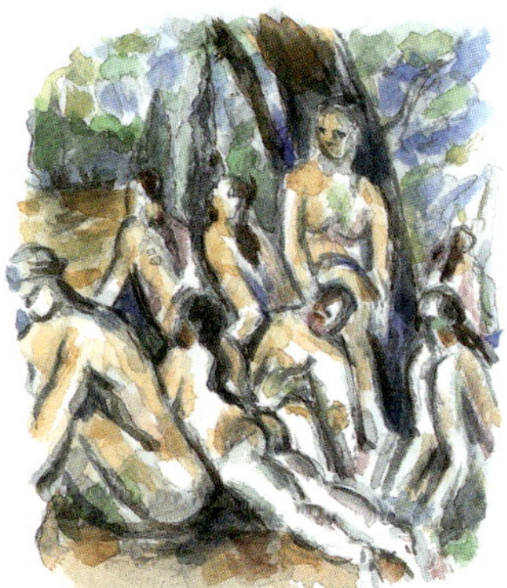

12 After Paul Cézanne. *Les Grandes Baigneuses*, c. 1906, detail. Oil on canvas, 208.5 x 251.5 cm. Philadelphia Museum of Art

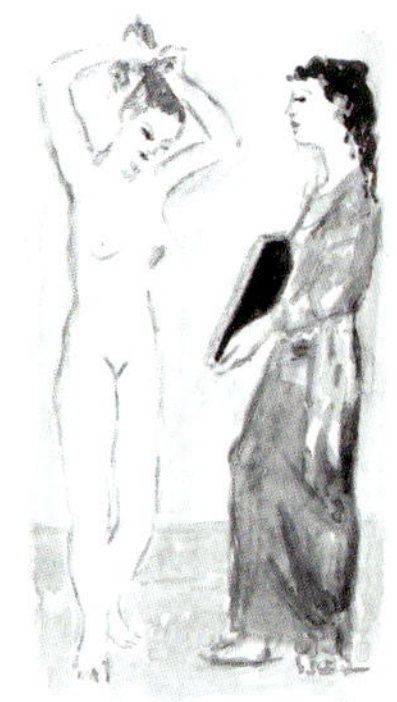

13 After Pablo Picasso. *La Toilette*, 1906, detail. Oil on canvas. Albright Knox Art Gallery, Buffalo

handedly, carved up the three-dimensional, illusionistic space that had dominated European art for a thousand years. In doing so, he reinvented art.

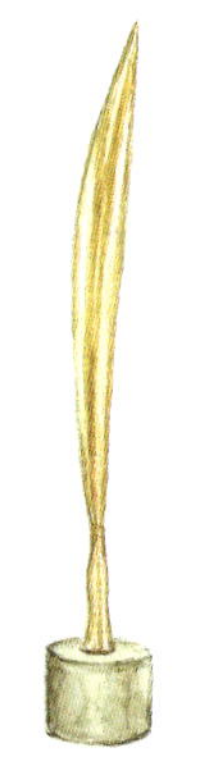

14 Constantin Brancusi. *Bird in Space*, 1925. Polished bronze. Philadelphia Museum of Art

Why should a painting look like a flower? It hasn't grown from a bud, nor is it made of tiny translucent cells flowing with sap, nor is it always a display to secure sexual congress, though it might sometimes be. Art could now be the natural product of artists – the human equivalent, to use Picasso's phrase, of "the song of a bird". He had opened the doors of the cage: the early twentieth century witnessed a great dawn chorus of individual creativity. Paul Klee (1879–1940) defined drawing as "taking a line for a walk". His small, desk-top pictures (ill. 15) were little theatres in which the actors were the lines, colours, shapes and textures that sprang to life at his touch, and told their stories. The sculptor

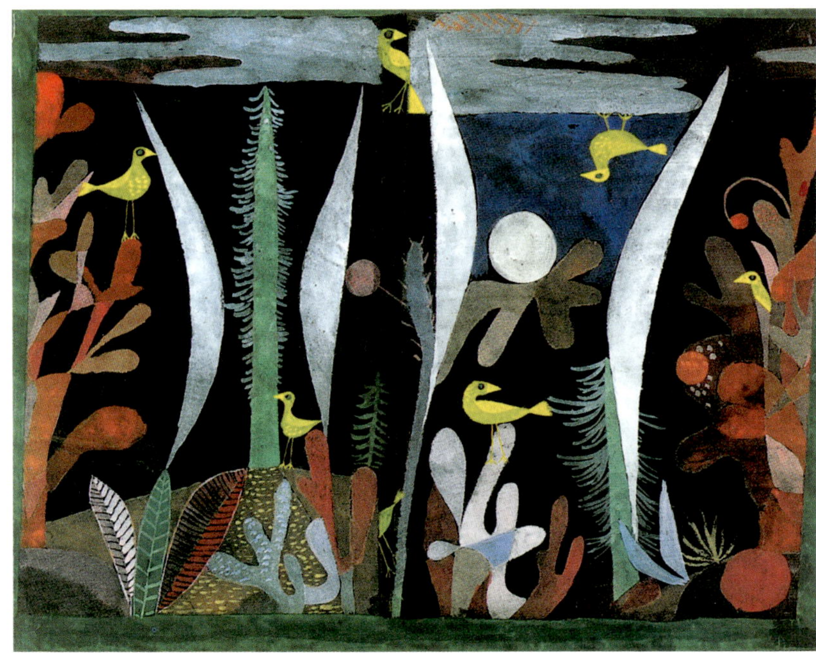

15 Paul Klee. *Landscape with Yellow Birds*, 1923. Watercolour and gouache on paper. Private collection

Constantin Brancusi (1876–1957) believed that "we mustn't try to force materials to speak our language", but should let them speak to us. He said of this shining bronze sculpture (ill. 14): "All my life I have sought the essence of flying. Don't look for mysteries. I give you pure joy." It was the joy of an inner life. And by the beginning of the twentieth century human inner life was also being examined; there were now no barriers to scientific enquiry.

Sigmund Freud (1856–1939) explored the motivations within the human psyche. His beautifully reasoned *Interpretation of Dreams* (1900) – often as gripping a read as a contemporaneous Sherlock Holmes detective story – provided evidence that dreams, like neuroses, are often disguised manifestations of repressed sexual desires. In time, Freud's work opened a door for a new generation of artists, allowing them to return, with relief, to the world of appearances – now radically changed to one in which nothing was as it seemed. At first glance the painting by René Magritte (1898–1967) *The Rape* (1934) (ill. 16) appears to be a girl's face, but then one realises that her eyes are actually her nipples, and her pinched mouth is her pubic triangle. Is it her look or your look that has made this transformation? The title might suggest the latter. Suddenly, in the twentieth century, the Evil Eye has returned with a vengeance – many would have said that it had never gone away. Surrealism, at its best, was an attitude towards life, not a style. Its aim was "to resolve the previously contradictory conditions of dream and reality into an absolute reality, a

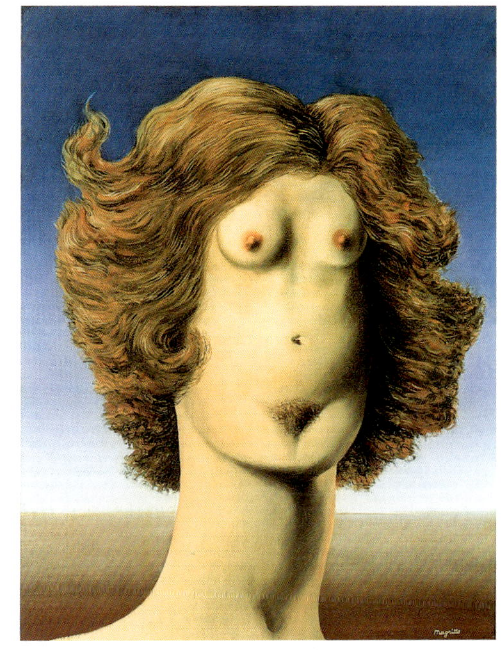

16 René Magritte. *The Rape*, 1934. Oil on canvas, 72.4 x 53.3 cm. Menil Foundation Collection, Houston, Texas

super-reality", a fuller, more honest, not so nicely polite view of ourselves and our desires. Its arch priest, the poet André Breton, wrote: "I have discarded clarity as worthless. Working in darkness I have discovered lightning." The age of the Enlightenment was finally over.

Max Ernst (1891–1976) began his career studying the new science of psychiatry, but he found academic life too constricting and, inspired by the drawings of mental patients, he turned to art. He was fascinated by microscopic life forms which he incorporated into his pictures, creating images, such as *The Entire City* (1935–36) (ill. 17) that marry the microcosm with the macrocosm and ominously leave no room for mankind. Salvador Dalí's pictures were equally calculated. Civil war broke out the year he painted *Soft Construction with Boiled Beans (Premonition of Civil*

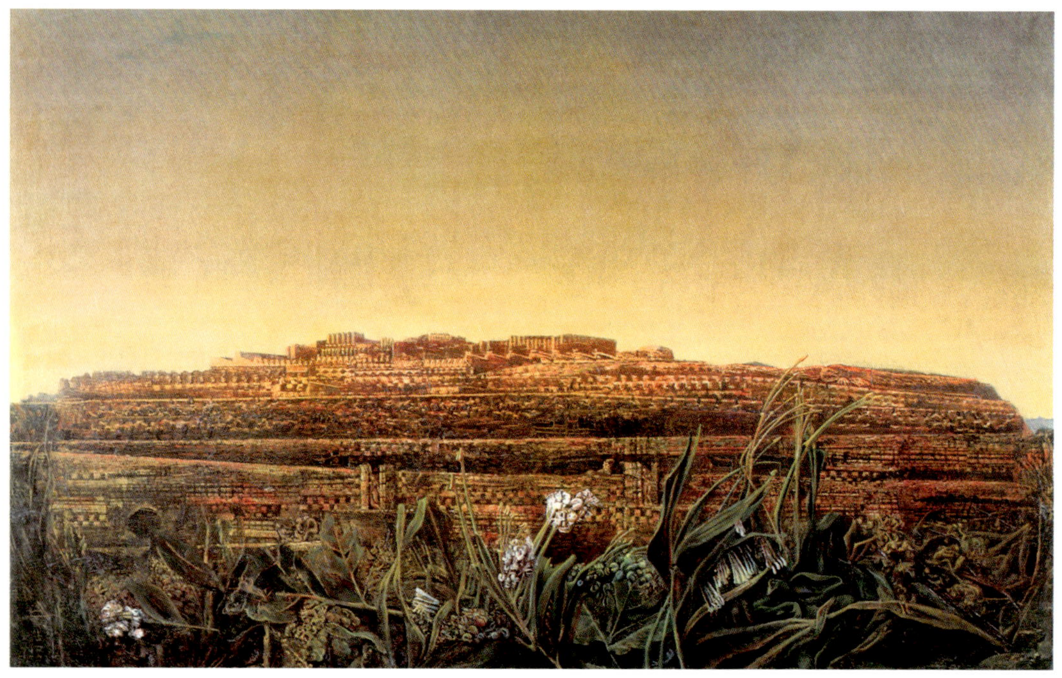

17 Max Ernst. *The Entire City*, 1935–36. Oil on canvas, 60 x 81 cm. Kunsthaus, Zurich

War) in 1936 (ill. 18), but he wasn't alone in predicting it. He'd already left Spain when trouble started in 1934. He described the picture later in these terms: "I showed a vast human body breaking into a monstrous excrescence of anus and legs tearing at one another in a delirium of auto-strangulation… As a background I painted a geological landscape that had been uselessly revolutionised for thousands of years." One senses in Dalí's intense landscapes a yearning for a time before we lost our belief in a God-created world. Had he lived at the time of Darwin, he might have been a Pre-Raphaelite. In 1940, he converted to Catholicism.

The way humanity saw itself changed dramatically in the twentieth century. We hovered somewhere, uncertain and isolated, between the galaxies of atoms within us and the galaxies of stars around us. Our world simultaneously expanded and contracted. We lived in vast cities but became more isolated. A now famous painting by Edward Hopper (1882–1967), *Nighthawks* (1942) (ill. 19), captures that moment in a New York diner late at night when everyone has become lost in their own thoughts and everything has fallen silent. The emotional truth of it—the solitariness one can feel in a large city—makes us mistake it for the rendition

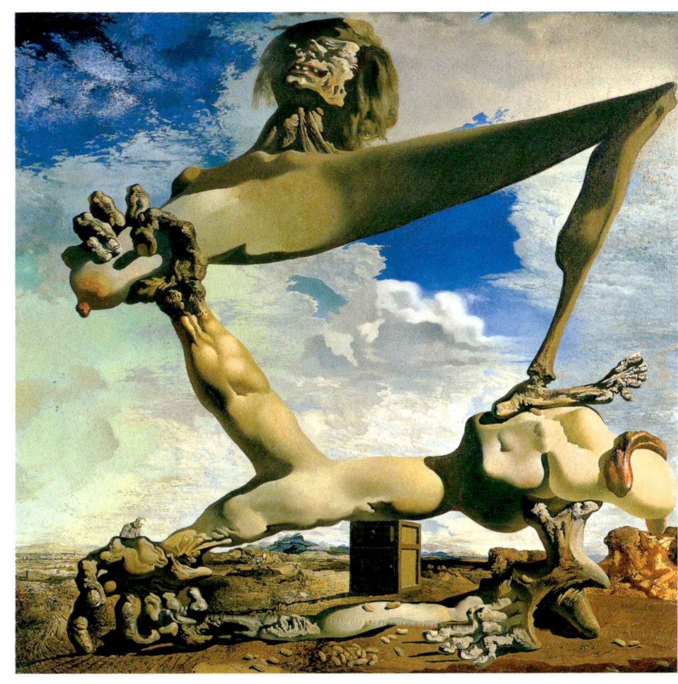

18 Salvador Dalí. *Soft Construction with Boiled Beans (Premonition of Civil War)*, 1936. Oil on canvas. Philadelphia Museum of Art

of an actual scene, though it's an imaginary composition which gestated slowly in Hopper's mind. It was inspired by van Gogh's *Night Café* (1888), which had been exhibited in New York a year before. It was as if Hopper were meditating on a contemporary combination of that eerie, silent interior with van Gogh's *Café Terrace at Night*, painted in the same year, which shows a café from the outside—its lamp flares under a brilliant gold awning while, above, the stars shine in the blue-black sky. In Hopper's painting we see the people in the interior, and there are no stars.

Western art fell apart in the 1940s. This was partly a delayed reaction to the undermining, in Christian countries, of values based on visual appearances. Most people found the more contorted modern art difficult, if not impossible to like. They yearned for the good old times when art was something they could understand and enjoy—when it was based on what they could see. In the 1920s and 30s, however, people had been getting used to the

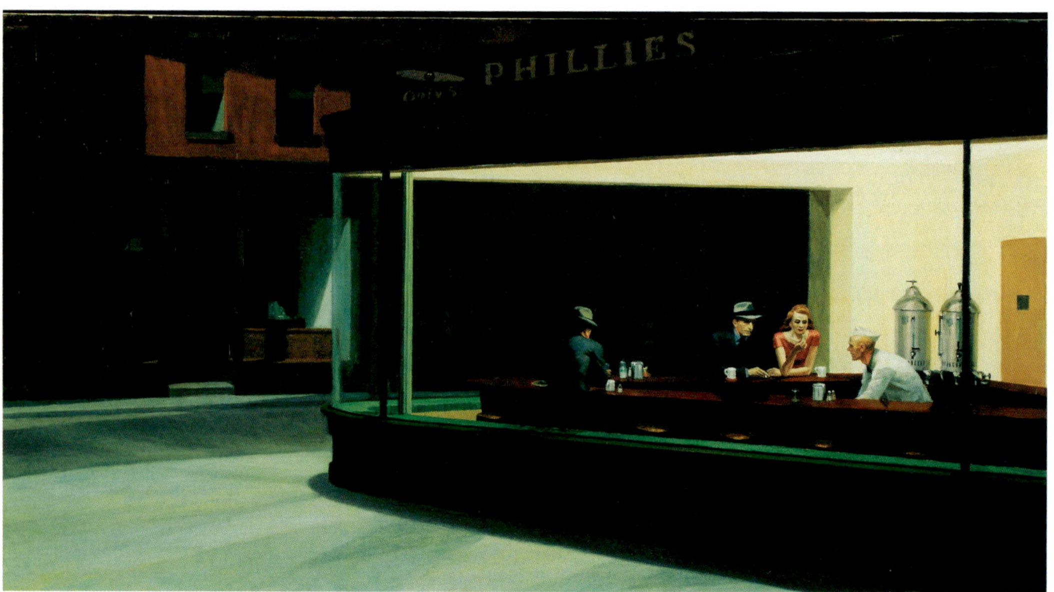

19 Edward Hopper. *Nighthawks*, 1942. Oil on canvas. The Art Institute of Chicago

new artistic freedoms. The exuberant, decorative abstractions of Matisse and his followers, such as Raoul Dufy, soon became very popular and began to influence fabric and wallpaper design. The calmer, more classical abstractions of Mondrian and the De Stijl group exerted a profound and continuing impact on modern architecture and product design. Cities were turning into walk-through Mondrians. Art Deco – which became *the* house style of those new temples of modern life, the cinemas – would have been inconceivable without the prior experimentation of the Cubists and Futurists. Even Picasso was becoming acceptable, if only as an *enfant terrible*; though many people who wanted an art that affirms rather than disturbs continued to find his work unpalatable. Dalí, however, whose work was never comfortable, enjoyed instant and far-reaching acclaim. So, all looked set for the exuberant rebirth of non-representational art, until Hitler and the Nazi party set the clock back half a century.

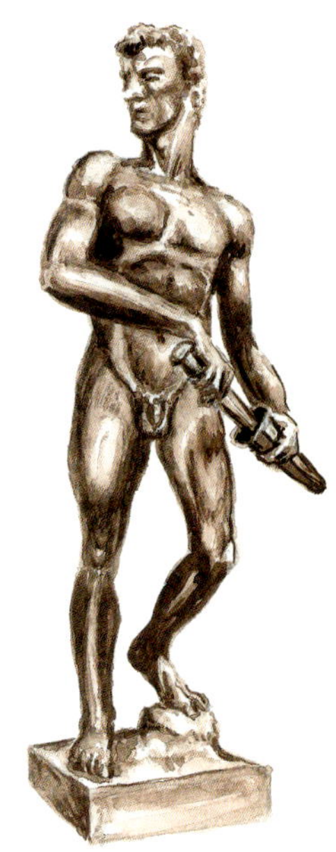
20 Arno Breker. *Preparedness*, c.1936, Bronze. Destroyed

Adolf Hitler (1889–1945) was a failed painter (his early works show mundane technical competence, but not a spark of creativity) who decided to become an artist of life. His agenda was almost entirely visual. Darwin had never argued that evolution was in any way progressive or purposeful. But Nazi doctrine transformed the concept of the survival of the fittest – those who were the best adapted to changing circumstances – into the glorification of strapping blonds with rippling torsos (ill.20). Millions of gypsies, people with disabilities, homosexuals and all followers of the Jewish faith were subjected to degrading visual examinations and then murdered because they didn't fit Hitler's picture of the master race that would rule for his promised millennium. Art had to fit the picture too. In 1937, the Nazis organised their exhibition of *Entartete Kunst* – art of degenerate races. Photographs of people with physical disabilities were shown next to Cubist and

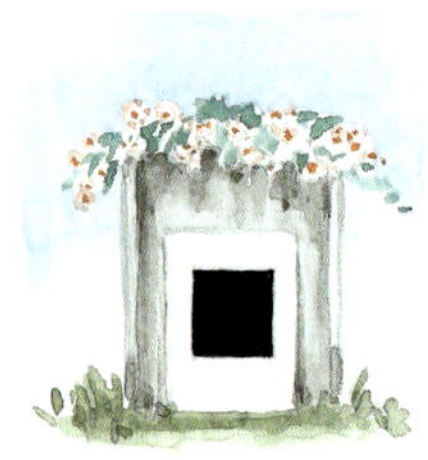

21 After a photograph showing Suetin's copy of the painting *Black Square* (1915) by Kasimir Malevich placed on Malevich's grave in Nemchikov, Russia, detail

Expressionist paintings. Kandinskys, Klees and Kirchners were hung at rakish angles, under captions that read "Mockery of German Womanhood" or "Complete Madness". Between 19 July and 30 November, 2,009,899 visitors flocked to see the show in Munich, making it ironically the most popular modern art show ever. Many must have attended out of fear, but most because they were genuinely bewildered by modern art, and many must have been relieved to learn that the Nazis said they didn't have to like it, or even look at it.

This attack on modern art might have been buried with Hitler, had not the Soviet, and later the Chinese communists, decided to promote Socialist Realism as the "art of the people". The Russian revolutionaries had briefly flirted with abstraction. They encouraged Kasimir Malevich (1878–1935) to evolve a new language of art for everyone, which would be abstract and classless. He saw his *Black Square* (1915) (ill. 21) as the beginning of a new art for everyone, but it marked his own end, for it was carried before his coffin and placed on his grave. Long before then the Soviets had decided to outlaw any art that was abstract and expressionist and went beyond appearances. Art became a victim of the division of the Cold

22 Mark Rothko. *Green on Blue (Earth Green and White)*, 1956. Oil on canvas, 228.6 x 161.3 cm. University of Arizona Museum of Art, Tucson

War. America outlawed representational art—Hopper's work was thought "too communist"—and promoted, instead, Abstract Expressionism, an uncomfortable amalgam of two contradictory creative processes: abstraction is a process of reduction, Expressionism one of addition. The works of gifted but essentially lesser followers of the abstract artist Mondrian, like Mark Rothko (1903–70) (ill.22), and of the Expressionist painter Kandinsky, like Jackson Pollock (1912–56) (ill.23) were vaunted and presented to the world as something absolutely original, which they weren't, except in scale.

Worse followed: the art world in the West became obsessed by two imperatives: art, to be modern, had to be new, and it had to shock. The idea was that modern art was progressing towards some wonderful epiphany, and that it was to be expected that each new advance would be greeted with howls of protest from the public. Artists in the West vied with each other to produce more and more abstract works, like Carl Andre's stacks of bricks, or more and more Expressionist works, like Julian Schnabel's paintings made of smashed plates. The new art historians and the

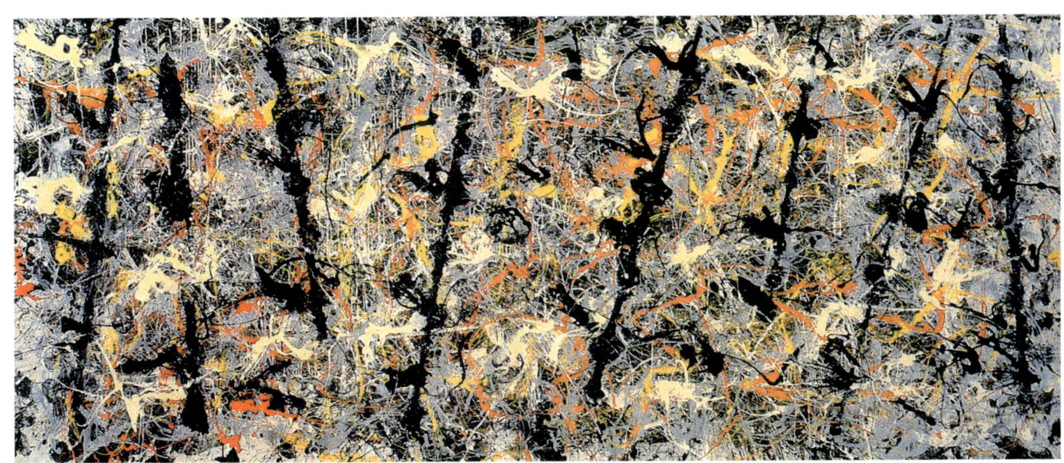

23 Jackson Pollock. *Blue Poles: Number II*, 1952. Enamel and aluminium paint with gloss on canvas, 211 x 463 cm. National Gallery of Australia, Canberra

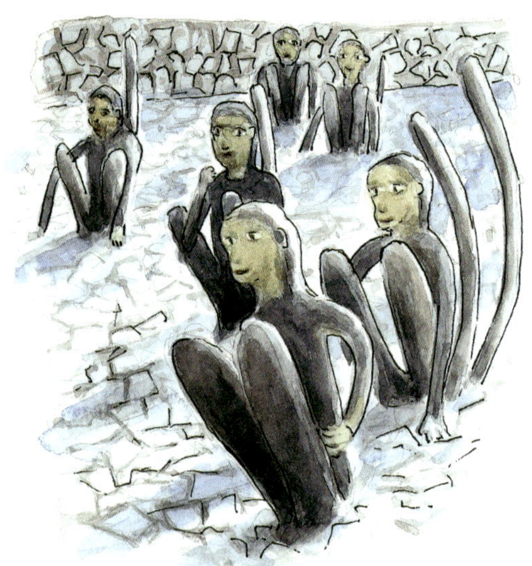

24 Nek Chand Saini. *Monkeys*, 1958–2000. The Rock Garden, Chandigarh, India

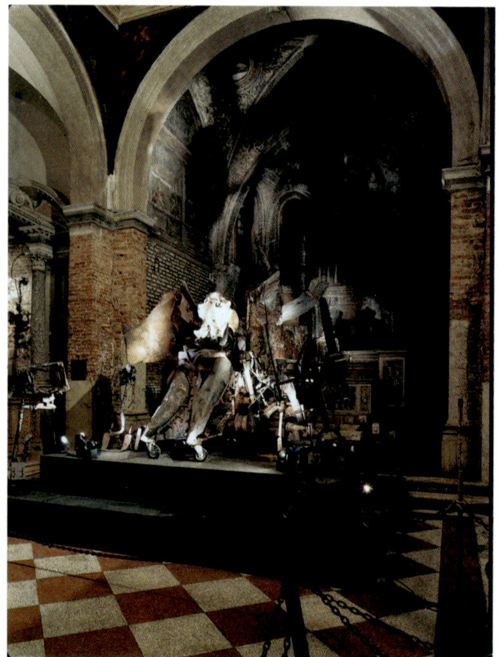

25 Jean Tinguely. *Mengele (High Altar)*, 1986. 300 x 440 x 420 cm. Jean Tinguely Museum, Basle

new modern art museums—neither of which had existed in any significant numbers before the Second World War—were there to record and collect each artist's contribution to the grand progression of modern art. It was the other side of the coin to Hitler's misreading of evolution as the manifestation of progress, not of the will to survive.

The trouble with these new galleries of modern art—insulated as they are from criticism by the need for public condemnation—is that anything exhibited in them automatically becomes a work of art because it's there. So a gents' urinal, a can filled with excrement, or an unmade, soiled bed acquires a spurious significance that it would not have if seen on a dump. Modern art curators have created quasi-sacred spaces that exist without a religious belief to sustain them, which are a sitting target for mountebanks and pseudo-shamans.

It is too soon to name the significant artists of our time. They'll almost certainly be found among those who have worked outside the self-important world of contemporary art galleries—artists like Jean Tinguely (1925–91), whose kinetic sculpture of Mengele (ill.25), who conducted horrific experiments on his patients as part of the Nazi programme to create a super race, is also an image of what mankind is doing to nature; Eduard Bersudsky (born 1939) who creates tragicomic kinetic sculptures (ill.24) expressing his horror at the oppressive regime he lived through in Russia, and Nek Chand Saini (born 1924), a road engineer in Chandigarh, who has created a huge garden in which animals (ill.26) are among the heavenly hosts; and Niki de Saint Phalle (1930–2002), whose Tarot Garden (ill.27) in Italy gives one a glimpse of what it might actually have been like to walk down the Street of the Dead in Teotihuacan, or stroll among the painted statues on the Acropolis in Athens.

Artists, poets and mystics have long tried to look at themselves from the outside. Humanity was given a chance to do just that during the Apollo space programme which achieved its objective on 20 July 1969 when Neil Armstrong set foot on the moon. The moon walks were a bit of a let-down – there was nothing much the astronauts could do except bounce about for a bit.

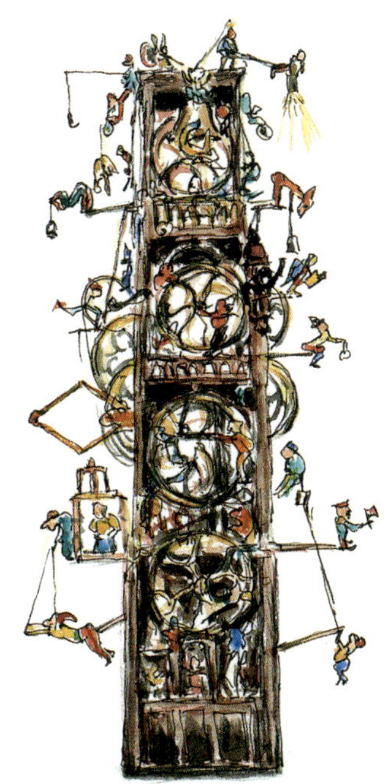

26 Eduard Bersudsky. *Tower of Babel*, 1986–89. Wood, metal, motors and paint, 3 m high. Sharmanka Theatre, Glasgow, Scotland

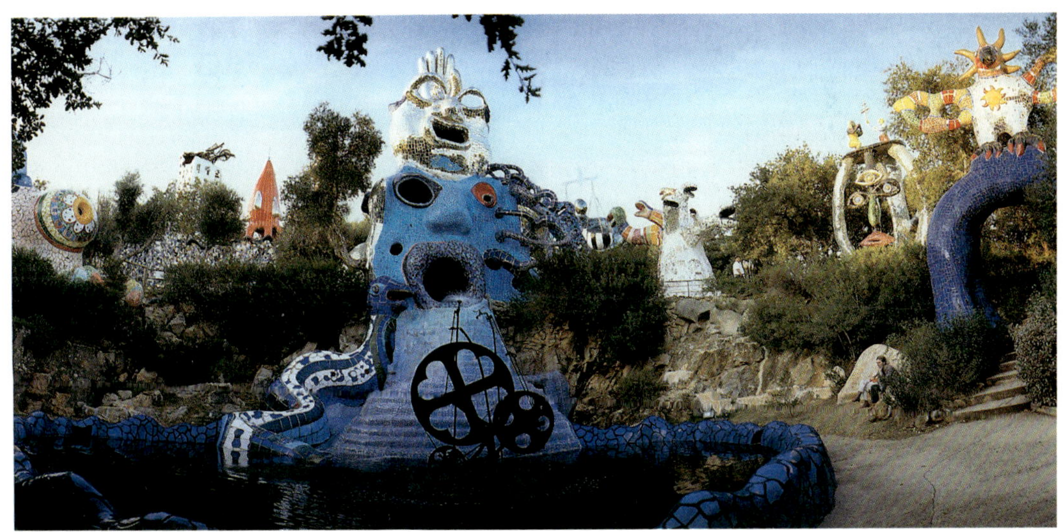

27 Niki de Sainte Phalle. Tarot Garden, 1979–98. Garavicchio, Italy

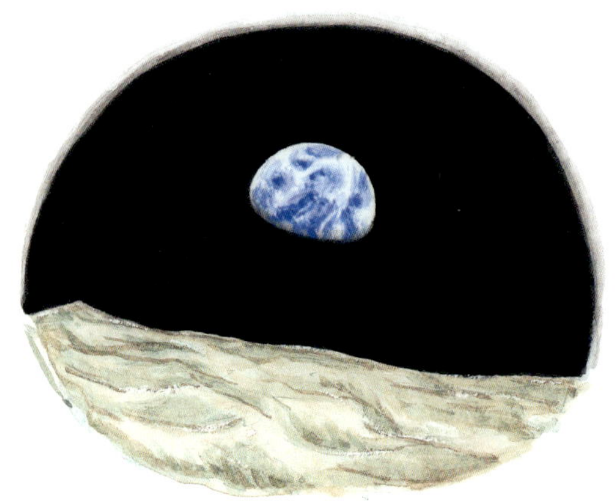

28 After a photograph of earthrise, taken by William A. Anders, 24 December 1968

But what the Apollo programme did achieve was to give us a totally different view of ourselves. On Christmas Eve 1968, Apollo 8 astronaut William A. Anders took a photograph from his module (ill.28) that has affected our world-view ever since. We see ourselves inhabiting a blue and white marbled jewel drifting in the wastes of space. We have become aware not just of our own, but of our planet's fragility.

The fragility of nature became a subject of scientific interest in the 1960s and 70s. Scientists realised that the structural laws of the universe which had been developed from Newton's theories didn't explain everything they could see. The Polish mathematician Benoit Mandelbrot was fond of saying that "a cloud is not a sphere". In fact it emerges out of and merges into infinitesimal patterns of wisps. Science till then had dismissed these as marginal, merely the frayed edges of the great and graceful smooth geometric forms that Newton believed were the true building blocks of nature. In the 1970s, the American mathematician Mitchell Feigenbaum became fascinated by the theories of the German poet Goethe who had tried to prove that Newton's view of nature was only partial. Goethe had conducted experiments to show that colour could be created by agitating the border between light and dark. Newton's laws of the spectrum have stood the test of all subsequent analysis, while Goethe's observations were dismissed as romantic wishful thinking, until Feigenbaum saw that there might be some truth in them.

Goethe had proposed a theory that a leaf represented the essential form of a plant, from which all its other forms had devel-

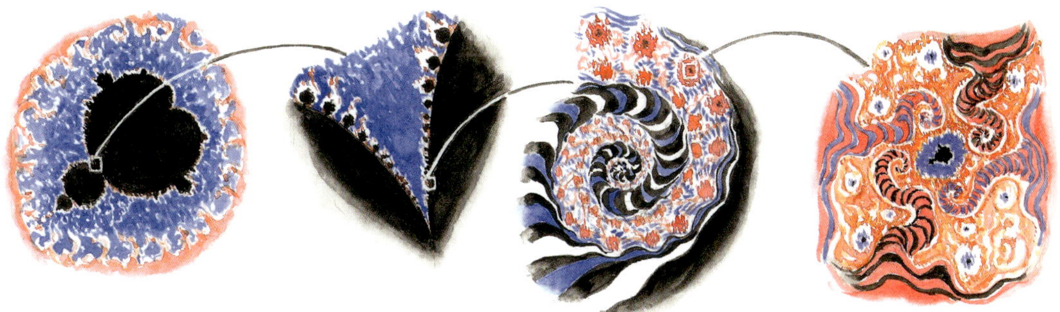

oped. Feigenbaum thought he could be right. During two months in 1976 he worked out a mathematical framework for the bewilderingly complex, multidimensional, universal processes of unpredictable flow—what came to be known as the chaos theory. Benoit Mandelbrot found a way of visualising this new type of geometry, which he called "fractal", to reveal the structure of natural boundaries. The closer we zoom in on the mathematical shapes in the Mandelbrot Set (ill. 29)—and we've only been able to do this since the development of computers—the more varied and complex these boundaries become. This fractal geometry explains many natural forms, such as the spines of mountain ranges, the infinite variety of snowflakes and the patterning on sea shells.

29 The Mandelbrot Set, a sequence of ever-decreasing details

In 1995, the palaeontologist Andrew Parker noticed microscopic parallel lines, astonishingly preserved on the fossils of sea creatures which had lived 515 million years ago. It occurred to him that they might be diffraction gratings like those found on some bird and insect wings today, which make them iridescent. He reconstructed models of these surfaces and placed them in shallow sea water in sunlight. Rainbows flashed from the far distant past (ill. 30). The moment was magical enough in itself, but it set Parker thinking. One of the great mysteries of evolution was why there had been an unprecedented and never repeated explo-

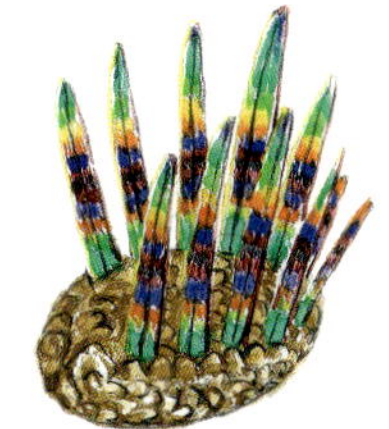

30 *Wiwaxia*, reconstruction of a Cambrian sea creature, 515 million B.C.E.

sion in living forms precisely 543 million years ago, an extraordinary Big Bang in evolution that lasted only about five million years, which came to be known as the Cambrian explosion. Evidence of this had worried Darwin, who thought that it might be used as a valid argument against his theory, and indeed its cause remained undiscovered until, in 2000, Parker presented his now widely accepted findings that this outburst of life-forms had been caused by the evolution of the eye.

The Precambrian world had been lived in underwater by jelly-bodied sliding, floating, swimming, creeping amoeba-like creatures, which were all blind. Some could sense light, as you can sense your hand moving in front of your closed eyes in bright sunlight, but none could see. Then eyes began to develop—and revealed good things to eat. There had been predators before, but they had found their food by chance or by groping, as jellyfish and starfish still do. But for creatures with eyes, the world became their oyster. Whole species must have been gobbled up. Animals and plants survived by adapting to sight—and the closing mouths or the embraces that followed gazes. Defensive surfaces hardened first—seashells, spines and sharp teeth—but, within geological minutes, the whole panoply of the coral reef had appeared under the sun-dappled sea, with all its strategies for using colour and form to attract, deceive and warn.

Darwin argued that the appearance of living things had nothing to do with their purpose, unless this gave them an evolutionary advantage. Peacocks' feathers had evolved, he argued, merely to attract peahens, just as *Wiwaxia* had, perhaps, waved its iridescent spines to impress a mate or frighten an attacker in the Cambrian sea, five hundred million years ago. But Mandelbrot's new mathematics mean that we have to take into account an additional reason for the splendour of nature. Perhaps Leonardo had been right, up to a point, to compare a growing seed with the human heart (p. 103, ill. 25) and Ruskin justified in marvelling at the glory of a peacock's breast feather (p. 248, ill. 30). D'Arcy Thompson (1860–1948) showed–in his book *On Growth and Form* (1917) how organisms and inorganic matter are subject to the same structural laws–how, for example, a drop of ink falling through water takes on the form of a jellyfish. It was obviously efficient for living organisms to obey the laws of natural physics, but these laws were thought to be marginal constraints, not central to any purpose. Yet it was this very belief in a uniform principle governing all natural forms that inspired the anonymous builders of Hindu temples, Islamic mosques, Christian cathedrals and Chinese imperial halls to examine in detail the patterns formed in nature by branches and flowers, scales and feathers, the eddies and flow of clouds and seas, in their attempt to express the endless, beautiful divisibility of god.

This begged the question: what was god? The Brahmins of India teach "that art thou"–the ultimate being out there, which lies beyond the visible world, is the same as that eternal being that lies within you. Japanese Shinto priests believed that, in the beginning, "chaos began to condense", but no-one could know the form it first took. It was only later that "the two spirits of the active and the passive developed and became the ancestors of all things". One of the oldest books in the world, first written down about 3,000 years ago, is the Chinese *Book of Changes*–a divination system based on a sequence of broken and unbroken lines (ill. 31)–perhaps the first digitisation. A random throw of coins or yarrow sticks connects the consultant to the cosmic order and informs them, through poetic allusions–water over fire spells danger, a wind under heaven calls for a meeting–what to do next in life. This duality is another manifestation of the Yin-Yang sym-

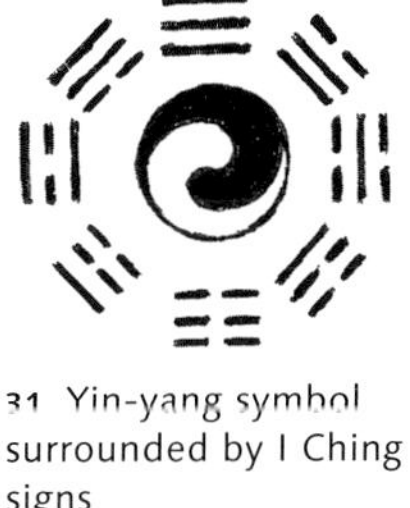

31 Yin-yang symbol surrounded by I Ching signs

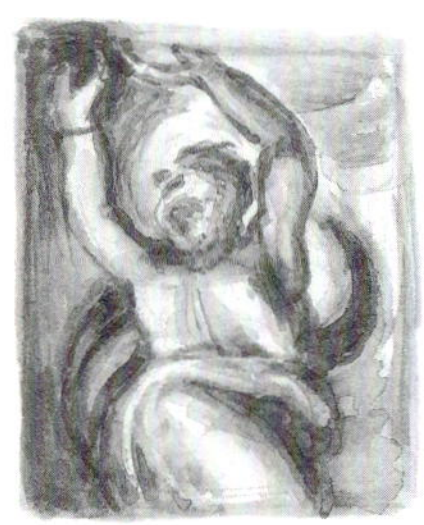

32 After Michelangelo. *God Dividing the Light from the Darkness*, 1508–12, Sistine Capel, Vatican, Rome

bol, representing the light, active force and the dark, receptive force, from whose ceaseless embrace all creation flows.

The twisted rice straw ropes (p. 168, ill. 17) that Shinto priests hang around sacred sites in Japan, the churning of the ocean that Hindus believed began the process of creation, and the snakes that entwine together to create the head, body and skirt of the great Aztec earth mother Coatlicue (p. 160, ill. 5), all suggest that people have long sensed the presence of an interlocking spiral at the heart of existence; Michelangelo used this form in his depiction of God dividing light from darkness (ill. 32) as did van Gogh in his inspired rendering of a spiralling galactic wind (ill. 33), which he could never have seen. Such an interlocking spiral has now been discovered in the structure of DNA (ill. 34). Van Gogh pondered, in his literal but wonderful way: "Why should the shining dots of the sky not be as accessible as the black dots on the maps of

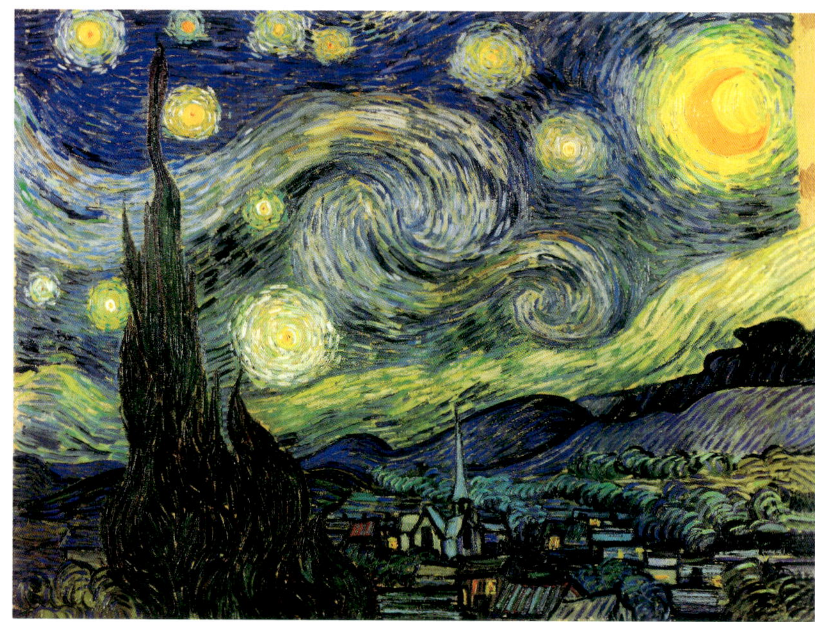

33 Vincent van Gogh. *Starry Night*, 1889. Oil on canvas, 73.7 x 92 cm. The Museum of Modern Art, New York

France? If we take a train to get to Tarascon or Rouen, we take death to reach a star." The black cypresses – to him the flames of death – would carry him there. In our hearts we still believe, with Walt Whitman (1819–92), that "a leaf of grass is no less than the journey-work of the stars", though we do not yet know how this could be so. Shortly before he died, Newton wrote: "As to myself, I seem to have been only like a boy playing on the seashore, and diverting myself in now and then finding a smoother pebble or a prettier shell than ordinary, whilst the great ocean of truth lay all undiscovered before me." We are back where this book started, with the Australian Aborigines (p. 25, ill. 11), gazing with wonder at the stars. Every discovery reveals a new mystery. And one of the greatest mysteries is now wonder itself.

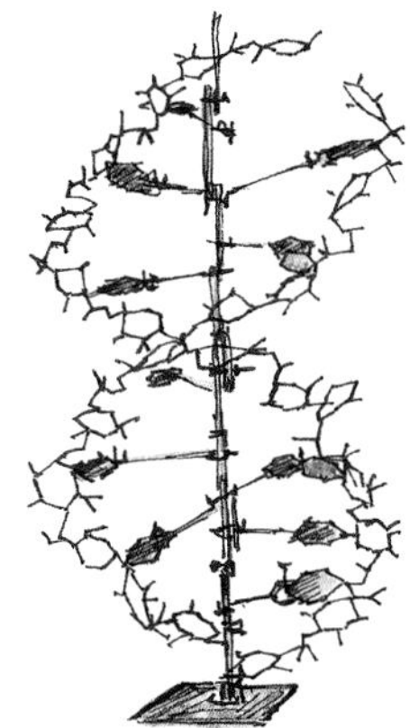

34 First model of DNA, by Francis Crick and James Watson

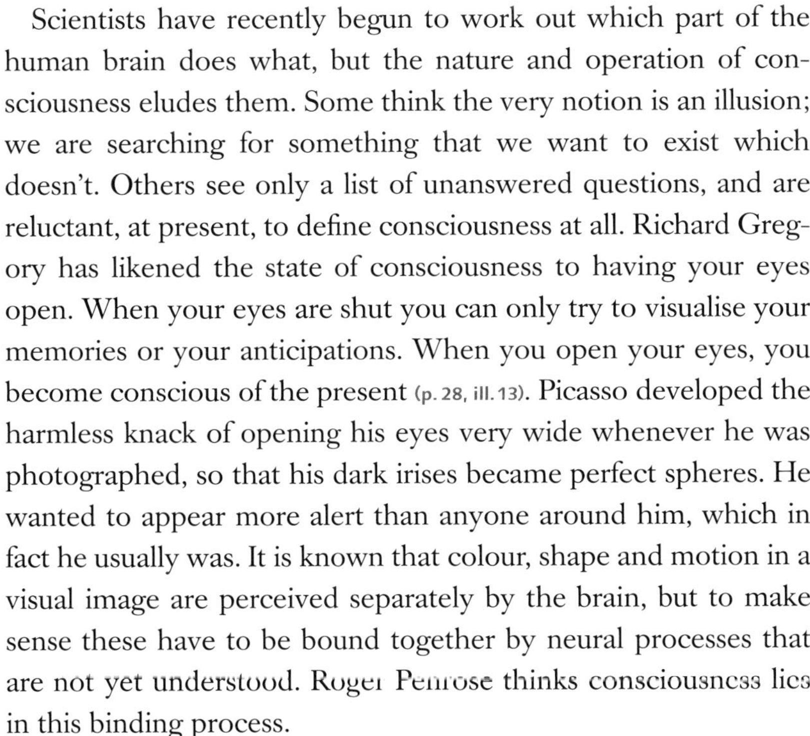

Scientists have recently begun to work out which part of the human brain does what, but the nature and operation of consciousness eludes them. Some think the very notion is an illusion; we are searching for something that we want to exist which doesn't. Others see only a list of unanswered questions, and are reluctant, at present, to define consciousness at all. Richard Gregory has likened the state of consciousness to having your eyes open. When your eyes are shut you can only try to visualise your memories or your anticipations. When you open your eyes, you become conscious of the present (p. 28, ill. 13). Picasso developed the harmless knack of opening his eyes very wide whenever he was photographed, so that his dark irises became perfect spheres. He wanted to appear more alert than anyone around him, which in fact he usually was. It is known that colour, shape and motion in a visual image are perceived separately by the brain, but to make sense these have to be bound together by neural processes that are not yet understood. Roger Penrose thinks consciousness lies in this binding process.

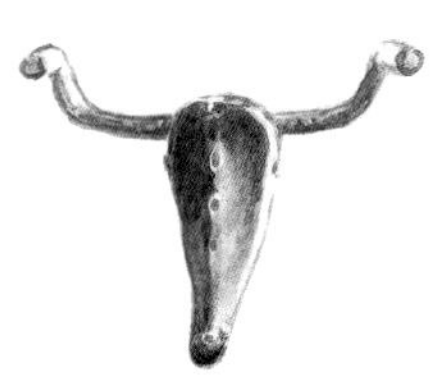

35 Pablo Picasso. *Head of a Bull*, 1943. Bicycle saddle and handlebars. Musée Picasso, Paris

It is this binding process that art reveals; vividly, for example, in Picasso's *Head of a Bull* of 1943 (ill.35), which is at once the sleek head of a wild bull of the type used for bullfighting in Spain, and the saddle and handlebars of a bicycle, used by young men for racing. Two ordinary objects have been magnetically fused together in the artist's mind to make a third that resonates down centuries of youthful heroics, back through the existing tradition of bullfighting in Spain to the paintings and bronzes of ancient Crete (ill.36) showing young men hurling themselves over the backs of bulls, back, even further, to the myth of the Minotaur, the bull-headed monster of that island who had to be fed every seven years with seven youths and seven maidens, perhaps to keep the heavenly bodies in their places. But the *Head of a Bull* also exposes, with stark clarity, the artist's creative process. Picasso was continually and genuinely surprised by how he got from here to there in his art. He was fond of asking: "If I knew what I was going to do next, what would be the point of doing it?" He often dated and even timed series of work because he thought that some day someone would understand this process of discovering. The chances are that they will, and that Picasso's works will be used to illustrate the operations of the conscious mind, in a state, perhaps, of heightened awareness.

You cannot create art of great beauty and power without intense attention and concentration. The cave painters of the Paleolithic age must have been on their toes—probably literally—to have been able to draw animals as if they were moving, especially with such sureness and economy. The precision of feeling in the gold mask of Tutankhamen, or a sculpture at Khajuraho showing Shiva and Parvati in a blissful, sexual embrace, or a drawing of a Star of Bethlehem flower by Leonardo springs not from the subject of the work of art but from the alertness of the artist who created it. Great works of art look complete; they look bound together in a way that enables them to emit an authority, a clarity which distinguishes them from the ordinary jumble of things. It is this clearness around them that enables you to see these works of art instantaneously as a whole, while responding to the feelings within them. They are like living things held up for all to look at, as if in a crystal sphere. The atmosphere around them is the light of art. Their creation – a process of clarification – is the product of the artists' hard work.

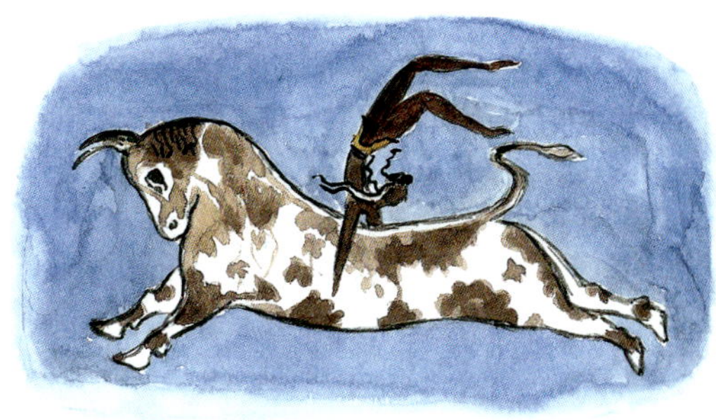

36 *Bull Rider*, c.1700 B.C.E., Knossos, Crete. Fresco

This light is nothing less than our consciousness, which somehow, through art, we have managed to make manifest so that we can communicate it to others. And it is into this light of consciousness that we have, at different times and in different places, condensed our visions of who we think we are and of what is important to us. These distilled images once glowed in a world bathed in wonder. Now most of them – the images in this book – linger like lost souls in the littered wasteland of our trampled universe. We might think we know the reason for all that we can see, but we can take heart from the fact that the ultimate cause is still a mystery. Strange things are going on in all dimensions far beyond the reach of our perception, and these might in time reveal new mysteries in the world we see around us, which now seems so drained of wonder that we hardly look at, and care little for it.

Wonder will perhaps be found again in the very process of seeing, of seeing not just through our eyes, but with our minds. The emotional and moral world of personal experience, which has been excluded for so long from the matter-of-fact investigations of science, is now coming under scientific scrutiny. But this is also the rich, colourful hunting-ground of the artist. It could be that consciousness, awareness of death and the making of art are all related, and that it is these characteristics that distinguish us from any other creature, including our nearest extinct relatives, the Neanderthals. A horizon over which we cannot see stretches before us: one in which human feelings and thoughts – the very nature of our experience – will, once again, be encompassed in wonder. There could, after all, be stars in our eyes.

Index of Proper Names, Monuments and Sites

Numbers in *italics* refer to illustrations

A

Aberlemno, pictish stone 32, *32*
Acropolis, Athens 273
Agamemnon 77
Ahhotep, Queen 123
Akhenaten 74, 75
Alhambra, Granada 179, *180*
Al-Khatib, Ibn 179
Altamira, cave 118, *118*
Altdorfer, Albrecht *220*, 227
Anders, William A. 274, *274*
Andre, Carl 271
Angelico, Fra 217
Angkor Thom, Cambodia 50, *51*
Angkor Wat, Cambodia 50
Antinous 27
Arena Chapel, Padua 189, *203*
Aretino, Pietro 151
Aristarchus of Samos 225
Aristotle 132, 221, 222, 224
Armstrong, Neil 273
Audubon, John James 240, *240*

B

Bacon, Roger 229
Baudelaire, Charles 261, 263
Bede, Venerable 186
Beijing, The Forbidden City 29, *29*, 50, *50*, *51*, 52, 53, 55, 85, *94*, 95, 97, 98, *98*, 183, 226
Bellini, Giovanni 204, *204*, 205
Bernini, Gianlorenzo *166*
Bersusky, Eduard 273, *273*
Besant, Annie 258
Bingen, Hildegard of 149, 195, 196
Blake, William 70, *70*, 82
Blavatsky, Madame 258, 260
Bohr, Niels 257
Bosch, Hieronymus *34*, *46*, *146*, 147, *214*, 215
Boswell, James 221
Botticelli, Sandro 81, *81*, *200*, 201
Braille, Louis 236
Brancacci Chapel / S. Maria del Carmine, Florence 202, *202*
Brancusi, Constantin *264*, 265
Breker, Arno *269*
Brendekilde, H.A. *135*
Breton, André 266
Breughel, Peter 84, *84*, *134*, *144*
Brunelleschi, Filippo 203
Buddha 17, 92, 96, 107, 148, 151, 152, 162-164, 174, 175, 185, 205, 213, *213*
Buffalmacco, Buonamico *135*
Buffon, Comte de 240, 241

C

Caesar, Julius 111, 202
Calvin, Johannes 189
Canaletto, Antonio 48
Caravaggio, Michelangelo Merisi da 218, *218*, 231, 219
Castello del Buonconsiglio, Trento 246, *246*
Cerne Abbas, Dorset/England 111, *111*
Cézanne, Paul 250, 251, 263, *263*
Charles I, King 129, *129*
Chartres, cathedral 10, 122, *123*, 176, *177*, *189*, *190*, 191
Chauvet, cave 24, *24*, 117
Cheops, pyramid 96
Chin-feng, Chang 247, *247*
Christian IV, King *126*
Church of Saints Cosmas and Damian, Rome *71*
Cicero 120
Claudius, Emperor 129
Columbus, Christopher 35, 43, 71, 72, 208, 226, 227, 240
Confucius 98, 122, 152, 170
Constable, John 97, *97*, 244
Constantine, Emperor 187
Copernicus, Nicolaus 227, 233
Cortés, Hernando 71
Crick, Francis *279*
Curtis, Edward S. *20*, 70, *71*, *105*, *128*, *138*

D

Dalí, Salvador 266, 267, *267*, 269
Daniken, Erich von 104
Dante Alighieri 215
Darwin, Charles 18, 44, 208, 244, 245, *245*, 246-248, 250, 267, 269, 276
Davies, John 172
Delacroix, Eugène 241
Democritus 47, 248, 257
Descartes, René 229, 235, 236
Diderot, Denis 236
Dioscorides 224
Dome of the Rock, Jerusalem 49, *50*
Donatello *143*
Dufy, Raoul 269
Dürer, Albrecht 206, 207, *207*, 208, 215, 216, *216*, 231, 244, *244*

E

Einstein, Albert 257
Elisabeth I, Queen 168
Engels, Friedrich 247
Epicurus 248
Epidaurus, theatre 12
Eratosthenes 225
Ernst, Max 266, *266*
Eyck, Hubert and Jan van *182*, 183, 188, *188*, 205, 207, *207*

F

Faraday, Michael 243
Feigenbaum, Mitchell 274, 275
Fiesole, Giovanni da 217
Firenze, Andrea da *130*
Flaccus, Valerius 27
Font de Gaume, cave 116, *116*
Fossum, petroglyphs *41*
Francesca, Piero della 50, *50*, 206, *206*
Francis I, King 216
Franck, Sebastian 205
Freud, Sigmund 265
Friedrich, Caspar David 242, *242*
Fyning, Dirich *126*

G

Gakutei *73*
Galilei, Galileo 27, 43, 203, 208, 228, *228*, 229, 219
Gauguin, Paul 254
George III, King 125
Ghandi, Mahatma 249
Ghent, cathedral of S. Bavon *182*
Gibbon, Edward 186, 188, 189, 201, 217
Giocondo, Franceso del 213
Giorgione 106, *106*, 183
Giotto 189, 203, *203*, 204
Gislebertus 28, *28*
Gizeh, pyramids 86, *86*
Goes, Hugo van der *6*, 14, *14*, *15*, *148*
Goethe, Johann Wolfgang von 237, 244, 274
Gogh, Theo van 79
Gogh, Vincent van 14, *16*, 17, *78*, 79, 83, 84, *84*, 250, 253, 254, *254*, 268, 278, *278*
Goya y Lucientes, Francisco José de 234, *234*, *235*
El Greco 263, *263*
Gregory, Pope 196
Gregory, Richard 279
Grünewald, Matthias *147*, 195, *195*

H

Hadrian, Emperor 27
Hagia Sophia, Istanbul 187, *187*
Harvey, William 238
Hawk, High 128, *128*
Henry VIII, King 111, *111*
Heraclides of Pontus 225
Hereford, cathedral *197*
Hildesheim, cathedral *145*
Hilliard, Nicholas 168, *168*
Hitler, Adolf 269, 270, 272
Hokusai, Katsushika 95, *95*
Holbein, Hans *111*, 155, *155*
Holmes, Sherlock 265
Hooke, Robert 229, *229*
Hopper, Edward 267, 268, *268*
Howard, Luke 97
Hua Shan *41*, 42
Hunefer, scribe 149, *149*
Hunt, William Holman *248*, 249, 250

I

Inayat Khan 239, *239*

J

Jahan, Shah 127, *127*
Jehangir 239
Julius II, Pope 164
Justinian, Emperor 187

K

K'ai, Liang *170*
K'uan, Fan *99*
Kaaper, Egyptian ritualist 22, *22*, 23
Kabah, Mecca 59
Kailash, temple *60*, 61, 62, *62*, 63
Kandinsky, Wassily 258, *258*, 259, 262, 270, 271
Kashan, Maqsud of 178, *178*
Keats, John 82
Khajuraho, India 108, *108*, 109, *109*, *110*, 280
Kircher, Athanasius 240, *241*
Kirchner, Ernst Ludwig 270
Klee, Paul 264, 264, 270
Knossos, Crete 280, *281*
Konrak, India *67*, 68, *68*
Krishna *90*, 91, *91*

L

Lao Zi 98, 148, *148*, 170
Lascaux, cave 116, *116*, 117, *117*, 200
Le Cap Blanc, Périgord 117
Lenin, Wladimir I. 135
Les Trois Frères, cave *119*, *138*, 139
Li Bo *170*
Limbourg Brothers *30*, *84*, *114*
Linnaeus, Karl (Carolus) 39, 238, 240
Louis XIV, King 233
Lucretius 22, 47, 57, 66, 83, 115
Luther, Martin 164, 189, 194

M

Machu Picchu 100, *100*, 101, *101*, 102, *102*
Magellan, Ferdinand 203, 226
Magritte, René 265, *265*
Malevich, Kasimir 270, *270*
Malin, David 25, *25*
Mamallapuram, India 91, *91*
Manet, Edouard 250

Mao (Mao Zedong) 135
Marcus Aurelius, Emperor 213
Mark Anthony 129
Marx, Karl 247, 248
Masaccio *145*, 201, *202*
Matisse, Henri 260, *260*, 261, 262, 269
Meacham, Joseph 165
Medici 81, 201
Michelangelo 149, *150*, 151, 157, *159*, 164, 278, *278*
Millet, Jean François 249, *249*, 250
Mondrian, Piet 258, 259, *259*, 260, 262, 269, 271
Monet, Claude 250, 251, *251*
Montezuma 193, 194
Morris, William 249
Muhammad 49
Mumtaz-Mahal 180
Munch, Edvard 254, *254*

N

Naumburg, cathedral 206, *206*
Nazca, Peru 176, *176*, 178
Nefertiti *74*, 75, *75*
Newton, Isaac 47, 233, 237, 274, 279
Nicholson, Ben 260
Nicole Le Cat, Claude *236*
Nike of Samothrace 130, *130*

O

Obiri, rock painting *41*
Oedipus 131
Olympus, Greece 95
Orissa, India *179*
Osiris 122, *122*, 149

P

Paine, Thomas 233
Pakal II, Mexico 104, *104*
Palmer, Samuel 82, *82*
Pantheon, Rome 187
Paracelsus 93
Parker, Andrew 275, 276
Parthenon, Athens 48, *49*, 66, *66*
Pascal, Blaise 230
Pech-Merle, cave *118*
Penrose, Roger 279
Phidias 7
Picasso, Pablo 7, 10, *256*, 261, 262, *262*, 263, *263*, 264, 269, 279, 280, *280*
Pieve die San Pietro, Gropina/Italy *120*
Pissarro, Camille 250
Plato 45, 172, 224
Pollock, Jackson 271, *271*
Pompeii 45, *45*, *126*
Pompey, Roman general 162
Prawn, Stephen *72*
Proust, Marcel 249
Ptolemy 227

R

Rahotep, Prince 22, *22*
Raleigh, Walter 124
Raphael, Santi 206, 249
Redouté, Pierre Joseph *238*, 239
Rembrandt van Rijn *230*, 231
Renegade Canyon *41*
Renoir, Auguste 250
Riley, Bridget 250
Rothko, Marc *270*, 271
Ruskin, John 248, *248*, 277
Rutherford, Ernest 257
Ryoan-ji, temple *97*

S

S. Maria Maggiore, Rome *195*
Sacsayhuaman, Cuzco/Peru 102, *102*, 183
Saini, Nek Chand 273
Saint Phalle, Niki de 273, *273*
Salisbury, cathedral 50, *50*
San Marco, Florence 217
Sanchi, stupa 98, *98*, 162, *163*
Santucci, Antonio *228*
Sargon II, palace *130*, 131
Schinkel, Friedrich von 241
Schnabel, Julian 271
Seneca 31
Seurat, Georges 250
Shah Jahan, Emperor 74, 179
Shakespeare, William 70, 123, 133, 169
Sheik el-Beled, *see* Kaaper
Siddharta 152
Sims, Paddy Japaljarri 25, *25*, 26
Sisley, Alfred 250
Socrates 152, 172
Song, dynasty 99
Spinoza, Baruch 230, 231
Sri Meenakshi-Sundareshwarar Temple, Madurai/India 48, 166, *166*, 167
St Augustine 185, 189
St Francis of Assisi 204
St Mark's Basilica, Venice 51, 67, 188, 192, *192*
St Peter's, Rome 48, 164
St Rupert 195
St Simeon Stylites 49
St Teresa of Avila 166, *166*
Stonehenge 50, 84, 85, *85*
Stubbs, George 125, *125*, 239
Sydney, Philip 212

T

Tagore, Rabindranath 181
Taj Mahal, Agra/India 50, 74, 179, 181, *181*
Tenochtitlan, Mexico City 50, 51, *51*, 54
Teotihuacan, Mexico 54, *54*, *55*, 55, 56, *103*, 273
Thompson, D'Arcy 277
Tinguely, Jean 272, *272*
Toft, Thomas *129*
Toledo, cathedral *213*
Tolstoy, Leo 249, 251
Tour, Georges de la 231
Trafalgar Square, London 49
Tuc d'Audoubert, cave 119, *119*

Turner, J.M. William *76*, 242, 243, *243*, 249, 250
Tutankhamen 8, 37, 38, *38*, *64*, 69, *69*, 75, 78, 280
Tyson, Edward 238

U

Urnes church, Norway *152*
Ussher, Archbishop 241
Utamaro, Kitagawa 112, *112*

V

Varanasi, India 56, *56*, 57, 58
Vasarely, Victor 250
Vasari, Giorgio 211, 213
Velázquez, Diego 231, 232, *232*
Venceslao, Maestro *246*
Venus of Laussel 90, *90*, 117
Venus of Milo *132*
Venus of Willendorf 113, *113*, 160
Vermeer, Jan *88*, *94*, 94
Versailles 233
Vespucci, Amerigo 201
Villa Imperiale, Sicily 223, *223*
Villa of Ariadne, Stabiae *80*
Villa of the Mysteries, Pompeii/Italy 112, *112*
Vinci, Leonardo da 7, 14, 18, 98, *99*, 103, *103*, *171*, 208–210, *210*, 211, *211*, 212, *212*, 213, 215-218, 229, 231, 235, 255, 276, 280
Voltaire 237

W

Watson, James *279*
Watts, G.F. 255, *255*
Wedgwood, Josiah *233*
Wells, cathedral *191*
Weyden, Rogier van der *193*
Whitman, Walt 279
Wood, Grant *165*
Wordsworth, William 243
World Trade Center, New York 48
Wren, Christopher 48
Wurm, Ole 197

Y

Yaxchilán, temple *105*, 142
Yuan, Wangshi 257

Z

Zamrak, Ibn 179
Zarathustra 185
Zhu Di 225, 226

For Daniel

Page 1 The Milky Way, our galaxy seen sidelong just before dawn; watercolour by the author

The Library of Congress Cataloguing-in-Publication data is available; British Library Cataloguing-in-Publication Data: a catalogue record for this book is available from the British Library; Deutsche Bibliothek holds a record of this publication in the Deutsche Nationalbibliografie; detailed bibliographical data can be found under: http://dnb.ddb.de

Prestel books are available worldwide. Please contact your nearest bookseller or one of the following Prestel offices for information concerning your local distributor:

Prestel Verlag
Königinstrasse 9, 80539 Munich
Tel. +49 (89) 38 17 09-0
Fax +49 (89) 38 17 09-35

Prestel Publishing Ltd.
4 Bloomsbury Place,
London WC1A 2QA
Tel. +44 (020) 7323-5004
Fax +44 (020) 7636-8004

Prestel Publishing
900 Broadway, Suite 603,
New York, NY 10003
Tel. +1 (212) 995-2720
Fax +1 (212) 995-2733

www.prestel.com

Design, layout and production
René Güttler
Cover design Liquid, Augsburg
Typesetting Fotosatz Huber, Germering
Origination ReproLine Mediateam, Munich
Printing Sellier, Freising
Binding Conzella, Pfarrkirchen

Printed in Germany on acid-free paper

ISBN 3-7913-3150-7

The illustrated works are watercolours, drawings, and photographs by the author, have been taken from the publisher's archive, or from the following sources (numbers refer to pages):

Archivi Alinari, Florence 232; The Art Institute of Chicago 19, 165; Artothek, Peissenberg 207 (24), 220; Leonardo Bezzola, Bätterkinden 272 (25); Detroit Institute of Arts 158 (3); Digital Image © 2005 The Museum of Modern Art/Scala, Florence 260, 262 (9), 278 (33); Gabriel Figueroa Flores 54f.; Fogg Art Museum, Harvard University, Cambridge, Mass. 16; Max Hirmer 133; Hirmer Verlag, Munich 190; Landesamt für Denkmalpflege und Archäologie Sachsen-Anhalt (photo: Juraj Lipták) 89; Jürgen Liepe 22 (6); Paul M.R. Maeyaert, Maarkedal (© St Baafskathedraal, Ghent, Belgium) 182, 188 (4), 193, 207 (25); Musée d'Unterlinden, Colmar (Octave Zimmermann) 147, 195 (11); Museum of Fine Arts, Boston 243; National Gallery of Australia, Canberra 271; Philadelphia Museum of Art 267; Giulio Pietromarchi 273 (27); Reunion musées nationaux, Paris 113 (43), 130 (34), 249, 256; Hickey Robertson, Houston 265; © 2005 Photo SCALA, Florence 6, 14, 15, 150, 171, 235; University of Arizona Museum of Art, Tucson 270; Vatican Museums, Rome 159